▲

Tevye
the Dairyman
————— a n d —————
The Railroad
Stories

▼

LIBRARY OF YIDDISH CLASSICS

Tevye the Dairyman

and

The Railroad Stories

Sholem Aleichem

Translated from the Yiddish with an
Introduction by Hillel Halkin

SCHOCKEN BOOKS NEW YORK

Library of Congress Cataloging-in-Publication Data
Sholem Aleichem, 1859–1916.
Tevye the dairyman and The railroad stories.
(Library of Yiddish classics)
Translation of Tevye der milkhiker and Ayznban geshikhtes: Ksovim
fun a komivoyazher.
I. Halkin, Hillel, 1939–   . II. Sholem Aleichem, 1859–1916.
Ayznban geshikhtes: Ksovim fun a komivoyazher. English. 1987. III. Title.
IV. Title: Railroad stories. V. Series.
PJ5129.R2T4518 1987   839′.0933   86–24835

Manufactured in the United States of America
ISBN 0-8052-0905-0 (Paperback)

24689753

The *Library of Yiddish Classics* is sponsored by the
Fund for the Translation of Jewish Literature.
Series editor: Ruth R. Wisse

We gratefully acknowledge the generosity of the late
M. H. Blinken and the Jewish Community Foundation of Montreal
in supporting the translation of this volume.

Contents

Introduction by Hillel Halkin   ix

Tevye the Dairyman

Tevye Strikes It Rich   *3*

Tevye Blows a Small Fortune   *20*

Today's Children   *35*

Hodl   *53*

Chava   *69*

Shprintze   *82*

Tevye Leaves for the Land of Israel   *97*

Lekh-Lekho   *116*

The Railroad Stories

To the Reader   *135*

Competitors   *136*

The Happiest Man in All Kodny   *143*

Baranovich Station   *152*

CONTENTS

Eighteen from Pereshchepena   *163*

The Man from Buenos Aires   *166*

Elul   *177*

The Slowpoke Express   *184*

The Miracle of Hoshana Rabbah   *186*

The Wedding that Came without Its Band   *194*

The *Tallis Koton*   *199*

A Game of Sixty-Six   *207*

High School   *217*

The Automatic Exemption   *229*

It Doesn't Pay to Be Good   *238*

Burned Out   *247*

Hard Luck   *255*

Fated for Misfortune   *259*

Go Climb a Tree If You Don't Like It   *269*

The Tenth Man   *274*

Third Class   *279*

Glossary and Notes   *285*

INTRODUCTION

▼

▲ 1 ▲

A little over a century ago, in 1883, an aspiring writer of comic talents named Sholem Rabinovich, who was then serving as a "crown rabbi," a state-appointed clerical functionary in a small Jewish community in the Ukraine, published a satirical account of local politics in the St. Petersburg *Yiddishe Folksblat* and playfully signed it "Sholem Aleichem"—that is to say, "Hello There!" It was not his first alias. He already had, and would continue to assemble, a precocious collection of pseudonyms, including such curiosities as "Solomon Bikherfresser" (Solomon Bookeater), "Baron Pipernoter" (Baron Ogre), "Terakhs an Eynikl" (Terach's Grandson), and "Der Yiddisher Gazlen" (The Robber Jew). Compared with these titles, however, which had at best a slapstick humor, the ancient Hebrew salutation first employed in the *Folksblat* (its Arabic cognate of *salaam aleykum* can be heard today throughout the Middle East) was a prescient choice. Meaning literally "peace be upon you," the phrase is used in Yiddish not as an everyday greeting but as a more emphatic one that is reserved for either old acquaintants long unmet or new ones just introduced; thus, besides encoding in the form of a pun Rabinovich's own name of "Sholem," it pithily anticipated the career of an author who, over the next three decades, was to come and go in the Yiddish press from one newspaper and magazine to another, delighting an ever-growing audience with his unpredictable appearances before vanishing again until the next time. Gradually he used the new pen name more and more. It did not replace its rivals all at once, but by 1894, the year in which the first chapter of what is possibly the greatest of all Jewish novels, *Tevye the Dairy-man,* appeared in the pages of the Warsaw yearbook *Der Hoyz-fraynt,* it had become an exclusive trademark recognized by Yiddish readers everywhere. Eventually his own friends and intimates took to calling him by it too. Whereas Sholem Aleichem had once been Sholem Rabinovich, Sholem Rabinovich was now Sholem Aleichem, the private man subsumed in the public identity of the world's most famous Yiddish writer.

Yet if comedy seems to imply a sufficient degree of well-being to make laughter possible, the debut of Sholem Aleichem as a comic Jewish writer did not come at an auspicious time. Indeed, coinciding as it did with the drastic deterioration in the Jewish situation in Russia that began in 1881 with the assassination of Alexander II and the bloody pogroms that followed, it could hardly have come at a worse one. Today, it is true, when modern Jewish history is read backwards in the monstrous light of the Holocaust, it is difficult to be as shocked as contemporaries were by the plight of Russian Jewry in the last decades of the Czarist Empire, during which the number of Jews murdered by Christian mob violence did not exceed several hundred. But in the context of its own time and place, the era of 1881–1917 in Russia was an exceedingly black period, the most savage experienced by Jews anywhere since the terrible massacres of Khmelnitsky's Cossacks in the Ukraine in 1648–1649. Moreover, not only were the pogroms that took place under Alexander III and his successor, Nicholas II, actually incited and approved by the Russian government, they were part of an official policy of anti-Semitism calculated to render life so intolerable for the country's Jewish inhabitants that, in the notorious words of Alexander III's adviser Constantine Pobyedonostzev, a third of them would be forced to emigrate, a third to convert, and a third to perish from hunger. One has to go back to the Spanish Inquisition and Expulsion of 1492 to find a previous instance of a European government setting out on a deliberate course of first terrorizing and then eliminating its Jewish population.

Such were the times that Sholem Aleichem wrote about—and that, remarkably for a humorist, he wrote about without either ridiculing or rose-tinting, neither saying to his reader, "Laugh and be above it," nor telling him, "Come, it's not as bad as you think; let me show you the brighter side." On the contrary: it was consistently his method, for all the near-manic exuberance of his prose, to confront the reader with reality in its full harshness, laughter being for him the explosive with which he systematically mined all escape routes away from the truth. Despite the exaggeration that is an ingredient of all humor, he had a reportorial passion for fact; more than one of his stories actually came from reading the morning newspaper. In the absence of other sources, one could infer much of the history and sociology of the Russian Jewry of his time from his work alone. And because, before one can fully appreciate this work's universal dimensions (of which he himself was well aware) one must read it as the specific anatomy of Russian Jewish existence that it was, a few more words about the latter may be helpful.

Russia did not develop a Jewish problem; it swallowed one whole. Unlike other European countries, whose Jewish populations were built up in medieval times by a slow process of migration, often initially encouraged by rulers wishing to benefit from Jewish commercial skills and contacts, the Russian state, which had traditionally barred Jews entirely, suddenly acquired large numbers of them, and without any desire to do so, by virtue of the three partitions of Poland in 1772, 1793, and 1795, and the revisions of them made by the Congress of Vienna in 1815. Overnight, as it were, the Jewish communities of eastern and central Poland, Lithuania, Latvia, Byelorussia, and the Ukraine found themselves on annexed Russian soil—beyond whose boundaries, however, the Czarist regime in St. Petersburg had no intention of letting them spread. And so by the end of the eighteenth century, there had come into being the human enclosure of the Pale of Settlement, that vast ghetto of western and southwestern Russia to which millions of Jews were confined by a jumble of confusing laws. Although it ran roughly along the lines of the new territories, the Pale as an entity was never clearly defined; its exact borders kept shifting as different parts of it were declared in or out of bounds according to the whims of bureaucrats, the outward pressure of the Jews bottled up inside it, and the counterpressure of anti-Jewish officials and Russian merchants fearing Jewish competition. Thus, for instance, the Ukrainian capital of Kiev, the "Yehupetz" of Sholem Aleichem's fiction and the city in which he lived for many years, was first opened to Jews (1794), then barred to them (1835), then put back on limits for temporary visits only (1862), then gradually reopened to Jewish residence by special permit, which depended on the petitioner's profession and the connections he happened to have. Even more filled with reversals was the history of Jewish residential rights in the Pale's rural villages, as opposed to its cities and towns. Originally left to the discretion of the local nobility in 1797, rural residence for Jews was denied in 1804, temporarily restored in 1807, redenied that same year, restored again in 1808, partially revoked once more in 1823, and so back and forth until 1910, when a final wave of rural expulsions began. Not all the restrictions on the books, of course, were always put into practice; yet even when they were not, the ever-present anxiety that they might be was enough to make a nightmare of the lives of great numbers of Jews who, generally for reasons of economic opportunity, were domiciled illegally.

Confinement to the Pale of Settlement, however, was not the worst of Russian Jewry's problems. Far more onerous was the fact that within the Pale itself, where most Jews lived in grinding poverty, they were discriminated against at every turn by an imperial administration that, lacking Pobyedonostzev's inclusive vision, could never quite make up its mind whether it wished to starve them or assimilate them, and so alternated between the most oppressive features of both approaches. Jews were excluded from local councils and trade guilds, even in towns where they formed a majority of the inhabitants. They were made to pay special and frequently humiliating taxes—a head tax, a property tax, a tax on the slaughter of kosher meat, a tax on Sabbath candles, a tax on the right to wear their traditional clothes. They were barred at different times and places from a wide range of occupations—law, agriculture, tavern keeping, the production and sale of liquor, the retailing of manufactured articles, the employment of their wives as market vendors. They were harassed in the education of their children, now forced to send them to Russianizing schools and now confronted with a system of quotas that made a Russian schooling almost impossible. And they were subjected to especially harsh draft laws, being inducted into the army in higher percentages and for longer terms of service than other sectors of the population. This last affliction reached a horrendous extreme in the reign of Nicholas I, who decreed in 1827 that an annual number of Jewish boys aged twelve and up should be taken to the army for premilitary training until they turned eighteen, at which time they were to be drafted for twenty-five years. These "cantonists," as the unfortunate children were called, rarely saw their homes again, and until its abolition by Alexander II in 1856, the institution of juvenile conscription struck terror into the hearts of Jewish families. Extortionate bribery, child snatching, and the physical mutilation of one's sons were some of the measures employed to ensure that the boy taken to the army was not one's own.

Under Alexander II, whose liberalizing tendencies were most prominently expressed by his emancipation of the Russian serfs, the condition of the Jews improved too; some of the discriminatory legislation against them was relaxed, and a more thorough removal of the rest was contemplated. Yet even before Alexander's assassination in 1881 by a bomb-throwing revolutionary, further progress had become mired in a welter of indecisive commissions of inquiry, and with the succession of his son, Alexander III, the anti-Jewish outlook of former years was revived with fresh vigor. There was now, moreover, a new factor that made this policy more brutal than ever: the desire to blame the Jews for the growing revolutionary movement, thus simultaneously discrediting the revolutionaries by painting them as Jewish conspirators, and deflecting the grievances of the Russian peasantry and working class from the government to the Jews. For the first time, government persecution of the Jews ceased to be a simple matter of social and economic containment and became a political tool. An idea of the cynical cruelty with which this tool was wielded can be gained even from an abbreviated chronology of the rash of anti-Semitic decrees and outbreaks that followed in the next several years:

1881/ Government-incited pogroms in Yelisavetograd, Kiev, and elsewhere in the Ukraine, as well as in Warsaw; the government officially blames them on Jewish economic exploitation of the masses, which have been driven to exact their just revenge.

1882/ Jews are again forbidden to settle in any of the rural sections of the Pale of Settlement (that is, in ninety percent of its area) or to buy property there. Jews already living in the villages are made subject to expulsion if they do not own their homes, if they move from village to village, or if they are absent from the village they live in for even a few days.

1883/ Pogroms in Rostov-on-Don; thousands of Jews living illegally in St. Petersburg are rounded up by the police and expelled.

1884/ Pogrom in Nizhni-Novgorod.

1887/ All high schools and universities within the Pale of Settlement (where Jews, though roughly a tenth of the inhabitants, form a majority of the literate population) are limited to a Jewish quota of ten percent of their student bodies.

1890/ Numerous towns in the Pale are reclassified as villages, from which Jews are therefore expelled; Jews are disqualified throughout the Pale of Settlement from voting for deputies in local elections.

1891/ Twenty thousand Jews are expelled from Moscow.

1894/ Jews are forbidden to change their names to non-Jewish ones; Jewish identity passes are marked with the word "Jew."

1899–1900/ More pogroms in the Ukraine; in Vilna a Jew is put on trial on the atavistic charge of attempting to murder a Christian girl in order to bake Passover matsoh from her blood. (This medieval "blood libel" was to be repeated in 1911 in the more famous case of Mendel Beilis, which attracted worldwide attention.)

1903/ The worst pogrom yet in Kishinev; forty-five Jews killed, eighty-six severely wounded, fifteen hundred Jewish houses and stores looted and demolished. Pogrom in Homel; when Jews try for the first time to defend themselves with arms, thirty-six are indicted for attacking Christians.

1904/ Outbreak of the Russo-Japanese war; Jews are called up in disproportionate numbers; the number of Jewish soldiers sent to the front is also disproportionately large.

Even the popular-backed Revolution of 1905, which broke out in the aftermath of Russia's defeat by Japan and led Nicholas II to grant a short-lived liberal constitution that aroused, among other things, extravagant hopes of a new age for Russia's Jews, only ended in the further shedding of Jewish blood: the ink on the constitutional manifesto had hardly dried when gangs of counter-revolutionary thugs known as "the Black Hundreds," organized with the complicity of the Czarist police, attacked Jewish neighborhoods all over Russia under the cover of nationalist slogans holding the Jews responsible for the country's troubles and accusing them of subverting the authority of the Czar in order to seize power themselves. The worst of these pogroms took place in Odessa, where over three hundred Jews were killed, thousands

injured, and tens of thousands left homeless. Another that occurred in Kiev was witnessed by Sholem Aleichem himself from
the window of the hotel in which he had taken refuge with his
family. Soon afterward he left Russia, never to return again except for brief visits until his death in New York in 1916.

In taking his departure, of course, Sholem Aleichem was join-
ing a flood of Jews heading westward; it is estimated that between
1881 and 1914, when World War I shut the gates of emigration,
nearly three million Jews left the Russian Empire, mostly for the
United States. This mass flight, however, only partially relieved
congestion within the Pale itself, both because of a high birthrate
and because economic pressures and the rural expulsions led to
an internal migration of Jews to the crowded quarters of the
larger towns, where mass proletarization took place. Despairing
of a future under the Czarist regime, many young Jews turned to
the revolutionary movement. If at the time of Alexander II's assassination the specter of Jewish insurrectionism had been largely
a red herring, by the first decade of the twentieth century it was
an unassailable fact. Jews were active in large numbers in the two
major underground parties, the Social Revolutionaries and the
Social Democrats, and in 1897 they formed a clandestine Marxist
organization of their own, the League of Jewish Workingmen, or
"Bund." Jewish youth that was not politically active was becoming
modernized too, so that a yawning gap developed between an
older generation that still clung to the traditional ways and a
younger one that was rapidly forsaking them. Russian began to
displace Yiddish in daily speech (it is an astounding symptom of
the times that Sholem Aleichem himself spoke Russian to his wife
and children!) and the medieval culture of Orthodox Judaism
that had remained intact for centuries was in the process of crum-
bling. Everywhere, battered from without and eroded from
within, Jewish life was in a state of flux, disarray, decomposition.

It has been commonly remarked that while in most humor the
self, be it individual or collective, laughs at that which is unlike it
and with which it does not identify, thereby proclaiming its own
superiority, in Jewish humor it laughs at itself—the explanation
for this presumably being that among a people with so long a
history of persecution, the most pressing task of humor has been
to neutralize the hostility of the outside world, first by internaliz-

ing it ("Why should I care what the world thinks of me, when I think even less of myself?") and then by detonating it through a joke ("Nevertheless, the world doesn't know what it's talking about, because in fact I am much cleverer than it is—the proof being that it has no idea how funny I am, and I do!"). There is doubtless much truth in this, provided one realizes that the type of humor in question is not historically very Jewish at all and first makes its appearance in Jewish literature in the course of the nineteenth century, especially in the second half. Before that, Jews reacted to hatred and oppression in a variety of ways—with defiance, with scorn, with anger, with bitterness, with vengefulness, with lamentation, with (and perhaps here the seeds of modern Jewish humor were first sown) copious self-accusation—but never, as far as can be determined from the literary sources, with laughter directed at themselves. This is strictly a latter-day method of coping (one prompted perhaps by the loss of the religious faith that had given meaning to Jewish tribulations in the past), and Sholem Aleichem is one of its great developers and practitioners.

The fact that the inner dialectic of such humor (which, despite its defensive function, can easily undermine the ego from within) became in the hands of Sholem Aleichem a therapeutic force of the first order is one of his most extraordinary achievements. It is a matter of record that the Jews of his time who read his work, or heard him read it himself at the many public performances that he gave, not only laughed until their ribs ached at his unsparing portrayals of their perversity, ingenuity, anxiety, tenacity, mendacity, humanity, unplumbable pain, and invincible hopefulness, they emerged feeling immeasurably better about themselves and their fate as Jews. His appearance in a Russian shtetl on one of his tours was a festive event: banquets were given in his honor, lecture halls were filled to overflowing, pleas for favorite stories were shouted at him from the audience, encores were demanded endlessly, crowds accompanied him to the railroad station to get a last glimpse of him before he went. Besides being a sensitive performer—contemporary accounts describe him as reading his stories aloud with great restraint and simplicity, never overacting or burlesquing them—he clearly touched his listeners in a place where nothing else, except perhaps their ancient prayers and rituals, was able to. He gave them a feeling of transcendence.

   This feeling, as has been stated, had nothing to do with the sense of being "above it all," with that comforting assurance given us by a great deal of comic literature that life is ultimately so silly a business that there is no point in taking it too seriously. Quite the opposite: Sholem Aleichem's humor demanded of its readers that they take life seriously indeed—nor, in any case, with pogroms and hunger often at the door, were they in any position not to. His comedy did not lift them *above* the suffering world that they were part of; it lifted them *together with it.* The laughter his work evoked was not that of contempt, or of embarrassment, or of relief, or even of sympathy, but rather of identification and acceptance. "You who have been through all this," it said, "and who know that such are our lives and that no amount of self-delusion can make them less so—you who have experienced fear, and humiliation, and despair, and defeat, and are aware that there is more yet to come—you to whom all this has happened and who still have been able to laugh—you, my friends, need no consolation, because you have already prevailed." Those who rose at the end of such an evening to give him a standing ovation were also paying tribute to themselves.

▲ 2 ▲

   Readers of *Tevye the Dairyman* who are familiar with the play or movie *Fiddler on the Roof* will notice that, in more ways than one, there is scant resemblance between Sholem Aleichem's novel and the charming musical based on it. (Indeed, this is true even of the musical's name, which does not come from the work of Sholem Aleichem at all but from the art of Marc Chagall with its recurrent motif of a sad-gay Jewish fiddler playing upon the rooftops of a Russian village.) To begin with, there is the tone: unlike *Fiddler* which, whether sad or gay, keeps within the range of the safely sentimental, *Tevye* has a giddy energy, a recklessness of language and emotion, a dizzy oscillation of wildly funny and wrenchingly painful scenes that come one on top of another without letup. In addition, the dramatic plot of *Fiddler on the Roof* is culled from just four of the eight *Tevye* episodes, the third, fourth, fifth, and eighth, so that Chapters 1, 2, 6, and 7 have no bearing on it. Lastly, in *Fiddler* Tevye has only three daughters, Tsaytl, Hodl, and Chava, whereas in *Tevye* . . . but how many daughters Tevye has in *Tevye* is a question we will come to in a moment. Suffice it to say first that, quite apart from the pointlessness of comparing two such different treatments simply because one derives from the other, similar departures from the text of *Tevye* (except for its being set to music) were made in 1914 by Sholem Aleichem himself for a dramatized version of the book that had a long stage life of its own. In fact, his cannibalization of the novel was even more extreme than the musical's: essentially it utilized only Chapters 5 and 8, and Tevye's daughters were reduced to two, Tsaytl and Chava, the plot revolving entirely around Chava and her marriage to and ultimate break-up with Chvedka, the Ukrainian villager, leaving Tsaytl in a mere supporting role. In sentimentality, too, Sholem Aleichem's play, written as it clearly was with one eye on the box office of the highly commercial Yiddish theater, is every bit the equal of *Fiddler on the Roof*, which is without a doubt the more stage-worthy of the two.

But how many daughters *does* the original Tevye have? As Professor Khone Shmeruk has shown in an absorbing study, the uncertain answer to this question casts considerable light on the composition of the book as a whole. In its opening episode, "Tevye Strikes It Rich," which first appeared in 1894 and was revised in 1897, the number of Tevye's daughters is given as seven. In Chapter 2, "Tevye Blows a Small Fortune," and Chapter 3, "Today's Children," which is about Tsaytl, Tevye's oldest daughter (both were published in 1899), no count is given at all. In "Hodl" and "Chava" (1904 and 1905) we again read of seven girls—yet in Chapter 6, "Shprintze" (1907), there are only six, the two youngest of whom are Beilke and Teibl, while in Chapters 7 and 8 (1909 and 1914) Teibl has vanished and only Beilke remains. What can be concluded from this? Clearly, it would seem, that Sholem Aleichem planned *Tevye* in several stages, each representing a modification of his previous conception. Indeed, the first episode, which was based on his acquaintance with an actual milkman whom he befriended one summer in the resort town of Boyarka near Kiev (the "Boiberik" of the novel), was no doubt written as an independent story with little or no thought of a sequel, its figure of seven nameless daughters being no more than a way of saying "many." Also probably meant to stand by itself was the second episode, in which Tevye meets Menachem Mendl, who was already the comic hero of another, epistolary work of fiction that Sholem Aleichem was working on at the time. By the third, or at the latest, fourth chapter, on the other hand, Sholem Aleichem had evidently decided to write a series about Tevye's daughters, which meant producing seven more stories, one for each of them; yet in Chapter 6, either tiring of the subject or feeling he was running out of material, he reduced their number to six, and in Chapter 7, he cut it again to five. This chapter, in fact, was evidently intended to conclude the Tevye cycle with Tevye's departure for Palestine, since in 1911, with Sholem Aleichem's authorization, it was printed together with the first six episodes as a book called *Tevye the Dairyman*—the first time such a title was used for the series as a whole. The eighth and last episode, added several years later, was apparently written as an afterthought (one motive, Shmeruk conjectures, being the desire to return Chava to the bosom of her family). Having written it, however, Sholem Aleichem must have planned at least one further installment, because he did not give this story, "Lekh-Lekho," a coda-like ending, as he did Chapter 7, and only subsequently sought to make up for the omission by adding a brief fragment that was published shortly before his death.*

---

*This fragment, which was given the tongue-twisting Hebrew name of *Vekhalaklakoys*, after the verse in Psalms 35:6, *Yehi darkom khoyshekh vekhalaklakoys*, "Let their path be dark and slippery," was written in 1914, the same year as "Lekh-Lekho," but not published until two years later. Though it seems to have been begun as a genuine sequel to "Lekh-Lekho," that is, as a ninth episode of *Tevye*, it is less than a third of the average length of the other stories, repeats much of the material in Chapter 8 without adding anything essentially new, and has a rather tired quality that contrasts with the sparkle of the rest of the book. Still, one cannot call it unfinished; on the contrary, it contains precisely the "finale" that Chapter 8 lacks. In the absence of explanatory biographical material, of which there appears to be none, one can only speculate what this fragment represents. My own guess is as follows: while Sholem Aleichem indeed intended to write a full-length sequel to "Lekh-Lekho" and began it immediately after finishing the latter, he soon, whether because of failing health or because he realized that the book had reached its natural conclusion and had nowhere else to go, gave it up—though not before hastening to write a proper end for it, his main concern being that *Tevye* should have one. Unhappy with the results, however, he refrained from publishing this, possibly hoping to revise and expand it; yet ultimately, seeing this was not to be, he consented to its publication in the days before his death. Subsequently, in all the Yiddish editions of *Tevye* printed after Sholem Aleichem's death, the *Vekhalaklakoys* fragment has appeared as its last chapter.

As the translator of *Tevye*, I was in a dilemma. On the one hand, *Vekhalaklakoys* was published by Sholem Aleichem himself in his lifetime, and without it *Tevye* has no real end; yet on the other hand, apart from its last page, not only does it add nothing to the remainder of the work, it qualitatively detracts from it. What was one to do? In the end I

Can a work of fiction begun with no overall plan, written in installments over a twenty-year period, and ending more than once, be called (as it has been here) a novel at all? There are critics whose answer is no. The noted Sholem Aleichem scholar Dan Miron, for instance, has written that the structure of *Tevye* is more "mythic" than novelistic, each of its episodes consisting of a pattern of rise, fall, and recovery that can repeat itself endlessly; Sholem Aleichem, Miron argues, could have brought *Tevye* to a close after its seventh chapter or gone on to write a tenth and eleventh—in terms of the book's form and thematic contents, it would hardly have mattered. But though it certainly is true that each episode of *Tevye* can be read as a story in itself (which is undoubtedly how some of its original readers, not all of whom were familiar with what came before, did read it), and true too that each shares basic patterns with the others, it is equally clear that each builds on the previous installments and that there is a definite development from one chapter to the next. Indeed, if what perhaps most characterizes the novel as a literary form is the flow of time in it, the fact that more than in any other artistic medium we see human beings exposed to time,

---

decided to follow the example of Frances Butwin's 1948 English translation of *Tevye* and to omit most of the fragment, some six pages of Yiddish text in all, retaining only the final coda, which I spliced on to the end of "Lekh-Lekho," adding several lines of my own to make the transition smoother. Though taking such a liberty in translating a classic of world literature may seem presumptuous to some readers, I would like to think that Sholem Aleichem might have welcomed it. Besides always being open to criticism of his work, frequently revising it as a result, he encouraged his Russian and Hebrew translators, whom he personally helped and advised, to be extremely free in their renditions. Anyone comparing his Yiddish with the Hebrew translations by his son-in-law Y. D. Berkovits, for example, and especially with Berkovits' translation of *Tevye*, in which Sholem Aleichem was an active collaborator, will be struck by the enormous differences between them. (Berkovits himself omitted the *Vekhalaklakoys* fragment entirely in his complete Hebrew edition of the novel, which he ended with "Lekh-Lekho," but this was apparently his own decision, made after Sholem Aleichem's death.) There will no doubt come a time for variorum editions of *Tevye* in which the full text of *Vekhalaklakoys* can appear alongside whatever ending the translator cares to give the book.

Apart from this fragment, I have departed (as did Berkovits) from the standard Yiddish text of *Tevye* in one other place. When the first episode of the book, "Tevye Strikes It Rich," was published in 1894, it was accompanied by a brief preface, purporting to be a letter written by Tevye to Sholem Aleichem, the literary purpose of which was to introduce Tevye to the reader. Though this preface was later republished as part of the novel as a whole, it was clearly written for "Tevye Strikes It Rich" alone, makes no reference to any of the stories that come after it, and cannot possibly be construed as applying to them. I have therefore omitted it.

shaped by time, worn by time, then *Tevye* is a novel *par excellence,* perhaps the only one ever written in real time, that is, according to a scale on which time for the author and time for his characters are absolutely equivalent. Sholem Aleichem and Tevye age together: a year in the life of one is a year in the life of the other, and twenty years in the life of one is twenty years in the life of the other. Even as Sholem Aleichem sits at his desk writing down Tevye's stories, Tevye continues to grow older by the amount of time that writing takes.

It is in part this aspect of Tevye that makes him so real a character, for despite the great misfortunes that befall him and his extraordinary resilience in confronting them, the years affect him much as they do most men: slowly, subtly, almost imperceptibly in the course of any one of the book's episodes—in which, as in the short story generally, time is not a significant factor—but enormously when regarded over the whole span of them. *Le plus ça change, le plus ça reste la même chose* is only one side of Tevye and of us all; *le plus ça reste la même chose, le plus ça change* is the other. He is, as Miron says, always Tevye; but who, meeting him in 1894 and again in 1914, would not be shocked by the difference—and not only because of the gray hairs? Tevye has changed internally—and with these changes, the novel's three internal levels of meaning all reach a climax too. Let us consider them.

The first of these is the story of Tevye and his family as a paradigm of the fate of Russian Jewry. It is a measure of Sholem Aleichem's great artistry that Tevye, Golde, and their daughters—and with what a bare minimum of strokes these last are sketched!—are all wonderfully alive and individualized human beings who never strike us as being anything but themselves. Yet this should not obscure the perception that they are also, like most of the other characters in the book, representative types of Russian Jewish life who, taken together, tell the tale of its destruction. Indeed, each of Tevye's daughters falls in love with and/or marries a man who can be said to embody a distinct historical force or mood, and if Tevye himself is the very incarnation of the traditional culture of the shtetl, then beginning with the novel's second chapter, every one of its episodes illustrates another phase of this culture's helpless disintegration. In "Tevye Blows a Small Fortune," for example, we see in the person of Menachem Mendl the economic collapse of a community that has been driven by the unnatural conditions imposed on it to seek its livelihood in the most pathetic kinds of nonproductive speculation. In "Today's Children" we read of that undermining of parental authority which, though still relatively mild in Tsaytl's case, will eventually bring Tevye's world crashing down on him. "Hodl" deals with the defection of Jewish youth to the revolutionary movement, and "Chava" with its loss to intermarriage. Shprintze's suicide is the outcome of a situation that at first resembles Tsaytl's and her other sisters', i.e., she has fallen in love with a young man whom Tevye originally disapproves of as a match for her—but precisely because of this parallel, the difference between Tsaytl's and Motl's behavior, on the one hand, and Shprintze's and Ahronchik's, on the other, shows how dramatically the lines of communication between generations have broken down in the space of a few years. In Beilke's story, "Tevye Leaves for the Land of Israel," we meet yet another new Jewish type, the contractor Podhotzur, a vulgar nouveau-riche assimilationist ruthlessly intent on climbing the social and economic ladder of a society making the transition from rural feudalism to urban capitalism. And finally, in "Lekh-Lekho," what is left of Tevye's life literally falls apart: expelled from the village in which he and his ancestors have lived since time immemorial, he is forced to become a homeless wanderer. Coming in the final chapter of the novel, this expulsion is the ultimate concretization of the ruin of an entire world.

In all this, Tevye's role is essentially passive; he schemes, he fantasizes, he makes a great fuss over things (although less so as the years go by and he grows more aware of his powerlessness)—yet each time the events, like his own unruly horse, simply run away with him, leaving him aghast and uncomprehending. And yet, as the Yiddish critic Y. Y. Trunk has perceptively observed, what makes him a genuinely tragic figure and not just the comic victim of a world beyond his control is that in every case it is he himself who brings about his downfall—a theme that comprises the second level of the book, that encompassing the relationships in Tevye's family, especially between him and his daughters. With his wife Golde, all in all, Tevye's relations are simple: they might be defined as those of a harmonious conjugal antagonism, a common enough modus vivendi among East European Jews that is composed on Tevye's side of equal parts genial misogyny and husbandly loyalty to hearth and home. This misogyny, however, runs only skin-deep, because, despite his protestations to the contrary (it is when he protests, in fact, that he most reveals his true feelings, a more direct expression of affection not being in his vocabulary), Tevye clearly loves his daughters to distraction. Nor does he just adore them; he admires and respects them with that unconventionally unsnobbish openness, that basic inclination to judge everyone on, and only on, his merits, which, beneath his facade of patriarchal autocracy and middle-class pretensions, is one of his most endearing traits. It is just this openness and capacity for love, however, that prove his undoing, for without his quite grasping the fact, these are the qualities that, absorbed from him by his daughters, make them act as they do in the face of his own apprehensions and objections. As is so often the case with parents and children, Tevye's daughters are much more like him than he is willing to admit; they are, in fact, the actors-out of the fantasies and values that he has transmitted to them. Does Tsaytl, disappointing her father, refuse to marry the rich Layzer Wolf and choose the poor Motl Komzoyl instead? But Tevye cannot stand Layzer Wolf, he truly likes Motl, and he himself has told Sholem Aleichem: "Money is a lot of baloney . . . what matters is for a man to be a man!" Is Tevye devastated because Hodl has linked her life with the young revolutionary, Pertchik? But besides having brought Pertchik into his home (for which, it is true, he blames himself—he just does not go beyond this), who if not Tevye has sat on his front stoop imagining what it would be like to trade places with the rich Jews of Yehupetz, living in their dachas while they bring him milk and cheese each day! Has Chava done the unthinkable, married a goy? Why, Tevye himself has wondered in the solitude of the forest, "What does being a Jew or not a Jew matter?" It is Tevye who in his fondness for Ahronchik has introduced him to Shprintze, and Tevye who, in his anger at Beilke for selling her soul to marry wealth, forgets that this is exactly the arrangement that he planned for Tsaytl long ago. Tevye knows that Beilke has sacrificed herself for his sake—yet it does not occur to him that she has done so because of the vision of magical riches that he himself has handed down to her.

In short, whether he is simply a natural democrat, or whether, staunchly traditional Jew though he is, he has unknowingly been affected by the liberal winds blowing in Russia, Tevye has fathered the daughters of his deepest dreams. Trunk puts it well when he writes of the man and his children, "Though consciously they have different outlooks on life, unconsciously they share the same sense of it." It is only in the novel's penultimate chapter, the story of Beilke, however, that Tevye achieves a belated insight concerning this fact, for then, seeing Beilke's unhappiness in her stultifyingly opulent surroundings and recalling the vivacious child who lived with him in semipoverty, he articulates at last what at heart he has always known, namely, that all that really matters in life is human love, warmth, and intelligence, thus realizing the pitifulness of his one great conscious obsession: to have a rich daughter. Fate, he tragically learns, not only mocks a man by withholding his desires, but also—and sometimes most of all—by granting them. And like any tragic hero's, Tevye's fate, as Trunk reminds us, is his character.

But what a disproportion between the two! What a character and what a fate! Surely no man, and most surely none as good as Tevye, deserves to see his daughters stricken, as he says, by a curse worse than any in the Bible . . . and this conviction of injustice, the subject of Tevye's running debate with God, forms the novel's third and most profound level of all. Sholem Aleichem, it is true, is not often thought of as a religious writer. Religious observance, though constantly referred to in his work as part of the everyday fabric of Jewish life, does not play an especially important role in it, and genuinely spiritual figures are rare there. Indeed, this was one of the reasons that Y. L. Peretz, his leading rival among the Yiddish writers of the day and the author of much edifying fiction, dismissed Sholem Aleichem as a basically lowbrow figure who never grappled with ultimate Jewish issues. Humor in general, though by no means an illegitimate medium for serious religious expression, is not commonly put to that purpose. Yet having said all this, I would submit that *Tevye the Dairyman,* the comitragic historical account of the death of an ancient culture and psychological analysis of a father's unhappy love for his daughters, is also one of the most extraordinary Jewish religious texts of our own, and perhaps of any, time.

Tevye is a God-arguer: as such he belongs in a long Jewish tradition that starts with Abraham and runs prominently on through Moses, through Job, through the Tannaitic rabbi Yehoshua ben Levi (who refused to accept a heaven-backed interpretation of Scripture even though it was supported by divine miracles), through Levi Yitzchak of Berdichev, the saintly Hasidic master who is said to have held a trial at which God was the absentee defendant, accused of having inflicted undeserved suffering on His people. Other religions may have their folktales about men who debate with and even rebuke God, but only in Jewish tradition, I believe, are such stories taken with high seriousness, the behavior in question being regarded—provided, of course that it comes from a spiritually ripe individual—as the highest form of religious service. Though it is Job's friends who keep telling him to accept God's judgment and Job who insists that he will not because that judgment is unjust, God Himself, after finally speaking to Job from the whirlwind, turns to his friends and says, "My wrath is kindled against you . . . for you have not spoken of Me what was right, as My servant Job has." And what is right, apparently, is to hold God to the highest standards of a man's conscience, even if He does not seem to behave by them.

It is worth considering this for a moment, for it presents an oddly paradoxical alternative, and by no means the main one adopted by Judaism either, to what have commonly been the standard responses of advanced cultures to the problem of innocent suffering in the world. Basically there have been three of these:

1. God exists, is good, and is all-powerful; what appears to us His injustice is either a legitimate testing of our character, a just retribution for our sins, or an illusion created by our inability to understand the workings of the Divinity.

2. God exists, is good, but is not all-powerful; beside Him are other, evil forces that contend with and sometimes best Him, thus gaining power over the world.

3. God does not exist and suffering is the result either of blind chance or of immutable laws working themselves out in the lives of men.

The first of these answers has been the one most often given by the major monotheistic religions; the second by Manichaeism, Gnosticism, Zoroastrianism, and various other dualistic beliefs; the third by modern science and, essentially, by Buddhism.

But there is also, as we have seen, a fourth possible response: God exists; He is good; He is all-powerful; therefore He must be just; but He is not just; therefore He owes man an explanation and man must demand it from Him.

This is Job's response. And it is also Tevye's.

Job is not one of the religious texts that Tevye is always quoting from, nor would it be likely to be. On the whole it was not a part of Scripture widely read by East European Jews, both because it was not linked to specific prayers, rituals, or holidays like other books in the Bible, and because its Hebrew is extremely difficult. But Tevye knows its story and, in "Shprintze," on his way home from his humiliating meeting with Ahronchik's uncle, when it seems to him that nothing worse can happen (little does he know that he is soon to receive the most terrible blow of all), his identification with it emerges. And yet though his suffering is truly Jobian, as is his reaction to it, how much more lonely and isolated a figure he is than Job! Job has his three friends, who despite their aggravating piety are a comfort merely by their presence, and he has his God, who finally speaks to him in a blazing epiphany that rewards him for all his anguish; Tevye, however, has no one. Alone in his village, without a Jew to speak to, without a synagogue to go to, without a God to be spoken to by, he must carry on the dialogue of Job all by himself, now being Tevye demanding to know what he has been punished for, now being his comforters patiently explaining that whatever God does is for the best, and now being God Himself threatening to blow him, little Tevye, away with a puff of His breath if he does not stop his tiresome complaining. All around him the world is as silent as the forest in which he has his deepest thoughts. There is not a consoling word. Man says nothing. God says nothing. The Messiah is a policeman with an eviction notice. And Tevye, who will not take nothing for an answer, goes on arguing with them all!

Did Sholem Aleichem think of this side of Tevye in more than just comic terms? Of course he did. Listen to what his son-in-law Y. D. Berkovits has to say about him at the time he was writing "Shprintze":

It goes without saying that none of these externals [Berkovits has been discussing Sholem Aleichem's attitude toward Jewish religious obser- vance] had very much to do with the inner religious feelings that existed in him and that frequently stirred him greatly. For that Sholem Aleichem had in his own way a most religiously sensitive per- sonality—of this I have not the slightest doubt. On the table by his bed always lay a small, open Bible that he would read now and then, especially at night when he had trouble sleeping. I suspected that he was mainly reading the Book of Job, and once indeed, when he began to test me on my knowledge of it, I was astounded by his familiarity with it, especially when I thought of how hard we had found it in the schoolroom when we were young.

One more word on the subject.

Not long ago I gave a talk on *Tevye the Dairyman* to a small audience in the town in Israel where I live. A lively discussion ensued, during which one of the participants, a professor of the history of science, exclaimed angrily, "But Tevye is a fool! Instead of realizing once and for all that there is no God, and that his own life is the best proof of it, he goes on wasting his energy on a God who doesn't exist." It was a perfectly natural comment and it led to an even more animated exchange, but as that went on, I kept asking myself, where have I heard those words before? And then it came to me: Job's wife! "And then his wife said to him, 'Do you still hold fast to your integrity? Curse God, and die!' "

For Job—and for Tevye—to curse God *is* to die, because neither can live in a world without Him. Even if God never answers, even if He never will, Tevye must go on debating with Him, for the minute he stops, his life has lost its meaning. And besides, who is to say when God answers and when He does not? In Job's case, you say, it was obvious: "And then the Lord answered Job out of the whirlwind." Yes: but had you or I been present in that whirlwind, would we have heard anything but wind? "So the Lord blessed the latter end of Job more than the beginning: for he had fourteen thousand sheep, and six thousand camels, and a thousand yoke of oxen, and a thousand she-asses. And he also had seven sons and three daughters." Tevye has exile and the road beneath his feet—and the daughter he loves most, Chava, restored to him from the dead. The Lord giveth and the Lord taketh away. And what shall Tevye call that which sometimes giveth again?

Tevye's habit of peppering his Yiddish speech with endless quotations from sacred Hebrew sources is his most distinctive verbal quirk and, on the whole, the thorniest problem he presents to the translator. It does not, however, make him unique. The tendency liberally to cite Scripture and liturgy was widespread among speakers of Yiddish, as it must always have been among observant Jews everywhere, who, merely in the course of their daily prayers and their weekly and yearly rituals, commit to memory an enormous number of texts. It was and is not unusual, for example, for a simple, uneducated Jew to know by heart the three daily Hebrew prayers, which even recited at breakneck speed would take a good half hour to get through, plus various other devotions, blessings, and bits of the Bible. In the work of Sholem Aleichem, too, Tevye is by no means the only chronic quoter, even if he is an extreme case for whom chapter and verse, depending on the situation and the person he is talking to, can serve any conceivable purpose: to impress, to inform, to amuse, to intimidate, to comfort, to scold, to ridicule, to show off, to avoid, to put down, to stake a claim of equality or create a mood of intimacy, and so on. He has, as his daughter Chava says, a quote for everything, and sometimes one quote for several things, for his stock is ultimately limited and he has to make the most of it.

In traditional Jewish terms, that is, Tevye is not nearly so erudite as the uninformed reader, or some of his own unversed acquaintances, may think. (Of course, such things are relative; there are not a few American Jewish congregations today in which he would have to be considered a highly learned Jew, second only—and not even always that—to the rabbi.) An analysis of his quotations shows that nearly all of them come from four basic sources, each read and heard year in and year out by the average Orthodox Jew: the daily and holiday prayer book; the Bible (especially the Pentateuch, portions of which are read every Sabbath; the Book of Esther, which is chanted on Purim; and Psalms, which observant Jews often recite as a paternoster when troubled or in their spare time); the Passover Haggadah; and *Pirkey Avot* or "The Ethics of the Fathers," a short Mishnaic tractate of rabbinic sayings that is printed in the Sabbath section of the prayer book. Of the rest of the Mishnah and of the Talmud, to say nothing of the many commentaries upon them—the real bread and butter, as it were, of a higher Jewish education—he appears to know next to nothing. Indeed, when he wishes to quote a line of Talmud to Layzer Wolf, he has to make it up out of whole cloth.

Yet if Tevye is no scholar, neither is he the Yiddish Mr. Malaprop that others, overly aware of these limitations, have taken him to be. To be sure, he does occasionally clown, deliberately inventing, confusing, or misattributing a quote in order to mock an ignoramus who will never know the difference, thus scoring a little private triumph of which he himself is the sole witness. On the whole, however—and certainly when directly addressing Sholem Aleichem, who is his superior in Jewish knowledge and whose approval he desires—his quotations are accurate, apropos, and show an understanding of the meaning of the Hebrew words, if not always of their exact grammar. Sometimes they are even witty, taking an ancient verse or phrase and deliberately wrenching it out of context to fit the situation he is talking about, as when, at the beginning of "Hodl," in discussing how hard it is for a Jewish youngster to be accepted by a Russian school, Tevye says, "*Al tishlakh yodkho:** they guard their schools from us like a bowl of cream from a cat." The words *al tishlakh yodkho* mean "lay not thine hand" and are found in the story of the sacrifice of Isaac in Chapter 22 of Genesis, in which, at the last second, just as Abraham is about to slaughter his son, an intervening angel cries out, "Lay not thine hand upon the lad, neither do thou anything unto him; for now I know that thou fearest God, seeing thou has not withheld thy son, thine only son, from Me." Tevye knows perfectly well where the phrase he is quoting comes from (the highly dramatic chapter is not only read once a year on the Sabbath like the rest of the Pentateuch, it is chanted a second time as a special selection for Rosh Hashanah)—but this does not keep him from putting it in the mouths of Czarist officials telling Jewish applicants to keep their hands off Russian schools!

Here too, it must be stressed, there is nothing particularly original about his method: Jews have been "deconstructing" biblical texts in this way practically since the Bible was written, and the vast corpus of rabbinical exegesis known as the midrash is based precisely on the enterprise of pouring new wine into old Scriptural bottles. Though these reinterpretations are not generally humorous, there is definitely a creative playfulness in the activity of midrash *per se,* which was, one might say, the ancient rabbis' chief form of recreation—and to this day, if one has the good luck to be among a group of knowledgeable Jews who are in a "midrashic" mood, one can witness this fascinating interplay of encyclopedic recall and wit in which biblical and rabbinic texts are caromed around and off each other as though they were billiard

---

*Tevye's Hebrew is transliterated here, as it is throughout, according to the Ashkenazic pronunciation of Eastern Europe, which is quite different from the way Hebrew is pronounced in Israel and by most Jews today.

balls. Tevye is not quite in this league, but it is one he aspires to, for a religiously educated Jew in the traditional culture of Eastern Europe belonged to a universally recognized aristocracy of the spirit, regardless of his economic status. The riches Tevye dreams of are a mirage; yet the opportunity to rise above his station by a vigorous display of a body of knowledge that, while not large, he is in total command of, is a subjective and objective reality that he exploits to the utmost, and sometimes a bit beyond.

How, though, can this reality be translated into English? Theoretically, the translator has four choices:

1. He can give Tevye's quotations in English instead of in Hebrew.
2. He can give them both in English and in Hebrew, the latter transliterated into Latin characters.
3. He can give them only in Hebrew (as in the original Yiddish text).
4. He can omit them entirely.

I have in fact utilized all these approaches. In some places, where a quotation of Tevye's is neither especially striking nor crucial, and where leaving it out does not adversely affect the tone or the significance of his remarks, I have done so. At a few points in the text I have translated his quotes into English, sometimes retaining the Hebrew as well and sometimes deleting it. In the great majority of cases, however, I have chosen Option 3 and, like the Yiddish text, given only Tevye's Hebrew, translations of which will be found in the glossary and notes at the back of the book. Though this may be the solution that seems at first glance to be the most inconvenient for the English reader, I preferred it for several reasons.

The first of these is that many of Sholem Aleichem's Yiddish readers also failed to understand some or all of Tevye's quotes. Sholem Aleichem had a mass audience, much of it composed of working men and women with little or no religious education, and if they did not mind being stumped by Tevye's Hebrew, neither need the English reader today.

Secondly, most of the characters in *Tevye the Dairyman*—in fact, nearly all of them—are simple Jews themselves who complain that they can't follow Tevye's quotations, from which they keep begging him to desist. For the English reader to be told what these mean at the same time that Tevye's family and acquaintances are baffled by them would create a rather odd effect.

Thirdly, translating Tevye's Hebrew in the text itself almost always results in the wrong tone, since the biblical and rabbinic passages that he cites have an archaic sound in English, which is not at all the case in the original. On the contrary, even when a Yiddish speaker did not know the meaning of a Hebrew verse, the feeling it suggested to him was generally the warm, homey one of religious rituals and synagogue services that he knew well.

Finally, as far as Jewish readers are concerned, modern Jewish history has ironically reversed the composition of Sholem Aleichem's public. Once he was read by Jews who knew more Yiddish than Hebrew; today he is mostly read by those who, if they know any Jewish language at all, know more Hebrew than Yiddish. It is my hope that many such readers who cannot read Sholem Aleichem in the original will nevertheless be able to enjoy Tevye's Hebrew wordplay in this English translation.

For those who cannot, there are two consolations. One is the glossary, which the reader is free to consult not only for the meaning and pronunciation of Tevye's Hebrew quotes, but also for explanations of historical references and Jewish customs that may elude him. The other is the fact that there is no need to skip over the Hebrew quotations just because one does not understand them. Read them aloud; savor them; try saying them as Tevye did. There is no way to reproduce in print the exact sights, smells, and tastes of Tevye's world, but a bit of the sound of it is in these pages.

▲ 3 ▲

Though there is only one Tevye, there was also only one Sholem Aleichem, and, as readers of the twenty *Railroad Stories* will notice, as prolifically creative as he was (the first posthumous, incomplete edition of his work ran to twenty-eight volumes!)—indeed, it would seem, as a prerequisite for such productivity—there are in his work certain basic themes and situations that occur again and again. Thus, one is reminded by the story "Eighteen from Pereshchepena" of the comic scene between Tevye and Layzer Wolf in which the two carry on a single conversation that each thinks is about something else; by the narrator's attitude toward women in "High

School" of Tevye's antifemale posturing; by Berl Vinegar's fast-talking of the priest in "The Miracle of Hoshana Rabbah" of Tevye's handling of Ivan Paparilo in the pogrom scene of "Lekh-Lekho," etc. Even Tevye's rampant quotationism has its parallel in the narrator of "Burned Out"—who, however, is even less of a "scholar" than Tevye and wildly throws Hebrew phrases about without always knowing what they mean. Such recurrent elements served Sholem Aleichem as modular blocks out of which he was able to construct an amazing variety of characters and plots.

Although *The Railroad Stories,* first assembled in book form in 1911, are contemporary with the *Tevye* episodes, their composition was not widely spaced like that of *Tevye* but rather concentrated in two intense bursts of activity, one in 1902 and one in 1909–1910. In the first period were written "High School," "The Automatic Exemption," "Burned Out," "Fated for Misfortune," and, though it was later slightly revised to form the collection's closing story, "Third Class." With the exception of "It Doesn't Pay to be Good," which dates from 1903, all the other stories belong to the second period. It was only then, indeed, that Sholem Aleichem decided to write a book of tales all told to or overheard by a traveling salesman on a train, which explains a fundamental difference between the 1902–1903 series and the 1909–1910 one; for in the latter group trains and train rides are generally intrinsic, whereas in the former they are not. The 1902–1903 stories, in other words, were not originally written with railroads in mind, to which they were adapted after the fact by the simple device of adding a brief descriptive opening paragraph placing them on a train. As for the order of the stories in the book, it was determined by Sholem Aleichem himself. While it does not strictly reflect the sequence in which they were written, it does have a chronological basis, the first eleven tales dating from 1909–1910, the next five from 1902–1903, and the next three from 1909–1910 again.

Like *Tevye,* nearly all *The Railroad Stories* are monologues; this was Sholem Aleichem's favorite form and one he repeatedly returned to. At first glance it may seem that the traveling salesman who records them is a more active party than the Sholem Aleichem who merely listens to Tevye, since he describes what he sees and occasionally participates in the conversation—yet this is but one side of the coin. Though Sholem Aleichem never speaks to Tevye, Tevye is always conscious of speaking to Sholem Aleichem; his idea of the educated, cultured, sophisticated author he is talking to colors all that he says, and more than once he insists that he would never confide such things to anyone else. The commercial traveler of *The Railroad Stories,* on the other hand, is simply someone to whom his fellow passengers can tell their tale, at times revealing to the book's readers aspects of themselves that he himself is naïvely unaware of. (Such as the fact, for example, that the "Man from Buenos Aires" is really a rich pimp engaged in the white slave trade, the shanghaiing of girls to Argentina to work as prostitutes there.) Who he is does not interest them in the least. A Jew meets another Jew on the train and straightaway begins to talk about himself.

Nevertheless, though the notion of trains running through Russia with almost no one in their third-class cars but Jews who tell each other stories may seem like an artificial literary convention, this is actually not the case. The Russia of Sholem Aleichem's day, especially in the provincial Pale of Settlement, had a relatively small Christian middle and lower-middle class. The great bulk of the population belonged to either the peasantry or the landed aristocracy, and of the two groups, the first rarely traveled, and the second never traveled third class. Jews were often merchants, but mostly petty ones who preferred to travel as cheaply as they could—and the fact that Jews, when traveling, tend even today to talk nonstop to each other is something that can be vouched for by anyone who has ever taken a crowded flight to Israel.

Nor is this the only example in *The Railroad Stories* of the way in which our distance from the times may mislead us into thinking that Sholem Aleichem was deliberately exaggerating for literary or comic purposes. Take, for instance, the seemingly surrealistic plot of "The Automatic Exemption," in which a father must run endlessly from draft board to draft board because a son who died in infancy still appears in the population registry; "the [Russian] government," writes the Jewish historian Simon Dubnow, "refused [in drafting Jews] to consider the fact that, owing to inaccurate registration, the conscription lists often carried the names of persons who had long since died, or who had left the country to emigrate abroad"; even the three hundred rubles that a lawyer tells the distraught father he will have to pay as a fine was the exact sum stipulated by Russian law for such cases! Or take the apparently farcical section of the story "High School" in which a

Jew must get a Christian drunk so that he will agree to send his son, at the Jew's expense, to a commercial school together with the Jew's son. Here is Dubnow again:

> In the commercial schools maintained by the commercial associations Jewish children were admitted only in proportion to the contributions of the Jewish merchants toward the upkeep of the particular school. In private commercial schools, however, percentages of all kinds, varying from ten to fifty percent, were fixed in the case of Jewish pupils. This provision had the effect that Jewish parents were vitally interested in securing the entrance of as many Christian children as possible in order to increase thereby the number of Jewish vacancies. Occasionally, a Jewish father, in the hope of creating a vacancy for his son, would induce a Christian to send his boy to a commercial school—though the latter, as a rule, offered little attraction for the Christian population—by undertaking to defray all expenses connected with his education.

This is not to say that there are not elements of farce in these stories, but they lie far more in the reaction of the characters than in the situation itself. Always a stickler for getting the details right (even the fabulous Brodsky of *Tevye* and "Go Climb a Tree If You Don't Like It" was a real Jewish sugar magnate of that name who lived in Kiev), Sholem Aleichem became even more so after leaving Russia in 1906, for he was afraid of being thought out of touch with the world he continued to write about. The Soviet Jewish critic Max Erik quotes a revealing letter written by him to an acquaintance in the White Russian town of Homel at the time that he was working on these tales:

> Perhaps you would consider doing something for me: I would like you to send me raw material from Homel, from Vitebsk, from Bialystok, from wherever you care to, as long as it is subject matter that I can use in my "Railroad Stories." I have in mind characters, encounters, anecdotes, comic and tragic histories, events, love affairs, weddings, divorces, fateful dreams, bankruptcies, family celebrations, even funerals—in a word, anything you see and hear about, have seen and heard about, or will see and hear about, in Homel or anywhere else. Please keep one thing in mind, though: I don't want anything imaginary, just facts, the more the better!

Two more examples of such (on our part) unsuspected factuality in these stories are of particular interest.

One concerns a matter of language. In the first of *The Railroad Stories*, "Competitors," we are presented with a woman train vendor who, when her tongue is unleashed, turns out to be a stupendous curser—and by no means a rote one, but a talented improviser who can match every phrase she utters with an appropriate imprecation. One of a kind, no? No. In a chapter devoted to curses in his *The World of Sholom Aleichem*, Maurice Samuel writes of what he calls the "apposite or apropos" curse in the Yiddish of Eastern Europe:

> The apposite or apropos curse is a sort of "catch," or linked phrase; it is hooked on to the last word uttered by the object of the curse. Thus, if he wanted to eat, and said so, the response would be: "Eat? May worms eat you, dear God!" Or: "Drink? May leeches drink your blood!" "Sew a button on for you? I'll sew cerements for you!" If the person addressed does not supply the lead, the curser does it for herself. "There runs Chaim Shemeral! May the life run out of him!" . . . "Are you still sitting? May you sit on open sores! Are you silent? May you be silent forever! Are you yelling? May you yell for your teeth! Are you playing? May the Angel of Death play with you! Are you going? May you go on crutches."

Indeed, in his autobiography *From the Fair*, Sholem Aleichem describes his stepmother as being just such an "apropos curser" and confesses to having modeled several characters on her—one of whom is no doubt the woman vendor from "Competitors."

Finally, there is the story "Elul," whose ending, if we do not know what lies behind it, must strike us as rather forced. After all, it does not seem quite credible for an apparently normal girl, even if her father is a smirking bully, suddenly to kill herself just because a jilted and possibly pregnant friend has done the same. But there is a clue here, and that is Mikhail Artsybashev's novel *Sanine*, which the two girls have been reading in secret. All but forgotten today, *Sanine* was a literary sensation when it appeared in 1907 (the shopboy Berl's "summary" of it, of course, is a hilariously garbled version of the story). Written during the period of Czarist reaction that followed the abortive Revolution of 1905 by an author who was himself a professed anarchist, the novel, with its curious combination of (for then) daring erotica, world-weary cynicism, and obsession with death, led to a wave of youthful suicides in Russia, comparable to that caused in Europe by *The*

Sorrows of Young Werther over a century before. The times were ripe for it; they were what Tevye's youngest daughter calls the disillusioned "Age of Beilke" as opposed to the idealistic "Age of Hodl"; and Etke, the daughter of the narrator, was patterned on cases of actual youngsters swept up in an adolescent death cult.

Apart from the fact that they are all monologues, *The Railroad Stories* do not fit into any one mold. Some, like "The Miracle of Hoshana Rabbah" and "*Tallis Koton*," are sheer hijinks; others, like "High School," have an aspect of social satire; still others, like "The Man from Buenos Aires," "A Game of Sixty-Six," "It Doesn't Pay to Be Good," and "Fated for Misfortune," belong to that ironic genre of gradual exposure wherein the reader comes to realize that the speaker is not the kind of man he is pretending to be. "The Automatic Exemption," "Burned Out," and "Go Climb a Tree If You Don't Like It" are comic studies in hysteria and mania; "The Happiest Man in All Kodny" is a piece of pure pathos with few comic lines in it; and yet another story, "The Tenth Man," is a single brilliant joke whose punch line is withheld till the last moment. Indeed, there are perhaps only two things that all these narrators have in common: each has his distinctive verbal tic or tics, one or more favorite expressions that keep recurring as a kind of nervous identification tag, and each has an obsessive, an uncontrollable, an insatiable, an almost maniacal need to talk.

▲ 4 ▲

This obsessive garrulousness is common in Sholem Aleichem and is in effect a precondition of the monologue, which can hardly be based on taciturn types. The speakers of his stories talk when they have something specific to say and they talk when they do not; in his famous monologue "The Pot," for example, a woman, whose nagging voice is all we ever hear, comes to see a rabbi about some minor matter of Jewish law, chatters on and on about one unrelated subject after another without ever coming to the point, and stops only when the rabbi, still not having gotten a word in edgewise, finally faints from exhaustion. . . . There is something of this pot woman in many of Sholem Aleichem's characters, who seem to be saying, "I talk, therefore I exist." Nothing frightens them so much as silence—most of all, their own.

Jews have perhaps always been a highly verbal people, certainly since the time when their religion became centered on a growing number of sacred texts and the constant exposition and reexposition of them; the vast "sea of the Talmud" itself, as it is called in Hebrew, is but the edited record of endless oral discussions and debates among the early rabbis, and for centuries, down to the yeshivas and synagogues of Sholem Aleichem's Eastern Europe, the most common method of studying the Law was to talk about it aloud in groups of twos and threes and fours. Here the spoken word is still a functional tool of analysis and communication. In Sholem Aleichem's world, however, it has become something else—or rather, many things: a club, a cloud, a twitch, a labyrinth, a smokescreen, a magic wand, a madly waved paper fan, a perpetual motion machine, a breastwork against chaos, the very voice of chaos itself. . . . His characters chute on torrents of words and seek to drag others into the current with them. And succeed. When the storyteller in "Baranovitch Station" breaks off his unfinished tale because it is time for him to change trains, his fellow passengers cannot believe that a Jew like themselves would rather stop talking in the middle of a sentence than miss his connection.

No one understood better than Sholem Aleichem that this astonishing verbosity, this virtuoso command of and abuse of language, was at once the greatest strength and the ultimate pathology of East European Jewish life. Reviled, ghettoized, impoverished, powerless, his Jews have only one weapon: the power of speech. And because it is a weapon that has come down to them honed by the expert use of ages, they wield it with the skill of trained samurai, men, women, and children. (One of Sholem Aleichem's most wonderful long monologues, the picaresque *Motl, Peysi the Cantor's Son,* is narrated by a ten- or eleven-year-old boy.) What can a Jew not accomplish with his tongue? He can outsmart a goy, bury an enemy, crush a wife or husband, conjure up a fortune, turn black into white, turn white into black . . . and believe it all has happened, so that the very sense of reality becomes distorted and defeat turns into victory, humiliation into triumph, grimy wretchedness into winged flight. Don Quixote would have felt at home in Kasrilevke and Anatevka. He might even have learned a few tricks there.

Yet can we be so sure that this defiant quixotism, when all is said and done, does not represent a real triumph of sorts? In a discussion of Sholem Aleichem's story "Dreyfus in Kasrilevke" (in which, being told by a fellow Kasrilevkite, who has just read it in the newspaper, that Dreyfus was found guilty, the town's Jews refuse to believe it), Professor Ruth Wisse writes:

> Here, too, the oppressed replace the world's reality with the reality of their argumentative concern. But the Sholem Aleichem story equates the Jews' far-sightedness with faith. . . . Dreyfus in Kasrilevke is judged by God's law; and is God's truth to be sacrificed for journalism?

And she quotes the final lines of the story:

> "Paper!" cried Kasrilevke. "Paper! And if you stood here with one foot in heaven and one foot on earth, we still wouldn't believe you. Such things cannot be! No, this cannot be! It cannot be! It cannot be!"
> Well, and who was right?

"It cannot be": such is the true human voice of Sholem Aleichem's world and the only one he really cared about. For a great writer, he was in some ways oddly limited: he rarely wrote more than cursory descriptions of people, places, and things and was not outstandingly good at them; abstract ideas did not interest him; and even his dialogue reverts quickly to monologue or peters out in misunderstandings and cross-purposes. As a consequence, those of his novels that are not monologic do not rank with the best of his work, and, when their comic thrust fails, they often lapse into sentimentality. (As all cynics are said to be wounded idealists, are not all humorists wounded sentimentalists?) The solo voice was his specialty: he had an uncanny ability to mimic it, to catch its rhythms and intonations, to study it as the mask and revelation of inner self. (Y. D. Berkovits relates how, upon emigrating westward in 1906 and first stopping in Austrian Galicia, whose Yiddish was quite different from that of Russia, Sholem Aleichem imitated the natives so well that soon they could not tell him from a local!) This voice is indomitable. It keeps on talking. It will not be stilled. "It cannot be!" is what it says, and in one way or another it is right.

Human speech, of which nearly all the fiction in this volume is composed, is both the easiest and the hardest language to translate: the easiest because it is usually syntactically so simple, the hardest because it carries the greatest freight of those localisms and culture-bound words of a community that can never have a true equivalent in other languages. And this is especially so of Yiddish, that Jewish tongue woven on a base of middle high German and richly embroidered with Hebrew and Slavic, whose syntax is far simpler than German's but which is culturally more remote from the languages of Christian Europe than any of them are from each other. True, one needn't exaggerate the difficulties: professional translators are used to insoluble problems, and they generally manage to solve them. There are, however, two aspects of Yiddish speech that, because they have no real parallel in English and cannot be satisfactorily approximated in it, deserve to be mentioned.

The first has to do with formulas for avoiding the evil eye. Superstition and the fear of provoking or attracting the attention of hostile forces, or simply of causing offense, are of course universal; but in Yiddish (perhaps because it was the language of a culture in which aggression, given little external outlet, was always felt to be threateningly close to the surface) this anxiety is so extreme that it dictates the use of a wide variety of appeasing expressions in daily speech. Thus, one should not mention a dead person one has known without adding *olov hasholom,* "may he rest in peace"; one does not boast of or express satisfaction with anything unless one says *kinnehoro,* "no evil eye" (i.e., touch or knock wood); if one mentions a misfortune to someone, one tells him *nisht do gedakht* or *nisht far aykh gedakht,* "it shouldn't happen here" or "it shouldn't happen to you"; if one makes a remark critical of somebody, one prefaces it with *zol er mir moykhl zayn,* "may he forgive me"; if the criticism is aimed at Providence, one says *zol mir got nisht shtrofn far di reyd,* "may God not punish me for my words." Moreover, such expressions cover only the specific case; if a person is talking about a deceased relative, for example, and mentions him ten times, it is good form to say *olov hasholom* after each. The result is that one or several sentences of spoken Yiddish can contain a whole series of such phrases that break the speech up into a sequence of fragments punctuated by anxious qualifications. The translator can and should retain some of these, but being overly faithful to them makes the English tiresome, and I have left quite a few out. Wherever the reader sees one such expression in the English, he can assume there may be more in the Yiddish.

Secondly, there is the widespread use in Yiddish of Hebrew, not in the form of quotations, as with Tevye, but of idioms that have become rooted in popular speech, commonly transplanted there from religious texts and prayers. These occupy an ambivalent position: on the one hand, they are understood and used even by uneducated speakers, yet on the other, their Hebrew etymology continues to be recognized and their sacral origins are not obscured, so that they often produce ironic or comic effects. For example, when the arsonist who narrates "Burned Out" relates his neighbors' suspicions of him, he does not say that they accuse him of "setting fire" to his house and store, but rather of "making *boyrey me'oyrey ho'eysh.*" Literally these Hebrew words mean "He Who creates the light of fire," but they belong to a blessing ("Blessed art Thou O Lord our God, King of the Universe, Who creates the light of fire") that is said every week in the *havdalah,* the ritual of ending the Sabbath on Saturday night, part of which involves lighting a candle (an act forbidden on the Sabbath itself) and holding one's hand up to the flame. What can the translator do with such untranslatabilities, which are not uncommon in Yiddish, and especially not in a comic Yiddish like Sholem Aleichem's? Shut his eyes and hope to think of something! And in this case I did, because suddenly I remembered a snatch of a comic ditty that I knew as a boy in New York about a Jew who burns down his store for the "inshurinks," just like the narrator of "Burned Out." It was sung in a Yiddish accent to the tune of the Zionist anthem *Hatikvah,* and one stanza of it went:

> *Vans I hed a kendy store, business it vas bed,*
> *Along came a friend of mine, vat you tink he said?*
> *"I hear you got a kendy store vat you don't vant no more;*
> *Take a metch, give a skretch, no more kendy store!"*

And so "to make *borey me'oyrey ho'eysh*" became "to give the match a scratch"—not an ideal solution perhaps, but certainly a passable one. One does the best one can. Sometimes it's a matter of luck.

I have been translating fiction for many years, but from Hebrew, not from Yiddish, and this volume is the first full-scale Yiddish translation I have attempted. I wish, therefore, to express my deepest thanks to the editor of this series, Ruth Wisse, both for trusting and encouraging me to undertake this translation and for going over it with a fine-tooth comb. She was the safety net above which I felt free to be as acrobatic as I liked, knowing I would always be caught if I fell. This book is hers too.

I also wish to thank Michael Stern of Washington, D.C., for kindly letting me use an unpublished paper tracing the sources of Tevye's Hebrew quotations, thus sparing me much arduous spadework; and my sister, Miriam Halkin Och, of Haifa University Library, for her generous help in obtaining bibliographical materials.

HILLEL HALKIN

Zichron Ya'akov, Israel
1986

▲

Tevye
the Dairyman

TEVYE STRIKES IT RICH

▼

If you're meant to strike it rich, Pani Sholem Aleichem, you may as well stay home with your slippers on, because good luck will find you there too. The more it blows the better it goes, as King David says in his Psalms—and believe me, neither brains nor brawn has anything to do with it. And vice versa: if it's not in the cards you can run back and forth till you're blue in the face, it will do as much good as last winter's snow. How does the saying go? Flogging a dead horse won't make it run any faster. A man slaves, works himself to the bone, is ready to lie down and die—it shouldn't happen to the worst enemy of the Jews. Suddenly, don't ask me how or why, it rains gold on him from all sides. In a word, *revakh vehatsoloh ya'amoyd layehudim,* just like it says in the Bible! That's too long a verse to translate, but the general gist of it is that as long as a Jew lives and breathes in this world and hasn't more than one leg in the grave, he musn't lose faith. Take it from my own experience—that is, from how the good Lord helped set me up in my present line of business. After all, if I sell butter and cheese and such stuff, do you think that's because my grand-mother's grandmother was a milkman? But if I'm going to tell you the whole story, it's worth hearing from beginning to end. If you don't mind, then, I'll sit myself down here beside you and let my horse chew on some grass. He's only human too, don't you think, or why else would God have made him a horse?

Well, to make a long story short, it happened early one summer, around Shavuos time. But why should I lie to you? It might have been a week or two before Shavuos too, unless it was several weeks after. What I'm trying to tell you is that it took place exactly a dog's age ago, nine or ten years to the day, if not a bit more or less.

I was the same man then that I am now, only not at all like me;
that is, I was Tevye then too, but not the Tevye you're looking at.
How does the saying go? It's still the same lady, she's just not so
shady. Meaning that in those days—it should never happen to
you!—I was such a miserable beggar that rags were too good for
me. Believe me, I'm no millionaire today either. If from now until
autumn the two of us earned a tenth of what it would take to make
me half as rich as Brodsky, we wouldn't be doing half badly. Still,
compared to what I was then, I've become a real tycoon. I've got
my own horse and wagon; I've got two cows that give milk, bless
them, and a third cow waiting to calve; forgive me for boasting,
but we're swimming in cheese, cream, and butter. Not that we
don't work for it, mind you; you won't find any slackers at my
place. My wife milks the cows; the girls carry the cans and churn
butter; and I, as you see, go to the market every morning and
from there to all the summer dachas in Boiberik. I stop to chat
with this person, with that one; there isn't a rich Jew I don't know
there. When you talk with such people, you know, you begin to
feel that you're someone yourself and not such a one-armed tailor
any more. And I'm not even talking about Sabbaths. On Sabbaths,
I tell you, I'm king, I have all the time in the world. Why, I can
even pick up a Jewish book then if I want: the Bible, Psalms,
Rashi, Targum, Perek, you name it . . . I tell you, if you could only
see me then, you'd say, "He's really some fine fellow, that Tevye!"

To get to the point, though . . . where were we? Oh, yes: in
those days, with God's help, I was poor as a devil. No Jew should
starve as I did! Not counting suppers, my wife and kids went
hungry three times a day. I worked like a dog dragging logs by the
wagonful from the forest to the train station for—I'm embarrassed even to tell you—half a ruble a day . . . and not even every
day, either. You try feeding a house full of little mouths on that,
to say nothing of a horse who's moved in with you and can't be put
off with some verse from the Bible, because he expects to eat and
no buts! So what does the good Lord do? I tell you, it's not for
nothing that they say He's a *zon umefarneys lakoyl,* that He runs this
world of His with more brains than you or I could. He sees me
eating my heart out for a slice of bread and says, "Now, Tevye, are
you really trying to tell me that the world has come to an end? Eh,
what a damn fool you are! In no time I'm going to show you what

God can do when He wants. About face, march!" As we say on
Yom Kippur, *mi yorum umi yishofeyl*—leave it to Him to decide who
goes on foot and who gets to ride. The main thing is confidence.
A Jew must never, never give up hope. How does he go on hoping, you ask, when he's already died a thousand deaths? But that's
the whole point of being a Jew in this world! What does it say in
the prayer book? *Atoh bekhartonu!* We're God's chosen people; it's
no wonder the whole world envies us . . . You don't know what
I'm talking about? Why, I'm talking about myself, about the miracle God helped me to. Be patient and you'll hear all about it.

Vayehi hayoym, as the Bible says: one fine summer day in the
middle of the night, I'm driving home through the forest after
having dumped my load of logs. I feel like my head is in the
ground, there's a black desert growing in my heart; it's all my
poor horse can do to drag his feet along behind him. "It serves
you right, you schlimazel," I say to him, "for belonging to someone like me! If you're going to insist on being Tevye's horse, it's
time you knew what it tastes like to fast the whole length of a
summer's day." It was so quiet you could hear every crack of the
whip whistle through the woods. The sun began to set; the day
was done for. The shadows of the trees were as long as the exile of
the Jews. And with the darkness a terrible feeling crept into my
heart. All sorts of thoughts ran in and out of my head. The faces
of long-dead people passed before me. And when I thought of
coming home—God help me! The little house would be pitch-
dark. My naked, barefoot kids would peek out to see if their
schlemiel of a father hadn't brought them some bread, maybe
even a freshly baked roll. And my old lady would grumble like a
good Jewish mother: "A lot he needed children—and seven of
them at that! God punish me for saying so, but my mistake was
not to have taken them all and thrown them into the river." How
do you think it made me feel to hear her say such things? A man is
only flesh and blood, after all; you can't fill a stomach with words.
No, a stomach needs herring to fill it; herring won't go down
without tea; tea can't be drunk without sugar; and sugar, my
friend, costs a fortune. And my wife! "My guts," says my wife,
"can do without bread in the morning, but without a glass of tea
I'm a stretcher case. That baby's sucked the glue from my bones
all night long!"

Well, one can't stop being a Jew in this world: it was time for the
evening prayer. (Not that the evening was about to go anywhere,
but a Jew prays when he must, not when he wants to.) Some fine
prayer it turned out to be! Right in the middle of the *shimenesre*,
the eighteen benedictions, a devil gets into my crazy horse and he
decides to go for a pleasure jaunt. I had to run after the wagon
and grab the reins while shouting "God of Abraham, Isaac, and
Jacob" at the top of my voice—and to make matters worse I'd
really felt like praying for a change, for once in my life I was sure
it would make me feel better . . .

In a word, there I was running behind the wagon and singing
the *shimenesre* like a cantor in a synagogue. *Mekhalkeyl khayim bekhesed,* Who provideth life with His bounty—it better be all of life,
do You hear me? . . . *Umekayeym emunosoy lisheyney ofor,* Who keep-
eth faith with them who slumber in earth—who slumber in earth?
With my troubles I was six feet underground already! And to
think of those rich Yehupetz Jews sitting all summer long in their
dachas in Boiberik, eating and drinking and swimming in luxury!
Master of the Universe, what have I done to deserve all this? Am I
or am I not a Jew like any other? Help! . . . *Re'ey-no be'onyeynu,* See
us in our affliction—take a good look at us poor folk slaving away
and do something about it, because if You don't, just who do You
think will? . . . *Refo'eynu veneyrofey,* Heal our wounds and make us
whole—please concentrate on the healing because the wounds we
already have . . . *Boreykh oleynu,* Bless the fruits of this year—
kindly arrange a good harvest of corn, wheat, and barley, although what good it will do me is more than I can say: does it
make any difference to my horse, I ask You, if the oats I can't
afford to buy him are expensive or cheap?

But God doesn't tell a man what He thinks, and a Jew had better
believe that He knows what He's up to. *Velamalshinim al tehi tikvoh,*
May the slanderers have no hope—those are all the big shots who
say there is no God: what wouldn't I give to see the look on their
faces when they line up for Judgment Day! They'll pay with back
interest for everything they've done, because God has a long
memory, one doesn't play around with Him. No, what He wants is
for us to be good, to beseech and cry out to Him . . . *Ov harakhamon,* Merciful, loving Father! . . . *Shma koyleynu*—You better listen
to what we tell You! . . . *Khus verakheym oleynu*—pay a little attention to my wife and children, the poor things are hungry! . . .

Retsey—take decent care of Your people again, as once You did long ago in the days of our Temple, when the priests and the Levites sacrificed before You . . .

All of a sudden—whoaaa! My horse stopped short in his tracks. I rushed through what was left of the prayer, opened my eyes, and looked around me. Two weird figures, dressed for a masquerade, were approaching from the forest. "Robbers!" I thought at first, then caught myself. Tevye, I said, what an idiot you are! Do you mean to tell me that after traveling through this forest by day and by night for so many years, today is the day for robbers? And bravely smacking my horse on the rear as though it were no affair of mine, I cried, "Giddyap!"

"Hey, a fellow Jew!" one of the two terrors called out to me in a woman's voice, waving a scarf at me. "Don't run away, mister. Wait a second. We won't do you any harm."

It's a ghost for sure! I told myself. But a moment later I thought, what kind of monkey business is this, Tevye? Since when are you so afraid of ghouls and goblins? So I pulled up my horse and took a good look at the two. They really did look like women. One was older and had a silk kerchief on her head, while the other was young and wore a wig. Both were beet-red and sweating buckets.

"Well, well, well, good evening," I said to them as loudly as I could to show that I wasn't a bit afraid. "How can I be of service to you? If you're looking to buy something, I'm afraid I'm all out of stock, unless I can interest you in some fine hunger pangs, a week's supply of heartache, or a head full of scrambled brains. Anyone for some chilblains, assorted aches and pains, worries to turn your hair gray?"

"Calm down, calm down," they said to me. "Just listen to him run on! Say a good word to a Jew and you get a mouthful of bad ones in return. We don't want to buy anything. We only wanted to ask whether you happened to know the way to Boiberik."

"The way to Boiberik?" I did my best to laugh. "You might as well ask whether I know my name is Tevye."

"You say your name is Tevye?" they said. "We're very pleased to meet you, Reb Tevye. We wish you'd explain to us, though, what the joke is all about. We're strangers around here; we come from Yehupetz and have a summer place in Boiberik. The two of us went out this morning for a little walk, and we've been going around in circles ever since without finding our way out of these woods. A little while ago we heard someone singing. At first we thought, who knows, maybe it's a highwayman. But as soon as we came closer and saw that you were, thank goodness, a Jew, you can imagine how much better we felt. Do you follow us?"

"A highwayman?" I said. "That's a good one! Did you ever hear the story of the Jewish highwayman who fell on somebody in the forest and begged him for a pinch of snuff? If you'd like, I'd be only too glad to tell it to you."

"The story," they say, "can wait. We'd rather you showed us the way to Boiberik first."

"The way to Boiberik?" I say. "You're standing on it right now. This is the way to Boiberik whether you want to go to Boiberik or not."

"But if this is the way to Boiberik," they say, "why didn't you say it was the way to Boiberik before?"

"I didn't say it was the way to Boiberik," I say, "because you didn't ask me if it was the way to Boiberik."

"Well," they say, "if it is the way to Boiberik, would you possibly happen to know by any chance just how long a way to Boiberik it is?"

"To Boiberik," I say, "it's not a long way at all. Only a few miles. About two or three. Maybe four. Unless it's five."

"Five miles?" screamed both women at once, wringing their hands and all but bursting into tears. "Do you have any idea what you're saying? *Only* five miles!"

"Well," I said, "what would you like me to do about it? If it were up to me, I'd make it a little shorter. But there are worse fates than yours, let me tell you. How would you like to be stuck in a wagon creeping up a muddy hill with the Sabbath only an hour away? The rain whips straight in your face, your hands are numb, your heart is too weak to beat another stroke, and suddenly . . . bang! Your front axle's gone and snapped."

"You're talking like a half-wit," said one of the two women. "I swear, you're off your trolley. What are you telling us fairy tales from the Arabian Nights for? We haven't the strength to take another step. Except for a cup of coffee with a butter roll for breakfast, we haven't had a bite of food all day—and you expect us to stand here listening to your stories?"

"That," I said, "is a different story. How does the saying go? It's no fun dancing on an empty stomach. And you don't have to tell me what hunger tastes like; that's something I happen to know. Why, it's not at all unlikely that I haven't seen a cup of coffee and a butter roll for over a year . . ." The words weren't out of my mouth when I saw a cup of hot coffee with cream and a fresh butter roll right before my eyes, not to mention what else was on the table. You dummy, I said to myself, a person might think you were raised on coffee and rolls! I suppose plain bread and herring would make you sick? But just to spite me, my imagination kept insisting on coffee and rolls. I could smell the coffee, I could taste the roll on my tongue—my God, how fresh, how delicious it was . . .

"Do you know what, Reb Tevye?" the two women said to me. "We've got a brilliant idea. As long as we're standing here chatting, why don't we hop into your wagon and give you a chance to take us back to Boiberik yourself? How about it?"

"I'm sorry," I say, "but you're spitting into the wind. You're going to Boiberik and I'm coming from Boiberik. How do you suppose I can go both ways at once?"

"That's easy," they say. "We're surprised you haven't thought of it already. If you were a scholar, you'd have realized right away: you simply turn your wagon around and head back in the other direction . . . Don't get so nervous, Reb Tevye. We should only have to suffer the rest of our lives as much as getting us home safely, God willing, will cost you."

My God, I thought, they're talking Chinese; I can't make head or tail of it. And for the second time that evening I thought of ghosts, witches, things that go bump in the night. You dunce, I told myself, what are you standing there for like a tree stump? Jump back into your wagon, give the horse a crack of your whip, and get away while the getting is good! Well, don't ask me what got into me, but when I opened my mouth again I said, "Hop aboard!"

They didn't have to be asked twice. I climbed in after them, gave my cap a tug, let the horse have the whip, and one, two, three—we're off! Did I say off? Off to no place fast! My horse is stuck to the ground, a cannon shot wouldn't budge him. Well, I said to myself, that's what you get for stopping in the middle of nowhere to gab with a pair of females. It's just your luck that you couldn't think of anything better to do.

Just picture it if you can: the woods all around, the eerie still-
ness, night coming on—and here I am with these two apparitions
pretending to be women . . . My blood began to whistle like a
teakettle. I remembered a story I once had heard about a coachman who was driving by himself through the woods when he
spied a sack of oats lying on the path. Well, a sack of oats is a sack
of oats, so down from the wagon he jumps, shoulders the sack,
barely manages to heave it into his wagon without breaking his
back, and drives off as happy as you please. A mile or two later he
turns around to look at his sack . . . did someone say sack? What
sack? Instead of a sack there's a billy goat with a beard. He reaches
out to touch it and it sticks out a tongue a yard long at him, laughs
like a hyena, and vanishes into thin air . . .

"Well, what are you waiting for?" the two women asked me.

"What am I waiting for?" I say. "You can see for yourselves
what I'm waiting for. My horse is happy where he is. He's not in a
frisky mood."

"Then use your whip," they say to me. "What do you think it's
for?"

"Thank you for your advice," I say to them. "It's very kind of
you to offer it. The problem is that my four-legged friend is not
afraid of such things. He's as used to getting whipped as I'm used
to getting gypped." I tried to sound casual, but I was burning with
a ninety-nine-year fever.

Well, why bore you? I let that poor horse have it. I whipped him
as long as I whipped him hard, until finally he picked up his heels
and we began to move through the woods. And as we did a new
thought occurred to me. Ah, Tevye, I said to myself, are you ever
a numbskull! Once a beggar, always a beggar, that's the story of
your life. Just imagine: here God hands you an opportunity that
comes a man's way once in a hundred years, and you forget to
clinch the deal in advance, so that you don't even know what's in it
for you! Any way you look at it—as a favor or a duty, as a service
or an obligation, as an act of human kindness or something even
worse than that—it's certainly no crime to make a little profit on
the side. When a soup bone is stuck in somebody's face, who
doesn't give it a lick? Stop your horse right now, you imbecile, and
spell it out for them in capital letters: "Look, ladies, if it's worth
such-and-such to you to get home, it's worth such-and-such to me
to take you; if it isn't, I'm afraid we'll have to part ways." On

second thought, though, I thought again: Tevye, you're an imbecile to call yourself an imbecile! Supposing they promised you the
moon, what good would it do you? Don't you know that you can
skin the bear in the forest, but you can't sell its hide there?

"Why don't you go a little faster?" the two women asked, poking
me from behind.

"What's the matter?" I said, "are you in some sort of hurry?
You should know that haste makes waste." From the corner of
my eye I stole a look at my passengers. They were women, all
right, no doubt of it: one wearing a silk kerchief and the other a
wig. They sat there looking at each other and whispering back
and forth.

"Is it still a long way off?" one of them asked me.

"No longer off than we are from there," I said. "Up ahead
there's an uphill and a downhill. After that there's another uphill
and a downhill. After that comes the real uphill and the downhill,
and after that it's straight as the crow flies to Boiberik . . ."

"The man's some kind of nut for sure!" whispered one of the
women to the other.

"I told you he was bad news," says the second.

"He's all we needed," says the first.

"He's crazy as a loon," says the second.

I certainly must be crazy, I thought, to let these two characters
treat me like this. "Excuse me," I said to them, "but where would
you ladies like to be dumped?"

"Dumped!" they say. "What kind of language is that? You can
go dump yourself if you like!"

"Oh, that's just coachman's talk," I say. "In ordinary parlance
we would say, 'When we get to Boiberik safe and sound, with
God's help, where do I drop *mesdames* off?' "

"If that's what it means," they say, "you can drop us off at the
green dacha by the pond at the far end of the woods. Do you
know where it is?"

"Do I know where it is?" I say. "Why, I know my way around
Boiberik the way you do around your own home! I wish I had a
thousand rubles for every log I've carried there. Just last summer,
in fact, I brought a couple of loads of wood to the very dacha
you're talking about. There was a rich Jew from Yehupetz living
there, a real millionaire. He must have been worth a hundred
grand, if not twice that."

"He's still living there," said both women at once, whispering and laughing to each other.

"Well," I said, "seeing as the ride you've taken was no short haul, and as you may have some connection with him, would it be too much for me to request of you, if you don't mind my asking, to put in a good word for me with him? Maybe he's got an opening, a position of some sort. Really, anything would do . . . You never know how things will turn out. I know a young man named Yisro'eyl, for instance, who comes from a town not far from here. He's a real nothing, believe me, a zero with a hole in it. So what happens to him? Somehow, don't ask me how or why, he lands this swell job, and today he's a big shot clearing twenty rubles a week, or maybe it's forty, who knows . . . Some people have all the luck! Do you by any chance happen to know what happened to our slaughterer's son-in-law, all because he picked himself up one fine day and went to Yehupetz? The first few years there, I admit, he really suffered; in fact, he damn near starved to death. Today, though, I only wish I were in his shoes and could send home the money he does. Of course, he'd like his wife and kids to join him, but he can't get them a residence permit. I ask you, what kind of life is it for a man to live all alone like that? I swear, I wouldn't wish it on a dog! . . . Well, bless my soul, will you look at what we have here: here's your pond and there's your green dacha!"

And with that I swung my wagon right through the gate and drove like nobody's business clear up to the porch of the house. Don't ask me to describe the excitement when the people there saw us pull up. What a racket! Happy days!

"Oy, Grandma!"

"Oy, Mama!"

"Oy, Auntie, Auntie!"

"Thank God they're back!"

"Mazel tov!"

"Good lord, where have you been?"

"We've been out of our minds with worry all day long!"

"We had search parties out looking for you everywhere!"

"The things we thought happened to you, it's too horrible for words: highwaymen or maybe a wolf! So tell us, what happened?"

"What happened? What happened shouldn't have happened to a soul. We lost our way in the woods and blundered about for miles. Suddenly, along comes a Jew. What, what kind of a Jew? A

Jew, a schlimazel, with a wagon and a horse. Don't think we had an easy time with him either, but here we are!"

"Incredible! It sounds like a bad dream. How could you have gone out in the woods without a guide? What an adventure, what an adventure. Thank God you're home safe!"

In no time lamps were brought out, the table was set, and there began to appear on it hot samovars flowing with tea, bowls of sugar, jars of jam, plates full of pastry and all kinds of baked goods, followed by the fanciest dishes: soup brimming with fat, roast meats, a whole goose, the best wines and salad greens. I stood a ways off and thought, so this, God bless them, is how these Yehupetz tycoons eat and drink. Why, it's enough to make the Devil jealous! I'd pawn my last pair of socks if it would help to make me a rich Jew like them . . . You can imagine what went through my mind. The crumbs that fell from that table alone would have been enough to feed my kids for a week, with enough left over for the Sabbath. Oh, my dear Lord, I thought: they say You're a long-suffering God, a good God, a great God; they say You're merciful and fair; perhaps You can explain to me, then, why it is that some folk have everything and others have nothing twice over? Why does one Jew get to eat butter rolls while another gets to eat dirt? A moment later, though, I said to myself, ach, what a fool you are, Tevye, I swear! Do you really think He needs your advice on how to run the world? If this is how things are, it's how they were meant to be; the proof of it is that if they were meant to be different, they would be. It may seem to you that they ought to have been meant to be different . . . but it's just for that you're a Jew in this world! A Jew must have confidence and faith. He must believe, first, that there is a God, and second, that if there is, and if it's all the same to Him, and if it isn't putting Him to too much trouble, He can make things a little better for the likes of you . . .

"Wait a minute," I heard someone say. "What happened to the coachman? Has the schlimazel left already?"

"God forbid!" I called out from where I was. "Do you mean to suggest that I'd simply walk off without so much as saying good-bye? Good evening, it's a pleasure to meet you all! Enjoy your meal; I can't imagine why you shouldn't."

"Come in out of the dark," says one of them to me, "and let's have a look at you. Perhaps you'd like a little brandy?"

"A little brandy?" I say. "Who can refuse a little brandy? God may be God, but brandy is brandy. Cheers!" And I emptied the glass in one gulp. "God should only help you to stay rich and happy," I said, "because since Jews can't help being Jews, someone else had better help them."

"What name do you go by?" asked the man of the house, a fine-looking Jew with a skullcap. "Where do you hail from? Where do you live now? What's your work? Do you have a wife? Children? How many?"

"How many children?" I say. "Forgive me for boasting, but if each child of mine were worth a million rubles, as my Golde tries convincing me they are, I'd be richer than anyone in Yehupetz. The only trouble is that poor isn't rich and a mountain's no ditch. How does it say in the prayer book? *Hamavdil beyn koydesh lekhoyl*—some make hay while others toil. There are people who have money and I have daughters. And you know what they say about that: better a house full of boarders than a house full of daughters! Only why complain when we have God for our Father? He looks after everyone—that is, He sits up there and looks at us slaving away down here . . . What's my work? For lack of any better suggestions, I break my back dragging logs. As it says in the Talmud, *bemokoym she'eyn ish,* a herring too is a fish. Really, there'd be no problem if it weren't for having to eat. Do you know what my grandmother used to say? What a shame it is we have mouths, because if we didn't we'd never go hungry . . . But you'll have to excuse me for carrying on like this. You can't expect straight talk from a crooked brain—and especially not when I've gone and drunk brandy on an empty stomach."

"Bring the Jew something to eat!" ordered the man of the house, and right away the table was laid again with food I never dreamed existed: fish, and cold cuts, and roasts, and fowl, and more gizzards and chicken livers than you could count.

"What will you have?" I was asked. "Come on, wash up and sit down."

"A sick man is asked," I answered, "a healthy one is served. Still, thank you anyway . . . a little brandy, with pleasure . . . but to sit down and make a meal of it, when back home my wife and children, they should only be healthy and well . . . so you see, if you don't mind, I'll . . ."

What can I tell you? They seemed to have gotten the hint,

because before I knew it my wagon was being loaded with goodies: here some rolls, there some fish, a pot roast, a quarter of a chicken, tea, sugar, a cup of chicken fat, a jar of jam . . .

"Here's a gift to take home to your wife and children," they said. "And now please tell us how much we owe you for your trouble."

"To tell you the truth," I said, "who am I to tell you what you owe me? You pay me what you think it was worth. What's a few kopecks more or less between us? I'll still be the same Tevye when we're done."

"No," they say, "we want you to tell us, Reb Tevye. You needn't be afraid. We won't chop your head off."

Now what? I asked myself. I was really in a pretty pickle. It would be a crime to ask for one ruble when they might agree to two. On the other hand, if I asked for two they might think I was mad. *Two* rubles for one little wagon ride?

"Three rubles!" The words were out of my mouth before I could stop them. Everyone began to laugh so hard that I could have crawled into a hole in the ground.

"Please forgive me," I said, "if I've said the wrong thing. Even a horse, which has four legs, stumbles now and then, so why not a man with one tongue . . ."

The laughter grew even louder. I thought they'd all split their sides.

"Stop laughing now, all of you!" ordered the man of the house. He pulled a large wallet from his pocket and out of it he fished— how much do you think? I swear you'll never guess—a ten-ruble note, all red as fire, as I hope to die! And do you know what else he says to me? "This," he says, "is from me. Now children, let's see what each of you can dig out of your pockets."

What can I possibly tell you? Five- and three- and one-ruble notes flew onto the table. I was shaking so hard that I thought I was going to faint.

"Well, what are you waiting for?" says the man of the house to me. "Take your money from the table and have a good trip home."

"God reward you a hundred times over," I said. "May He bring you good luck and happiness for the rest of your lives." I couldn't scoop up that money (who could even count it?) and stuff it into my pockets fast enough. "Good night," I said. "You should all be happy and well—you, and your children, and their children after them, and all their friends and relations."

I had already turned to go when the older woman with the silk kerchief stopped me and said, "One minute, Reb Tevye. There's a special present I'd like to give you that you can come pick up in the morning. I have the strangest cow; it was once a wonderful beast, it gave twenty-four glasses of milk every day. Someone must have put a hex on it, though, because now you can't milk it at all— that is, you can milk it all you want, you just can't get any milk from it . . ."

"I wish you a long life," I said, "and one you won't wish was any shorter. We'll not only milk your milk cow, we'll milk it for milk. My wife, God bless her, is such a wizard around the house that she can bake a noodle pudding from thin air, make soup from a fingernail, whip up a Sabbath meal from an empty cupboard, and put hungry children to sleep with a box on the ear . . . Well, please don't hold it against me if I've run on a little too long. And now good night to you all and be well," I said, turning to go to the yard where my wagon was parked . . . good grief! With my luck one always has to expect a disaster, but this was an out-and-out misfortune. I looked this way, I looked that way—*vehayeled eynenu:* there wasn't a horse in sight.

This time, Tevye, I thought, you're really in a fix! And I remembered a charming story I once read in a book about a gang of goblins who played a prank on a Jew, a pious Hasid, by luring him to a castle outside of town where they wined and dined him and suddenly disappeared, leaving a naked woman behind them. The woman turned into a tigress, the tigress turned into a cat, and the cat turned into a rattlesnake . . . Between you and me, Tevye, I said to myself, how do you know they're not pulling a fast one on you?

"What are you mumbling and grumbling about?" someone asked me.

"What am I mumbling about?" I said. "Believe me, it's not for my health. In fact, I have a slight problem. My horse—"

"Your horse," he says, "is in the stable. You only have to go there and look for it."

I went to the stable and looked for him. I swear I'm not a Jew if the old fellow wasn't standing there as proud as punch among the tycoon's thoroughbreds, chewing away at his oats for all he was worth.

"I'm sorry to break up the party," I said to him, "but it's time to go home, old boy. Why make a hog of yourself? Before you know it, you'll have taken one bite too many . . ."

In the end it was all I could do to wheedle him out of there and into his harness. Away home we flew on top of the world, singing Yom Kippur songs as tipsily as you please. You wouldn't have recognized my nag; he ran like the wind without so much as a mention of the whip and looked like he'd been reupholstered. When we finally got home late at night, I joyously woke up my wife.

"Mazel tov, Golde," I said to her. "I've got good news."

"A black mazel tov yourself," she says to me. "Tell me, my fine breadwinner, what's the happy occasion? Has my goldfingers been to a wedding or a circumcision?"

"To something better than a wedding and a circumcision combined," I say. "In a minute, my wife, I'm going to show you a treasure. But first go wake up the girls. Why shouldn't they also enjoy some Yehupetz cuisine . . ."

"Either you're delirious, or else you're temporarily deranged, or else you've taken leave of your senses, or else you're totally insane. All I can say is, you're talking just like a madman, God help us!" says my wife. When it comes to her tongue, she's a pretty average Jewish housewife.

"And you're talking just like a woman!" I answered. "King Solomon wasn't joking when he said that out of a thousand females you won't find one with her head screwed on right. It's a lucky thing that polygamy has gone out of fashion." And with that I went to the wagon and began unpacking all the dishes I'd been given and setting them out on the table. When that gang of mine saw those rolls and smelled that meat, they fell on it like a pack of wolves. Their hands shook so that they could hardly get a grip on it. I stood there with tears in my eyes, listening to their jaws work away like a plague of starving locusts.

"So tell me," says my woman when she's done, "who's been sharing their frugal repast with you, and since when do you have such good friends?"

"Don't worry, Golde," I say. "You'll hear about it all in good time. First put the samovar on, so that we can sit down and drink a glass of tea in style. Generally speaking, you only live once, am I right? So it's a good thing that we now have a cow of our own that gives twenty-four glasses of milk every day; in fact, I'm planning to go fetch her in the morning. And now, Golde," I said to her, pulling out my wad of bills, "be a sport and guess how much I have here."

You should have seen her turn pale as a ghost. She was so flabbergasted that she couldn't say a word.

"God be with you, Golde, my darling," I said. "You needn't look so frightened. Are you worried that I stole it somewhere? Feh, you should be ashamed of yourself! How long haven't you been married to me that you should think such thoughts of your Tevye? This is kosher money, you sillyhead, earned fair and square by my own wits and hard work. The fact is that I've just saved two people from great danger. If it weren't for me, God only knows what would have become of them . . ."

In a word, I told her the whole story from beginning to end, the entire rigamarole. When I was through we counted all the money, then counted it again, then counted it once more to be sure. Whichever way we counted, it came to exactly thirty-seven rubles even.

My wife began to cry.

"What are you crying like a fool for?" I asked her.

"How can I help crying," she says, "if the tears keep coming? When the heart is full it runs out at the eyes. God help me if something didn't tell me that you were about to come with good news. You know, I can't remember when I last saw my Grandma Tsaytl, may she rest in peace, in a dream—but just before you came, I dreamed that I saw a big milk can filled to the brim, and Grandma Tsaytl was carrying it underneath her apron to keep the Evil Eye from seeing it, and all the children were shouting, 'Look, Mama, look . . .' "

"Don't go smacking your lips before you've tasted the pudding, Golde, my darling," I said to her. "I'm sure Grandma Tsaytl is enjoying her stay in Paradise, but that doesn't make her an expert on what's happening down here. Still, if God went through the trouble of getting us a milk cow, it stands to reason He'll see to it that the milk cow will give milk . . . What I wanted to ask you, though, Golde my dear, is what should we do with all the money?"

"It's funny you ask me that, Tevye," she says, "because that's just what I was going to ask you."

"Well, if you were going to ask me anyway," I say, "suppose I ask you. What do you think we should do with so much capital?"

We thought. And the harder we thought, the dizzier we became planning one business venture after another. What didn't we deal in that night? First we bought a pair of horses and quickly sold them for a windfall; then with the profit we opened a grocery store in Boiberik, sold out all the stock, and opened a dry-goods store; after that we invested in some woodland, found a buyer for it, and came out a few more rubles ahead; next we bought up the tax concession for Anatevka, farmed it out again, and with the income started a bank . . .

"You're completely out of your mind!" my wife suddenly shouted at me. "Do you want to throw away our hard-earned savings by lending money to good-for-nothings and end up with only your whip again?"

"So what do you suggest?" I said. "That it's better to go bankrupt trading in grain? Do you have any idea of the fortunes that are being lost right this minute on the wheat market? If you don't believe me, go to Odessa and see for yourself."

"What do I care about Odessa?" she says. "My greatgrandparents didn't live there and neither will my greatgrandchildren, and neither will I, as long as I have legs not to take me there."

"So what do you want?" I ask her.

"What do I want?" she says. "I want you to talk sense and stop acting like a moron."

"Well, well," I said, "look who's the wise one now! Apparently there's nothing that money can't buy, even brains. I might have known this would happen."

To make a long story short, after quarreling and making up a few more times, we decided to buy, in addition to the beast I was to pick up in the morning, a milk cow that gave milk . . .

It might occur to you to ask why we decided to buy a cow when we could just as well have bought a horse. But why buy a horse, I ask you, when we could just as well have bought a cow? We live close to Boiberik, which is where all the rich Yehupetz Jews come to spend the summer in their dachas. And you know those Yehupetz Jews—nothing's too good for them. They expect to have everything served up on a silver platter: wood, meat, eggs, poultry, onions, pepper, parsley . . . so why shouldn't I be the man to walk into their parlor with cheese, cream, and butter? They like to eat well, they have money to burn, you can make a fat living from them as long as they think they're getting the best—and believe me, fresh produce like mine they can't even get in Yehupetz. The two of us, my friend, should only have good luck in our lives for every time I've been stopped by the best sort of people, Gentiles even, who beg to be my customers. "We've heard, Tevye," they say to me, "that you're an honest fellow, even if you are a rat-Jew . . ." I ask you, do you ever get such a compliment from Jews? My worst enemy should have to lie sick in bed for as long as it would take me to wait for one! No, our Jews like to keep their praises to themselves, which is more than I can say about their noses. The minute they see that I've bought another cow, or that I have a new cart, they begin to rack their brains: "Where is it all coming from? Can our Tevye be passing out phony banknotes? Or perhaps he's making moonshine in some still?" Ha, ha, ha. All I can say is: keep wondering until your heads break, my friends, and enjoy it . . .

Believe it or not, you're practically the first person to have heard this story, the whole where, what, and when of it. And now you'll have to excuse me, because I've run on a little too long and there's a business to attend to. How does the Bible put it? *Koyl oyreyv lemineyhu,* it's a wise bird that feathers its own nest. So you'd better be off to your writing, and I to my milk cans and jugs . . .

There's just one request I have, Pani: please don't stick me in any of your books. And if that's too much to ask, do me a favor and at least leave my name out.

And oh yes, by the way: don't forget to take care and be well!

(1894, 1897)

TEVYE BLOWS A SMALL FORTUNE

▼

Raboys makhshovoys belev ish: "Many are the thoughts in a man's heart but the counsel of the Lord shall prevail"—isn't that what it says in the Bible? I don't have to spell it out for you, Pani Sholem Aleichem, but in ordinary language, that is, in plain Yiddish, it

means the best horse can do with a whipping and the cleverest
man with advice. What makes me say that? Only the fact that if I
had had enough sense to go ask some good friend about it, things
would never have come to this sorry state. You know what,
though? When God decides to punish a man, He begins by re-
moving his brains. How many times have I said to myself, Tevye,
you jackass, would you ever have been taken for such a ride if you
weren't the big fool you are? Just what was the matter, touch
wood, with the living you were already making? You had a little
dairy business that was, I swear, world-famous in Boiberik and
Yehupetz, to say nothing of God knows where else. Just think how
fine and dandy it would be if all your cash were stashed quietly
away now in the ground, so that no one knew a thing about it.
Whose business was it anyway, I ask you, if Tevye had a bit of
spare change? . . . I mean that. A fat lot anyone cared about me
when—it shouldn't happen to a Jew!—I was six feet underground myself, dying from hunger three times a day with my wife
and kids. It was only when God looked my way and did me a favor
for a change, so that I managed to make a little something of
myself and even to put away a few rubles, that the rest of the
world sat up and noticed me too. They made such a fuss over Reb
Tevye then that it wasn't even funny. All of a sudden everybody
was my best friend. How does the verse go? *Kulom ahuvim, kulom
brurim*—when God gives with a spoon, man comes running with a
shovel. Everyone wanted me for a partner: this one to buy a
grocery, that one a dry-goods store, another a house, still another
a farm—all solid investments, of course. I should put my money
into wheat, into wood, into whatnot . . . "Brothers," I said to them,
"enough is enough. If you think I'm another Brodsky, you're
making a terrible mistake. I'd like to inform you that I haven't
three hundred rubles to my name, or even half of that, or even
two-thirds of that half. It's easy to decide that someone is worth a
small fortune, but come a little closer and you'll see what cock-
and-bull it is."

In short, our Jews—don't even mention them!—put the
whammy on me. The next thing I know, God sends me a relative—
and a real kissing cousin too, let me tell you, the horse's own tail, as
they say. Menachem Mendl was his name: a wheeler, a dealer, a
schemer, a dreamer, a bag of hot air; no place on earth is bad
enough to deserve him! He got hold of me and filled my head with

such pipe dreams that it began to spin like a top . . . I can see, though, that you want to ask me a good question: why does a Tevye, of all people, get involved with a Menachem Mendl? Well, the answer to that is: because. Fate is fate. Listen to a story.

One day early last winter I started out for Yehupetz with some merchandise—twenty-five pounds of the very best butter and a couple of wheels of white and yellow cheese such as I only wish could be yours. I hardly need say that I sold it all right away, every last lick of it, before I had even finished making the rounds of my summer customers, the dacha owners in Boiberik, who wait for me as though I were the Messiah. You could beat the merchants of Yehupetz black and blue, they still couldn't come up with produce like mine! But I don't have to tell you such things. How does the Bible put it? *Yehalelkho zor*—quality toots its own horn . . .

In a word, having sold everything down to the last crumb and given my horse some hay, I went for a walk about town. *Odom yesoydoy mi'ofor*—a man is only a man: it's no fault of his own if he likes to get a breath of fresh air, to take in a bit of the world, and to look at the fine things for sale in Yehupetz's shopwindows. You know what they say about that: your eyes can go where they please, but please keep your hands to yourself! . . . Well, there I was, standing by a moneychanger's window full of silver rubles, gold imperials, and all sorts of bank notes, and thinking: God in heaven, if only I had ten percent of what I see here, You'd never catch me complaining again. Who could compare to me then? The first thing I'd do would be to make a match for my eldest daughter; I'd give her a dowry of five hundred rubles over and above her trousseau, her bridal gown, and the wedding costs. Then I'd sell my nag and wagon, move to town, buy a good seat in the front row of the synagogue and some pearls, God bless her, for my wife, and make a contribution to charity that would be the envy of any rich Jew. Next I'd open a free school for poor children, have a proper tin roof made for the synagogue instead of the wreck it has now, and build a shelter for all the homeless people who have to sleep on the floor there at night, the kind any decent town should have. And lastly, I'd see to it that that no-good Yankl was fired as sexton of the Burial Society, because it's high time he stopped swilling brandy and guzzling chicken livers at the public expense . . .

"Why, hello there, Reb Tevye!" I heard someone say behind me. "What's new with a Jew?"

I turned around to look—I could have sworn that the fellow was familiar. "Hello there, yourself," I said. "Don't I know you from somewhere?"

"From somewhere?" he answers. "From Kasrilevke! I'm an acquaintance of yours. In fact, I'm actually your second cousin once removed. Your wife Golde is my third cousin on her father's side."

"Say there," I say. "You aren't by any chance Boruch Hirsh and Leah Dvossi's son-in-law, are you?"

"You guessed it," he says. "I'm Boruch Hirsh and Leah Dvossi's son-in-law. And my wife, Shayne Shayndl, is Boruch Hirsh and Leah Dvossi's daughter. Do you know me now?"

"Do I?" I say. "Your mother-in-law's grandmother, Soreh Yente, and my wife's aunt, Frume Zlote, were, I believe, real first cousins—which makes you Boruch Hirsh and Leah Dvossi's middle son-in-law indeed. The only trouble is that I've forgotten your name. It's slipped right out of my mind. What exactly did you say it was?"

"My name," he says, "is Menachem Mendl. Boruch Hirsh and Leah Dvossi's Menachem Mendl, that's how I'm known in Kasrilevke."

"In that case, my dear Menachem Mendl," I say to him, "you deserve a better hello than the one I gave you! Tell me, how are you? How are your mother-in-law and your father-in-law? How is everyone's health? How is business?"

"Eh," he says. "As far as health goes, we're all still alive, God be praised. But business is nothing to speak of."

"It's sure to pick up," I say, glancing at his clothes. They were patched in several places and his boots, the poor devil, were a safety hazard. "Leave it to God," I said. "Things always look up in the end. It's written in the Bible, *hakoyl hevel*—money never follows a straight line. One day you're up, the next you're down. The main thing is to keep breathing. And to have faith. A Jew has to hope. So what if things couldn't be worse? That's why there are Jews in the world! You know what they say: a soldier had better like the smell of gunpowder . . . Not that that has anything to do with it—why, all of life is but a dream . . . Tell me, though, my good fellow: what are you doing here, right smack in the middle of Yehupetz?"

"What do you mean, what am I doing here?" he says. "I've been here, let me see, it's been nearly a year and a half now."

"Is that so?" I say. "Do you mean to tell me that you live here?"

"Sshhh!" he says to me, looking all around. "Not so loud. You're right, I do live here, but that's strictly between the two of us."

I stood staring at him as though at a madman. "If you're hiding from the law," I said to him, "are you sure that the main street of Yehupetz is the place for it?"

"Ask me no questions, Reb Tevye," he says. "That's how it is. I can see that you don't know very much about our legal system here. If you'll just let me explain it to you, you'll understand in a jiffy how a man can live here and not live here at one and the same time . . ." With which he launched into such a brief explanation, that is, such a long song and dance, about what he had been through trying to get a permit to live in Yehupetz that I said:

"Listen, Menachem Mendl, I have an idea. Why don't you come spend a day with us in the village? It will be a chance to rest your weary bones. You'll be a most welcome guest. In fact, the old lady will be tickled pink to have you."

Well, it didn't take much to convince him, and the two of us set out for my place. There was some to-do when we got there. A guest! A genuine third cousin! That may not seem like much, but kinfolk are best folk, as they say. What a carnival! How are things in Kasrilevke? How is Uncle Boruch Hirsh? How is Aunt Leah Dvossi? How is Uncle Yosl Menashe? How is Aunt Dobrish? What are all the children doing? Who's died? Who's been married? Who's divorced? Who's sick or expecting? "Golde," I said at last, "what's a wedding more or a circumcision less to you when we have nothing to put in our mouths? *Koyl dikhfin yeysey veyitzrokh*— it's no fun dancing on an empty stomach. If there's a bit of borscht around, that will do nicely, and if there isn't, no matter—we'll start right in on the knishes, or the kreplach, or the knaidlach, or the varnishkes, or the pirogen, or the blintzes. You needn't limit yourself to one course, but be quick."

In a word, we washed our hands and sat down to a fine meal. "Have some more, Menachem Mendl," I said when I was done. "It's all vanity anyway, if you don't mind my quoting King David. It's a false and foolish world, and if you want to be healthy and enjoy it, as my Grandma Nechomeh used to say—oh, she was a smart one, all right, sharp as a whistle!—then you must never forget to lick the pot clean." My poor devil of a guest was so hungry that his hands shook. He didn't stop praising my wife's cooking and swearing up and down that he couldn't remember when he had last eaten such delicious dairy food, such wonderful knishes and tasty varnishkes. "Don't be silly, Menachem Mendl," I said. "You should try her pudding or her poppy cake—then you would know what heaven on earth is really like."

After the meal we chatted a bit as people do. I told him about my business and he told me about his; I talked about everything under the sun and he talked about Yehupetz and Odessa, where he had been, as they say, through thick and thin, now on top of the world and now in the pits, one day a prince, and the next a pauper, and then a prince again, and once more without a shirt on his back. Never in my life had I heard of such weird, complicated transactions: stocks and shares, and selling long and short, and options and poptions, and the Devil only knows what else. And for the craziest sums too, ten and twenty thousand rubles, as though money were water! "To tell you the truth, Menachem Mendl," I said, "you must have a marvelous head on your shoulders to figure all that out. There's one thing I don't get, though: if I know your wife as I think I do, how does she let you run around loose like this without coming after you on a broomstick?"

"Ah, Reb Tevye," he says with a sigh, "I wish you hadn't mentioned that. She runs hot and cold, she does, mostly freezing. If I were to read you some of the letters she writes me, you'd see what a saint I am. But that's neither here nor there. What's a wife for, if not to put a man in his place? Believe me, I have a worse problem than her, and that's my mother-in-law. I don't have to describe her to you—you know her well enough yourself."

"What you're trying to tell me," I say, "is that she's just like it says in the Bible, *akudim nekudim uvrudim.* Or to put it in plain language, like an abcess on a blister on a boil."

"Reb Tevye," he says, "you've hit the nail on the head. And if you think the boil and the blister are bad, wait until you hear about the abcess."

In a word, we stayed up gabbing half the night. By then I was dizzy from all his wild stories about the thousands of rubles he had juggled as though he were Brodsky. All night long my head was in a whirl: Yehupetz . . . gold imperials . . . Brodsky . . .

Menachem Mendl and his mother-in-law . . . It wasn't until the next morning, though, that he finally got to the point. What was the point? It was, said Menachem Mendl, that since money was so scarce in Yehupetz that you couldn't even give away your goods, "You, Reb Tevye, have a chance not only to make a nice killing but also to help save my life, I mean literally to raise me from the dead!"

"And you," I said to him, "are talking like a child. Are you really so foolish as to believe that I'm sitting on Yehupetz's millions? I only wish the two of us could earn in a year a tenth of what I'd need to be half as rich as Brodsky."

"Of course," he said. "You don't have to tell me that. But what makes you think I have such big sums in mind? Let me have a hundred rubles and in a couple of days I'll turn them into two hundred for you, into three hundred, into six hundred, into seven. In fact, I'll make it an even thousand."

"That may very well be," I said. "All things are possible. But do you know when they are? When there's a hundred in the first place. When there isn't, it's *begapoy yovoy uvegapoy yeytsey*. Do you know what Rashi has to say about that? That if you invest a fever, you'll get consumption for your profit."

"Come, come," he says to me. "A hundred rubles, Reb Tevye, you're sure to find. With your business, your reputation, touch wood . . ."

"What's my reputation got to do with it?" I ask. "A reputation is a wonderful thing to have, but would you like to know something? It's all I do have, because Brodsky has all the rest. If you must know exactly, it may be that I could squeeze together somewhere in the neighborhood of roughly more or less a hundred rubles, but I can also think of a hundred different ways to make them disappear again, the first of which is marrying off my eldest daughter . . ."

"But that's just it!" he says. "Listen to me! When will you have another opportunity, Reb Tevye, to invest a hundred rubles and wind up, God willing, with enough money to marry off every one of your daughters and still have plenty to spare?" And for the next three hours he's off on another serenade about how he can turn one ruble into three and three into ten. "The first thing you do," he says, "is take your hundred and buy ten whatchumacallits with it."

(That wasn't his word, I just don't remember what he called them.) "You wait a few days for them to go up, and then you send off a telegram with an order to sell and buy twice as much. Then you wait a few more days and send a telegram again. Before you know it, your hundred's worth two, your two hundred four, your four hundred eight, and your eight a thousand and six. It's the damnedest thing! Why, I know people who just the other day were shop clerks in Yehupetz without a pair of shoes on their feet; today they live in mansions with walls to keep out beggars and travel to the baths in Germany whenever their wives get a stomachache. They ride around town in rubber-wheeled droshkies—why, they don't even know you anymore!"

Well, so as not to make a short story long, he gave me such an itch to be rich that it wasn't any laughing matter. Why look a gift horse in the mouth? I told myself. Maybe he's really meant to be your good angel. What makes you think you're any worse than those shop clerks in Yehupetz who are living on easy street? He's certainly not lying, because he could never make up such fairy tales in a million years . . . It just may be, I thought, that Tevye's lucky number has come up at last and he's finally going to be somebody in his old age. How long does a man have to go on working himself to the bone—day and night, horse and wagon, cheese and butter, over and over again? It's high time, Tevye, for you to relax a bit, to drop in on a synagogue and read a book now and then like any respectable Jew. What are you so afraid of? That nothing will come of it? That you'll be fleeced like a lamb? That your bread, as they say, will fall with the butter side down? But what's to keep it from falling with the butter side up? "Golde," I asked the old lady, "what do you think? How does our cousin's plan strike you?"

"What should I think?" she said. "I know that Menachem Mendl isn't some fly-by-night who's out to put one over on you. He doesn't come from a family of fishmongers. His father was a fine Jew, and his grandfather was such a crackerjack that he kept right on studying Torah even after he went blind. Even his Grandmother Tsaytl, may she rest in peace, was no ordinary woman . . ."

"I'm talking Purim costumes and you're talking Hanukkah candles!" I said. "What do his Grandmother Tsaytl and her honey cakes have to do with it? Next you'll be telling me about her saint of a grandfather who died with a bottle in his arms! Once a woman, always a woman, I tell you. It's no coincidence that King Solomon traveled the whole world and couldn't find a single female with all her marbles in her head!"

In a word, we decided to go halves: I would invest the money and Menachem Mendl the brains, and we would split what God gave us down the middle. "Believe me, Reb Tevye," he said to me, "I'll be fair and square with you. With God's help, you'll soon be in clover."

"Amen," I said, "the same to you. May your mouth be up against His ears. There's one thing that still isn't clear to me, though: how do we get the cat across the river? I'm here, you're there, and money, as you know, is a highly perishable substance. Don't take offense, I'm not trying to outfox you, God forbid. It's just that Father Abraham knew what he was talking about when he said, *hazoyrim bedimoh berinoh yiktsoyru*—better twice warned than once burned."

"Oh," he says to me, "you mean we should put it down in writing. With the greatest of pleasure."

"Not at all," I say. "What good would that do? If you want to ruin me, a piece of paper won't stop you. *Lav akhboroh ganvo*—it's not the signature that counts, it's the man that signs. If I'm going to hang by one foot, I may as well hang by two."

"Leave it to me, Reb Tevye," he says. "I swear by all that's holy—may God strike me down if I try any monkey business! I wouldn't even dream of such a thing. This is strictly an aboveboard operation. God willing, we'll split the take between us, half and half, fifty-fifty, a hundred for me, a hundred for you, two hundred for me, two hundred for you, three hundred for me, three hundred for you, four hundred for me, four hundred for you, a thousand for me, a thousand for you . . ."

In a word, I took out my money, counted it three times with a trembling hand, called my wife to be a witness, explained to him once more how I had sweated blood for it, and handed it over to him, making sure to sew it into his breast pocket so that no one could steal it on the way. Then I made him promise to write me every detail by the end of the following week and said goodbye to him like the best of friends, even kissing him on the cheek as cousins do.

Once he was gone and we were alone again, I began having such wonderful thoughts and sweet dreams that I could have wished they'd go on forever. I imagined ourselves living in the middle of town, in a huge house with a real tin roof, and lots of wings, and all kinds of rooms and alcoves and pantries filled with good things, and my wife Golde, a regular lady now, walking from room to room with a key ring in her hand—why, she looked so different, so high-and-mighty with her pearls and double chin, that I hardly recognized her! And the airs she put on, and the way she swore at the servants! My kids waltzed around in their Sabbath best without lifting a finger, while geese, chickens, and ducks cackled in the yard. The house was all lit up; a fire glowed in the fireplace; supper was cooking on the stove, and the kettle whistled like a horse thief. Only, who's that sitting in a house frock and skullcap at the dining table, surrounded by the most prominent Jews in Yehupetz, all begging for his attention? Why, I do believe it's Tevye! "Begging your pardon, Reb Tevye . . ." "No offense meant, Reb Tevye . . ." "That would be most kind of you, Reb Tevye . . ."

"Damn it all!" I said, snapping out of it. "The Devil take every last ruble on earth!"

"Who are you sending to the Devil?" asked my Golde.

"No one," I said. "I was just thinking—dreaming—of pie in the sky . . . Tell me, Golde, my darling, you wouldn't happen to know by any chance what this cousin of yours, Menachem Mendl, does for a living, would you?"

"May all my bad dreams come true for my enemies!" says my wife. "What? Do you mean to tell me that after talking and talking with that fellow all day and all night, I should tell you what he does for a living? God help me if I understood a thing about it, but I thought you two became partners."

"So we did," I said. "It's just that you can have my head on a platter if I have the foggiest notion what it is that we're partners in. I simply can't make heads or tails of it. Not that that's any reason for alarm, my dear. Something tells me not to worry. I do believe, God willing, that we're going to be in the gravy—and now say amen and make supper!"

In short, a week went by, and then another, and then another—and not a peep from my partner! I was beside myself, I went about like a chicken without its head, not knowing what to think. It can't be, I thought, that he simply forgot to write; he knows perfectly well that we're waiting to hear from him. And suppose he's skimmed all the cream for himself and claims we haven't earned a kopeck's profit, what can I do about it—call him a monkey's uncle? . . . Only I don't believe it, I told myself, it simply isn't possible. Here I've gone and treated him like one of the family, the good luck that I've wished him should only be mine— how could he go and play such a trick on me? . . . Just then, though, I had an even worse thought: the principal! The Devil take the profit, Menachem Mendl could have it, *revakh vehatsoloh ya'amoyd layehudim*—but God protect my principal from him! You old fool, I said to myself, you sewed your whole fortune into his jacket with your own two hands! Why, with the same hundred rubles you could have bought yourself a team of horses such as no Jew ever horsed around with before, and traded in your old cart for a new droshky with springs in the bargain!

"Tevye," says my wife, "don't just stand there doing nothing. Think!"

"What does it look like I'm doing?" I asked. "I'm thinking so hard that my head is falling off, and all you can tell me is, think!"

"Well," she says, "something must have happened to him. Either he was stripped bare by thieves, or else he's taken ill, or else, God forgive me, he's gone and died on us."

"Thieves? That's a good one! What other cheery thoughts do you have, light of my life?" I asked—though to myself I thought, who knows what a man can meet up with when he's traveling? "Why is it that you always have to imagine the worst?"

"Because," she says, "it runs in his family. His mother, may she speak no ill of us in heaven, passed away not long ago in her prime, and his three sisters are all dead too. One died as a girl; one was married but caught a cold in the bathhouse and never recovered from it; and one went crazy after her first confinement and wasted away into nothing . . ."

"May the dead live in Paradise, Golde," I said, "because that's where we'll join them some day. A man, I tell you, is no different from a carpenter; that is, a carpenter lives till he dies, and so does a man."

In a word, we decided that I should pay a call on Menachem Mendl. By now I had a bit of merchandise, some Grade A cheese, cream, and butter, so I harnessed the horse to the wagon and *vayisu misukoys*—off to Yehupetz I went. I hardly need tell you that

I was in a black and bitter mood, and as I drove through the forest my fears got the better of me. No doubt, I thought, when I ask for my man in Yehupetz I'll be told, "Menachem Mendl? There's someone who's made it to the top. He lives in a big house and rides about in droshkies—you'll never recognize him!" Still, I'll pluck up my nerve and go straight to his house. "Hey, there, uncle," says the doorman, sticking an elbow in my ribs, "just where do you think you're going? It's by appointment only here, in case you didn't know."

"But I'm a relative of his," I say. "He's my second cousin once removed on my wife's side."

"Congratulations," says the doorman. "Pleased to meet you. I'm afraid, though, that you'll have to cool your heels all the same. I promise you your health won't suffer from it."

I realize that I have to cross his palm. How does the verse go? *Oylim veyordim*—if you want to travel, you better grease the wheels. At once I'm shown in to Menachem Mendl.

"A good morning to you, Reb Menachem Mendl," I say to him.

A good what to who? *Eyn oymer ve'eyn dvorim*—he doesn't know me from Adam! "What do you want?" he says to me.

I feel weak all over. "But how can it be, Pani," I say, "that you don't even know your own cousin? It's me, Tevye!"

"Eh?" he says. "Tevye? The name rings a bell."

"Oh, it does, does it?" I say. "I suppose my wife's blintzes, and knishes, and knaidlach, and varnishkes all happen to ring a bell too . . . ?"

He doesn't answer me, though, because now I imagine the opposite: as soon as he catches sight of me, he greets me like a long-lost friend. "What a guest! What a guest! Sit down, Reb Tevye, and tell me how you are. And how is your wife? I've been looking all over for you, we have some accounts to settle." And with that he dumps a bushel of gold imperials out on the table. "This," he says, "is your share of the profit. The principal has been reinvested. Whatever we make we'll keep on sharing, half and half, fifty-fifty, a hundred for me, a hundred for you, two hundred for me, two hundred for you, three hundred for me, three hundred for you, four hundred for me, four hundred for you . . ."

He was still talking when I dozed off, so that I didn't see my old dobbin stray from the path and run the wagon into a tree. It gave

me such a jolt in the pants that I saw stars. Just look how everything turns out for the best, I told myself. You can consider yourself lucky that the axle didn't break . . .

Well, I arrived in Yehupetz, had my goods snatched up in no
time as usual, and began to look for my fine friend. One, two,
three hours went by in roaming the streets of the town—*vehayeled
eynenu,* there's neither hide nor hair of him. Finally I stopped
some people and asked, "Excuse me, but do you by any chance
know of a Jew around here whose given name is Menachem
Mendl?"

"Menachem Mendl?" they say to me. "We know no endl Menachem Mendls. Which one are you looking for?"

"You mean what's his last name?" I say. "It's Menachem Mendl.
Back home in Kasrilevke he's called after his mother-in-law, that
is, Leah Dvossi's Menachem Mendl. In fact, his father-in-law—
and a fine old man he is—is called Leah Dvossi's Boruch Hirsh.
Why, Leah Dvossi is so well known in Kasrilevke that she herself is
called Leah Dvossi's Boruch Hirsh's Leah Dvossi. Do you know
who I'm talking about now?"

"We follow you perfectly," they say. "But that still isn't enough.
What's his line? What does he deal in, this Menachem Mendl of
yours?"

"What's his line?" I say. "His line is gold imperials, and now and
then poptions. And telegrams to St. Petersburg and Warsaw."

"Is that so?" they say, holding their sides. "If it's the Menachem
Mendl who'll sell you a bird in the bush at half price that you're
looking for, you'll find him over there with all the other bushmen,
on the other side of the street."

One is never too old to learn, I thought, but *bushmen?* Still, I
crossed to the opposite sidewalk, where I found myself among such
a mob of Jews that I could hardly move. They were packed together as at a fairgrounds, running around like crazy and climbing
all over each other. What bedlam! Everyone was shouting and
waving his hands at once. "Up a quarter! . . . Give me ten! . . .
Word of honor! . . . Put it there! . . . Cash on the barrelhead! . . .
Scratch that! . . . You double-dealer! . . . You four-flusher! . . . I'll
bash your head in! . . . You should spit in his eye! . . . He'll lose his
shirt! . . . What a chiseler! . . . You're a bankrupt! . . . You're a
bootlicker! . . . So's your old man! . . . " They looked about to come
to blows. *Vayivrakh Ya'akoyv,* I told myself: you better scram while

you can, Tevye, my friend. If only you had listened to what the Bible says, you would never have believed in False Profits. So this is where the gold imperials grow on trees? This is the business you invested in? A black day it was that you became a businessman!

In a word, I had moved on a bit and come to a big display window full of pants when whose reflection did I see in it but Mr. Moneybags' himself! My heart sank to my stomach. I thought I would die! We should only live to meet our worst enemies crawling down the street like Menachem Mendl. You should have seen his coat! And his shoes! And the face on him—why, a corpse in the grave looks better. Nu, Tevye, I thought, *ka'asher ovadeti ovadeti*—you're up the creek this time for sure. You can kiss every cent you ever had goodbye. *Loy dubim veloy ya'ar*—the principal's gone with the profit and all that's left you is troubles!

He too must have been stunned to see me, because we just went on standing there without a word, staring at each other like two roosters, as if to say, you know and I know that it's all over with the two of us; there's nothing for it now but to take a tin cup and start going from door to door with it . . .

"Reb Tevye," he said in such a whisper that I could hardly hear him. "Reb Tevye! With luck like mine it's better not to be born. I'd rather hang than have to live like this . . ."

He couldn't get out another word. "There's no doubt, Menachem Mendl," I said, "that you deserve as much. You should be taken right now and given such a whipping in the middle of Yehupetz, in front of everyone, that you'd soon be paying a call on your Grandmother Tsaytl in the next world. Do you have any idea what you've done? You've taken a house full of people, live, feeling human beings who never did you an ounce of harm, and slit their throats without a knife! How in the world am I supposed to show my face now to my wife and kids? Perhaps you can tell me that, you thief, you, you swindler, you murderer!"

"It's the truth," he says, flattening himself against the wall. "So help me God, every word of what you say is true!"

"Hell itself," I say, "hell itself, you cretin, is too good for you!"

"It's the truth, Reb Tevye," he says. "So help me God, before I'll go on living like this any longer, I'll . . . I'll . . ."

And he hung his head. I stood there looking at the schlimazel pressed against the wall with his hat falling off, every sigh and groan of his breaking my heart. "Well," I said, "come to think of it, there's no sense in blaming you either. After all, it's ridiculous to suppose you did it on purpose, because you were a partner just like me, the business was half yours. I put in the money, you put in the brains, and don't we both wish we hadn't! I'm sure you meant well, *lekhayim veloy lamoves*. If we blew a small fortune, that's only because we weren't meant to make a big one. How does the verse go? *Al tis'haleyl beyoym mokhor*—the more man plans, the harder God laughs. Take my dairy business, for example. You would think it was pretty solid—and yet just last autumn, it shouldn't happen to you, a cow dropped dead on me for whose carcass I was lucky to get fifty kopecks, and right after her, a red heifer that I wouldn't have sold for twenty rubles. Was there anything I could do about it? If it's not in the cards, you can stand on your head and say the alphabet backwards—it doesn't help a damn bit. I'm not even asking what you did with the money that I bled for. I know as much as I want to, that it went to buy birds in a bush, whole flocks of them, and that I'll never get to see a single one. And whose fault is it? It's my own, for having been taken in by a lot of hot air. Take it from me, the only way to make money is to work your bottom off. Which is where you, Tevye, deserve to get a swift kick! But what good does it do to cry about it? It's just like it says in the Bible, *vetso'akoh hane'aroh*—you can scream till you burst, who says that anyone is listening? Wisdom and second thoughts are two things that always come too late. Tevye just wasn't meant to be upper crust, that's not how God wanted it. *Hashem nosan vehashem lokakh,* the Lord giveth and the Lord taketh away—in which case, says Rashi, cheer up, my friend, and let's go have a little shot of brandy! . . ."

And that, Pani Sholem Aleichem, is how I blew all my money. But if you think I've been eating my heart out over it, you have another guess coming. You know the Bible's opinion: *li hakesef veli hazohov*—money is a lot of baloney. What matters is the man who has it—I mean, what matters is for a man to be a man. Do you know what I still can't get over, though? Losing my dream! If only you knew how badly, oh Lord, how really badly I wanted to be a rich Jew, if only for just a few days! But go be smarter than life. Doesn't it say *be'al korkhekho atoh khai*—nobody asks if you want to be born or if you want your last pair of boots to be torn. "Instead of dreaming, Tevye," God was trying to tell me, "you should have stuck to your cheese and butter." Does that mean I've lost faith and stopped hoping for better times? Don't you believe it! The more troubles, the more faith, the bigger the beggar, the greater his hopes. How can that be, you ask? But I've already gone on enough for one day, and I'd better be off and about my business. How does the verse go? *Koyl ha'odom koyzev*—there isn't a man who hasn't taken a beating sometime. Don't forget to take care and be well!

(1899)

TODAY'S CHILDREN

▼

Say what you will about today's children, Pani Sholem Aleichem, *bonim gidalti veroymamti:* first you have them, then you break your back for them, make every sacrifice, put yourself through the mill . . . and for what? So that maybe, you think, if you've managed to get ahead a bit in life, you can help them get somewhere too. I wouldn't dream of having Brodsky for my in-law, of course, but that doesn't mean I have to settle for just anyone, because I'm not such a nobody myself; and since I don't come, as my wife likes to put it, from a long line of fishmongers, I had hoped for some luck with my daughters. How was that? In the first place, because God gave them good looks, and a pretty face, the saying goes, is half a dowry. And secondly, because even if, with God's help, I'm no longer the Tevye I once was, someone like me still rates a good match even in Yehupetz, don't you think? The trouble is that the same merciful God who's always practicing His miracles on me, first seeing how quick He can raise a man up and then how fast He can dump him back down, has let me know in no uncertain terms, "Tevye, stop being so ridiculous as to think you can run the world!" . . . Well, wait till you hear how the world runs itself without me. And who, naturally, does it run right over first? Why, your schlimazel of a Tevye, of course!

But why make a short story long? I'm sure you remember, though I would much prefer to forget, what happened with my cousin Menachem Mendl—how I wish I had never heard that name!—and with the fine business in gold imperials and poptions that we did in Yehupetz. It shouldn't happen to my worst enemy! For a while I went about moaning and groaning that it was all over with me and my dairy, until the wife said to me, "Tevye, you're a fool to carry on as though the world has come to an end. All you're doing is eating your heart out. Why not just pretend we've been burgled, it could happen to anyone . . . If I were you, I'd go see Layzer Wolf the butcher in Anatevka. He keeps saying he needs to talk to you urgently."

"What can be so urgent?" I asked. "If he's got it into his head that I'm going to sell him our brown cow, he can take a stick and beat it out again."

"What's so precious about our brown cow?" says my wife. "All the rivers of milk and mountains of butter we get from her?"

"No, it isn't that," I say. "It's just a sin to hand over a poor innocent beast to be slaughtered. Why, it says in our holy Bible—"

"For goodness' sake, Tevye," she says, "that's enough! The whole world knows what a professor of Bible you are. Listen to a simple woman like me and go see Layzer Wolf. Every Thursday when I send our Tsaytl to his butcher shop for meat, it's the same thing again: would she please tell her father to come at once, he has something important to say to him . . ."

Well, sometimes you have to do what you're told, even if it's by your own wife; I let myself be talked into going to see Layzer Wolf in Anatevka, which is a couple of miles away. When I got there, he was out.

"Where's Layzer Wolf?" I asked the pug-nosed woman who was busy doing the housework.

"He's at the slaughterhouse," she says. "He's been there all morning slaughtering an ox, but he should be back soon."

While I waited for him I wandered about the house, taking in the furnishings. I only wish I had half as much! There was a cupboard full of copper that you couldn't have bought for two hundred and fifty rubles; not just one samovar but two; and a brass tray, and another tray from Warsaw, and a set of cups with gilt edges, and a pair of silver candlesticks, and a cast-iron menorah, and all kinds of other things, more bric-a-brac than you could count. God in heaven, I thought, I should only live to see my daughters own such things! Some people have all the breaks. Not only is Layzer Wolf rich, with a grand total of two children, both married, he even has the luck to be a widower . . .

Well, before long the door opened and in came Layzer Wolf himself, fit to be tied at the slaughterer for having been so unkind as to declare unkosher an ox the size of an oak tree because of a tiny scar on its lung no bigger than a hairpin. A black hole should open up in the earth and swallow him alive! . . . "Am I glad to see you, Reb Tevye!" he says. "It's easier to raise the dead. What's new with a Jew?"

"What should be new?" I say. "The harder I work, the less I have to show for it. It's like it says in the Bible: *loy mi'uktsokh veloy miduvshokh.* I not only have no money, I also lack health, wealth, and happiness."

"It's a sin to be ungrateful, Reb Tevye," he says. "Compared to what you once were, and let's hope won't be again, you're not doing half bad these days."

"It's the other half that worries me," I say. "But I have nothing to complain about, thank God. *Askakurdo dimaskanto dikarnaso difarsmakhto,* as the Talmud puts it . . ." And I thought: may your nose stick to your backside, you meat hacker, you, if there's such a line of Talmud in the world . . .

"You're always quoting something," Layzer Wolf says. "I envy you, Reb Tevye, for being able to read the small print. But what good does all that book learning do you? Let's talk about something more practical. Have a seat, Reb Tevye." And before I can have one, he bellows, "How about some tea!"

Out of nowhere, as if she had been hiding beneath the floorboards, the pug-nosed woman appears, snatches a samovar like the wind snatching a leaf, and disappears into the kitchen.

"Now that we're alone with only four eyes between the two of us," says Layzer Wolf to me, "you and I can talk business. It's like this: I've been wanting to speak to you for quite a while, Reb Tevye. I even asked your daughter several times to have you come see me. You see, lately I've had my eye on—"

"I know you have," I said. "But it won't do you any good. It's out of the question, Layzer Wolf, simply out of the question."

"But why?" he asks, giving me an astonished look.

"Because there's no hurry," I say. "She's still young. The river won't catch fire if we wait a little longer."

"But why wait," he says, "if you have an offer for her now?"

"In the first place," I say, "I just told you. And in the second place, it's a matter of compassion. I simply don't have the heart."

"Just listen to him talk about her!" says Layzer Wolf with a laugh. "A person might think you had no others. I should imagine, Reb Tevye, that you have more than enough of them, touch wood."

"I can use every one I have," I say. "Whoever envies me should know what it costs just to feed them."

"Envy?" says Layzer Wolf. "Who's talking envy? On the contrary, it's just because they're such a fine bunch that I . . . do you get me? Have you ever thought for a minute, Reb Tevye, of all I can do for you?"

"Of course I have," I say. "And I've gotten a headache each time I did. Judging by all you've done for me in the past, you might even give me free ice in the middle of the winter."

"Oh, come," he says, sweet as sugar. "Why harp on the past? We weren't in-laws then."

"In-laws?" I say. "What kind of in-laws?"

"Why, how many kinds are there?" he says.

"Excuse me, Reb Layzer Wolf," I say, "but do you have any idea what we're talking about?"

"I should say I do, Reb Tevye," he says. "But perhaps you'd like to tell me."

"With pleasure," I say. "We're talking about my brown cow that you want me to sell you."

"Hee hee hee," he says, chortling. "Your brown cow, no less, that's a good one . . . ho ho ho!"

"But what do you think we were talking about, Reb Layzer Wolf?" I say. "Why not let me in on the joke?"

"Why, about your daughter!" he says. "We've been talking all along about your Tsaytl! You know I'm a widower, Reb Tevye—it shouldn't happen to you. Well, I've made up my mind; why try my luck again far from home, where I'll have to deal with all sorts of spooks, flukes, and matchmakers? Here we are, the two of us, both from the same place, I know you and you know me—to say nothing of the party in question, who I've taken quite a fancy to. I see her every Thursday in my butcher shop and we've even exchanged a few words; she's on the quiet side, I must say, but not bad, not bad at all! And as for me, touch wood, you can see for yourself: I'm comfortably off, I have a couple of shops, I even own my own house. I don't mean to boast, but it has some nice furnishings too, and there are hides stored away in the attic, and a bit of cash in a chest. Reb Tevye, why haggle like gypsies about it? Come, let's shake hands and be done with it, do you get me?"

In short, I sat there listening and couldn't say a word, the whole thing bowled me over so. For a minute I thought: Layzer Wolf . . . Tsaytl . . . why, he's old enough to be her father . . . But it didn't take me long to think again. My God, I told myself, what a godsend! She'll be sitting pretty with him, on top of the world! So what if he's a tightwad? These upside-down days, that's actually considered a virtue. *Odom koroyv le'atsmoy*—charity begins at home . . . It's true the man is a trifle common—but since when can everyone be a scholar? There are plenty of rich Jews, fine people, in Anatevka, Mazapevka, and even in Yehupetz, who wouldn't know a Hebrew letter if one fell on them; that still doesn't keep them from being thought highly of—I should only be as respected as they are! How does the verse go? *Im eyn kemakh eyn Toyroh*—it's all very well to know the Bible by heart, but you still can't serve it for dinner . . .

"Nu, Reb Tevye," says Layzer Wolf. "Why don't you say something?"

"What's there to shout about?" I say, playing hard to get. "One doesn't decide such things on the spur of the moment. It's no laughing matter, marrying off your eldest daughter."

"That's just it!" he says. "She's your eldest. Once she's my wife, God willing, marrying off your second and your third and your fourth will be no problem, do you get me?"

"Amen," I say. "It's easy as pie to marry off a daughter. God simply has to find her the right man."

"But that isn't what I meant, Reb Tevye," he says. "I meant that you not only needn't put up a penny's dowry for your Tsaytl, or buy her the things a girl needs for her wedding, because I'll take care of all that myself—you can also trust me to beef up your wallet while I'm at it . . ."

"Hold on there!" I said. "You'll forgive me for saying so, but you're talking just like in a butcher shop. What's this about beef in my wallet? You should be ashamed of yourself! My Tsaytl, God forbid, is not up for sale to the highest bidder."

"Ashamed?" he says. "And here I thought I was only being nice! I'll tell you what, though: for you, I'll even be ashamed. Far be it from me to object to your saving me money. Let's just be quick about it, the sooner the better! I want a woman in my house, do you get me?"

"I certainly do," I say. "For my part, I won't stand in your way. But I'll have to talk it over with the missus, because such things are her department. One doesn't give away one's eldest daughter every day. You know what Rashi says about it: *Rokheyl mevakoh al boneho*—that means there's no one like a mother. And we'll have to ask Tsaytl too, of course. You don't want this to be the sort of wedding where everyone turns up but the bride . . ."

"What kind of a man are you!" he says. "Who asks? Go home and tell them, Reb Tevye, tell them it's all been decided and that I'll be waiting beneath the wedding canopy."

"You musn't talk like that, Reb Layzer Wolf," I say. "A young girl isn't a widow, to be married off at the drop of a hat."

"Of course she's not," he says. "A girl is a girl and a hat is a hat. That's why I want it settled quickly, because there's still a whole lot to talk about, pots, pans, and petticoats. But first, Reb Tevye, what say we drink to it, eh?"

"Why not?" I say. "I never turn down a drink. Among friends it's always appropriate. A man is only a man, as they say, but brandy is still brandy. You'll find that in the Talmud too." And with that I began spouting whole passages of Gemara, mixed in with some prayers and a bit of the Haggadah, such as no one ever dreamed of before . . .

In a word, we put a few drops of brandy beneath our belts without keeping count of how many and then, when old Pug Nose brought the samovar, switched to tea-and-brandy punch, jabbering away all the while in the friendliest of fashions about the wedding, and God knows what else, and the wedding again, until I said, "I hope you realize, Reb Layzer Wolf, what a diamond it is that you're getting."

"You hope I realize?" he says. "Do you think I would have asked for her if I didn't?"

"A diamond," I say, raising my voice, "and twenty-four carats too! You better take good care of her and not act like the butcher you are . . ."

"Don't you worry about that, Reb Tevye," he says. "She'll eat better by me every day of the week than by you at your Passover seder!"

"Eat!" I say. "How much can a person eat? A rich man can't eat the gold in his safe, nor a poor man the stones in his shoes. Just how do you think a Jew as crude as yourself is even going to appreciate her cooking? Why, the hallahs she bakes, her gefillte fish . . . good Lord, Reb Layzer Wolf, her gefillte fish . . . lucky is the man who gets to taste it . . ."

"Reb Tevye," he says, "you'll forgive me for saying so, but what does an old prune like you know about it? You don't know the first thing about anything, Reb Tevye, you don't even know the first thing about me!"

"If you were to give me all the rice in China," I say, "I wouldn't take it for my Tsaytl. Listen here, Reb Layzer Wolf, I don't care if you have two hundred thousand to your name, you aren't worth the little toe of her left foot!"

"Believe you me, Reb Tevye," he says, "if you didn't happen to be older than me, I'd tell you to your face what a fool you are."

Well, we must have gone at it hammer and tongs until we were good and sozzled, because when I arrived home it was late at night and my feet felt made out of lead. My wife, may her life be a long one, saw right away how pie-eyed I was and gave me the welcome I deserved.

"Ssshhh, don't be angry with me, Golde," I said, feeling so merry that I could have broken right into a jig. "Stop screaming at me, light of my life, and wish me a mazel tov instead!"

"A mazel tov?" she says. "I'll wish you a mazel tov you'll never forget! I'll bet you went and sold our poor brown cow to Layzer Wolf, after all."

"Oh, it's worse than that," I say.

"What?" she says. "You swapped her for a cow of his? Just wait till the poor devil finds out how you cheated him!"

"You're not even warm yet," I say.

"For God's sake," she says, "out with it! Do I have to pay you money for each word?"

"Mazel tov to you, Golde!" I said again. "Mazel tov to us both. Our Tsaytl is engaged."

"My God, are you ever potted!" she says. "It's no joke, the man's hallucinating! How many drinks did you say you had?"

"Layzer Wolf and I had more than one between us," I say, "and a bit of punch to wash it down with, but I swear I'm as sober as can be. It's my pleasure to inform you, my dear brother Golde, that our Tsaytl has had the good fortune to be betrothed to Layzer Wolf himself!"

And with that I told her the whole story from beginning to end, the who, where, when, and all the rest of it, not leaving out an iota. "So help me God now and forever, Tevye," she said when I was done, "if something didn't tell me all along that's what Layzer Wolf wanted. You know what, though? I was frightened to think that maybe nothing would come of it . . . Oh, thank You, dear God, thank You, thank You, merciful Father! It should only be for the best. Tsaytl should live to grow old and be happy with him, because Frume Soreh, rest her soul, didn't have such a wonderful time of it; but then she was, God forgive me, an impossible woman who couldn't get along with a soul, not at all like our Tsaytl. Oh, thank You, thank You, God! What did I tell you, Tevye, you dummy! What's the use of worrying? If it's written in the stars, it will walk right in without knocking . . ."

"There's no doubt about that," I said. "It even says in the Bible—"

"Spare us your Bible!" she says. "We have to start planning for the wedding. First we should make a list for Layzer Wolf of all the things that Tsaytl will need. Linen goes without saying. And she doesn't have a spare set of underthings, not even an extra pair of socks. And then there's dresses—a silk one for the wedding and two woolen ones, one for summer and one for winter—and house frocks, and lingerie, and a fur coat . . . no, I want two: a plain cat fur for everyday and a good fox fur for Sabbaths and holidays. She'll need high-heeled boots too, and a corset, and gloves, and handkerchiefs, and a parasol, and all kinds of other things that a young lady can't do without . . ."

"Golde, my dearest," I said to her, "since when are you such an expert on high fashion?"

"And why shouldn't I be?" she says. "Don't you suppose I have eyes? Don't you think I've seen what they wear back home when they step out in Kasrilevke? Just you leave it to Layzer Wolf and me. He's no pauper, and you can bet he won't want the whole world calling him cheap. If you have to eat pork, you might as well eat it till it's running down your chin . . ."

In short, we talked all night long until I said, "Round up what cheese and butter there is, my wife, and I'll take it to Boiberik. Not that everything isn't fine and dandy right here, but we can't just forget about the business. *Haneshomoh lokh,* it says—our souls may be God's but someone better look after our bodies."

And so at the crack of dawn, before it was light out, I harnessed my horse and wagon and set out for Boiberik. I arrived at the marketplace—oho! (is there any place in the world where a Jew can keep a secret?)—everyone knows all about it and is congratulating me from all sides.

"Mazel tov, Reb Tevye," they say. "When will the wedding be?"

"Mazel tov to you too," I say. "But I'm afraid it's a case of the son growing up before the father has been born."

"There's no use trying to pull our leg, Reb Tevye," they say. "You'll have to stand us all drinks, you lucky devil. Why, the man is a gold mine!"

"When the gold gives out," I say, "a mine's just a hole in the ground. Which is no reason, of course, to be piggish with one's friends. As soon as I've finished my route, the food and drinks are on me. We'll live it up and to hell with it! *Tsoholoh vesomeykhoh,* my friends—if beggars can't be choosers, they may as well be boozers."

In a word, I finished my rounds in a jiffy as usual and went off to drink a toast with my dear brothers. We wished each other the happiness we all deserved and I started out for home, a bit tipsy and as merry as a lark. I rode through the forest, the summer sun shining down, the trees casting their shadows on either side of the path, a good smell of pine needles all around—this is the life, I thought! I even let go of my horse's reins and stretched out like a count in a carriage. "Run along without me," I told the old boy, "it's time you knew the way yourself"—and with that I threw back my head and broke into a little tune. I had such a holiday feeling in my heart that I even began to sing melodies from the prayer book. There I sat, staring up at the sky and thinking of the words of the *hallel* prayer. *Hashomayim shomayim ladoynai*—the heavens belong to God . . . *veha'orets nosan livney odom*—but the earth He's given to us, the human race, so that we can bury each other six feet deep in it and fight for the honor of crying by the grave . . . *Loy hameysim yehallelu yoh*—the dead don't praise God, and why should they? . . . *Ve'anakhnu nevoreykh yoh*—yet we poor folk who are still barely alive can't thank Him enough if He does us a single favor . . . *Ohavti ki yishma*—of course I love Him; wouldn't you if He had cupped a hand to His

ear just to listen to your prayers? . . . *Ofafuni khevley moves*—there
I was, a poor wretch surrounded by worries: one day a cow dies
on me out of the blue, the next it's my luck to run into a schlimazel of a cousin, a Mr. Menachem Mendl of Yehupetz, who walks
off with my last cent . . . *Ani omarti bekhofzi*—why, I thought the
sky had fallen in . . . *Koyl ha'odom koyzev*—and that I couldn't
trust a living soul anymore . . . So what does God do? *Oydkho ki
anisoni*—He taps Layzer Wolf on the shoulder and tells him to
marry my Tsaytl, all expenses paid . . . Which is why I thank
You, dear Lord, for having looked down on Your Tevye and
decided to lend him a hand. At last I'll have some pleasure from
my children! When I'll come to visit my Tsaytl in her new home,
God willing, I'll find a grand lady with everything a person could
ask for, closets full of fine linen, cupboards full of jam and
schmaltz, cages full of chickens, ducks, and geese . . .

Well, at that very moment my horse took a notion to practice
his downhill gallop. Before I could even look around, I was flat
on my back with all my jugs and milk cans, staring up at my
wagon on top of me. It was all I could do to crawl out from
under it, more dead than alive, and chew the idiot out. "You
should sink to the bottom of the sea and be eaten by vultures!
Who asked you, you moron, to prove you could be a racehorse?
You almost did me in for good, you Satan, you!" I gave it to him
for all he was worth—and the old fellow must have realized what
a dirty trick he had played, because he stood there with his head
bowed as though waiting to be milked. "The Devil take you and
keep you!" I said a last time, righting and reloading the wagon.
"Giddyap!" I cried—and we were off again. I knew it wasn't a
good omen, though. Suppose, I thought, something has gone
wrong at home . . .

And so it had. I had traveled another mile or so and wasn't far
from our village when I saw the figure of a woman coming toward
me. I drove a little nearer—it was Tsaytl! I don't know why, but I
felt a twinge when I saw her. I jumped to the ground and called,
"Tsaytl, is that you? What are you doing here?"

Her only answer was to throw herself on me and sob.

"For the love of God, Daughter," I said, "what are you crying
for?"

"Oh, Papa," she said, the tears running down her cheeks. "Oh,
Papa."

I had a black feeling. My heart sank. "Tsaytl," I said, taking her in my arms to hug and kiss her, "what is it?"

"Oh, Papa," she said, "oh, dearest, darling Papa, I don't care if I have to live on bread and water, just have pity on me and my youth . . ."

She was crying so hard that she couldn't say any more. God help us, I thought, for by now I had guessed what it was. The Devil himself had made me go to Boiberik that morning!

"But what is there to cry about, you silly?" I said, stroking her hair. "Why cry? You have no call to: if you say no, it's no; we won't marry you off with a shotgun. We meant well. We thought it was all for the best. But if your heart tells you not to, what more can we do? It simply wasn't meant to be in the first place . . ."

"Oh, Papa," she says, "oh, thank you, thank you so much!"— and she throws herself on me again, crying and kissing me until we're both wet all over.

"Come," I say, "enough is enough. *Hakoyl hevel*—even chicken soup with kreplach gets to be tiresome after a while. Into the wagon with you and home you go! Your mother must be good and worried."

Once the two of us were aboard, I did my best to calm her. "Look, it's like this," I said. "Your mother and I meant no harm. God knows our only thought was of you. If it didn't work out, God musn't have wanted it to. You, Tsaytl, just weren't meant to be a fine lady with a house full of grand things and two old parents who could finally enjoy themselves a bit after keeping their nose to the grindstone all their poor, luckless, miserable, penniless lives . . ."

"Oh, Papa," she said, starting to cry again. "I'll hire myself out, I'll get down on my knees and scrub floors, I'll shovel dirt if I have to . . ."

"But why are you still crying, you little ninny?" I said. "I was talking to God, not to you. I'm feeling so low that I have to have it out with someone—and considering all He's done for me, it might as well be with Him. He's supposed to be our merciful Father; well, He's had such mercy on me that I hope I've seen the last of it—and He better not charge me extra for saying that. A lot of good it does to complain to God about God! I suppose, though, that that's how it's meant to be: He's up in His heaven and I'm down below, with one foot already in the grave—which still leaves me the other to stand on while I tell the world about His justice . . . Only come to think of it, I really must be a big fool to carry on like this. What am I talking about? Where does a little worm like me crawling about on the earth get off telling God, who can blow me away to kingdom come with one puff of His breath, how to manage His affairs? If this is how He's arranged them, who am I to say otherwise? Forty days before a child is a twinkle in its mother's eyes, forty days beforehand, so it says in our holy books, an angel comes along and proclaims: 'Tsaytl the daughter of Tevye to Berl the son of Shmerl'—and Layzer Wolf the butcher, if he doesn't mind my saying so, can go look for his intended up another tree. I can promise him she won't fly away . . . I only hope, Tsaytl, that God sends you a proper young man, the sooner the better, amen. And now pray for me that your mother doesn't scream bloody murder, because something tells me that I'm in for it . . ."

In short, as soon as we got home I unhitched the horse and sat down outside to have myself a think what fairy tale to tell the wife—anything to keep me out of trouble. It was evening and the sun was going down; from far away came the croaking of the frogs; my fettered horse stood nibbling grass; the cows, back from pasture, were waiting with their feedbags to be milked; all around me the greenery gave off a smell like Paradise. And as I sat there thinking about things, it struck me how cleverly the good Lord had made His world, so that every creature, from man to beast, could earn its keep. Only there were no free lunches! You want to eat, Mrs. Cow? Then let's have some milk, help a poor Jew support his wife and kids! You want some grass, Mr. Horse? Then please be so kind as to trot over to Boiberik with these milk cans! And you too, Mr. Man, you want some bread for your belly? Then off your butt and milk the cows, carry the cans, churn the butter, make the cheese, harness the horse, go early each morning to the dachas in Boiberik, scrape and bow to the rich Jews there, smile at them, fawn on them, make them feel special, be sure they're satisfied—and whatever you do, don't step on anyone's toes . . . Except that here we come to one of the Four Questions: *ma nishtanoh*—where does it say in the Bible that Tevye has to work his bottom off and be up at the crack of dawn every day when even God is still snoozing away in bed? Where does it say that the rich Jews of Yehupetz must have fresh cheese and butter each morning for the rolls they eat with their coffee? Where does it say that I have to be dead on my feet to deserve a plate of grits and some soup that's more water than barley, while they, the same Jews, can stretch and yawn without lifting a finger and be served with roast duck, juicy knishes, varnishkes, and blintzes? Am I less of a Jew than they are? When will justice be done, so that Tevye too can spend a summer vacation in a dacha in Boiberik! . . . Who, though, you ask, would bring him his cheese and butter? Who would milk the cows? Why, the Yehupetz tycoons, of course! . . . But I have to admit that was such a weird thought that it made me laugh out loud. How does the proverb go? If God were to listen to what each fool has to say, He would have to create a new world every day . . .

"Good evening, Reb Tevye!" I heard someone greet me.

I turned around and saw a familiar face, Motl Komzoyl, a tailor boy from Anatevka.

"Well, well, well, look who's here!" I said. "If I sat here long enough, I bet even the Messiah would turn up. Have a seat on God's earth, Motl. What brought you here of all places?"

"What brought me here? Why, my feet," he says, sitting down on the grass and glancing at my girls, who were busy with the jugs and cans. "I've been meaning to drop by for a while, Reb Tevye, but I haven't had a free moment. As soon as I finish one piece of work, it's time to start on another. I'm in business for myself now and thank God there's plenty of it—in fact, all we tailors are swamped. There's been nothing but weddings all summer long. First Berl Fonfatsh married off his daughter; then Yosl Sheygetz; then Yankl Piskatsh; then Moyshe Gorgel; then Meir Kropeve; then Chayim Lushik; why, even Trihobikhe the Widow has gone and gotten herself hitched."

"It certainly looks like the whole world is marrying," I said. "I must be the only one not throwing a wedding this summer. I suppose God is too busy for one more."

"Not at all, Reb Tevye," he says, eyeing my girls again. "You're wrong there. You can have a wedding whenever you want. It's entirely up to you."

"Just what are you trying to tell me?" I asked. "You don't happen to have a match for my Tsaytl, do you?"

"One just her size!" he says in tailor talk.

"A serious proposal?" I say, thinking: bless my soul if he isn't about to offer me Layzer Wolf the butcher!

"The perfect fit!" he says with another look at my girls.

"Where does this match of yours come from?" I ask him. "I'm warning you right now that if he smells of the meat counter, I don't want to hear another word!"

"God forbid!" he says. "There's not an ounce of meat on him. As a matter of fact, Reb Tevye, it's someone you know well."

"And you're sure it's on the up-and-up?" I say.

"Why, it's so far up it's heavenly!" he says. "It's a dream—custom-made and alterations free."

"In that case," I say, "perhaps I can ask you who it is."

"Who is it?" he says, stealing a sideways glance once more. "The match I have in mind for you, Reb Tevye, is none other than myself."

I wouldn't have jumped to my feet any faster if he had poured boiling water over me. He jumped up too, and we stood facing each other like a pair of fighting cocks.

"Are you crazy?" I said. "Since when can you be the matchmaker, the father-in-law, and the groom all rolled into one? I suppose you want to be the rabbi and the bandleader too! I never in all my life heard of a young man making matches for himself."

"All your enemies, Reb Tevye," he says, "should be as crazy as you think I am. You can take my word for it that they don't come any saner than me. In fact, it's a sign of my sanity that I want to marry your Tsaytl—and the proof is that even the richest Jew in Anatevka, Layzer Wolf, wants to take her off your hands free of charge. Do you think that's a secret? Why, the whole town knows about it! And as for what you say about a matchmaker, I'm surprised at you, Reb Tevye. I wouldn't have thought that a Jew like yourself had to be spoon-fed . . . But why beat around the bush? The truth of the matter is that your daughter Tsaytl and I decided to get married a year ago."

I tell you, he might as well have knifed me in the heart! In the first place, how could a tailor boy like Motl even dream of being my son-in-law? And in the second place, what kind of *decided to get married a year ago?*

"Well," I said to him, "and just where does that leave me? Did it ever occur to you that I might also be asked—that I might happen to have an opinion on my daughter's future too?"

"Of course it did," he says. "That's why I'm here, to ask you. As soon as I heard that Layzer Wolf was interested in your daughter, who I've been in love with for over a year, as you know—"

"So far," I say, "all I know is that Tevye has a daughter named Tsaytl and that you're Motl Komzoyl the tailor boy. But what do you have against her that you want to marry her?"

"You don't understand," he says. "I'm not just telling you that I love your daughter. I'm telling you that she loves me too. It's been over a year since we swore to be husband and wife. I had meant to talk to you about it long ago, but I kept putting it off until I had saved up a few rubles to buy a sewing machine and outfit myself properly, because anyone who's anyone these days owns at least two suits and a pair of matching vests . . ."

"Tfu!" I said. "A child like you ought to be spanked. What exactly do you propose to live on after the wedding—the money you'll get from pawning your stomachs, since you won't be needing them anyway? Or do you plan to feed your wife matching vests?"

"Reb Tevye, I'm amazed at you," he says. "I don't believe you had a house to call your own when you were married, either—and yet just look at you now! What's good enough for other Jews is good enough for me. And besides, I have a profession . . ."

Well, to make a long story short, he talked me into it. After all, why pretend: what do most Jewish children have in the bank when they marry? If everyone acted sensibly, there wouldn't be a Jewish wedding in the world.

One thing still bothered me, though: I simply couldn't understand how they had decided such a thing on their own. What has the world come to when a boy meets a girl and says to her, "Let's you and I get married, just the two of us"? You'd think it was as simple as eating an onion! . . . But when I saw my Motl standing there with his head bowed contritely, looking so serious and sincere, I couldn't help thinking that maybe I had the wrong attitude. What was I being so snooty about and who did I think I was, the great-grandson of Rabbi Tsatskeleh of Pripichek? One might suppose I was giving my daughter a huge dowry and buying her a grand trousseau . . . Motl Komzoyl may be only a tailor, I thought, but he's a fine, hardworking boy who'll support his family, and he's as honest as the day is long, why look down on him? Tevye, I said to myself, stop hemming and hawing and sign on the dotted line! How does the Bible put it? *Solakhti kidvorekho*—congratulations and good luck to you both!

But what was I going to do about the wife? I was sure to get it in the neck from her unless I could make her see the light. "You know what, Motl?" I said to my future son-in-law. "You go home and leave the rest of it to me. There's one or two people I need to have a word with. As it says in the Book of Esther, *vehashtiyoh kedos*—there's a right and a wrong way to do everything. Tomorrow, God willing, if you haven't changed your mind, you and I will meet again . . ."

"Changed my mind?" he says. "*I* should change my mind? May sticks and stones break all my bones if I do a thing like that!"

"There's no need for oaths," I say, "because I believe you without them. Now run along home, and sweet dreams . . ."

And with that I went to bed too. But I couldn't fall asleep. I was thinking so hard of plan after plan that I was afraid my head would explode. Until finally I hit on the right one. What was it? Be patient and you'll hear what a brainstorm Tevye had.

In a word, in the middle of the night, when the whole house was sound asleep, snoring and whistling to wake the dead, I suddenly sat up in bed and began to shout at the top of my voice, "Help! Help! For God's sake, help!"

Everyone woke up, of course, and quickest of all, my wife Golde. "My God, Tevye," she said, shaking me, "wake up! What is it? What are you screaming for?"

I opened my eyes, glanced all around as though looking for someone, and gasped in a trembling voice, "Where is she?"

"Where is who?" asks my wife. "Who are you looking for?"

"For Frume Soreh," I say. "Layzer Wolf's Frume Soreh was just here."

"You must have a fever," she says. "God help you, Tevye, Layzer Wolf's Frume Soreh passed away years ago."

"I know she did," I say. "But she was just standing here by my bed, talking to me. And then she grabbed me by the throat and tried to choke me!"

"Oh, my God, Tevye," she says, "you're delirious. It was only a dream. Spit three times against the Evil Eye, tell me what you dreamed, and you'll see that it's nothing to be afraid of."

"God bless you, Golde," I say. "If it weren't for you, I would have croaked on the spot from sheer fright. Bring me a glass of water and I'll tell you my dream. But I'll have to ask you, Golde, to control yourself and not panic, because our holy books say that no dream can come true more than seventy-five percent, and that the rest of it is pure poppycock, such stuff and nonsense that only a fool would believe in . . . And now listen. At first I dreamed that we were having some sort of celebration, a wedding or an engagement party, I'm not sure which. All sorts of people were there, the rabbi too, even a band of musicians. Then a door opened and in came your Grandmother Tsaytl, God rest her soul . . ."

As soon as I mentioned her grandmother, my wife turned as white as the wall and cried out, "How did she look and what was she wearing?"

"She looked," I said, "like your enemies should, as yellow as wax, and she was wearing something white, it must have been a funeral shroud . . . 'Mazel tov!' she says to me. 'I'm so pleased to hear that you've chosen a fine young man for your Tsaytl, your eldest daughter who's named for me. He's called Motl Komzoyl, after my cousin Mordechai, and he's an excellent fellow, even if he is a tailor . . .' "

"Why in the world," says my Golde, "is she bringing us a tailor? We've always had teachers in our family, cantors, beadles, even undertakers—I won't say that some of them weren't poor, but we never, God forbid, had a shoemaker or a tailor."

"Don't interrupt me, Golde," I said. "Your Grandmother Tsaytl must know what she's talking about—though in fact I also said, 'Grandma, I'm afraid you've got it wrong: Tsaytl's fiancé is a butcher, not a tailor, and his name is Layzer Wolf, not Motl Komzoyl . . .' 'No,' says your Grandma Tsaytl. 'No, Tevye, *you've* got it wrong: Tsaytl's young man is called Motl. He's a tailor, all right, and he and she, God willing, will have a long and happy life together . . .' 'Right you are, Grandma,' I say. 'But what exactly do you propose that we do about Layzer Wolf? I hope you realize that I've given him my word . . .' No sooner had I said that than I looked up—your Grandmother Tsaytl was gone! Now Frume Soreh was standing in her place, and this is what she said to me: 'Reb Tevye! I've always thought you were a learned, honorable Jew; would you kindly explain to me, then, how you can let your daughter take over my house, sit in my chairs, carry my keys, walk around in my coats, put on my jewelry, and wear my pearls?' 'But why blame me?' I say to her. 'That's what your Layzer Wolf wants.' 'Layzer Wolf?' she says. 'Layzer Wolf will come to no good end, while as for your daughter Tsaytl—I feel sorry for your daughter, Reb Tevye, because she won't live out three weeks with him. If she does, I promise you that I'll come to her in person the next night and throttle her, like this . . .' And with those very words, Golde, Frume Soreh grabbed me by the throat and began to squeeze so hard that if you hadn't waked me when you did, I'd be in the world to come now."

"Tfu! Tfu! Tfu!" goes my wife, spitting three times. "May the river drown it, may the earth swallow it up, may the wind carry it off, may the forest blot it out, and no harm come to us and our children! May the butcher have black dreams himself! He should break a hand and a foot before anything happens to Motl Komzoyl's little finger, even if he is a tailor! Believe me, if he's named after my cousin Mordechai he doesn't have a tailor's soul. And if my grandmother, may she rest in peace, has taken the trouble of coming all the way from the next world to wish us a mazel tov, we'd better say mazel tov ourselves. It should only turn out for the best. They should have lots of happiness, amen and amen!"

Why make a short story long? I must be made of iron if I could manage to lie there under the blankets without bursting from laughter. *Borukh shelo osoni ishoh*—a woman is always a woman . . . Needless to say, we celebrated the engagement the next day and the wedding soon after, and the two lovebirds are as happy as can be. He tailors in Boiberik, going from dacha to dacha for work, and she's busy day and night, cooking, and baking, and washing, and scrubbing, and fetching water from the well. They barely manage to get by. In fact, if I didn't bring them some produce now and then, and sometimes a bit of cash, they'd be in a real fix—but listen to her and she's sitting on top of the world as long as she has her Motl . . .

Well, go argue with today's children! It's like I said at the beginning, *bonim gidalti veroymamti:* you can slave for them, you can knock your head against the wall—*veheym poshu vi*, they still think they know better than you do. No, say what you will, today's children are too smart for their own good. But I'm afraid I've chewed your ear off even more than usual today. Please don't hold it against me—you should only take care and be well!

(1899)

▼

Yoou've been wondering, have you, Pani Sholem Aleichem, where I've been all this time? Tevye's changed quite a bit, you say, grown suddenly gray? Ah, if only you knew the troubles, the heartache, that I've been through! It's written that *odom yesoydoy mi'ofor vesoyfoy le'ofor,* that a man can be weaker than a fly and stronger than steel—I tell you, that's a description of me! Maybe you can tell me, though, why it is that whenever something goes wrong in this world, it's Tevye it goes wrong with. Do you think that's because I'm a gullible fool who believes whatever he's told? If only I'd managed to remember what our rabbis said a thousand times, *kabdeyhu vekhoshdeyhu*—a man musn't trust his own dog . . . But what can I do, I ask you, if that's my nature? And besides, I'm a man of faith, as you know, I have no complaints against God. Not that they would do me the least bit of good if I had them! Whatever He does must be for a reason, though. It's like the prayer book says, *haneshomoh lokh vehaguf shelokh*—what does a man ever know and what is he really worth? My wife and I quarrel about that. "Golde," I'm always telling her, "it's a sin even to think such things. There's a story in the Talmud that—" "Leave me alone with your Talmud!" she says. "We have a daughter to marry off, and after her, touch wood, two others, and after them three more, if first they don't break a leg . . . ." "You musn't talk that way, Golde," I say. "Our rabbis warned against it. In the Talmud it also says—" But she never lets me finish. "A house full of growing daughters," she says, "is all the Talmud I need to know!" Go argue with a woman, I tell you!

In short, I don't have to remind you that I have, touch wood, some fine goods at home, each better-looking than the other. God forgive me for boasting. It's not a man's job to praise his own daughters, but you should hear the whole world tell me what knockouts they are! And most of all my Hodl, who's next after Tsaytl, the one who fell for the tailor, if you recall. I can't begin to tell you how gorgeous she is—I mean Hodl, my second daughter; she's like the Bible says of Queen Esther, *ki toyvas mar'eh hi*—prettier than a picture! And if looks aren't bad enough, she has the brains to go with them; she reads and writes both Yiddish and Russian and swallows books like hot cakes. What, you may ask, do a book and a dairyman's daughter have in common? Well, I ask them the same riddle—I mean all those nice Jewish youngsters who, begging your pardon, don't own a pair of britches for their backsides, yet only want to study all day long. *Kulonu khakhomim, kulonu nevoynim,* as it says in the Haggadah—nowadays everyone wants to be a student. Where? How? Why, a cow can sooner jump over a roof than a Jew get into a Russian university! *Al tishlakh yodkho:* they guard their schools from us like a bowl of cream from a cat. Not that it keeps us from studying anyway—and plain ordinary boys and girls too, the children of tailors and shoemakers, God help me if I don't see them everywhere! They leave home for Yehupetz or Odessa, they live there in attics and garrets, they eat the ten plagues of Egypt with the eleventh for dessert, they go for months on end without seeing a scrap of meat, a single roll and a herring is a feast for a dozen of them. *Vesomakhto bekhagekho*—life for them is one big holiday . . .

Well, one such character turned up in our neck of the woods, a real vagabond, too. In fact, I once knew his father, a man who peddled homemade cigarettes and was a beggar seven times over. But that's a whole other story—and besides, if the Talmud tells us that Rabbi Yochanan the Cobbler made a living patching shoes, a person can be permitted a father who didn't make one selling cigarettes. What annoyed me was something else: where did a pauper like him get off thinking he was a student? Not that he was born feebleminded, God forbid, because he had a good head on his shoulders. And though his name was Pertchik, we all called him Peppercorn, because that's exactly what he looked like: a small, black, puny little ragamuffin. Still, they don't come any brighter, and when he let loose with his tongue . . . whew, you had better step back!

Listen to how I met him. *Vayehi hayoym,* one fine day I'm on my way home from Boiberik, having sold a bit of merchandise, a whole wagon full of cheese, cream, butter, and other such vegetables. As usual I was thinking about the world's problems, such as why in Yehupetz they had it so good, whether Tevye ever would, what my horse would say if he could, and so on and so forth. It was summertime; the sun was shining down; the flies were biting; and the whole wide world seemed such a delicious place that it made you want to sprout wings and fly off into it . . .

Just then I looked ahead and saw a young man trudging along by the side of the path, a bundle under one arm, all sweaty and falling off his feet. "Hurry up or you'll be late for the wedding!" I called out to him. "Come to think of it, hop aboard; I'm going your way and my wagon is empty. You know what the Bible says: help the jackass of your neighbor if you pass him on the road, and your jackass of a neighbor too."

He laughed and jumped into the wagon without having to be asked twice.

"Where might a young fellow like you be coming from?" I asked.

"From Yehupetz," he says.

"And what might a young fellow like you be doing in Yehupetz?" I ask.

"A young fellow like me," he says, "is preparing for his entrance exams."

"And what," I ask, "might a young fellow like you be planning to study?"

"A young fellow like me," he says, "hasn't decided that yet."

"In that case," I ask, "why's a young fellow like you beating his brains out?"

"Don't you worry, Reb Tevye," he says. "A young fellow like me knows what he's doing."

"Tell me," I say, "since you seem to be a personal acquaintance of mine, just who exactly are you?"

"Who am I?" he says. "A human being."

"I already guessed as much," I said, "because you didn't look like a horse to me. What I meant was, whose child are you?"

"Whose child?" he says. "I'm a child of God's."

"I knew that too," I say. "After all, it's written, *vaya'as eloyhim*— and God made every creeping thing. I mean, who's your family? Are you from hereabouts or from elsewhere?"

"My family," he says, "is the human race. But I was born and raised around here. You even know me."

"Then out with it!" I say. "Who is your father?"

"My father," he says, "was named Pertchik."

"The devil take you!" I say. "Did you have to take all day to tell me that? Are you Pertchik the cigarette maker's boy, then?"

"Yes," he says. "I'm Pertchik the cigarette maker's boy."

"And you're truly a student?" I ask.

"Yes," he says. "I'm truly a student."

"And what exactly do you live on?" I ask.

"I live," he says, "on what I eat."

"Good for you!" I say. "Two and two is four, four and four is eight, and ate and ate and had a tummy ache. But tell me, my fine friend, what exactly is it that you eat?"

"Whatever I'm given," he says.

"Well, at least you're not choosy," I say. "If there's food, you eat, and if there isn't, you bite your lip and go to bed hungry. I suppose it's worth all that to be a student. After all, why shouldn't you be like the rich Jews of Yehupetz? *Kulom ahuvim, kulom brurim,* as it says . . ."

Sometimes I like to cite a verse or a prayer. Do you think that Pertchik took it lying down? "Those Jews," he says, "will never live to see the day when I'll be like them. I'll see them all in hell first!"

"Why, bless my soul if you don't seem to have something against them," I say. "I hope they haven't gone and put a lien on your father's estate."

"It's their estates," he says, "that will be yours, and mine, and everyone's some day."

"You know what?" I say. "I'd leave that sort of talk to your worst enemies. I can see one thing, though—and that's that with a tongue like yours, you're in no danger of getting lost in the shuffle. If you're free tonight, why don't you drop over? We can chat a bit, and have some supper while we're at it . . ."

You can be sure I didn't have to repeat the invitation. My young man made sure to turn up at dinnertime sharp, just when the borscht was on the table and the knishes were sizzling in the pan. "You've timed it perfectly," I said. "If you'd like to wash your hands and say the Lord's blessing, go ahead, and if not—that's fine with me too, I'm not God's policeman. No one's going to whip me in the next world for your sins in this one."

Well, we ate and we talked—in fact, we talked on and on, because something about the little fellow appealed to me. I'm damned if I know what it was, but it did. You see, I've always liked a man I can have a Jewish word with; here a verse from the Bible, there a line from the Talmud, even a bit of philosophy or what-have-you; I can't help being who I am . . . And from then on the

boy began dropping in regularly. As soon as he finished the private lessons that he gave for a living each day, he would come to
us to rest up and have something to eat. (Mind you, I wouldn't
wish such a living on anyone, because in the most generous of
cases, I assure you, our local squires pay eighteen kopecks an hour
to have their sons taught, for which they expect their letters to be
addressed, their telegrams corrected, and their errands run in the
bargain. And why not? Doesn't it say *bekhoyl levovkho uvekhoyl naf-*
shekho—if you expect to eat, expect to pay the bill too!) The boy
could count himself lucky to take his meals with us and tutor my
girls in return for them. An eye for an eye, as it says—one good
turn deserves another. Before we knew it, he had all but moved in
with us; whenever he arrived, someone would run to bring him a
glass of milk, and my wife made sure he always had a clean shirt
and two whole socks, one for each of his feet. It was then that we
started calling him Peppercorn. He really did seem like one of the
family, because at bottom, you know, he was a decent sort, a
simple, down-to-earth boy who would have shared all his worldly
possessions with us, just as we shared ours with him, if only he had
had any . . .

The one thing I didn't like about him was his habit of disap-
pearing now and then. Suddenly he would vanish—*vehayeled ey-*
nenu, Peppercorn was nowhere to be found. "Where have you
been, my wanderbird?" I would ask him when he came back.
Peppercorn kept silent as a fish, though. I don't know about you,
but secretive people annoy me. Even God, when He created the
world, did it out loud, or else how would we know all about it? But
I will say this for Peppercorn: when he opened his mouth, it
erupted like a volcano. You wouldn't have believed the things that
came out of it then, such wild, crazy ideas, everything backwards
and upside down with its feet sticking up in the air. A rich Jew, for
instance—that's how warped his mind was!—wasn't worth a row
of beans to him, but a beggar was a big deal, and a workingman—
why, a workingman was king, he was God's gift to the world—the
reason being, I gathered, that he worked.

"Still," I would say, "when it comes to livelihoods, you can't
compare work to making money."

That would get him so mad that he'd go all out to convince me
that money was the root of all evil. All the monkey business in
the world, he said, was due to it and nothing honest could ever

come of it. And he would give me ten thousand proofs and demonstrations that stuck to me like a radish to a wall. "Stop talking like a madman," I would say. "I suppose it's dishonest of my cow to give milk and of my horse to pull my wagon for me?" I had some idiot question like that for every idiot statement that he made; trust Tevye not to let him get away with anything. If only Tevye hadn't trusted Peppercorn! . . . And he wasn't embarrassed to speak his mind, either. One evening, for instance, as we were sitting on the front stoop of my house and philosophizing away, he says to me, "You know what, Reb Tevye? You have some wonderful daughters."

"You don't say!" I said. "Thanks for letting me know. They have a wonderful father to take after."

"Especially your second eldest," he says. "What a head she has! She's perfection itself."

"So what else is new?" I say. "The apple fell close to the tree." Between you and me, though, my heart swelled with pleasure. Show me the father who doesn't like to hear his kids praised! Was I a prophet that I should have known what a crazy love affair would come of it? Listen and I'll tell you all about it.

In a word, *vayehi erev vayehi voyker*—one afternoon as I was making my rounds of the Boiberik dachas, someone hailed me in the street. I looked around to see who it was—why, it's Efrayim the Matchmaker! Efrayim the Matchmaker, you should know, is a Jew who makes matches. "Begging your pardon, Reb Tevye," he says, "but I'd like to have a word with you."

"With pleasure," I say, reining in my horse. "I hope it's a good one."

"Reb Tevye, you have a daughter," he says.

"I have seven, God bless them," I say.

"I know you do," he says. "So do I."

"In that case," I say, "we have fourteen between the two of us."

"All joking aside," he says, "what I want to talk to you about is this: being as you know a matchmaker, I have a match for you—and not just any match either, but something really exclusive, extraprime and superfine!"

"Perhaps you can tell me," I say, "what's hiding under the label, because if it's a tailor, a shoemaker, or a schoolteacher, he can save himself the trouble and so can I. *Revakh vehatsoloh ya'amoyd layehudim mimokoym akher*—thank you very kindly but I'll look for a son-in-law elsewhere. It says in the Talmud that—"

"Good Lord, Reb Tevye," he says, "are you starting in on the Talmud again? Before a body can talk with you, he has to spend a year boning up. The whole world is nothing but a page of Talmud to you. If I were you, I'd listen to the offer I'm about to make you, because it's going to take your breath away."

And with that he delivers himself of an after-dinner speech about the young man's credentials. What can I tell you? Champagne and caviar! In the first place, he comes from the best of families, not from the hoi polloi—and that, I want you to know, is what matters most to me, because although we have all kinds in my family, *akudim nekudim uvrudim*—well-off folk, working folk, even some pretty common folk—I'm far from a nobody myself . . . Secondly, Efrayim tells me, his man can parse a verse with the best of them, he knows how to read the small print—and that's no trifle with me either, because I'd sooner eat a buttered pig than sit down to a meal with an illiterate. A Jew who can't read a Jewish book is a hundred times worse than a sinner. I don't give a hoot if you go to synagogue or not; I don't even care if you stand on your head and point your toes at the sky; as long as you can match me quote for quote and line for line, you're a man after my own heart, that's just the way Tevye is . . . And finally, says Efrayim, the fellow is rolling in money; why, he rides about in a droshky pulled by a pair of horses who leave a trail of smoke wherever they go—and that, I thought, is certainly no crime either. Any way you look at it, it's an improvement on being poor. How does the Talmud put it? *Yo'oh aniyuso leyisro'eyl,* not even God likes a beggar. And the proof of it is that if He liked them, He wouldn't make them beg . . .

"Is that all?" I say. "I'm waiting to hear more."

"More?" he says. "What more can you want? He's crazy in love, he's dying to have you. That is, I don't mean you, Reb Tevye, I mean your daughter Hodl. He says he wants a beauty . . ."

"Does he now?" I say. "He should only deserve to have her. But just who is this hotshot of yours? A bachelor? A widower? A divorcé? Or the Devil's own helper?"

"He's a young bachelor," he says. "That is, he's not so young as all that, but a bachelor he certainly is."

"And what might his God-given name be?" I ask.

That, though, was something I couldn't get out of him for the life of me. "Run your daughter down to Boiberik," Efrayim says, "and I'll be glad to tell you."

"*Run* my daughter down to Boiberik?" I say. "Do you think she's a horse being brought to a fair?"

Well, a matchmaker, as you know, can talk a wall into marrying a hole in the ground; we agreed that after the Sabbath I would run my daughter down to Boiberik. I can't tell you what sweet dreams that gave me. I imagined Hodl trailing smoke in a droshky, and the whole world burning up too, but with envy— and not just for the droshky and the horses, but for all the good I would do once I was the father of a rich woman. Why, I'd become a real philanthropist, giving this beggar twenty-five rubles, that one fifty, that one over there an even hundred; I'd let everyone know that a poor man is a human being too . . . That's just what I thought as I traveled home that evening. "Giddyap," I told my horse, giving him a taste of the whip. "If you want your oats tonight, you'd better dance a little faster, because *im eyn kemakh eyn Toyroh,* by me there's no something for nothing."

In a word, there I was talking to him in Horsish when who do I see slipping out of the forest but a young couple, a boy and a girl, deep in talk and walking so close that they're practically hugging. Who can that be in the middle of nowhere, I wondered, squinting into the setting sun at them. Why, I could have sworn it was Peppercorn! But who was the schlimazel out with at this hour? I shaded my eyes with my hand and looked again: who was the female? My God, I said to myself, can that be Hodl? Yes, it's her, all right, or else I'm not a Jew . . . so these are the grammar lessons he's been giving her! Ah, Tevye, I thought, are you ever a jackass—and I stopped my horse and called out to them, "A good evening to you both! What's the latest war news from Japan? I hope it isn't too nosy of me to ask what you're doing here, because if you happen to be looking for pie in the sky, it's already been eaten by Brodsky . . ."

In short, I gave them such a hearty greeting that the two of them were left speechless, *loy bashomayim veloy ba'orets,* neither here nor there, embarrassed and blushing all over. For a moment they just stood there, staring down at the ground. Then they looked up at me, so that now we were staring at each other.

"Well," I said, half in anger, half in jest, "you're looking at me as though you hadn't seen me in a donkey's years. I can assure you that I'm the same Tevye as always, not a hair more or less of me."

"Papa," says my daughter Hodl to me, blushing even brighter. "You can wish us a mazel tov."

"I can?" I say. "Then mazel tov, you should live to be one hundred and twenty! Only what might I be congratulating you for? Have you found a buried treasure in the forest or been rescued from some great danger?"

"You can wish us a mazel tov," says Peppercorn, "because we're engaged to be married."

"You're engaged to be *what*?" I say. "What are you talking about?"

"To be married," he says. "Isn't that a custom you're familiar with? It means that I'll be her husband and she'll be my wife."

That's just what he said to me, Peppercorn did, looking me straight in the eye. So I looked him straight back and said, "Excuse me, but when was the engagement party? It's rather odd that you forgot to invite me to it, because if she'll be your wife, I just might be your father-in-law." I may have seemed to be making a joke of it, but the worms were eating my heart. Say what you will, though, Tevye is no woman; Tevye hears it out to the end. "I'm afraid I still don't get it," I said. "Whoever heard of a match without a matchmaker, without even a betrothal?"

"What do we need a matchmaker for?" says Peppercorn. "We're as good as married already."

"Oh, you are?" I say. "Will wonders never cease! And why have you kept it such a secret until now?"

"What was there to shout about?" he says. "We wouldn't have told you now either, but seeing as we're about to be parted, we decided to make it official."

That was already too much for me. *Bo'u mayim ad nefesh*, as it says: I felt cut to the quick. That he should tell me they were as good as married already—somehow I could still put up with that, how does the verse go? *Ohavti es adoyni, es ishti:* he loves her, she loves him, it's been known to happen before. But *make it official?* What kind of Chinese was that?

Well, even my young man must have seen how befuddled I was, because he turned to me and said: "You see, it's like this, Reb Tevye. I'm about to leave these parts."

"When?"

"Any day now."

"And just where," I asked, "are you off to?"

"I can't tell you that," he says. "It's confidential."

Would you believe it? *Confidential:* put that in your pipe and smoke it! Along comes a black little ragamuffin of a Peppercorn and informs me all in one breath that he's my son-in-law, and that he's making it official, and that he's going away, and that where is confidential! It made my gorge rise. "Look here," I said to him, "I understand that a secret is a secret—in fact, you're one big secret to me . . . But just tell me one thing, brother: you pride yourself on your honesty, you're so full of humanity that it's coming out of your ears—how can you marry a daughter of mine and run out on her the same day? You call that honest? You call that human? I suppose I should count myself lucky that you haven't robbed me and burned my house too."

"Papa!" says Hodl to me. "You don't know how happy it makes us to finally tell you the truth. It's such a load off our minds. Come, let me give you a kiss." And before I know it she grabs me from one side, he grabs me from the other, and we all begin to kiss so hard that pretty soon they're kissing each other. A scene from the theater, I tell you! "Don't you think that's enough for a while?" I finally managed to say. "It's time we had a practical talk."

"About what?" they ask.

"Oh," I say, "about dowries, trousseaus, wedding costs, everything from soup to nuts . . ."

"But we don't want any soup or nuts," they say.

"What do you want, then?" I ask.

"An official wedding," they say. Did you ever hear of such a thing in your life?

Well, I don't want to bore you. All my arguments did as much good as last winter's snow. We had an official wedding. Take my word, it wasn't the wedding that Tevye deserved, but what doesn't pass for a wedding these days? A funeral would have been jollier. And to make matters worse, I have a wife, as you know, who can be a royal pain. Day in and day out she kept after me: how could I ever permit such a higgledy-piggledy, such a slapdash affair? Go try explaining to a woman that time is of the essence! There was nothing for it but to smooth things over with a tiny little fib about a childless old aunt of Peppercorn's in Yehupetz, oodles of money, a huge inheritance that would be his one bright day in the middle of the night—anything to take the heat off me . . .

That same day, a few hours after the splendid wedding, I harnessed my horse to the wagon and the three of us, myself, my daughter, and my heir-in-law, piled into it and drove to Boiberik. As I sat there stealing a glance at them, I thought, how clever it is of God to run His world according to the latest fashions! And the weird types He puts in it! Why, right next to me was a freshly married couple, still wet behind the ears, so to speak, one of them setting out for the Devil knows where and the other not shedding a tear for him, not even one for the record—but Tevye was no woman, Tevye would wait and see . . . At the station were a few youngsters, born-and-bred Kasrilevkites to judge by the state of their boots, who had come to say goodbye. One, wearing his shirt down over his pants and looking more like a Russian than a Jew, stood whispering with my wanderbird. I do believe, Tevye, I told myself, that you've married into a gang of horse thieves, or purse snatchers, or housebreakers, or at the very least, highway murderers . . .

On the way back from Boiberik I couldn't restrain myself any longer, and I told my Hodl what I thought of them. She laughed and tried explaining to me that they were the best, the finest, the most honorable young people in the world, and that they lived their whole lives for others, never giving a fig for their own skins. "For example," she says, "that one with the shirt hanging out: he comes from a rich home in Yehupetz—but not only won't he take a penny from his parents, he refuses even to talk to them."

"Is that a fact?" I say. "I do declare, honorable is hardly the word! Why, with that shirt and long hair, all he needs is a half-empty bottle of vodka to look the perfect gentleman."

Did she get it? Not my Hodl! *Eyn Esther magedes*—see no evil, hear no evil. Each time I took a dig at her Peppercorn's friends, back she came at me with capital, the working class, pie in the sky. "What do I care about your working class," I said, "if it's such a military secret? There's an old saying, you know, that if you scratch a secret, you'll find a thief. Tell me the truth, now: where is Peppercorn going and why is he going there?"

"Ask me anything but that," she says. "Better yet, don't ask me anything. Just pray that there'll be some good news soon . . ."

"Amen," I say. "I only hope God's listening. My enemies should worry about their health as much as I'm beginning to worry about the little game that you and your friends are playing . . ."

"The trouble is, you don't understand," she says.

"What's to understand?" I say. "I'd like to think I understand harder things."

"It's not something you can grasp with just your head," she says. "You have to feel it—you have to feel it with all your heart!"

And on she went, my Hodl, her face flushed and her eyes burning as she talked. What a mistake it was to go and have such daughters! Whatever craziness they fall for, it's head and heart and body and soul and life and limb all together . . .

Well, let me tell you, a week went by, and then another, and still another, and another, and another—*eyn koyl ve'eyn kosef,* there's not a letter, not a single word. That's the last of Peppercorn, I thought, looking at my Hodl. There wasn't a drop of blood in her poor cheeks. All the time she did her best to keep busy about the house, because nothing else helped take her mind off him—yet couldn't she have said something, couldn't she at least have mentioned his name? No, not one syllable: you'd think that such a fellow as Peppercorn was a pure figment of my imagination . . .

One day when I came home, though, I could see that my Hodl had been crying; her eyes were swollen with tears. I asked around and was told that not long before, a character with long hair had been in the house and spoken to her in private. Oho, I said to myself, that must be our fine friend who goes about with his shirt hanging out and tells his rich parents to jump in the lake! And without thinking twice I called my Hodl out to the yard and put it straight to her. "Tell me," I asked her, "have you heard from him?"

"Yes," she said.

"And where," I ask, "is your true love?"

"He's far away," she says.

"And what," I ask, "might he be doing there?"

"He's doing time," she says.

"Time?"

"Time."

"But where?" I ask. "For what?"

Hodl didn't answer. She looked straight at me and said nothing.

"Just explain one thing to me, Daughter," I said. "I don't need you to tell me that he's not doing time for horse theft. And if he isn't a thief and he isn't a swindler, what good deeds has he been put away for?"

Eyn Esther magedes—mum's the word! Well, I thought, if you don't want to talk, you don't have to; he's your bit of bad luck, not

mine; may the Lord have mercy on him! . . . My heart didn't ache
any less, though. After all, she was my daughter. You know what
it says in the prayer book: *kerakheym ov al bonim*—a father can't
help being a father . . .

In short, the summer passed, the High Holy Days came and
went, and it was already Hoshana Rabbah, the last day of Sukkos.
It's my habit on holidays to give myself and my horse a breather,
just like it says in the Bible: *atoh*—you yourself; *veshorkho*—and
your wife; *vekhamorkho*—and your horse too . . . Besides, there's
nothing to do then in Boiberik anyway; as soon as Rosh Hashanah
comes along, all the dacha owners take off like a pack of hungry
mice and Boiberik turns into a ghost town. It's a good time to stay
home and relax a bit on the front stoop. In fact, it's my favorite
season. Each day is a gift. The sun's not as hot as an oven anymore
and has a mildness about it that makes being out-of-doors a pleasure. The leaves are still green, the pine trees give off a good tarry
smell, and the whole forest is looking its best, as if it were God's
own sukkah, a tabernacle for God. It's there that He must celebrate the holiday, not in the city, where there's such a commotion
of people running about to earn their next meal and thinking
only of money, of how to make more and more of it . . . And at
night you might think you were in Paradise, the sky such a deep
blue and the stars twinkling, sparkling, winking on and off at you
like eyes; sometimes one shoots through the air as fast as an ar-
row, leaving behind a green trail—that's a sign that someone's
luck has run out. Every Jew has his star . . . why, the whole sky is
Jewish . . . I hope it's not mine that just fell, I prayed, suddenly
thinking of Hodl. Lately she'd seemed cheerier, livelier, more her
old self again. Someone had brought her a letter, no doubt from
her jailbird. I would have given the world to know what was in it,
but I was blamed if I was going to ask. If she wasn't talking,
neither was I; I'd show her how to button up a lip. No, Tevye was
no woman; Tevye could wait . . .

Well, no sooner had I thought of my Hodl than she appeared
by my side. She sat down next to me on the stoop, looked around,
and said in a low voice, "Papa, are you listening? I have to tell you
something. I'm saying goodbye to you tonight . . . forever."

She spoke in such a whisper that I could barely hear her, and
she gave me the strangest look—such a look, I tell you, as I'll
never forget for as long as I live. The first thing to flash through

my mind was that she was going to drown herself . . . Why did I
think of drowning? Because there was once an incident not far
from here in which a Jewish girl fell in love with a Russian peasant
boy, and, not being able to marry him . . . but I've already told you
the end. The mother took it so hard that she fell ill and died, and
the father let his business go bankrupt. Only the peasant boy got
over it; he found himself another and married her instead. As for
the girl, she went down to the river and threw herself in . . .

"What do you mean, you're saying goodbye forever?" I asked,
staring down at the ground to hide my face, which must have
looked like a dead man's.

"I mean," she said, "that I'm going away early in the morning.
We'll never see each other again . . . ever."

That cheered me up a bit. Thank God for small comforts, I
thought. Things could have been worse—though to tell you the
truth, they conceivably could have been better . . .

"And just where," I inquired, "are you going, if it's not too
much of me to ask?"

"I'm going to join him," she said.

"You are?" I said. "And where is he?"

"Right now he's still in prison," she said. "But soon he's being
sent to Siberia."

"And so you're going to say goodbye to him?" I asked, playing
innocent.

"No," she says. "I'm going with him."

"Where?" I say. "What's the name of the nearest town?"

"We don't know the exact place yet," she says. "But it's awfully
far away. Just getting there alive isn't easy."

She said that, did my Hodl, with great pride, as if she and her
Peppercorn had done something so grand that they deserved a
medal with half a pound of gold in it. I ask you, what's a father to
do with such a child? He either scolds her, you say, or spanks her,
or gives her an earful she'll remember. But Tevye is no woman; it
happens to be my opinion that anger is the worst sin in the book.
And so I answered as usual with a verse from Scripture. "I see,
Hodl," I told her, "that you take the Bible seriously when it says, *al
keyn ya'azoyv ish es oviv ve'es imoy*, therefore a child shall leave its
father and its mother . . . For Peppercorn's sake you're throwing
your papa and your mama to the dogs and going God only knows
where, to some far wilderness across the trackless sea where even

Alexander the Great nearly drowned the time he was ship-
wrecked on a desert island inhabited by cannibals . . . And don't
think I'm making that up either, because I read every word in a
book . . ."

You can see that I tried to make light of it, though my heart was
weeping inside me. But Tevye is no woman; Tevye kept a stiff
upper lip. And she, my Hodl, was not to be outdone by me. She
answered whatever I said point by point, quietly, calmly, intelli-
gently. Say what you will about them, Tevye's daughters can
talk! . . . Her voice shook dully, and even with my eyes shut, I felt
that I could see her, that I could see my Hodl's face that was as
pale and worn as the moon . . . Should I have thrown myself on
her, had a fit, begged her not to go? But I could see it was a lost
cause. Damn them all, every one of those daughters of mine—
when they fall for someone, they do it hook, line, and sinker!

In a word, we sat on the stoop all night long. Much of the time
we said nothing, and even our talk was in bits and snatches. Sometimes I listened to Hodl, and sometimes she listened to me. I
asked her one thing: whoever heard of a girl marrying a boy for
the sole purpose of following him to the North Pole? I tried using
reason to convince her how unreasonable it was, and she tried
using reason to convince me that reason had nothing to do with it.
Finally, I told her the story of the duckling that was hatched by a
hen; as soon as it could stand on its feet it toddled down to the
water and swam away, while its poor mother just stood there and
squawked. "What, Hodl, my darling, do you have to say about
that?" I asked. "What is there to say?" she said. "Of course, I feel
sorry for the hen; but just because the hen squawks, is the duckling never to swim?" . . . Now, is that an answer or isn't it? I tell
you, Tevye's daughters don't mince words!

Meanwhile time was going by. The dawn began to break. Inside
the house my wife was grumbling. She had let us know more than
once that it was time we called it a night—and now, seeing all the
good it had done, she stuck her head out the window and bawled
with her usual tact, "Tevye! What in God's name do you think
you're doing out there?"

"Ssshhh, don't make so much noise, Golde," I said. "*Lomoh rogshu,* says the Bible—have you forgotten that it's Hoshana Rabbah?
On the night of Hoshana Rabbah one isn't supposed to sleep,
because it's then that the Book of Life is shut for the year . . . And

now listen, Golde: please put up the samovar and let's have tea, because I'm taking Hodl to the station." And right on the spot I made up another whopper about Hodl having to go to Yehupetz, and from there to somewhere else, on account of Peppercorn's inheritance; in fact, she might very well have to spend the winter there, and maybe even the summer, and possibly the winter after that—which was why she needed a few things for the trip, such as linens, a dress, some pillows and pillowcases, and whatever else a young lady had to have . . .

Those were my orders—the last of which was that there better not be any tears, not when the whole world was celebrating Hoshana Rabbah. "No crying allowed on a holiday!" I said, "It's written in the Talmud, black on white." It could have been written in solid gold for all anyone listened to me. Cry they did, and when the time came to part, such a wailing broke out as you never heard in all your life. Everyone was shrieking: my wife, my daughters, my Hodl, and most of all, my eldest, Tsaytl, who spent the holiday at our place with her Motl. The two sisters hugged each other so hard that we could barely tear them apart . . .

I alone stayed strong as steel—that is, I steeled myself, though I was about as calm as a boiling kettle inside. But do you think I let anyone see it? Not on your life! Tevye is no woman . . . Hodl and I didn't say a word all the way to Boiberik, and only when we were nearly at the station did I ask her one last time to tell me what her Peppercorn had done. "It's got to be something!" I said.

She flared up at that; her husband, she swore, was as clean as the driven snow. "Why," she said, "he's a person who never thinks of his own self! His whole life is for others, for the good of the world—and especially for the workers, for the workingman . . ."

Maybe some day I'll meet the genius who can explain to me what that means. "You say he cares so much about the world?" I said. "Well, maybe you can tell me why, if he and the world are such great friends, it doesn't care more about him . . . But give him my best wishes, and tell your Alexander the Great that I'm counting on his honor, because he is the very soul of it, isn't he, to see to it that my daughter isn't ruined and that she drops her old father a line now and then . . ."

I was still in the middle of the sentence when she hugged me and burst into tears. "We'd better say goodbye now," she said. "Be well, Papa. God knows when we'll see each other again . . ."

That did it! I couldn't keep it in a second longer. You see, just then I thought of my Hodl when I held her as a baby in my arms . . . she was just a tiny thing then . . . and I held her in these arms . . . please forgive me, Pani, if . . . if I . . . just like a woman . . . but I want you to know what a Hodl I have! You should see the letters that she writes me . . . she's God's own Hodl, Hodl is . . . and she's with me right here all the time . . . deep, deep down . . . there's just no way to put it into words . . .

You know what, Pani Sholem Aleichem? Let's talk about something more cheerful. Have you heard any news of the cholera in Odessa?

(1904)

CHAVA

▼

H oydu lashem ki toyv—whatever God does is for the best. That is, it had better be, because try changing it if you don't like it! I was once like that myself; I stuck my nose into this, into that, until I realized I was wasting my time, threw up my hands, and said, Tevye, what a big fool you are! You're not going to remake the world . . . The good Lord gave us *tsa'ar gidul bonim*, which means in plain language that you can't stop loving your children just because they're nothing but trouble. If my daughter Tsaytl, for example, went and fell for a tailor named Motl Komzoyl, was that any reason to be upset? True, he's a simple soul, the fine points of being a Jew are beyond him, he can't read the small print at all—but what of it? You can't expect the whole world to have a higher education. He's still an honest fellow who works hard to support his family. He and Tsaytl—you should see what a whiz she is around the house!—have a home full of little brats already, touch wood, and are dying from sheer happiness. Ask her about it and · she'll tell you that life couldn't be better. In fact, there's only one slight problem, which is that her children are starving . . .

Ad kan hakofoh alef—that's daughter number one. And as for number two, I mean Hodl, I hardly need tell you about her. You already know the whole story. She's lost and gone forever, Hodl is; God knows if I'll ever set eyes on her again this side of the world to come . . . Just talking about her gives me the shakes, I feel my world has come to an end. You say I should forget her? But how do you forget a living, breathing human being—and especially a child like Hodl? You should see the letters she sends me, it's enough to melt a heart of ice! They're doing very well there, she writes; that is, he's doing time and she's doing wash. She takes in laundry, reads books, sees him once a week, and hopes, so she says, that one glorious day her Peppercorn and his friends will be pardoned and sent home; then, she promises, they'll really get down to business and turn the world upside down with its feet in the air and its head six feet in the ground. A charming prospect, eh? . . . So what does the good Lord do? He's an *eyl rakhum vekhanun,* a merciful God, and He says to me, "Just you wait, Tevye. When you see what I have up my sleeve this time, you'll forget every trouble you ever had . . ." And don't think that isn't just what happened! I wouldn't tell anyone but you about it, because the shame is even worse than the sorrow, but *hamekhaseh ani mey'Avrohom*—do you and I have any secrets between us? Why, I don't keep a thing from you! There's just one request I have, though—that this stay between the two of us, because I'll say it again: as bad as the heartache has been, the disgrace is far worse.

In a word, *rotsoh hakodoysh borukh hu lezakoys,* God wanted to do Tevye such a big favor that He went and gave him seven daughters—and not just ordinary daughters either, but bright, pretty, gifted, healthy, hardworking ones, fresh as daisies, every one of them! Let me tell you, I'd have been better off if they all were as ugly as sin . . . You can take the best of horses—what will it amount to if it's kept in a stable all day long? And it's the same with good-looking daughters if you raise them among peasants in a hole like this, where there's not a living soul to talk to apart from the village elder Anton Paparilo, the village scribe Chvedka Galagan, and the village priest, damn his soul, whose name I can't even stand to mention—and not because I'm a Jew and he's a priest, either. On the contrary, we've known each other for ages. I don't mean that we ever slapped each other's backs or danced at each other's weddings, but we said hello whenever we met and stopped to chat a bit about the latest news. I tried avoiding long discussions with him, though, because they always ended up with the same rigamarole about my God, and his God, and how his God had it over mine. Of course, I couldn't let it pass without quoting some verse from the Bible, and he couldn't let that pass without insisting he knew our Scriptures better than I did and even reciting a few lines of them in a Hebrew that sounded like a Frenchman talking Greek. It was the same blessed routine every time—and when I couldn't let *that* pass without putting him in his place with a midrash, he'd say, "Look here, your Middyrush is from your Tallymud, and your Tallymud is a lot of hokum," which got my goat so that I gave him a good piece of my mind off the top of it . . . Do you think that fazed him, though? Not one bit! He just looked at me, combed his beard with his fingers, and laughed right in my face. I tell you, there's nothing more aggravating than being laughed at by someone you've just finished throwing the book at. The hotter under the collar I'd get, the more he'd stand there and grin at me. Well, if I didn't understand what he thought was funny then, I'm sorry to say I do now . . .

In short, I came home one evening to find Chvedka the scribe, a tall young goy with high boots and a big shock of hair, standing outside and talking to my third daughter, Chava. As soon as he saw me he about-faced, tipped his hat, and took off.

"What was Chvedka doing here?" I asked Chava.

"Nothing," she says.

"What do you mean, nothing?" I ask.

"We were just talking," she says.

"Since when are you and he on such talking terms?" I ask.

"Oh," she says, "we've known each other for a while."

"Congratulations!" I say. "You've found yourself a fine friend."

"Do you know him, then?" she says. "Do you know who he is?"

"Not exactly," I say, "because I haven't read up on his family tree yet, but that doesn't keep me from seeing what a blue blood he is. In fact, if his father isn't a drunk, he may even be a swineherd or a handyman."

Do you know what my Chava says to me? "I have no idea who his father is. I'm only interested in individuals. And Chvedka is no ordinary person, that I'm sure of."

"Well, then," I say, "what sort of person is he? Perhaps you could enlighten me."

"Even if I told you," she says, "you wouldn't understand. Chvedka is a second Gorky."

"A second Gorky?" I say. "And who, pray tell, was the first?"

"Gorky," she says, "is only just about the most important man alive."

"Is he?" I say. "And just where does he live, this Mr. Important of yours? What's his act and what makes him such a big deal?"

"Gorky," she says, "is a literary figure, a famous author. That means he writes books. He's a rare, dear soul, even if he comes from a simple home and never had a day's schooling in his life. Whatever he knows, he taught himself. Here, this is his picture . . ."

And she takes out a little photograph from her pocket and shows it to me.

"This tsaddik is your Rabbi Gorky?" I say, "I could swear I've seen him somewhere before. You can search me, though, if I remember whether he was toting sacks at the train station or hauling logs in the forest . . ."

"And is it so shameful," says my Chava, "for a man to work with his own two hands? Whose hands do you work with? Whose hands do we all?"

"Of course," I answer. "You're quite right. It even says as much in the Bible: *yegia kapekho ki toykheyl*—if you don't work yourself to the bone, no one will throw you one, either . . . But what's all that got to do with Chvedka? I'd feel better if you and he were friend-lier at a distance. Don't forget *meyayin boso ule'on atoh hoyleykh*—just think of who you are and who he is."

"God," says my Chava, "created us all equal."

"So He did," I say. "He created man in His likeness. But you had better remember that not every likeness is alike. *Ish kematnas yodoy,* as the Bible says . . ."

"It's beyond belief," she says, "how you have a verse from the Bible for everything! Maybe you also have one that explains why human beings have to be divided into Jews and Christians, masters and slaves, beggars and millionaires . . ."

"Why, bless my soul," I say, "if you don't seem to think, my daughter, that the millennium has arrived." And I tried explaining to her that the way things are now is the way they've been since Day One.

"But why are they that way?" she asks.

"Because that's how God made them," I say.

"Well, why did He make them like that?"

"Look here," I say, "if you're going to ask why, why, why all the time, we'll just keep going around in circles."

"But what did God give us brains for if we're not supposed to use them?" she asks.

"You know," I say, "we Jews have an old custom that when a hen begins to crow like a rooster, off to the slaughterer she goes. That's why we say in the morning prayer, *hanoyseyn lasekhvi binoh*—not only did God give us brains, He gave some of us more of them than others."

"When will the two of you stop yackety-yacking already?" calls my Golde from inside the house. "The borscht has been on the table for an hour and you're still out there singing Sabbath hymns."

"Well, well, well," I say, "strike up the band! Our rabbis weren't kidding about *shivoh dvorim bagoylem*—anyone can be a nincompoop, but being a woman helps. Here we are talking about the universe and all you can think of is your borscht."

"You know what?" says my Golde. "Better my borscht without the universe than the universe without my borscht."

"Mazel tov," I say, "a philosopher is born before our eyes! It's enough my daughters all think they're a mental notch above the angels without you deciding to join them by flying head first up the chimney . . ."

"As long as you're on the subject of flying," she says, "why don't you go fly a kite!"

I ask you, is that any way to talk to a hungry man?

Well, let's leave the princess in her castle and get back to the young prince—I mean to the old priest, God rot his soul! As I was driving home near our village with my empty milk cans one evening, who should ride by in his iron buggy, that combed beard of his blowing in the wind, but His Eminence in person. Damn your eyes, I think, it's just my luck to run into you!

"Good evening there!" he says to me. "Didn't you recognize me?"

"They say that's a sign you're about to come into money," I said to him, tipping my hat and making as if to drive on.

"Hold on a minute, Tevel," he says. "What's the hurry? I'd like a word or two with you."

"If it's a good word, why not?" I say. "Otherwise let's make it some other time."

"What other time did you have in mind?" he says.

"How about the day the Messiah comes?" I say.

"But he already has come," says the priest.

"I believe," I say, "that I've heard that opinion from you before. So tell me, Father, what else is new?"

"That's just what I wanted to see you about," he says. "I'd like to speak to you privately about your daughter Chava."

That made my heart skip a beat! What business of his was my daughter? "My daughters," I said to him, "don't need to be spoken for. They're quite capable of speaking for themselves."

"But this isn't a matter that can be left up to her," he says. "It involves others too. I'm talking about something of great importance. Her whole life depends on it."

"What makes you such a party to her life?" I say. "I should think she had a father to be that, may he live to a ripe old age . . ."

"So she does," he says. "You're certainly her father. But you don't see what's been happening to her. Your daughter is reaching out toward a new life, and you either don't understand her or else don't want to understand."

"Whether I do or don't understand her or want to is a story in itself," I say. "But what does it have to do with you, Father?"

"It has a great deal to do with me," he says, "because she's in my charge right now."

"She's in your *what?*" I say.

"My custody," he says, looking right at me and running a hand through that fine, flowing beard of his.

I must have jumped a foot in the air. "What?" I said. "My child in your custody? By what right?" I was beside myself, but he only smiled at me, cool as a cucumber, and said, "Now don't go losing your temper, Tevel. Let's talk this over calmly. You know I have nothing against you, God forbid, even if you are a Jew. You know I think a great deal of you Jews. It just pains me to see how stubbornly you refuse to realize that we Christians have your good in mind."

"I wish you wouldn't talk about my good," I say, "because instead of telling me what you just did, Father, it would have been kinder to poison me or put a bullet in my head. If you're really such a good friend of mine, do me one favor: leave my daughter alone!"

"Don't talk like a fool," he says to me. "No harm will come to your daughter. In fact, this is the happiest moment of her life.

She's about to be married—and to a young man any girl would envy her for."

"My best wishes," I say, pretending to smile, though I'm burning up like hellfire inside. "And just who, if you don't mind my asking, might this young man of hers be?"

"You probably know him," he says. "He's a fine, upstanding fellow, and educated too, entirely self-taught. He's in love with your daughter and wants to marry her. The only problem is, he's not a Jew."

Chvedka! I thought, feeling hot and cold flashes all over. It was all I could do not to fall right out of my wagon. I'd be hanged if I was going to show it, though, so I grabbed my horse's reins, gave him a lash of the whip, and *holakh Moyshe-Mordekhai*—away I went without so much as a by-your-leave.

I came home—the house was a wreck. My daughters were sprawled out on the beds, crying into the pillows, and my wife Golde looked like death warmed over. I began searching all over for Chava. Where could she be?

But Chava wasn't anywhere, and I saw I could save myself the trouble of asking about her. I tell you, I knew then what it must feel like to turn over in the grave! I had such a fire in my bones without knowing what to do with it that I could have punched myself in the nose—instead of which I went about shouting at my daughters and taking it out on my wife. I couldn't sit still for a minute. When I went out to the stable to feed the horse and saw he had slipped a foot through the slats of his stall, I took a stick and began to skin him alive. "I'll put the torch to you next, you moron, you!" I screamed. "You'll never see a bag of oats again in your life! If you're looking for trouble, you'll get it: blood, darkness, death—all the ten plagues of Egypt!"

After a while, though, it occurred to me that I was flaying a poor dumb beast who had never hurt a fly. I threw him some hay, promised him the sun would rise again in the morning, and went back inside, where I laid my aching body down while my head . . . but I tell you, I thought my head would burst from trying so hard to figure things out! *Ma pishi uma khatosi*—was I really the world's greatest sinner, that I deserved to be its most-punished Jew? God in heaven, *mah onu umeh khayeynu*—who am I that You don't forget me even for a second, that You can't invent a new calamity, a new catastrophe, a new disaster, without first trying it out on me?

There I lay as though on a bed of hot coals when I heard my wife Golde let out a groan that could have torn your heart in two. "Golde," I said, "are you sleeping?"

"No," she says. "What is it?"

"Nothing," I say. "We're ruined, that's all. Maybe you have some idea what we should do?"

"God help us all if you have to ask me for ideas," she says. "All I know is that she rose this morning a healthy, normal child, dressed herself, and then suddenly burst out crying and began to hug and kiss me without telling me why. I thought she had gone mad. 'Chava,' I asked, 'what's wrong?' She didn't say a word except to tell me she was going out to the cows—and that was the last I saw of her. I waited an hour, I waited two, I waited three . . . where could she have gone? She wasn't anywhere to be seen. So I called the girls and told them, 'Listen, I want you to run over to the priest's and—' "

"But how, Golde," I interrupted, "did you guess she was at the priest's?"

"How did I guess she was at the priest's?" she says. "So help me God! Do you think I'm not a mother? Do you think I don't have eyes in my head?"

"If you have eyes and you're a mother," I say, "what made you keep so quiet? Why didn't you say something to me?"

"What could I have said?" she says. "You're never home. And even if I had said it, would you have heard it? All you ever do when you're told anything is spout some verse from the Bible. You Bible a person half to death and think you've solved the problem."

That's just what she said, my Golde, as she lay there crying in the dark . . . and I thought, in a way she's right, because what can a woman really know? It broke my heart to hear her sighing and snuffling away, though, so I said, "Look here, Golde. You're angry at me for always quoting the Bible, but I have to quote it one more time. It says *kerakheym ov al bonim*—as a father loves his own child. Why doesn't it also say *kerakheym eym al bonim*—as a mother loves her own child, too? Because a mother isn't a father. A father speaks to his children differently. Just you wait: tomorrow, God willing, I'm going to have a talk with her."

"If only you would!" she says. "And with him too. He's not a bad sort for a priest. He has human feelings. If you throw yourself at his feet, he may pity you."

"What?" I say. "I should go down on my knees before a priest? Are you crazy or are you crazy? *Al tiftakh peh lasoton*—just suppose my enemies got wind of it . . ."

"What did I tell you?" she says. "There you go again!"

We spent the whole night talking like that. As soon as the cock crowed, I rose and said my prayers, took down my whip from the wall, and drove straight to the priest's. A woman may be only a woman, but where else should I have gone—to hell in a bucket?

In short, I drove into his yard and had a fine good morning said to me by his dogs, who set about straightening my caftan for me and sniffing my Jewish feet to see if they were edible. It's a good thing I had my whip with me to remind them that Scripture says, "And against the Children of Israel not a dog stuck out its tongue" . . . The racket we made brought the priest and his wife running from their house. It was all they could do to break up the party and get me safely indoors, where they received me like an honored guest and put the samovar up for tea. But tea, I told them, could wait; first I had something to talk to the priest about. He didn't have to guess what that was; with a wink he signaled his wife to leave the room—and as soon as the door shut behind her, I came straight to the point without shilly-shallying. The first thing I wanted to know was, did he or did he not believe in God? Next I asked him, did he have any idea what it felt like for a father to be parted from a child he loved? Then I insisted on his telling me where he drew the line between right and wrong. And finally, I demanded to know, with no ifs or buts, what he thought of a man who barged uninvited into another man's house and turned it upside down—the benches, the tables, the beds, everything . . .

You can be sure he wasn't prepared for all that. "Tevel," he said, "how does a clever fellow like you expect to ask so many questions at once and get answers to them all in one breath? Be patient and I'll deal with each one of them."

"Oh no you won't, Father dear," I said. "You won't deal with any of them. And do you know why not? Because I already know all your answers by heart. I want you to tell me one thing: is there or is there not any chance of my getting my daughter back?"

"But what are you saying?" he says. "Your daughter isn't going anywhere. And nothing bad will happen to her. Far from it!"

"Yes," I say. "I already know all that. You have only her good in mind. But that's not what I'm talking about. I want to know where my daughter is and whether I can get to see her."

"Ask me anything but that," he says to me.

"That's spoken like a man at last," I say, "short and sweet! You should only be well, Father—and may God pay you back with lots of interest for what you've done."

I came home to find my Golde in bed, cried dry and curled up like a ball of black yarn. "Get up, woman," I said to her. "Take off your shoes and let's begin the seven days of mourning as we're supposed to. *Hashem nosan vehashem lokakh,* the Lord giveth and the Lord taketh away—we're not the first and we won't be the last. Let's just pretend there was never any Chava to begin with, or that she's gone off like Hodl to the far ends of the earth where we'll never see her again . . . God is merciful, He knows what He's doing . . ."

Though I meant every word of it, I had a lump like a bone in my throat. Mind you, Tevye is no woman; Tevye doesn't break down and cry. Still, that's easier said than done when you have to live with the shame of it . . . and just try not breaking down yourself when you've lost your own daughter, and a jewel like Chava at that, who always had a special place in my and her mother's heart, more than any of her sisters. Don't ask me why that was. Maybe it had to do with her being a sickly child who came down with every illness in the book; why, the times we sat up all night with her, trying to snatch her from the very jaws of death, watching her fight for her life like a trampled little bird—but if God only wills it, He can even resurrect you from the grave, and *loy omus ki ekhyeh,* if your number hasn't come up yet, there's no reason to say die . . . And maybe it also had to do with her always having been such a good, dependable child who loved her parents body and soul. How then, you ask, could she have gone and done such a thing? Well, to begin with, it was just our rotten luck; I don't know about you, but I believe in fate. And then too, someone must have put a hex on her. You can laugh all you want at me, but (though I'm not such a yokel as to believe in haunts, spooks, ghosts, and all that hocus-pocus) witchcraft, I tell you, is a fact—because how do you explain all this if it isn't? And when you hear what happened next, you'll be as sure of it as I am . . .

In a word, our rabbis meant it when they said, *be'al korkhekho atoh khai*—a man must never say the jig is up with him. There's no wound in the world that time doesn't heal and no misfortune that can't be gotten over. I don't mean to say you forget such things, but what good does it do to remember them? And *odom kiveheymoh nidmeh*—if you want to eat, you can't stop slaving like a donkey. We took ourselves in hand, my wife, my girls, and I, went back to work, and *oylom keminhogoy noyheyg*—life went its merry way. I made it clear to them all that I never wanted to hear of Chava again. There simply was no such person.

And then one day, having built up a fresh stock of merchandise, I set out for my customers in Boiberik. I received a hero's welcome when I got there. "What's new with a Jew, Reb Tevye? Where have you been all this time?" "What should be new?" I said. "The more things change, the more they stay the same. I'm still the same sap I always was. A cow just died on me, that's all."

Well, everyone had to know, of course, which cow it was, and what it had cost, and how many cows I had left. "What is it with you, Reb Tevye," they asked, "that all the miracles happen to you?" They laughed and made a big joke of it, the way rich people do with us poor devils, especially if they've just had a good meal, and are feeling full and cozy, and the sun is shining outside, and it's time for a little snooze. Not that Tevye begrudges anyone a bit of fun at his expense. Why, they can croak, every last one of them, before they'll know what I'm feeling! . . .

When I had finished my rounds, I started back with my empty cans. Once I was in the forest I let go of my horse's reins and let him amble along and munch on some grass while I sat there thinking of one thing and another: of life and death, and of this world and the next, and of what both were all about, and so on and so forth—all to keep my mind off Chava. Yet as though to spite me, my thoughts kept coming back to her. I couldn't stop picturing her, as tall, fresh, and lovely as a young willow, or else as a tiny baby, a sick little rag doll of a thing, a teeny chick that I could hold in one hand with its head against my shoulder. *What is it you want, Chavaleh? Something to suck on? A bit of milk to drink?* . . . For a moment I forgot what she had done, and then I missed her terribly. As soon as I remembered, though, the blood rushed to my head and I began to rage like the Devil at her, and at Chvedka, and at the whole world, and at myself for not being able to forget her. Why couldn't I get her out of my mind, tear her from my heart? It's not as if she didn't deserve it! Was it for this I had been such a good Jew all my life, had bled myself white and raised seven daughters—for them to break away in the end like the leaves that fall from a tree and are carried off by the wind? Why, just think of it: here a tree grows in the forest, and here along comes a woodsman with an axe and begins to hack off its branches one by one . . . what good is the tree without its branches? Far better, woodsman, for you to chop it down all at once and have done with it! Who needs a branchless tree sticking up in the middle of the forest?

There I was arguing with myself when suddenly I noticed that my horse had come to a halt. Red light! What could it be? I looked ahead . . . Chava! The same Chava as always, not a hair more or less of her . . . why, even her dress was the same. My first thought was to climb down and grab her in my arms, but right away I thought again. What sort of woman are you, Tevye? I asked myself—and I jerked the reins to the right and cried, "Giddyap there, you moron!" Well, no sooner did my horse veer to the right than Chava ran in front of it again, gesturing as if to say that she had something to tell me. I could feel my heart split in two, my arms and legs wouldn't obey me . . . in a second I knew I would jump right out of the wagon . . . Just then, though, I got a grip on myself and jerked the reins back to the left. Back to the left runs Chava, a wild look in her eyes, her face the color of death . . . What do I do now, I wondered, hold my ground or full speed ahead? Before I could make up my mind she grabbed the horse by its bridle and cried, "Papa! May I hope to die if you drive away now! Oh, Papa, Papa, I beg you, at least listen to me first . . ."

Oho, I thought, so you think you can make me knuckle under? Well, guess again, my darling! If that's your idea of your father, it just shows how little you know him . . . And I began to whip my horse for all he was worth. He lunged forward, all right, though he kept looking back and pointing his ears at her. "Giddyap!" I cried again. "*Al tistakeyl bakankan*—keep your eyes on the road, you smart aleck! . . ." Do you think I didn't want to turn around too and take one last look at my daughter? But Tevye is no woman, Tevye puts Satan behind him . . .

Well, I won't bore you with more details. Why waste your time?

I can only say that if I have any sins to account for after my death, I'm already paid up for them in advance more than all the torments of hell; just ask me and I'll tell you a few things . . . All the way home I kept imagining that my Chava was running after me and screaming, "Oh, Papa, Papa . . ." Tevye, I said to myself, enough is enough! What harm would it do to stop for a minute and listen? Maybe she really has something important to say to you. Maybe she's sorry and wants to come home. Maybe her life with him is such hell that she needs your help to run away . . . I thought of a thousand such maybes, I pictured her again as a child, the words *kerakheym ov al bonim* kept running through my head—could there be anywhere a child so bad that a father still couldn't love it? What torture to think that I was the only exception . . . why, a monster like me wasn't fit to walk the earth! "What are you doing, you crazy old loon?" I asked myself. "Why are you making such a production of this? Stop playing the tyrant, turn your wagon around, and make up with her! She's your own child, after all, not some street waif . . ."

I tell you, I had even weirder thoughts than that in the forest. What did being a Jew or not a Jew matter? Why did God have to create both? And if He did, why put such walls between them, so that neither would look at the other even though both were His creatures? It grieved me that I wasn't a more learned man, because surely there were answers to be found in the holy books . . .

In a word, to take my mind off it all I began to chant the *ashrey*—that is, to say the afternoon prayer like any other good Jew. What use was it to pray out loud, though, when everything inside me was crying Cha-va? The louder I prayed, the more it sounded like Cha-va, and the harder I tried not to think of her, the more clearly I saw her and heard her begging me, "Papa, Papa, please . . ." I stopped my ears, I shut my eyes, and I said the *shimenesre,* beating my breast in the confessional without knowing for what sins . . . My life is a shambles and there's no one I can even talk to about it. I never told a living soul about meeting Chava in the forest or anything else about her, though I know exactly where she and he are living and even what they're doing there. Just let anyone try to worm it out of me, though! My enemies won't live to see the day that I complain. That's the sort of man Tevye is . . .

Still, I'd give a great deal to know if everyone is like me or if I'm the only madman of my kind. Once, for example . . . but do you promise not to laugh at me? Because I'm afraid you'll laugh . . . Well, once I put on my best clothes and went to the station in order to take the train there—I mean, to where he and she live. I stepped up to the window and asked for a ticket. "Where to?" says the ticket seller. "To Yehupetz," I say. "Yehupetz?" he says. "I never heard of such a place." "Well, it's no fault of mine if you haven't," I say—and I turn right around, walk home again, take off my best clothes, and go back to work, to my little dairy business with its horse and wagon. How does the saying go? *Ish lefo'aloy ve'odom le'avoydosoy*—the tailor to his needle and the shoemaker to his bench . . .

Ah, you're laughing at me anyhow? What did I tell you! I even know just what you're thinking: you're thinking what a screwball Tevye is . . . If you ask me, then, *ad kan oymrim beshabbes hagodol*—it's time to call it quits for the day. Be healthy and well, and drop me a line now and then. For God's sake, though, remember what I told you: you're not to breathe a word about any of this, or put it in any of your books! And if you absolutely must write about it, write that it happened to somebody else, not to me. As it says in the Bible, *vayishkokheyhu*—me, Tevye the Dairyman, please forget . . .

(1905)

SHPRINTZE

▼

Why, Pani Sholem Aleichem, what a pleasure to run into you! I haven't seen you in a dog's age. My oh my, the water that's flowed under the bridge since we last met! What you and I and Jews everywhere haven't been through these past years: pogroms in Kishinev, riots, troubles, the new Constantution—dear Lord, it doesn't stop . . . Don't take it wrong, but I'm surprised to see you haven't changed a bit, there's still not a gray hair on you! I only wish you could say the same of me. *Harey ani keven shivim shonoh*—I haven't even turned sixty, and just look how old and gray I am. It's no laughing matter what we go through with our children, and who has less to laugh about than me? The latest nightmare with my daughter Shprintze is worse than anything that came before—yet here I am, still alive and kicking, as if nothing had happened at all. *Be'al korkhekho atoh khai*—how does that little song go?

> What do I care if the weather is sunny
> When I'm all out of luck and all out of money . . .

In a word, *rotsoh hakodoysh borukh hu lezakoys*—God wanted to do us Jews a favor and so He sent us a new catastrophe, a Constantution. Believe me, that's all we needed! You should see what a panic the rich Yehupetz Jews are in, how they're all running abroad—that is, to the baths in Germany to take care of their nerves, their stomachs, their livers, their whoosywhatsis . . . And what with everyone leaving Yehupetz, you'd think, wouldn't you, that all the fresh air and green trees and dachas of Boiberik couldn't keep it from going to the dogs. You know what the good news is, though? That there's a *borukh merakheym al ha'orets,* a merciful God up above Who looks after us poor country folk and makes sure we keep our noses to the grindstone. Have we ever had a summer season here! They've come flocking to Boiberik from Odessa, from Rostov, from Yekaterinoslav, from Mogilev, from Kishinev—thousands of them, Jews filthy with money! It seems that the Constantution is even worse where they are, because they haven't stopped heading in this direction. But why, you ask, are they all running here? For the same reason, I tell you, that we're all running there! It's an old Jewish custom to pick up and go elsewhere at the first mention of a pogrom. How does the Bible put it? *Vayisu vayakhanu, vayakhanu vayisu*—or in plain language, if you come hide in my house, I'd better go hide in yours . . . Which is why Boiberik, I want you to know, has become a real metropolis, bursting with men, women, and children. Now children, mind you, like to eat; to eat you need cheese, cream, and butter; and where do you get such stuff if not from Tevye? Like it or not, Tevye's all the fashion nowadays. It's "Tevye, come here," and "Tevye, go there," and Tevye, Tevye, Tevye all day long. If that's how God wants it, who are you and I to object?

Well, *vayehi hayoym*—once upon a time not very long ago, I brought some produce to a new customer, a wealthy young widow from Yekaterinoslav who had come to Boiberik for the summer with her son, a fellow named Ahronchik. Needless to say, her first acquaintance in all of Boiberik was me. "You've been recommended," she says, "as being the best dairyman around." "And why shouldn't I have been?" I answer. "It's no coincidence that King Solomon said a good reputation is louder than a trumpet. If you have a minute to spare, I even have a nice little midrash . . ." But she didn't, because she was, she told me, a widow, and such things were not her cup of tea. In fact, she wouldn't know what to do with a midrash if I were to put one on her plate; all she wanted was good cheese and fresh butter. Just try having a serious talk with a woman . . .

In short, I began coming around to that widow from Yekaterinoslav twice a week, every Monday and Thursday like clockwork, without her having to order in advance. It got so that I was practically one of the household; I poked around in it a bit, saw how things were done there, and even gave a bit of advice. The first time I did that, I got a good chewing out from the servant: who did I think I was, sticking my nose into other people's business? The second time I was listened to, and the third time the widow actually asked my opinion about something, having seen by now who Tevye was. The long and short of it was that one day she approached me with her greatest problem: Ahronchik! Although he was, she said, over twenty years old, all he cared about was horses, fishing, and bicycles, apart from which nothing mattered to him. He didn't have the slightest interest in business or making money, or even in managing the handsome estate he had inherited from his father, which was worth a good million rubles. His one pleasure was to spend it, and liberally at that.

"Tell me," I said, "where is the young man now? If you let me have a few words with him, I might talk to him a bit, set him straight with a verse from the Bible, maybe even with a midrash . . ."

"If I know my son," she laughed, "a horse will get you further than a midrash."

We were still talking about him when—speaking of the Devil!—in walks Ahronchik himself, a tall, handsome, ruddy-faced young man with a broad sash around his waist, a pocket watch tucked into it, and sleeves rolled up past his elbows.

"Where have you been?" asks his mother.

"Out fishing in the skiff," he says.

"Can't you think of anything better to do?" I say. "Why, back in Yekaterinoslav they're Constantutioning the pants off of you, and all you can do is catch fish?"

I glanced at my widow—she turned as red as a beet and every other color of the rainbow. She must have been sure that her son would grab me by the collar and give me the heave-ho in a hurry. Which just goes to show how wrong she was. There's no way to scare Tevye. When I have something to say, I say it.

Well, when the young fellow heard that, he stepped back a bit, put his hands behind his back, looked me up and down from head to foot, let out a funny sort of whistle, and suddenly began to laugh so hard that the two of us were afraid he had gone mad before our eyes. Shall I tell you something, though? From then on he and I were the best of friends. And I must say that the better I knew him, the better I liked him, even if he was a bit of a windbag, the worst sort of spendthrift, and a little thick between the ears. For instance, let him pass a beggar in the street, and he'd stick a hand into his pocket and fork up a fistful of change without even bothering to count it! Did you ever hear of such a thing? Once I saw him take a brand-new jacket off his back and give it away to a perfect stranger—I ask you, how dumb can you get . . . ? I felt good and sorry for his mother, believe me. She kept asking me what she should do and begging me to take him in hand. Well, I didn't say no to that. Why refuse her a favor when it didn't cost me a red cent? So from time to time I sat down with him and told him a story, fed him a parable, slipped him a verse from the Bible, even let him have a midrash or two, as only Tevye can do. I swear, he actually liked it and wanted to know if I talked like that at home. "I'd sure like to visit you there, Reb Tevye," he said.

"Well," I said, "anyone wanting to visit Tevye only has to get to Tevye's village. Between your horses and your bicycles you can certainly make it, and in a pinch you're a big enough boy to use your own legs. Just cut through the forest and you're there."

"When is a good time to come?" he says.

"You can find me at home any Sabbath or holiday," I say. "But wait, I have an idea! The Friday after next is Shavuos. If you'd like to take a walk over to my place then, my wife will serve you such blintzes fit for princes as *lo blintzu avoyseynu bemitsrayim!*"

"Just what does that mean?" he asks. "I'm not too strong on chapter-and-verse, you know."

"I certainly do," I say. "But if you'd had the schooling I did, you'd know enough to be the rabbi's wife."

He laughed at that and said, "All right, then, you've got yourself a guest. On the first day of Shavuos, Reb Tevye, I'll be over with three friends of mine for blintzes—and they better be hot!"

"Hotter than hellfire," I promised. "Why, they'll be jumping right out of the frying pan at you!"

Well, as soon as I came home that day I whistled up my wife and said to her, "Golde, we're having guests for Shavuos!"

"Mazel tov," she says. "Who are they?"

"I'll tell you everything in good time," I say. "Just make sure you have enough eggs, because butter and cheese, thank God, are no problem. You'll be making blintzes for four extra mouths—but such mouths, you should know, that understand as much about eating as they don't understand about the Bible."

"I might have guessed it," she says. "You've been to Hunger-land again and found some new slob of a Hungarian."

"Golde," I said, "you're nothing but a big cow yourself. First of all, even if we did treat some poor hungry devil to blintzes on Shavuos, what harm would it do? And second of all, you may as well know, my most Esteemed, Honored, and Beloved Wife, that one of our guests will be the widow's son, that Ahronchik I've been telling you about."

"Then why didn't you say so in the first place?" she says.

What money doesn't do to some people! Even my Golde becomes a different woman as soon as she gets a whiff of it. But that's the world we live in—what can you or I do about it? As it says in the prayer book, *kesef vezohov ma'asey yedey odom*—money can dig a man's grave faster than a shovel.

In short, Shavuos time came around. I don't have to tell you how green and bright and warm and beautiful our village is then! Your richest Jew in town should only have such a blue sky above him, such a green forest all around, such a good smell of pine trees, such a carpet of grass that the cows smile at you when they chew it as if to say, "Just keep us rolling in clover and we'll keep you swimming in milk . . ." No, say what you will, I wouldn't swap places with you in town if you promised me the best job in the world. Can you also promise me such a sky there? *Hashomayim*

shomayim ladoynai—why, in the village the sky is God's own! You
can crane your neck in town till it breaks, what do you manage to
see? Walls, roofs, chimneys, but never a single tree! And if by
some miracle one grows there, you have to tend it like a sick
child . . .

In a word, our guests couldn't get over our village when they
came to visit on Shavuos. They arrived riding horses, all four of
them—and I do mean horses! Why, the nag that Ahronchik alone
was sitting on was such a thoroughbred that you couldn't have
bought it for three hundred rubles.

"Welcome, my friends," I said to them. "I see no one bothered
to tell you that a Jew doesn't ride on Shavuos. Well, we won't let
that spoil the holiday. Tevye's no saint himself, and if you're
whipped for it in the world to come, it won't be any skin off my
back . . . Golde! Put up the blintzes and have the girls carry out
the table and put it on the grass—our house isn't such a museum
piece that we have to show it off to visitors . . . Shprintze! Teibl!
Beilke! Where are you all? Let's get cracking . . ."

I stood there giving orders and pretty soon out of the house
came the table, benches, a tablecloth, plates, spoons, forks, and
saltshakers, and right on the heels of it all, my Golde with the
blintzes—and such piping-hot, mouth-watering, straight-from-
the-frying-pan, sweeter-than-manna-tasting blintzes they were
that our guests couldn't stop eating or praising them . . .

"What are you standing there for?" I said to my Golde. "Don't
you know that since Shavuos has two days, everything else about it
has to be doubled too? Bring some more blintzes and we'll have a
second round!"

Well, in a shake of a lamb's tail my Golde filled the platter with
more blintzes and my Shprintze brought them to the table. Just
then I glanced at Ahronchik, and what do I see? He's staring at
my Shprintze, his eyes are glued to her so hard he can't pull them
away. What did he suppose he was looking at? "Eat up," I said to
him. "Why aren't you eating?"

"Why, what does it look like I'm doing?" he says.

"It looks like you're looking at my Shprintze," I say.

Everyone burst out laughing at that, my Shprintze too. We were
all so gay, so happy, enjoying such a fine Shavuos . . . how was I
supposed to know it would end in such a nightmare, in such a
tragedy, in such a horror story, in such a punishment from God

that it's left me a wreck of a man? I'll tell you what, though. We men are fools. If we had any brains to speak of, we'd realize that things are the way they were meant to be, because if they were meant to be different, they wouldn't be the way they are . . . Doesn't it say in the Book of Psalms, *hashleykh al hashem*—trust no one but God? Just leave it to Him: He'll see to it that the worms are eating you like fresh bagels, and you'll thank Him for it too. And now listen to what can happen in this world of ours—and listen carefully, because you haven't heard anything yet.

Vayehi erev vayehi voyker—one evening when I came home from Boiberik, bushed from the heat and from running between dachas all day long, I spied a familiar horse tied to the gate by the house. In fact, I could have sworn it was Ahronchik's thoroughbred that I had priced at three hundred rubles! I went over to it, slapped it on the rear with one hand while scratching its head with the other, and said, "Well now, old fellow, what brings you to our neck of the woods?" To which it bobbed its chin quite handsomely and gave me a clever look as if to say, "Why ask me, when I happen to have a master?"

Well, I went inside, collared my wife, and said to her, "Golde, my dearest, what is Ahronchik doing here?"

"How am I supposed to know?" she answers me. "I thought he was one of your crowd."

"Where is he?" I asked.

"He went for a walk in the forest with the girls," my Golde tells me.

"What on earth made him do a thing like that?" I wondered out loud, and asked her for something to eat. When I had had my fill, I sat there thinking, Tevye, why are you so nervous? Since when is a visitor dropping by any reason to be so on edge? If anything . . . but I never finished the thought, because just then I looked outside and saw the bonnie young lad with my girls, who were carrying wild flowers they had picked. Teibl and Beilke were walking in front, and Shprintze was bringing up the rear with Ahronchik.

"A good evening!" I said to him.

"And to you, too," he replied. He stood there a little awkwardly with a blade of grass in his mouth, stroking his horse's mane; then he said, "Reb Tevye, I have an offer to make you. Let's you and I swap horses."

"Don't you have anyone better to make fun of?" I asked him.

"But I mean it," he says.

"Do you now?" I say. "Do you have any idea what this horse of yours is worth?"

"What would you price him at?" he asks.

"He's worth three hundred rubles if a cent," I say, "and maybe even a little bit more."

Well, Ahronchik laughed, told me his horse had cost over three times that amount, and said, "How about it, then? Is it a deal?"

I tell you, I didn't like it one bit: what kind of business was it to trade such a horse for my gluepot? And so I told him to keep his offer for another day and joked that I hoped he hadn't come just for that, since I hated to see him waste his time . . .

"As a matter of fact," he says to me, as serious as can be, "I came to see you about something else. If it's not too much to ask of you, perhaps the two of us could take a little walk."

He's got walking on the brain today, I thought, but I agreed to go for a stroll in the forest with him. The sun had set long ago; the woods were getting dark; frogs croaked from the river; and the smell of so many green, growing things was like heaven itself. Ahronchik and I walked side by side without exchanging a word. Suddenly he stopped short, let out a cough, and said, "Reb Tevye! What would you say if I told you I'm in love with your Shprintze and want to marry her?"

"What would I say?" I said. "I'd tell them to move over and make room for one more in the loony bin."

"What is that supposed to mean?" he says, staring at me.

"It means," I say, "exactly what it sounds like."

"But I don't get it," he says.

"That," I say, "just goes to show that you're even less of a genius than I thought. You know, there's a verse in the Bible that says, 'The wise man has eyes in his head.' That means you can talk to him with a wink, while the fool must be talked to with a stick."

"I'm speaking in plain language," he says, beginning to get sore, "and all I'm hearing from you is jokes from the Bible."

"Well," I said, "every cantor sings the best he can and every preacher toots his own horn. If you'd like to know how well you're tooting yours, I suggest you have a talk with your mother. She'll set you straight in a jiffy."

"Do you take me," he says, "for a little boy who has to get permission from his mother?"

"Of course I do," I say. "And your mother's sure to tell you you're a dunce. And she'll be right."

"She will be?" he says.

"Of course she will be," I say. "What kind of husband will you make my Shprintze? What kind of wife will my Shprintze make you? And most of all, what kind of in-law will I make your mother?"

"If that's what you're thinking, Reb Tevye," he says, "you're making a big mistake. I'm not an eighteen-year-old, and I'm not looking for in-laws for my mother. I know who you are, I know who your daughter is, and I like what I see. That's what I want and that's what I'm going to—"

"Excuse me for interrupting," I say, "but there's one thing I still have to ask you. I can see there's no problem on the groom's side, but have you bothered to clear this with the bride's side?"

"I don't know what you're talking about," he says.

"I'm talking about my daughter Shprintze," I say. "Have you talked this over with her? And if so, what does she say?"

Well, he gave me an insulted look but said with a smile, "What kind of a question is that? Of course I've talked it over with her— and not just once, either. I'm here every day."

Did you ever hear the likes of it? He's there every day and I know nothing about it! Tevye, you two-footed animal, I told myself, you deserve to eat hay with your cows! If that's how you let yourself be led about by the nose, you'll be bought and sold like the donkey you are! . . . I didn't say anything to Ahronchik as we walked back, though. He said goodbye to the girls, jumped on his horse, and *holakh Moyshe-Mordekhai*—away to Boiberik he went . . .

And now, as you writers like to say in your books, let's leave the young prince on his horse and get back to the princess in her castle, that is, to my Shprintze. "Tell me, Daughter," I said to her, "there's something I want to ask you: how could you and Ahronchik have discussed such a matter without even letting me know?"

Did you ever hear a tree talk? That's how my Shprintze answered me. She just blushed, stared down at her feet like a newlywed, and didn't open her mouth. Mum's the word! . . . Well, I thought, if you won't talk to me now, you'll do it later. Tevye is no woman; Tevye can wait. But I kept an eye out, looking for a chance to be alone with her again, and as soon as I found it one day outside the house, I said to her, "Shprintze, I want you to tell me: do you think you really know him, this Ahronchik?"

"Of course I do," she says.

"And do you know that he's a penny whistle?" I say.

"What's a penny whistle?" she asks.

"A penny whistle," I say, "is something hollow that makes a lot of noise."

"That isn't so," she says to me. "Arnold is a fine person."

"Arnold?" I say. "Since when is that phony called Arnold?"

"Arnold," she says, "is not a phony. Arnold has a heart of gold. It's not his fault if he grew up in a house full of vile people who only think of money all the time."

"Well, well, well," I said. "Look who's the philosopher now! I suppose you think that having money is a sin too . . ."

In a word, I could see that they both were too far gone to be talked out of it. I know my girls. Didn't I once tell you that when Tevye's daughters, God help us, fall for someone, they fall with everything they have? And so I told myself, you fool, you, why must you always think you know best? Why can't you admit the whole thing may be providential? Why isn't it possible that quiet little Shprintze is meant to be your salvation, your reward for all your hardship and your heartache, so that at last you can enjoy yourself in your old age and live like a human being for once? Suppose your daughter is fated to be a millionairess—is that really so terrible? Is it such a blow to your dignity? Does it say anywhere in the Bible that Tevye must always be a beggar who spends his whole life hauling cheese and butter to keep the rich Jews of Yehupetz from dying of hunger? Who's to say that God hasn't fingered you to do a little good in His world before you die—to give a bit of money to charity, to take someone needy under your wing, even to sit down with educated Jews and study some Torah . . .

I swear, those were only some of the sweet thoughts that ran through my head. You know what it says in the morning prayer: *raboys makhshovoys belev ish*—or as they say in Russian, a fool can get rich just by thinking . . . And so I stepped into the house and took my wife aside for a little talk. "Just suppose," I said to her, "that our Shprintze should become a millionairess?"

"What's a millionairess?" asks my Golde.

"A millionairess," I say, "is a millionaire's wife."

"And what's a millionaire?" she asks.

"A millionaire," I say, "is a man who's worth a million."

"And how much is a million?" she asks.

"Look," I say, "if you're such a cow that you don't know what a million is, it's a waste of time talking to you."

"So who asked you to talk to me?" she says. I couldn't argue with that.

In a word, another day went by in Boiberik and I came home again. "Was Ahronchik here?" No, he wasn't . . . Another day. "Was he here today?" No, he wasn't . . . Though I could have found some excuse to drop in on the widow, I wasn't keen on it: I didn't want her to think that Tevye was fishing for a match with her—and one that she needed *keshoyshanoh beyn hakhoykhim,* like a wagon needs a fifth wheel . . . (Not that she had any reason to be ashamed of me, mind you, because if I wasn't a millionaire myself, I would at least have an in-law who was, while the only in-law she'd have would be a poor beggar of a dairyman; I ask you, then, whose connections would be better, mine or hers?) . . . To tell you the honest truth, though, if I wanted that match at all, it was less for the match's sake than for the feeling of satisfaction it would give me. "The Devil take you all!" I'd be able to say to all the rich Jews of Yehupetz. "Until now it's been nothing but Brodsky, Brodsky, Brodsky, but now you see who Tevye really is . . ."

So I thought, driving home from Boiberik. As soon as I walked in the door, my Golde met me with a bombshell. "A messenger, a Russian, was just here from Boiberik, from the widow! She begs you to come for God's sake as quickly as you can, even if it's the middle of the night! Harness the horse and go, it must be something important."

"Where's the fire?" I asked. "Can't it wait until morning?" Just then, though, I glanced at my Shprintze—and while she didn't say a word, her eyes said it all, everything! No one knew that child's heart the way I did—which was why I had sounded off to her about Ahronchik, because I was afraid that nothing would come of it. (Not that I couldn't have saved my breath, since for the past three days my Shprintze had been wasting away like a candle!) . . . And so I harnessed the horse again and set out that same evening for Boiberik. What can be so urgent, I wondered as I drove there. If they want to shake hands on it and have a proper betrothal, it's they who should come to me, because I'm the bride's father . . . only that was such a preposterous thought that it made me laugh out loud: who ever heard of a rich man going to a poor one for a betrothal? Did I think that the world had already come to an end, as that scamp of a Peppercorn said it would, and that the tycoon and the beggar were now equals, *sheli shelkho* and *shelkho sheli*—you take what's mine, I take what's yours, and the Devil take the hindmost? People were born with brains in this world and yet, oh, my goodness—what jackasses there were in it! . . .

I was still trying to figure it all out when I arrived in Boiberik, drove straight to the widow's dacha, and parked my horse in front of it.

"Where is the widow?" I asked at the door.

"The widow's not here."

"Where is her son?"

"He's not here either."

"Then who asked me to come?"

"I did," says a round tub of a man with a stringy beard and a fat gold watch chain on his stomach.

"And just who are you?" I ask.

"I'm the widow's brother, Ahronchik's uncle," he says. "I was cabled to come from Yekaterinoslav, and I've just arrived."

"In that case," I say, sitting down in a chair, "welcome to Boiberik."

"Have a seat," he says.

"Thank you," I say, "but I already have one. So how's the Constantution in your parts?"

He didn't answer that. He just settled himself into a rocking chair with his hands still in his pants pockets and his stomach sticking out beneath his watch chain and said without wasting any words, "I'm told they call you Tevye."

"They do indeed," I said. "And when they call me to the Torah in the synagogue, it's even Reb Tevye the son of Shneyur Zalman."

"Well, then, Reb Tevye," he says to me, "listen here. Why beat around the bush? Let's get right down to business, as they say . . ."

"And why not?" I say. "There's a time for everything, as King Solomon once said—and if it's business time, it's time for business. And a businessman is what I happen to be . . ."

"I can see you are," he says, "and that's why I'll get down to brass tacks with you. I want you to tell me perfectly honestly, just what is this going to cost us?"

"I can tell you perfectly honestly," I say, "that I have no idea what you're talking about."

"Reb Tevye!" he says to me again, his hands still in his pockets. "I'm asking you in plain language. How much is this affair going to cost us?"

"Well, now," I say, "that all depends on what sort of affair you have in mind. If you're thinking of the fancy wedding that folks like you are accustomed to, I'm afraid it's a bit beyond my budget."

"Either you're playing dumb," he says to me, giving me the once-over, "or else you really are dumb. Only, how dumb can you be to have set my nephew up in the first place by pretending to invite him over for blintzes in order to introduce him to a young beauty who may or may not be your real daughter . . . I won't go into that now . . . and who got him to fall for her and maybe even—it's easy to see how she could—fell for him? Of course, I don't mean to imply it wasn't kosher . . . she may be a perfectly respectable girl, for all I know . . . I really don't want to go into that. But how could you have allowed yourself to forget who you are and who we are? Where does a sensible Jew like yourself get off thinking that a dairyman, a common cheesemonger, can marry into a family like ours? . . . He's given her his word, you say? Then he'll just have to take it back again! It's no tragedy, believe me. Of course, it has to cost something . . . there's breach of promise and all that . . . and I assure you, we're prepared to be reasonable. A young woman's honor is not the same as a young man's, even if she isn't your real daughter . . . but I would definitely prefer not to go into that . . ."

Good God, I thought, what does the man want from me? He didn't stop chewing my ear off. I shouldn't imagine for a minute that making a scandal by claiming his nephew was engaged to my daughter would get me anywhere . . . If I thought I could bilk his sister, I had another guess coming . . . Although with a bit of good will on my part, she was certainly good for a few rubles, for a charitable gesture, so to speak . . . I was, after all, a fellow human being, they would be glad to lend a helping hand . . .

And would you like to know what my answer to all that was? My answer, the shame of which I'll never live down to my dying day, was nothing! My tongue clove to my mouth, as the Bible says—the cat had got it but good. I simply rose from my chair, went to the door—and exit Tevye. I ran from there as fast as I could, as though from a fire or a prison, while the man's words kept buzzing in my ears: *perfectly honestly . . . who may or may not be your real daughter . . . bilk a widow . . . a charitable gesture, so to speak . . .* I went over to my wagon, laid my head on it, and—but promise not to laugh at me!—I cried and cried until I had no tears left. Then I climbed aboard, whipped my poor devil of a horse to within an inch of his life, and asked God an old question about an old, old story: what did poor Job ever do to You, dear Lord, to make You hound him day and night? Couldn't You find any other Jews to pick on?

Well, I came home and found that gang of mine merrily eating supper. Only Shprintze was missing. "Where's Shprintze?" I asked.

"What happened in Boiberik?" they all wanted to know. "What did they want there?"

"Where's Shprintze?" I asked again.

"What happened in Boiberik?" they said again.

"What happened in Boiberik?" I said. "What should have happened there? Everything is quiet, thank God, there isn't a sign of a pogrom yet . . ."

Just then Shprintze walked in. She glanced at me and sat quietly down at the table as if none of this concerned her in the least. You couldn't tell a thing from looking at her, but that silence of hers was too much, there was something unnatural about it . . . And in the days that followed I didn't like it one bit, either, the way she went through the motions of things without seeming to have a will of her own. If she was told to sit, she sat; if she was told to eat, she ate; if she was told to go, she went; if she was told to come back, back she came. It made my heart ache to see her. I was burning up inside without knowing at whom . . . ah, dear God, I thought, Master of the Universe, whose sins are You punishing me for?

Well, would you like to hear the end? It's one that I wouldn't curse my worst enemy with, that I wouldn't curse anyone with, because there's no curse in the whole Bible like a curse on your own child. For all I know, in fact, someone may have put one on me . . . You say you don't believe in such things? Then maybe you'll explain to me why it happened. Go ahead, I'm listening . . .

But what good will all the philosophy do us? You may as well hear the end of it. One evening I was driving home from Boiberik in my usual grand mood: the shame, the humiliation of it all, to say nothing of my feelings for my daughter! . . . (Whatever happened, you ask, to the widow and her son? Just go try finding them! They skipped town without so much as an adieu. I'm embarrassed to tell you, but they even stuck me with an unpaid dairy bill. It wasn't that that riled me, though—no doubt they simply forgot; it was their not having bothered to let me know. Why, to think of their picking up and leaving like that without even saying goodbye!) . . . What she, my daughter, went through, no one knew but me, because I was her father and a father knows in his heart. Don't imagine, though, that she ever said a word to me about it. Do you think she complained? Do you think she cried even once? If you do, you don't know Tevye's daughters! She just flickered out like a candle, without a word of protest, keeping it all to herself except for a sigh now and then—but such a sigh, I tell you, as could break a heart of iron . . .

In short, I was driving home with my horse, thinking about the whole miserable business and asking God all kinds of questions that He kindly let me answer for myself. My problem wasn't God, though—with Him I had somehow made my peace. My problem was men. Why did they have to be so bad when they could just as well have been good? Why did they have to ruin their own and other people's lives instead of being happy with what they had? Could God have created them on purpose to make them miserable? But what good could that possibly do Him . . .?

Just then I drove into our village and saw a crowd of people down by the dam on the river, men, women, and lots of children. What could have happened? There wasn't any sign of a fire—it must be a drowning, I thought. Someone went for a swim in the river and didn't come out. You never know where the Angel of Death will make a date with you . . .

And then all of a sudden I saw my Golde running toward the river, her arms waving in the air and her kerchief falling off, and after her Teibl and Beilke, all three screaming, shrieking, "Shprintze!" I jumped out of that wagon so fast it's a wonder I'm still in one piece and ran to the river myself, but it was too late to help my Shprintze anymore . . .

What was it I wanted to ask you? Oh, yes: have you ever seen a drowned man? Never? Well, mostly one dies with one's eyes shut, but a drowned man's eyes are always open. I just thought you might know why that was . . .

I hope you'll forgive me for taking so much of your time. It's not as if I had nothing better to do myself, because I have a horse and some merchandise waiting. The world hasn't changed any. You still have to think of the next ruble and put the past behind you. What was, is dead and buried, and a living man doesn't spit out his soul because it hurts. You can't outsmart fate. There's no getting around what it says in the morning prayer: *koyl zman shehaneshomoh bekirbi*—whatever breathes has to eat, so giddyap, Tevye!

Be well, and if you should ever happen to think of me, I only hope it isn't too badly.

(1907)

TEVYE LEAVES FOR THE LAND OF ISRAEL

▼

Why, if it isn't Reb Sholem Aleichem! How on earth are you? What a surprise, of all places! I never would have dreamed it, would you? How I've wondered why I haven't seen you in ages, neither in Boiberik nor in Yehupetz. I even thought you might have cashed in your chips and left us for that world where we'll never hunger or eat again, not even a radish with chicken fat . . . except that then I said to myself, "Since when would someone like Sholem Aleichem go do a dumb thing like that? He's an intelligent man, after all, if nothing else . . ." And now here you are, alive and well, thank God! How does the saying go? *Turo beturo*—two mountains never meet, but a man and a man sometimes do . . . Only, why are you looking at me as if you didn't know me, Pani? It's me, your good old friend Tevye! *Al tistakeyl bakankan*—don't let my new coat fool you: I'm still the same old schlimazel, there's not a hair more or less of me. It's just that a man seems more of a somebody when he's dressed in his Sabbath best, he can even make you think he's in the money—and one has to look presentable when traveling, especially on a long journey like mine, all the way to the Land of Israel. That's not an outing to sneeze at, is it? I suppose you must be wondering how a small-timer like Tevye who spent his whole life selling dairy can afford to travel like a Brodsky in his old age. Well, if you don't mind moving your suitcase a bit, I'll sit myself down beside you and tell you a story about what the good Lord can do.

The first first of all, it should never happen to you, is that I'm a widower now. My Golde, God rest her, is dead. She was a simple soul, subtle you couldn't call her; but you won't find a greater saint anywhere. I only hope she puts in a good word for her daughters where she is, because the Lord knows she went through enough for them. In fact, they may be the reason she's there now, because she couldn't stand their being scattered from east of the sun to west of the moon a minute longer. "So tell me," she would say to me, "what will I have left to live for one day when there won't be a mouse in the house? Why, even a cow grieves when her calves are taken away . . ."

Those were her very words, my Golde's, and you should have heard her cry when she said them. I felt so sorry to see her pining away in front of me that I said to her, "Eh, Golde, my dearest. It says in the prayer book, *im kevonim im ka'avodim*—it's no different without children than with them. Either way there's a great, kind, merciful God above. I only wish I had a ruble for every dirty trick He's played on us . . ."

But my wife, may she forgive me, was a female through and through. "It's a sin to talk that way, Tevye," she said. "You mustn't be sinful."

"What did I say wrong?" I asked her. "Did I say anything against God? I'm sure that if He chose to make a wonderful world like this in which children aren't children anymore and parents are nothing at all, He knew exactly what He was doing . . ."

She didn't follow a word of that, though, because she only said to me in a whisper, looking at me with two eyes that could have crumbled a stone, "Oh, Tevye, I'm dying. Who'll cook your supper when I'm gone?"

Well, Tevye is no woman. I came right back at her with a saying, then with a verse from the Bible, then with a midrash, then with my own two cents. "Golde," I said, "you've been a good wife to me all these years. Please don't go playing jokes on me now that I'm old."

Just then I took a look at her—uh-oh! I didn't like what I saw.

"Golde," I said, "what's the matter?"

"Nothing," she says to me, barely able to talk. But she didn't look long for this world, so I harnessed the horse, drove to town, and came back with the best doctor I could find. We entered the house . . . oh, lordy! My Golde was lying on the floor with a candle burning by her head, looking like a pile of dirt that had been covered with a black cloth. I stood there thinking, *ki zeh koyl ha'odom*—so this is all a human being is! Dear God, what have You done to Your Tevye this time? How is an old ruin like me going to live out his years now?

Well, I threw myself down on the floor beside her—and a fat lot of good it did. Do you hear me, Pani? Once you've looked death in the eye the way I have, it's hard to have faith anymore. You can't help wondering, *mah onu umeh khayeynu*—what's the point of the whole circus, this whole big yackety racket of a world on wheels? Why, it's nothing but vanity, one big zero with a hole in it!

In short, I hired a Jew to say the mourner's prayer every day in the synagogue and paid him the whole year in advance. What else could I do if God had punished me with no sons, only daughters, one female after another—it shouldn't happen to a living soul! I don't know if everyone goes through hell with his daughters or if it's just been my own rotten luck, but you can't really blame either, because the luck came from God and my daughters meant me no harm. In fact, I'd gladly settle for half of all the good things they've wished me. If anything, they were too devoted to me, and too much is as bad as not enough . . .

For example, take my youngest, Beilke. You simply have no idea what a gem she is! You've known me since before the Flood, as they say, and you know I'm not a father who goes around bragging about his kids—but on the subject of Beilke there's a thing or two, or even three, that I have to tell you, because while God may have made a lot of Beilkes in His time, He never made another Beilke like mine. And I'm not even talking about her looks, though if each of my daughters is a famous beauty, Beilke can put them all in her little pocket. Still, beauty isn't the word for her, because King Solomon had it right when he said that Charm

is a liar and Beauty a cheat—no, what I'm talking about is character, pure and simple . . . and when it comes to character, my
Beilke is pure gold! She's always thought the world of me, but
ever since her poor mother passed away I've been the apple of her
eye. Why, she wouldn't let a speck of dust fall on me! I've often
thought that God is just like He's said to be in the Rosh Hashanah
prayer, a *makdim rakhamim leroygez*—He never hits a man over the
head without first sending him the right medicine for it. The
problem is that it's not always clear which is worse, the blow or the
medicine. How was I to know that Beilke would sell herself down
the river so that I could live out the rest of my life in the Land of
Israel? Mind you, that's only a manner of speaking, because she's
no more to blame for it than you are. It's all his fault, her Prince
Charming! Far be it from me to wish him ill, but I wouldn't mind
it one bit if a whole armory blew up beneath his feet. And yet to
tell you the truth, when I think the matter over, the real guilty
party may be me. Why, there's even a saying in the Talmud . . .
but it's a pretty pass we've come to, Reb Sholem Aleichem, when I
have to quote the Talmud to you!

In short, I'll try not to make it a long story. A couple of years
went by and my Beilke grew into a young woman, while I carried
on with my business as usual, taking my cheese, cream, and butter
to Boiberik in the summer and, in the winter, to Yehupetz—may
it end up like Sodom beneath a sea of salt! I can't even bear to
think of that town anymore . . . that is, I don't mean the town, I
mean the Jews who live in it . . . that is, I don't mean them either, I
mean Efrayim the Matchmaker, may his grandfather break a leg
in the grave! Just listen to what a Jew, and a matchmaker yet, can
do to you.

Vayehi hayoym, one day after the summer season I'm on my way
to Yehupetz with some merchandise, when who do I see but Haman in person—I mean Efrayim the Matchmaker. I believe I once
told you about him. He's the sort of terrible pest you can't help
stopping to talk to, that's the strange power he has over you. And
so I said to my horse, "Whoaa, there, old fellow, pull over and I'll
give you a snack," waved to Efrayim, said hello to him, and
straightaway began to gab. "How's business?" I asked.

"Business," he says, letting out a juicy sigh, "is terrible."

"How come?" I ask.

"No customers," he says.

"None at all?" I ask.

"Not one," he says.

"But how can that be?" I ask.

"That can be," he says, "because matches aren't made around here any more."

"Where are they made, then?" I ask.

"Abroad," he says.

"And what happens," I ask, "to a Jew like me whose great-grandmother can't afford to travel?"

"For a Jew like you, Reb Tevye," says Efrayim, handing me a pinch of snuff, "I have a special offer, local goods."

"Which is?" I say.

"Which is," he says, "a childless widow, a cook in the best houses, net worth five hundred rubles."

"Reb Efrayim," I say, staring at him, "who do you think this match is for?"

"Who do I think it's for?" he says. "Why, for you!"

"The Devil take you!" I say, flicking the whip at my horse to start him up again. "May my enemies have as bad dreams all year long as I'll have of your widow tonight."

"No offense meant, Reb Tevye," says Efrayim. "I didn't mean to hurt your feelings. Who were *you* thinking of?"

"Who?" I say. "Of my youngest daughter, who else?"

"Why, of course!" he says, jumping a foot in the air while giving himself a box in the ear. "What luck you've reminded me of her! She should live to be one hundred and twenty, Reb Tevye."

"Amen," I say. "So should you. In fact, you should live till the Messiah comes. But what's all the excitement about?"

"Reb Tevye," he says, "do I have something good for you! Do I have something sensational! Do I have something you won't find better anywhere!"

"And just who might this gift from God be?" I ask.

"Do I have," says Efrayim, "the perfect match for your youngest daughter! He's a steal, a catch, a rare find, a colossus, a prince among men, a millionaire, a second Brodsky, a contractor named Podhotzur!"

"Podhotzur?" I say. "The name rings a bell from the Bible."

"What Bible?" he says. "Leave the Bible out of it for once. He's a contractor! He builds houses, bridges, factories! He was out near Japan during the war and came back from there with a fortune!

He rides around in a droshky with two horses faster than greased lightning! He has more doormen in front of his house than you have buttons on your shirt! He has his own private bathtub! He has furniture from Paris! He wears a diamond on his pinky! . . . And he's still a spring chicken, a bachelor, straight off the shelf, the genuine article! All he's looking for is someone with looks. He's willing to take her barefoot and naked, but she's got to be a raving beauty."

"Whoaa!" I say to him. "If you don't stop for breath, we'll end up in Hotzenklotz. If I'm not mistaken, you once offered me the same bill of goods for my second daughter, Hodl . . ."

Well, when he heard that the man hugged his ribs and began to laugh so hard that I was sure he would get a stroke. "Good Lord," he finally managed to wheeze, "that's such ancient history that my grandma was in diapers when it happened. The fellow you're thinking of went bust during the war and ran away to America."

"May his memory be a blessing," I say. "And suppose this contractor of yours should decide to follow in his footsteps?"

That got his dander up. "What are you talking about, Reb Tevye?" he says. "That first case was a crook, a swindler, a bankrupt! My man Podhotzur is a builder. He has army contracts, companies, an office, a staff, a . . ."

What can I tell you? Efrayim pulled me out of the wagon in his enthusiasm, grabbed me by the collar, and began to shake me so hard that a policeman came along and almost jugged us both for disorderly conduct. It's a good thing I remembered my Bible. *Lanokhri toshikh*, it says. Why are some palms like bridges? Because they have to be crossed when you come to them . . .

In a word, I don't want to bore you. This Podhotzur was engaged to my Beilke and *loy orkhu hayomim*—after a while the wedding was held. What makes me say after a while? Because Beilke would sooner have died than had Podhotzur for a husband. The more he showered her with presents, gold watches, diamond rings, the less she could stomach him. There was no need to put it in writing—it was written all over her face, which was wet with the silent tears she cried. Finally, I made up my mind to talk to her. I tried to be casual. "Listen, Beilke," I said to her, "I'm beginning to think that you're as much in love with this Podhotzur of yours as I am."

"Why do you say that?" she says, turning red as fire.

"Because you're certainly not crying for your health every night," I say.

"*I'm* crying?" she says.

"Well, I wouldn't exactly call it crying," I say. "It's actually more like weeping. Do you think that sticking your head under the pillow is enough to hide your tears from me? Do you think your father was born yesterday, or that his brains are so addled he can't see that you're doing all this for his sake? Do you suppose it's your job to see to it he has a place to lay his head in his old age so that he needn't go begging from door to door? You're a fool if you do! God's still in His heaven, and Tevye is no charity case and no sponger. Money is a lot of hooey anyway, just like the Bible says. Why, look at your sister Hodl! She hasn't a penny to her name, she lives in a hole in the wall at the far end of nowhere—and yet she keeps writing us how happy she is with her schlimazel of a Peppercorn . . ."

Shall I give you three guesses what my Beilke answered me? "Don't go comparing me to Hodl," she says. "In Hodl's day the world was on the brink. There was going to be a revolution and everyone cared about everyone. Now the world is its own self again, and it's everyone for his own self again, too." That's what she said, my Beilke—just go figure out what she meant!

Well, if you think that by now you're an expert on Tevye's daughters, you should have seen Beilke at the wedding—a princess! I stood there feasting my eyes on her and wondering, can this really be my Beilke? Who taught her to stand like that, to walk like that, to carry herself like that, to wear a dress like that, as if wedding gowns had been invented just for her? It wasn't much of a feast, though, because at 6:30 p.m. on the day of the wedding the two of them waved goodbye and *holakh Moyshe-Mordekhai*—off they went by night express to Nitaly, or Italy, or however the Devil that place is called that everyone goes to these days.

They didn't return until Hanukkah, when I received an urgent message from them to please, please come to Yehupetz at once. However you look at it, I thought, if they simply wanted to see me, they could have said as much; why the double "please" and the "at once"? There must be a special reason . . . but what? And I began to imagine all kinds of things, some good and some bad. Suppose, for instance, that they were already fighting like alley cats and had decided to get a divorce . . . Right away, though, I told myself,

Tevye, you dumbbell, why must you always imagine the worst!
How do you know what they want you for? Maybe they miss
you . . . Maybe Beilke would like to have her father nearby . . .
Maybe Podhotzur is planning to take you into his business and
give you a nice fat job . . .

One way or another, I had better go, so I harnessed up and
vayeyleykh khoronoh—off to Yehupetz I went. On the way my excitement got the best of me and I began to imagine leaving the
village, selling my cows, my horse, my wagon, the whole kit and
caboodle, and moving to Yehupetz, where I would first become
Podhotzur's foreman, then his bookkeeper, and finally a partner
in his business who rode around with two bolts of greased lightning, one a chestnut and one a dapple-gray . . . at which point,
though, I caught myself and thought: *mah zeh ve'al mah zeh*—
where does a small potato like Tevye get off being such a big shot?
Who needs the rat race, the hullabaloo, the night life, the rubbing
elbows with millionaires, the whole *lehoyshivi im nedivim*, when all I
want is to enjoy a peaceful old age in which I can study a bit of
Mishnah now and then and recite a few chapters of Psalms? It's
about time, Tevye, I said to myself, that you thought of the next
world too. King Solomon knew what the score was when he said
that a man is nothing but a jackass; he forgets that no matter how
long he lives, there comes a day when he doesn't anymore . . .

I was still mulling it all over when I arrived safe and sound in
Yehupetz, right at Podhotzur's door. Believe me, if I wanted to
boast about his *royv godloy veroyv oshroy*, his house and all its trim-
mings, it wouldn't be hard. Suffice it to say that while I've never
had the honor of dining with Brodsky, finer than Podhotzur's his
place can't possibly be. You'll get an idea what a mansion it was if I
tell you that the doorman, a lummox with silver buttons down his
chest, wouldn't agree to let me in for love or money. What was I to
do? The door was made of glass, and the lummox, damn his hide,
stood on the other side of it brushing off his clothes. I winked at
him; I talked to him in sign language; I put on a whole panto-
mime to tell him that the lady of the house was my own natural-
born daughter . . . none of which meant a thing to that dumb
Russian, because he sign-languaged right back to me that I could
go take a powder. What a schlimazel I felt like: imagine needing a
letter of recommendation to get to see your own child! A sad day

it is, Tevye, for your gray hairs, I told myself, when this is what things have come to . . .

Just then, though, I looked through the glass door again and saw a girl bustling about inside. That must be the chambermaid, I thought, because she has the eyes of a thief (all chambermaids do—my business has brought me to a lot of rich houses and I've seen a lot of chambermaids in my day)—and so I winked at her too as if to say, "Open up there, my little pussycat . . ."

Well, she noticed me, opened the door a crack, and asked me in Yiddish, "Who are you looking for?"

"Is this the Podhotzur place?" I said.

"Who are you looking for?" she asked again, raising her voice.

"When you're asked a question," I said, raising my voice louder than hers, "it's considered polite to answer before asking one of your own. Is this the Podhotzur place?"

"That it is," she says.

"In that case," I say, "you and I are practically related. Please be so kind as to tell Madame Podhotzur that she has a guest; her father Tevye has arrived and has been standing outside like a beggar for quite some time, because he failed to pass muster with that silver-buttoned sheygetz of yours, who isn't worth the nail on your little finger . . ."

The girl burst out laughing like a shiksa herself, shut the door in my face, ran upstairs, ran back down, opened the door again, and let me into a palace the likes of which my ancestors never saw in their dreams. There was silk and satin and crystal and gold all over, and you could hardly feel yourself walk, because wherever you put your big feet they sank into carpets softer than snow that must have cost a small fortune. And the clocks! There were clocks on the walls, clocks on the tables, clocks everywhere; Father Time himself wouldn't have known what to do with so many of them. I began to cross the floor with my hands behind my back, taking it all in, when suddenly, in every direction, I saw other Tevyes with their hands behind their backs just like me. One was heading this way, another that, another toward me, another away . . . the Devil take them, there were mirrors all around! Leave it to that fat cat of a contractor to wallpaper his house with clocks and mirrors . . .

The thought of that fat, bald, whinnying loudmouth of a Pod-hotzur reminded me of the first time he came driving his two speed demons to visit us in the village. He sprawled out in a chair as if he owned it, introduced himself to my Beilke, and then took me aside to shout a secret in my ear that could have been heard on the far side of Yehupetz. What was it? It was that my daughter had swept him off his feet and he wanted to marry her "pronto." His losing his footing was only natural, but that "pronto" of his was like a blunt knife in my heart. What kind of way was that to talk about a wedding? Where did I come in? And where did Beilke? I was about to pin his ears back with a verse or two from the Bible when I thought, *lomoh zeh anoykhi*—what's the point, Tevye, of butting in between these children? A lot it helped for you to think your other daughters' marriages were your business! You made more noise than a kettledrum, you quoted the Bible forwards and backwards, and who came out looking like a fool? Why, Tevye, of course!

But let's get back to the prince and the princess, as you writers like to say. I came to Yehupetz and was received with open arms. "How are you? . . . It's so good to see you! . . . How have you been? . . . Sit down, sit down! . . ." In short, the usual routine. You can be sure I wasn't going to be the first to ask *mah yoym miyomim,* why the rush invitation, because Tevye is no woman, Tevye knows how to wait. Meanwhile a servant in white gloves came to announce that food was on the table, and the three of us rose and went to a room that was all solid oak: the table was oak, and the benches were oak, and the walls were oak, and the ceiling was oak, all painted and lacquered and varnished and stained and carved and chiseled and paneled. The oak table was set for a king, with tea, and coffee, and chocolates, and pastries, and the best French cognac, and the most expensive pickled herring, and all kinds of fruits that I'm ashamed to admit my Beilke never saw in her father's home in her life. I was poured glass after glass of cognac, and I drank toast after toast, and I thought, looking at my Beilke, why, it's just like the prayer book says: *mekimi mi'ofor dal*—when God decides to help a poor person—*meyashpoys yorim evyoyn*—He goes the whole hog. That's certainly my Beilke that I'm looking at, but it's not like any Beilke that I've ever seen before.

As a matter of fact, when I compared the Beilke I knew to the Beilke I saw, I had the sinking feeling that I had driven a bad bargain and was left holding the bag. Do you know what it was like? It was like swapping my trusty old nag for a newborn colt without knowing what would come of it, a real horse or a wooden one. Ah, Beilke, Beilke, I thought, just look at you now! Do you still remember sitting up nights by our smoky oil lamp, sewing and humming an old tune? Plunking yourself down on a three-legged stool and milking a cow faster than it could shake its tail at you? Rolling up your sleeves and cooking me a good, down-to-earth borscht, or a dish of bean fritters, or a platter of cheese blintzes, and calling, "Papa, wash up and come eat"? Those words were such music to my ears—and now here was this woman sitting like a queen with her Podhotzur while two servants waited on the table, making a great clatter with the dishes, and where was my Beilke? You see, she didn't say a single word; Podhotzur was talking for the two of them, he didn't stop blabbing for a minute! In all my life I've never seen a man run on at the mouth like that about the Devil only knows what, and all the time with that high-pitched whinny of his. It's not everyone who can be the only person to laugh at his own jokes and still go right on telling them . . .

Apart from the three of us, there was another diner at the table, a man with red, jowly cheeks. I hadn't the vaguest notion who he was, but he was no mean eater, because all the time that Podhotzur kept talking, he kept putting it away. You know what the rabbis say about *shloyshoh she'okhlu,* three men who eat at one table? Well, with someone like him you didn't need the other two . . .

In a word, I'm being eaten at on one side of me and talked to on the other—and such talk it was, too, as went in one ear and straight out the other: construction contracts, tenders, specifications, government ministries, Japan . . . The one thing that interested me was Japan, because I took part in the Japanese war myself. That is, back then, when horses were in such short supply that the army was beating the bushes for them, some quartermaster came around to me, took my nag for a physical, measured him up, down, and sideways, put him through his paces, and gave him an honorable discharge. "I could have told you that you were wasting your time," I said to him, "because it says in the Bible, *yoydeya tsaddik nefesh behemtoy*—a righteous man knows the soul of his beast, and Tevye's horse was never meant to be a hero." But you'll have to excuse me, Pani Sholem Aleichem, for getting side-tracked. Let's go back to our story.

Well, we wined and dined and asked the Lord's blessing, and
when we rose from the table Podhotzur took me by the arm and
steered me into a special office that was done up like all get-out
with guns and swords all over the walls and little toy cannons on
the desk. He plumped me down on a sofa soft as butter, took two
big, juicy cigars from a gold box, lit one for himself and one for
me, sat down facing me, crossed his legs, and said, "Do you have
any idea why I sent for you?"

Aha, I thought, now he's about to talk turkey! I played innocent, though, and answered him, "How should I know? Am I my
son-in-law's keeper?"

"I have something of a private nature to discuss with you," he
says.

It's a job for sure! I tell myself. To him, though, I only say, "If
it's something good, I'll be happy to hear it."

Well, he took the cigar from his mouth, did Mr. Podhotzur, and
began to deliver a lecture. "You're an intelligent man," he says,
"and so you won't mind my speaking to you frankly. You know
that I run a big business, and that when one runs a business as big
as mine—"

This is where I come in, I thought—and so I said, interrupting
him, "That's exactly what the Talmud means by *marbeh nekhosim
marbeh da'ogoh!* I suppose you're familiar with the passage?"

You couldn't say he wasn't honest. "To tell you the truth," he
says with that little whinnying laugh, "I never studied a page of
Talmud in my life. I wouldn't know what a Talmud looked like if
you showed me one."

Do you see who I was up against now? You'd think, wouldn't
you, that if God had punished him by making him an ignoramus,
he would at least keep his trap shut about it!

"Well," I said, "I thought as much. You didn't look like much of
a Talmudist to me. But why not finish what you were saying?"

"What I was saying," he says, "is that with a business like mine, a
reputation like mine, a public position like mine, I can't afford to
have a cheesemonger for a father-in-law. The governor of the
province is a personal friend of mine, and I'm perfectly capable of
having a Brodsky, even a Rothschild, as my guest . . ."

I swear, I'm not making up a word of it! I sat there staring at
that shiny bald head of his and thinking, you may very well be
palsy-walsy with the governor and have Rothschild over for tea,

but you still talk just like a guttersnipe! "Look here," I said, trying not to sound too annoyed, "I can't help it, can I, if Rothschild insists on dropping in on you!" Do you think he got it, though? *Loy dubim veloy ya'ar*—it just sailed right by him.

"I would like," he says, "for you to leave the dairy line and engage in something else."

"And what exactly do you suggest that I engage in?" I asked.

"In anything you like," he says. "Do you think the world is short of things to do? I'll help you out with money, as much as you need, if you just agree to give up your cheesemongering. Come to think of it, I have an even better idea: how would you like to go pronto to America?"

And he sticks his cigar between his teeth again and gives me a shiny-headed look.

Well, you tell me: how does one answer a young whippersnapper like that? At first I thought, why go on sitting here like a golem, Tevye? Pick yourself up, walk through the door, shut it behind you, and *holakh le'oylomoy*—goodbye and good riddance! That's how hot under the collar he made me. The nerve of that contractor! Who did he think he was, telling me to give up a perfectly good living and go to America? Just because Rothschild was about to ring his doorbell, did that mean Tevye had to be sent packing to the other side of the globe? My blood began to boil; I was getting angrier by the minute, and now I was good and mad at my Beilke, too. How can you sit there like the Queen of Sheba surrounded by a thousand clocks and mirrors, I thought, when your father Tevye is being dragged over hot coals to the whipping post? May I hope to die if your sister Hodl isn't better off than you are! What's true is true: she may not live in a castle full of gewgaws, but at least that Peppercorn of hers is a human being—in fact, too much of one, because he never thinks of himself, only of others. And the head on that boy's shoulders . . . it's not a shiny pot of wet noodles like some people's . . . and the tongue on him . . . why, he's solid gold! Try polishing him off with a quotation and three more come flying back at you! Just you wait, you Putzhoddur, you, I'll let you have such a verse from the Bible that you'll see fireworks before your eyes . . .

And having thought it all over I turned to him and said, "Look here, I don't hold it against you that you think the Talmud is mumbo-jumbo. When a Jew sits in Yehupetz expecting Rothschild any minute, he can afford to keep the Talmud in his attic. Still, even you can surely understand a simple line of Scripture such as every Russian peasant boy knows. I'm referring, of course, to what Onkelos has to say in his Targum about what the Bible has to say in the Book of Genesis about Laban the Aramean: *miznavto dekhazirto loy makhtmen shtreimilto . . .*"

"I'm afraid," he says, looking at me sideways like a rooster, "that that's a bit over my head. What does it mean?"

"It means," I say, "that you can't make a fur hat out of a pig's tail."

"And what," he asks, "am I supposed to understand by that?"

"You're supposed to understand," I say, "that I'm not being shipped off to America."

Well, he laughed that whinnying laugh of his and said to me, "All right. If America is out, how about Palestine? Isn't that where all the old Jews like you go to die?"

The minute he said that, I felt it drive home like a nail. Hold on there, Tevye, I told myself. Maybe that's not such a weird idea. There just may be something in it. With all the pleasure you've been getting from your children, why not try your luck elsewhere? You're a jackass if you think you have anyone or anything to keep you here. Your poor Golde is six feet under, and between you and me, so are you; how long do you intend to go on drudging? . . . And by the way, Pani Sholem Aleichem, you should know that I always had a hankering to be in the Holy Land. I would have given anything to see the Wailing Wall, Rachel's Tomb, the Cave of the Patriarchs, the River Jordan, Mount Sinai, the Red Sea, the Ten Plagues, and all the rest of it with my own eyes. In fact, I was so carried away thinking of that blessed land of Canaan where the milk and honey flow that I had all but forgotten where I was when Podhotzur brought me back to it by saying, "Well, how about it? Why not decide pronto."

"I can see," I said, "that everything is pronto with you. Make haste while the sun shines, eh? Still, if you ask me, there's a small problem here, because one can't get to Palestine on an empty pocket . . ."

Well, he gave his little whinny again, rose from his seat, went to his desk, opened a drawer, took out a billfold, and counted out a very tidy sum. I must say I was no slouch myself: I took that wad of bills—the things one doesn't do for money!—stuck it deep in my pocket, and began to set the record straight with a midrash that interested him about as much as a cat's miaow. "That," he said without even letting me finish, "should get you to Palestine with plenty to spare. If you need more once you're there, just write and I'll send it to you pronto. And I trust I needn't remind you to catch the first train you can, because you're an honest, responsible fellow."

That's what he said to me, Mr. Hodputzer, whinnying so hard that I felt it right in the gut. Why don't you crack him on the snout with this wad of his, I thought, and tell him, begging your pardon, to stick it up his honest, responsible you-know-what, because Tevye is not for sale! Before I could open my mouth, though, he rang for Beilke and said to her, "Guess what, my sweet! Your father is leaving us. He's selling everything he owns and setting out for Palestine."

I tell you, it was like a bad dream! I looked at my Beilke, waiting for her to say something, to bat an eyelash at least. But she just stood there stock-still, not a drop of blood in her cheeks, glancing back and forth from her husband to me without so much as a word. I stared at her without saying one either, so that there we both were with our tongues stuck to the roofs of our mouths. My head was spinning, pounding away as though I had been breathing coal gas. What can be wrong with me, I wondered; if it's the cigar I smoked, he's been smoking one himself, and talking non-stop in the bargain, though his eyelids keep drooping as if he were itching to snooze. "You take the express train to Odessa," he says to me, "and from there a ship sails to Jaffa. The best time to go is right now, because later there are winds . . . and snow, and . . . and storms . . . and . . . and . . ." He was so sleepy he could barely get the words out, but he didn't stop jabbering for a second. "Just don't forget to notify us when you're ready to leave . . . We'll come to say goodbye at the station . . . Who knows when we'll meet again . . ." And he yawns in my face, gets up from his chair, and says to my Beilke, "And now, my sweet, you spend some time with your father while I go lie down for a while . . ."

I swear, I thought, that's the first sensible thing you've said; now at last I can get it all off my chest. And I turned to my Beilke to let out what had been building up in me all day—but before I could even begin, she threw her arms around me and started to cry. Did I say cry? My daughters, bless them, are all the same; for a while they manage to put on a brave face, but sooner or later every one of them gushes like a geyser. Take my second oldest, Hodl, for example; at the very last minute, just as she's setting out for Siberia with her Peppercorn, she breaks down and bawls like a baby! Only there's really no comparison, because when it comes to crying, Hodl can't hold a candle to Beilke.

I'll tell you the honest truth: I myself am no weeping willow. The last good cry I remember having, in fact, was when I found my poor Golde dead on the floor, and before that, when my Hodl left me standing in the station, all alone like a fool with my horse. There may have been a few other times when my eyes were a wee bit wet, but that's all; on the whole, it's not like me to blubber. But Beilke's tears threw me so that I couldn't hold my own in any longer, let alone say a cross word to her. I'm not a man who needs things spelled out for me: my name is Tevye. And I knew why she was crying: it was for *kheyt shekhotosi lefonekho,* for the sin of not listening to a father—so that instead of letting her have what she deserved and giving that Hodderputz hell, I tried cheering her up with some story or other, as only Tevye can do. She listened to me, did my Beilke, and said, "No, Papa, that's not why I'm crying. I'm not blaming myself or anyone. It just breaks my heart to know that you're going away because of me, and that there's not a thing I can do about it."

"There, there," I told her. "You're talking like a little girl. Have you forgotten that God is still in His heaven and your father is still a young man? Why, it's child's play for me to travel to Palestine and back again, just like it says in the Bible: *vayisu vayakhanu*—and the Children of Israel knew not if they were coming or going . . ."

Yet the words were no sooner out of my mouth than I thought, Tevye, that's a big fat lie! You're off to the Land of Israel for good—it's bye-bye Tevye forever . . . She must have read my mind, too, for she said to me, "Please, Papa. It's no use trying to comfort me as you would a child with some fairy tale that ends happily ever after—although if you like fairy tales, I can tell you one myself. I'm warning you, though, Papa, that this fairy tale is a sad one."

That's just what she said, my Beilke; Tevye's daughters don't mince words. And with that she began to tell me a story, a case history, a tale from the Arabian Nights, about how her Podhotzur was a self-made man who had pulled himself up from the bottom rung by his own bootstraps and now only wanted to hobnob with all the Brodskys of the world . . . Money, she said, was no object to him; he gave it away by the barrelful; only money, it seemed, was not enough, one needed a pedigree too—and Podhotzur was determined to prove that he wasn't just some rich upstart but the last of a long line of famous Podhotzurs and the son of a wealthy contractor himself. "And that," says my Beilke, "is though he knows that I know that his father was a fiddler at weddings. Worse yet, he goes about telling everyone that his father-in-law is a millionaire too . . ."

"Who, me?" I say. "Well, I always thought that someday I would get to be one."

"I can't tell you how I blush, Papa," she says, "when he introduces me to his friends with the most outrageous lies about my distinguished father, and all my uncles, and my whole family— and I have to sit there and put up with it, because he's eccentric that way."

"By you," I say, "he's eccentric. By me he's a charlatan and a fraud."

"But he's not, Papa," says my Beilke. "You don't know him. He's not such a bad man as you think. He's just unpredictable. He has a big heart and he's generous. If you catch him in the right mood, it's enough to make a long face for him to give you the shirt off his back. And I'm not even talking about myself—for me the sky's the limit! You mustn't think I have no influence with him. Why, not long ago I made him promise to do all he could to free Hodl and her husband from Siberia. He swore to me that money wouldn't stand in his way. His one condition was that they go to Japan when Peppercorn gets out."

"Why to Japan?" I asked. "Why not to India, or to Mesopotamia, or to Timbuktu?"

"Because," she says, "he has businesses there. He has businesses everywhere. He spends more on telegrams in a single day than it would cost us to live on for a year. But what good does all that do me if I can't be myself?"

"The rabbis," I said, "put that very well. *Im eyn ani li mi li*—if you can't be yourself, don't expect me to be."

And I tried to make a joke of it with a quote thrown in here and there, though my heart bled for my daughter to see what unhappiness money had bought her. "Your sister Hodl," I said, "would never have gotten into such a—"

"I already told you, Papa," said my Beilke, interrupting me, "not to compare me to Hodl. Hodl lived in the Age of Hodl and Beilke lives in the Age of Beilke. The distance between the two is as great as from here to Japan."

I ask you, is that Japanese or not?

Well, I see you're getting off at the next station, Pani. Just give me two more minutes. I left my lucky youngest daughter's house with a bellyful of her sorrows, a shattered, a devastated man; flung my cigar, which had only given me a headache, on the ground; and yelled at it, "You should go straight to hell, you and your father and all your uncles!"

"Whose uncles did you say, Reb Tevye?" I heard a voice ask behind me. I turned around—why, it's Efrayim the Matchmaker, the Devil take him and keep him!

"Well, well, a fellow Jew!" I say. "What are you doing here?"

"What are you doing here?" he asks.

"Visiting my daughter," I say.

"And how is she?" he asks.

"How should she be?" I say. "Not everyone has luck like hers."

"I can see you're happy with my merchandise," he says.

"Happy," I say, "is not the word. You should only be as happy yourself."

"Thank you for your kind wishes," he says. "Perhaps you'd like to add a small remittance to them."

"Are you trying to tell me," I say, "that you never were paid your matchmaker's fee?"

"That Podhotzur of yours," he says, "should only be worth as much as he paid me."

"You mean he short-changed you?" I ask.

"Not at all," he says. "What he gave me just wasn't enough."

"Why not?"

"Because there's not a kopeck left of it."

"How come?"

"I married off a daughter myself."

"Mazel tov!" I say. "May God grant you pleasure from her."

"A fine lot of pleasure He's already granted me," he says. "I wound up with a gangster for a son-in-law. He beat my daughter black and blue and ran away with all her money to America."

"But why didn't you stop him?" I say.

"Why, what could I have done?" he asks.

"Well," I say, "you might have salted him away in a pickle barrel."

"I see you're in a gay mood today, Reb Tevye," says Efrayim.

"It would be a fit punishment for God," I say, "if He had to feel half as gay as I do."

"Is that so?" he says. "And here I was thinking how lucky you were to be a rich Jew. Well then, how about a pinch of snuff to cheer you up?"

I took the snuff, said goodbye to the matchmaker, drove home to my village, and began to sell all the worldly goods I had accumulated over the years. Mind you, that's easier said than done. Every pot and pan, the silliest little item, cost me a year of my life; if it didn't remind me of my poor Golde, it reminded me of my daughters, may they live. The cruelest blow of all, though, was getting rid of my horse. I felt like a traitor to him. You see, we had suffered together for so many years, slaved together, been through so much together—and here I was, putting him on the block! In the end I sold him to a water carrier, because dealing with coachmen was too aggravating. You should have heard the guff I had to take from them. "God help us, Reb Tevye," they said to me, "do you call that thing a horse?"

"And what does it look like to you," I say, "a chandelier?"

"Not at all," they say. "A chandelier doesn't have four legs. In fact, for a horse we'd give him ninety-nine out of a hundred."

"You would?" I say.

"Yes," they say. "He'll live to be a hundred and he's already ninety-nine. His lips are gray, there's not a tooth in his mouth, and his ribs shake like an old woman's on a cold winter night."

That's coachmen's talk, in case you didn't know. I swear to you that my nag understood every word of it, just like it says in the Bible: *veyoda shor koyneyhu*—even a dumb beast knows when it's been put up for sale. And the proof of it was that when I slapped the water carrier on the back to congratulate him, my horse turned his old head to me and gave me a silent stare that said, "*Zeh khelki mikoyl amoli*—is this how you thank me for all I've done for you?" I took one last look at his new owner leading him away and beginning none too gently to teach him his new trade, and I thought as I stood there all alone, God Almighty, how cleverly

You run this world of Yours: here You create a horse and here You create a Tevye, and one fate is enough for them both! The only difference is that a man has a mouth and can grumble till he's hoarse, while a horse can't grumble till he's man. That's why he's only a horse.

You see the tears in my eyes, Pani Sholem Aleichem, and you must be thinking, how Tevye misses his horse! But what makes you think it's just my horse? I miss everything, there's not one thing it doesn't grieve me to think of. I miss my horse, I miss my village, I miss its elder, I miss its policeman, I miss the dachas of Boiberik, I miss the rich Jews of Yehupetz, I even miss Efrayim the Matchmaker, may the cholera carry him off! When you get right down to it, he's nothing but a miserably poor Jew himself who's out to make a living like the rest of us. Don't ask me what I'll do in the Land of Israel if I get there safely, God willing, but I do know one thing for sure, and that's that right off I plan to visit Mother Rachel in her grave. I'll pray there for the daughters I'll probably never see again, and I'll think of him, too—I mean Efrayim the Matchmaker—and of you, and of Jews everywhere. Here, let's shake on that! Be well, and have a good trip, and give my very best to any of our friends you may happen to meet on your way.

(1909)

LEKH-LEKHO

▼

Greetings, Pani Sholem Aleichem, greetings to you and yours! I've been looking for you everywhere, because I have some fresh goods for you. Where have you been? Why haven't I seen you? I've been told you were traveling all over the world, to all kinds of far places, each of the hundred-and-seven-and-twenty lands of King Ahasuerus . . . But am I imagining it, or are you really giving me a strange look? You seem to be trying to make up your mind if it's me or not. It's me, Pani Sholem Aleichem, it's me—

your old friend Tevye in person, Tevye the Dairyman! That is, I'm still Tevye, though I'm not a dairyman any more; I'm just a plain everyday Jew, and an old one too, as you can see, though to go by my age, no older than it says in the Haggadah: *harey ani keven shivim shonoh*—why, I'm not even pushing seventy yet . . . So why, you ask, all the white hair? Believe me, my dear friend, I didn't grow it for fun. It's partly from my own private sorrows— God forgive me for putting myself first!—and partly from those of Jews everywhere. What times we live in! What a miserable time to be a Jew! . . . I can see, though, that you're itching to ask me something. I suppose it's because you remember having said goodbye to me as I was leaving for the Land of Israel. You must be thinking that I'm back from there, and you can't wait to hear news of the Wailing Wall, Mother Rachel's Tomb, and all those other places. Well, let me assure you that if you've got the time for me, I've got the news for you. In fact, if you listen to me carefully, with a real *shmo'eyni*, as Father Abraham says, you'll soon say your- self that God's in His heaven, man is a jackass, and all is right with the world.

In a word, what Bible reading are you up to in the synagogue this week, the first chapter of Leviticus? Well, I'm a bit behind, because I'm still back in the third chapter of Genesis. That's the chapter of Lekh-Lekho, you know, where God shows Abraham the door. *Lekh-lekho*—get thee out, Tevye—*meyartsekho*—from your land—*umimoyladitkho*—and from the village you were born in and lived in your whole life—*el ha'orets asher arekko*—to wherever your legs will carry you . . . And when did it occur to the powers- that-be to tell me that? Not a minute before I'm so old, weak, and lonely that I'm a real *al tashlikheynu le'eys ziknoh,* as it says in the Rosh Hashanah prayer . . . Only I'm getting ahead of myself, be- cause I was telling you about my trip and what's new in the Land of Israel. Well, what should be new there, my dear friend? It's a land flowing with milk and honey—if you don't believe me, you can read up on it in the Bible. There's only one thing the matter with it, which is that it's there and I'm here . . . and not only am I still here in Russia, I'm still a schlimazel in Russia, and a schlimazel I'll be till I die! Just think of it: there I was with one foot practi- cally in the Holy Land already—I had only to buy a ticket, board a ship, and heigh-ho!—when what does the good Lord decide to do? It shouldn't happen to you or to anyone, but one night my son-in-law, Motl Komzoyl, the tailor from Anatevka, gets it into his head to go to bed well and wake up dead in the morning. I don't mean to say he was the picture of health before that. He was a workingman, after all, who spent day and night *al hatoyroh ve'al ha'avoydoh,* patching pants with his needle and thread. Well, the long and short of it was that he came down with the dry cough, and coughed and coughed until he coughed his lungs out. Nothing helped him one bit, not the doctors with their medicines, or the quacks with their snake oils, or the goat's milk, or the chocolate with honey. He was a fine young man; a bit simple perhaps, without any learning, but also without any guile; and was he ever crazy about my Tsaytl! He lived his whole life for her and her children, and he would have done anything for me, too . . .

In a word, *vayomos Moysheh*—Motl passed on and left me with a pretty kettle of fish to fry. How could I even think of a pilgrimage to the Holy Land when I had a house full of little pilgrims myself? You can't just let your widowed daughter and all her orphans go hungry—although on the other hand, I was about as much use to them as a sack full of holes. I couldn't bring Tsaytl's husband back to life for her, or restore the children's father from the dead; I was a mere mortal myself, and an old one at that, who wanted only to rest his weary bones and feel for once that he was a human being and not a donkey. I had had enough of this workaday, dog-eat-dog world; it was high time to start thinking of the next one. And besides, I had already held a clearance sale of everything I owned; my horse, as you know, was given his walking papers, and every one of my cows was sold too, except, that is, for two little calves, who needed their victuals if anything was to come of them . . . and now, all of a sudden, here I was running an orphanage in my old age, the father of a house full of children! And do you think that was all? Don't jump to any hasty conclusions. The real music hasn't begun yet, because it never rains in Tevye's life but it pours, like that time a cow of mine died and another cow thought it such a grand notion that the next day she went and died too . . . Well, that's how God chose to make this world of His, and that's how it always will be. Why spit into the wind?

In short, I told you how my youngest daughter Beilke struck it rich by landing that fat cat of a Podhotzur who made a pile as a war contractor. He heard of her from Efrayim the Matchmaker,

damn his soul, fell for her head over heels, and went down so
hard on his knees to ask me for her hand that he nearly split his
shins. And he took her without a penny's dowry, and rained
pearls and diamonds on her too—you'd normally call that a stroke
of good luck, wouldn't you? Well, all that luck, let me tell you,
went right down the drain in the end—and what a drain it was,
God save us all from such a filthy mess! When He decides to give
the wheel of fortune a spin so that the butter side is down, it's like
reciting the *hallel* prayer: you can't say *mekimi,* "He who raiseth the
lowly," without adding *mi'ofor dal,* "from the dirt"—and bang,
that's just where you find yourself, right smack on your bottom
again! Oh, God likes to play games with us, He does. He's got a
favorite He plays with Tevye called *Oylim Veyordim,* which means
in plain language Upsy-Daisy—now you're up, and now you're
pushing daisies . . . which is exactly what happened to that contractor. Perhaps you remember my telling you about his seven-
teen servants and his little mansion with its mirrors, clocks, and
toys. La-di-da! You may also remember my asking my Beilke—
begging her, in fact—to make sure he bought the house outright
and registered it in her name. Well, she listened to me the way a
dead man listens in the grave. What does a father know about
such things? Nothing times nothing, of course! And do you know
what happened in the end? Exactly what you'd wish on your worst
enemy! He not only went so broke that he had to sell every last
clock and mirror, even the pearls and diamonds he bought my
Beilke, he had to run for dear life from his creditors too, and light
out for never-never land—I mean for America, where else do all
the hard-luck cases go? And don't think they had it easy there,
either. They ran out of what little money was left, and when the
larder was empty they had to go to work—and I do mean work,
the worst sort of slave labor, just like we Jews did in Egypt, both
him and her! Lately, she writes, things are looking up, thank God;
they're both making socks in a sweatshop and doing well; which
means in American that they're breaking their backs to keep the
wolf from the door . . . although the lucky thing is, she writes, that
there are only two of them, they haven't any little mouths to feed.
What doesn't go by the name of luck these days! I ask you, doesn't
his great-aunt's grand-uncle deserve to break a leg? . . . No, I
don't mean that Podhotzur, I mean Efrayim the Matchmaker, for
palming off such a match on me and getting us all into this pickle!

Would it have been such a tragedy if my Beilke had married a workingman like my Tsaytl or a tutor like my Hodl? Not that they're sitting on top of the world themselves . . . one is a widow and the other is in Outer Nowhere . . . but these things come from God, a man can't do anything about them. Would you like to know something? The most sensible one of us all was my Golde. She saw what was coming and decided to clear out of this ridiculous world in time, because she knew it was a thousand times better to be breakfasted on by the worms than to go through what her Tevye has gone through with his daughters. Well, you know what our rabbis said: *be'al korkhekho atoh khai*—no one asks you if you want to live or not, and neither would you, if only you minded your own business . . .

I can see I've digressed, though. *Nakhzor le'inyoneynu harishon,* then—let's leave the prince on his horse, as you writers like to say, and see what the princess is up to. Where were we? Yes, in the chapter of Lekh-Lekho. But before we get to Lekh-Lekho, suppose we have a look, if you don't mind, at the story of the Amalekites in the Book of Exodus. I know that the way things are done in this world, and the way they always have been, Genesis comes before Exodus, but in this case the Amalekites came first. And I suggest you listen to the lesson they taught me, because it may come in useful some day.

In short, let's go back to the days after the Japanese war, when the Constantution was in the headlines and we Jews were having a fine old time of it, first in the big cities and then in the smaller towns to which the pogroms spread. They never reached my own village, though, and they never could have. Would you like to know why not? For the simple reason that I was the only Jew among Christians and on good terms with every one of them. Why, Uncle Tevel was king of the roost there, a friend in need and indeed! Did someone want advice? "Let's go ask Tevel." A remedy for baldness? "Tevel's sure to know." A little loan to tide him over? Try Tevel again. Why be afraid of a silly thing like a pogrom when my Christian neighbors had promised me over and over that I had nothing to worry about—they simply wouldn't allow it. And in the end they didn't. Listen to a crazy story.

One day when I came home from Boiberik—I was in my heyday then, selling cheese, cream, butter, and such stuff—I unharnessed my horse, gave him some hay and oats, and was about to wash up and have a bite myself when what do I see in my front yard but a big mob of peasants. The whole village was there from top to bottom, from Ivan Paparilo the elder to Trokhim the shepherd, all with an odd holiday air. For a second my heart skipped a beat, because I knew there was no holiday in sight. They've come to give you a Bible lesson, I thought, and "Then came Amalek and fought with Israel" is their text . . . only then I thought again: shame on you, Tevye! They may be Christians and you may be a Jew, but you've lived your whole life peacefully among them without a hair of your head being harmed. And so I stepped outside and acted my friendliest. "Welcome!" I said to them. "What brings you here, dear neighbors? What's the good word? What's new in the world?"

"We've come to you, Tevel," says Ivan Paparilo, stepping forward and getting right down to it, "because we want to have a pogrom."

How's that for an opener? There's nothing like breaking it gently!

Well, I don't have to tell you what I felt like. Don't think I let them see it, though. Far from it: Tevye was no crybaby. "Congratulations!" I said to them in my cheeriest voice. "What's taken you so long, though, my children? Everywhere else the pogroms are already over."

But Ivan Paparilo was in no mood to joke. "You see, Tevel," he said, "we've finally made up our minds. Since you Jews have been beaten up everywhere, why let you get away with it here? We just aren't certain what kind of pogrom to have. Should we just smash your windows, should we tear up your pillows and blankets and scatter all the feathers, or should we also burn down your house and barn with everything in them?"

This time my heart did a flip-flop. I looked at all those good people whispering to each other as they stood leaning on their staffs and I thought, Tevye, this is serious! It's *bo'u mayim ad nefesh* for sure, just like it says in the Bible—you're in for it this time, all right. You'd better watch what you say, because who knows what these pigs' snouts might do to you! And you'd better say it fast too, because this is no time to play guessing games with the Angel of Death . . .

Why make a short story long, my dear friend? It was a miracle from God that I kept my wits about me, got a grip on myself, and said, not sounding the least bit put out, "Listen to me, dear neigh-

bors and villagers. If that's what you've decided, who am I to
object? You must have good reasons for thinking that Tevye deserves to see his life go up in smoke. I just hope you realize,
though, that there is a higher power than your village council in
this world. You do know there's a God above, don't you? Mind
you, I'm not talking about my God or your God—I'm talking
about the God of us all, He who sits in His heaven and sees every
low-down trick that we play on each other here on earth . . . It
may very well be that He wants you to punish me for being guilty
of nothing at all. But the opposite may also be true, my dear
friends, and He may not want you to lift a finger against me. Who
can know what God's will is? Is there anyone here who would like
to explain to us how God makes up His mind?"

Well, they must have seen there was no outtalking Tevye, because he said to me, did Ivan Paparilo, "Look, Tevel, it's like this.
We have nothing against you personally. You're not at all a bad
sort for a kike. It's just that that has nothing to do with it. A
pogrom is a pogrom, and if the village council has voted to have
one, then that's what must be. We'll have to smash your windows
at least, because if anyone passing through here sees there's been
no pogrom yet, we'll be in hot water ourselves."

I swear to God and hope to die, those were his very words!
You're a Jew who's been all over, Pani Sholem Aleichem, you tell
me: is Tevye right or not when he says there's a great God up
above?

That's the story of the Amalekites—and now let's get back to
Lekh-Lekho. You see, I was only recently given a lesson in its real
meaning, against which none of the commentaries I knew helped
one bit. Let me tell it to you exactly as it happened, blow by blow
ka'asher ohavti, the way you like a story told.

Vayehi bimey Mendel Beilis—it happened back at the time of the
Beilis case, when Mendel Beilis was atoning for all our sins by
going through the torments of hell and the whole world was talking of nothing else. One hot summer day I was sitting on my front
stoop, the wheels spinning round in my head. How can it be, I
thought, how is it possible that such a thing can happen in times
like these, in such an intelligent world full of smart people? And
where is God in all this—where, oh where, is our old Jewish God?
Why doesn't He do something? Why doesn't He say something?
Why, why, why, why, why . . .

Well, once you get on the subject of God, you beat your brains
out about other things too. What was life all about? Was there
more of it after death? Why hadn't the Messiah come yet? Ai, I
thought, wouldn't it be clever of him, the Messiah, to come riding
down to us on his white horse right this minute! Just think how
grand that would be! Why, we've never needed him so badly!
There's no knowing what goes on in the mind of a rich Jew, of a
Brodsky in Yehupetz, for example, or of a Rothschild in Paris—
the Messiah may be the furthest thing from it; but we poor Jews of
Kasrilevke, and of Mazapevke, and of Zlodeyevke, and even of
Yehupetz, and yes, of Odessa too, can't wait for him any longer—
no, we absolutely can't wait another day! The only hope left us is
for God to work a miracle and send us the Messiah right away . . .

There I sat thinking all this when I happened to look up—and
what do you suppose I saw? A white horse with a rider on it right
in front of my house! "Whoaa," he tells it, jumping down and
tying it to the gate, while to me he says, "*Zdrastvoy,* Tevel!"

"*Zdrastvoytye,* Officer, *Zdrastvoytye,*" I say, giving him a friendly
greeting. It seems I only need think of the Messiah for Haman to
appear right away—I mean the village policeman. "Welcome, sit
down," I say. "What's the good word? What's new in the big
world, Officer?" Believe me, my heart was in my throat—what
could he possibly have come for? He took his time telling me, too.
He lit himself a cigarette slow and easy, blew out the smoke, and
spat on the ground before saying, "Tell me, Tevel, how much
time would you say you needed to sell your house and everything
in it?"

"But why," I said, staring at him, "should I sell my house? Is it in
anyone's way?"

"No," he says, "it isn't. It's just that I've come to expel you from
the village."

"Is that all?" I say. "And what good deeds have I done you to
deserve such an honor?"

"It's not my doing," he says. "It's the provincial governor's."

"The governor's?" I say. "What does the governor have against
me?"

"It's not against you," he says. "And it's not just here, either. It's
in every village in the area, in Zlodilevka, and in Rabilevka, and in
Kostolomevka, and even in Anatevka, which has been considered
a town until now. You all have to leave. Every one of you Jews."

"Even Layzer Wolf the butcher?" I ask. "And lame Naftoli Gershon? And the rabbi? And the slaughterer?"

"Everyone," he says, knifing the air with his hand.

Well, that made me feel a little better. *Tsoras rabbim khatsi nekhomoh,* as they say—misery never minds a bit of company. Still, I was burning up inside. "Tell me, Officer," I said to him, "are you aware of the fact that I've been living in this village longer than you have? Do you know that my father lived hereabouts too, and my grandfather before him, and my grandmother also, rest her soul . . ."

I didn't stop there, either; I went on to list every member of my family who had ever lived and died in those parts. I must say he heard me out, but all he said when I finished was, "You're a smart Jew, Tevel, and you've got the gift of the gab. But what do I care about your grandmother and your grandfather and all their old wives' tales? They flew away to heaven long ago, and you had better pack your things and fly away to Berdichev."

That made me even angrier. It was bad enough to get such wonderful news from that big goy in the first place without his making a joke of it. He could fly away somewhere himself! "Officer!" I said. "In all the years you've been the law around here, have you ever heard a single soul in the village complain that I stole anything, or pilfered anything, or cheated anyone, or took the smallest item that didn't belong to me? Go on, ask everyone if I wasn't on better terms with them than their own next-door neighbors. In fact, how many times did I come on their behalf to ask you to stop being such a brute to them . . ."

Well, that didn't sit too well with him, because he got to his feet, snuffed out his cigarette with his fingers, threw it away, and said, "Listen, I don't have time to chew the fat with you all day. I have a written order, and that's that. Here, this is where you sign. I'm giving you three days to clear out. That should be enough to sell all your things and pack."

"So you're giving me three days, are you?" I said, seeing it was a lost cause. "Well, for each of them I wish you a whole year of as much happiness as you've brought me. May God pay you back with interest for being the bearer of such good tidings." And I proceeded to give him a good tongue-lashing, as only Tevye can do. What did I have to lose? Had I been twenty years younger, and still had my Golde—had I been, that is, the Tevye I once was—oho, I wouldn't have taken it lying down: why, I would have settled his hash in a minute! But the way things stood . . . *mah onu umeh khayeynu*—just take a look at me now: I'm a shadow of myself, a walking corpse, a decrepit shell of a man! Dear Lord God, I thought, wouldn't You like to play one of Your jokes on a Brodsky or a Rothschild for a change? Why doesn't anyone give them a lesson in Lekh-Lekho? They could use it more than me. In the first place, it's high time they too had a taste of what it's like to be a Jew. And secondly, let them see for once in their lives what a great God we have watching over us . . .

In a word, it was one big waste of breath. There's no arguing with God, and you can't tell Him how to run this world of His. When He says *li hashomayim veli ha'orets,* I'm boss of heaven and earth, all you can do is listen. No sooner said than done with Him! . . . So I went inside and told my daughter Tsaytl, "Tsaytl, we're moving to town. Enough of this country life. It's time to look for greener pastures . . . You get busy packing the linens, the samovar, and everything else, and I'll take care of selling the house. We've just gotten a written order to be out of here in three days and find another roof for our heads."

My daughter burst out crying, and as soon as they saw her, the children began howling so loudly that you might have thought it was the day of mourning for the Temple. That was already too much for me, and I let it all out on her. "What do you want from my life?" I asked her. "What in the world are you wailing for, like an old cantor on Yom Kippur? Do you think I'm God's only child? Do you think He owes me special consideration? Do you think there aren't lots of other Jews who are being expelled just like us? You should have heard what the policeman told me. Would you believe that even a town like Anatevka has been declared a village, glory be, so that the Jews can be kicked out of it too? Since when am I less of a Jew than they are?"

I was sure that would cheer her up, but my Tsaytl is only a woman. "How are we going to move in such a hurry?" she asked. "Where will we ever find a town to live in?"

"Don't be a sillyhead," I said. "When God came to our great-great-great-grandfather, I mean to Father Abraham, and told him *lekh-lekho meyartsekho,* get thee out of thy land, did Abraham ask Him where to? God told him exactly where to, *el ha'orets asher arekko*—which means in plain language, hit the road! We'll go where all the other Jews go—that is, where our two feet take us. What's good enough for them is good enough for us. What makes you think you're more privileged than your sister Beilke the millionairess? If sweating for a living with her Podhotzur in America isn't beneath her dignity, neither is this beneath yours . . . Thank the good Lord that we at least have something to fall back on. There's some money that I saved over the years, there's what we got for the horse and cows, and there's what we'll get for the house. Every little bit helps—why, we ought to be counting our blessings! Even if we didn't have a penny to our name, we'd still be better off than Mendel Beilis . . ."

In a word, after managing to convince her that it was pointless to be obstinate and that, if a policeman comes along with an eviction order, it's only sporting to sign without being piggish about it, I went off to the village to see Ivan Paparilo, an ox of a man who had been dying to have my house for years. Naturally, I didn't breathe a word of what had happened—any way you look at it, a Jew is still smarter than a goy. "You must have heard, Ivan, old man," I said to him, "that I'm about to say goodbye to you all."

"How come?" asks Ivan.

"I'm moving to town," I say. "I want to be among Jews. I'm not such a young man any more—why, I might kick off any day . . ."

"But you can kick off right here," says Ivan. "Who's stopping you?"

"I believe I'll leave that to you to do," I say, thanking him all the same for his kind offer. "You can even have my turn. I myself would rather die among my own. I just thought, though, that you might like to buy my house and garden. I wouldn't dream of selling them to anyone else, but for you I'll make an exception."

"How much do you want for them?" he asks.

"How much will you give me?" I say.

Well, we haggled a bit back and forth, I driving the price up by a ruble and he knocking it down by two, until at last we shook hands on it. I made sure he paid a good chunk in advance so that he couldn't back out—I tell you, a Jew is smarter than a goy!—and, the whole shebang sold in one day for hard cash, although for a song, of course, off I went to hire a wagon for what little we had left in the house. And now listen, Pani Sholem Aleichem, to what can happen in this world. Just bear with me a little longer, because I don't want to keep you, and it won't take but a minute or two.

It was time for the last goodbyes. The house looked more like a ruin than a home. The bare walls seemed to have tears running down them, and there were bundles all over the floor. The cat sat on the mantel above the stove looking like a little orphan . . . I tell you, it made me so sad that I had a lump in my throat; if I hadn't been ashamed to be seen by my own daughter, I would have sat down and sobbed like a child. Why, I had grown up in this place, I had died a thousand deaths in it, and suddenly, out of nowhere— *lekh-lekho!* Say what you will, it was a depressing situation. But Tevye is no woman. And so I pulled myself together, kept my chin up, and called to my daughter, "Tsaytl, where are you? Come here for a minute."

Tsaytl came out of the other room, all red-eyed and runny-nosed. Aha, I thought, she's been weeping like an old woman at a funeral again! I tell you, it's no joke with these females; tears are cheap with them, they cry before you even know it. "You little ninny!" I said to her. "What are you crying for this time? Can't you see how foolish you're being? Why, just think of Mendel Beilis . . ."

She wouldn't listen to me, though. "Papa," she said, "you don't even know why I'm crying."

"Of course I do," I said. "How could I not know? You're crying for the house. You were born here, you grew up here—it's upsetting. Believe me, even if I weren't Tevye, even if I were someone else, I would still kiss these bare walls and empty shelves, I would get down on my knees and kiss the ground! It hurts me to part with every nook and cranny as much as it hurts you, you silly thing, you. Why, just look at that cat sitting like an orphan over the stove. It's only a dumb animal, it can't talk—but how can you help feeling sorry for it, being left all alone without a master . . ."

"Papa," she says. "There's someone you should be feeling even sorrier for."

"Why, who's that?" I say.

"It's the one person," says my Tsaytl, "who'll be left behind like a stone by the roadside when we're gone."

I had no idea who she meant. "What person?" I asked. "What stone? What are you yattering about?"

"Papa," she said, "I'm not yattering. I'm talking about our Chava."

I swear to you, hearing that name was like being dowsed with boiling water or clubbed on the head! I turned to my daughter in a fury and said, "What the devil does Chava have to do with this? I thought I told you that I never wanted to hear her mentioned again!"

Do you think that fazed her? Not my Tsaytl! Tevye's daughters are no pushovers. "Papa," she says, "instead of being so angry, why don't you think of what you yourself have always told us about human beings loving and pitying each other as a father does his own child?"

Did you ever hear anything like it? That made me see so red that I really blew my top. "You're talking to me about pity?" I said. "Where was her pity for me when I groveled like a dog before that damn priest and all but kissed his feet, with her sitting, I'll bet, right in the next room and hearing every word? Where was her pity when her poor mama, God rest her, lay here dead on the floor? Where was she then? Where was she all the nights I couldn't sleep because of her? Why, it makes me sick to this day just to think of what she did to us, of who she threw us over for . . . When, I ask you, did she ever pity us?"

I was in such a blind rage that I couldn't say another word—but don't think that scared Tevye's daughter! "But you've always told us, Papa," says my Tsaytl, "that even God must forgive a person who's honestly sorry for what he's done."

"Sorry?" I say. "It's too late for that! Once the branch tears itself from the tree, that's the end of it. Let the fallen leaf rot where it fell. I don't want to hear another word—*ad kan oymrim beshabbes hagodol.*"

Well, when she saw she was getting nowhere, because there's no outarguing Tevye, she threw herself at my feet and began kissing my hand. "Papa," she said, "I'll die if you turn her away again, like you did that time in the forest when you practically drove your horse over her and rode off . . ."

"What are you doing to me?" I said. "Why are you sucking my blood like this? Why are you torturing me?"

She wouldn't give up, though. She just kept clinging to my hand. "I'll die right here and now," she says, "if you don't forgive her! She's your daughter as much as I am!"

"But what do you want from me?" I say. "She's not my daughter anymore. She died long ago."

"She did not!" says Tsaytl. "She did not die and she is your daughter as much as ever, because the minute she heard we had to leave, she made up her mind to come with us. Whatever happens to us, she said to me, will happen to her too—if we're homeless, so will she be—and the proof of it, Papa, is, that's her bundle right there on the floor . . ."

She said it all in one breath, did my Tsaytl, pointed to a bundle tied with a red kerchief, and, before I could get in a word edgewise, threw open the door to the other room and called out—I swear to God she did, as I'm sitting here before you!—"Chava! . . ."

What can I tell you, my dear friend? It was just like in one of your books. Out of the other room she came, my daughter Chava, as unspoiled and beautiful as ever—a little more careworn perhaps, a little less bright-eyed, but with her head held high, like a queen. For a minute she just stared at me, the same as I did at her. Then she held out her hands, though all she could say was a single whispered word:

"Pa-pa . . ."

Please don't think any worse of me for having tears in my eyes now. If you suppose I shed any then, though, or was the least bit sentimental, you have another guess coming. Of course, what I felt like inside was something else. You're a father of children yourself, and you know as well as I do that no matter what a child may have done, when it stands there looking right through you and says "Papa" . . . well, go be a hero and tell it to disappear! Still, the blood went to my head when I thought of the fine trick my Chava had played on us . . . and of that Chvedka Galagan, may he roast . . . and that damn priest . . . and all my grief . . . and my poor dead Golde . . . You tell me: how, how can you ever forget such a thing? And yet on the other hand, how can you not? A child is a child . . . *kerakheym ov al bonim* . . . when God Himself is an *eyl erekh apoyim,* a long-suffering Lord, how can a man harden his heart? And especially since she was sorry for all she had done and wanted only to return to her father and her God . . .

What do you say, Pani Sholem Aleichem? You're a Jew who writes books and gives the whole world advice—what should Tevye have done? Taken her in his arms, hugged her and kissed her, and told her, as we say on Yom Kippur, *solakhti kidvorekho*—come to me, you're my own flesh and blood? Or turned a deaf ear as I did once before and said, *lekh-lekho*—get lost and stay lost! Put yourself in Tevye's place and tell me honestly, in plain language, what you would have done . . .

Well, if you can't answer that right off the bat, you're welcome to think about it, but meanwhile I have to be off, because my grandchildren are getting impatient. Just look at them looking at their grandpa! I want you to know that grandchildren are a thousand times more precious and lovable than children. *Bonim uvney vonim*, your own children's children—that's nothing to sneeze at, you know! Be well, then, and don't hold it against me if I've run on a little too long—it will give you something to write about. If God has no objections, I'm sure we'll meet again someday . . .

What did you say? I didn't finish the story of the Amalekites? I never told you if they smashed my windows? Well, as a matter of fact they didn't, because it was decided to leave that up to me. "They're your windows, Tevel," said Ivan Paparilo, "and you might as well smash them yourself. As long as those damn officials can see there's been a pogrom . . . And now, bring out the samovar and let's all have tea. And if you'd be so kind as to donate half a bucket of vodka to the village, we'll all drink to your health, because you're a clever Jew and a man of God, you are . . ."

I ask you, Pani Sholem Aleichem, you're a person who writes books—is Tevye right or not when he says that there's a great God above and that a man must never lose heart while he lives? And that's especially true of a Jew, and most especially of a Jew who knows a Hebrew letter when he sees one . . . No, you can rack your brains and be as clever as you like—there's no getting around the fact that we Jews are the best and smartest people. *Mi ke'amkho yisro'eyl goy ekhod*, as the Prophet says—how can you even compare a goy and a Jew? Anyone can be a goy, but a Jew must be born one. *Ashrekho yisro'eyl*—it's a lucky thing I was, then, because otherwise how would I ever know what it's like to be homeless and wander all over the world without resting my head on the same pillow two nights running? You see, ever since I was given that lesson in Lekh-Lekho, I've been on the go; there hasn't been a place I could point to and say, "Tevye, we're here; now sit down and relax." But Tevye asks no questions; if he's told to keep moving, he does. Today, Pani Sholem Aleichem, we met on the train, but tomorrow may find us in Yehupetz, and next year in Odessa,

or in Warsaw, or maybe even in America . . . unless, that is, the
Almighty looks down on us and says, "Guess what, children! I've
decided to send you my Messiah!" I don't even care if He does it
just to spite us, as long as He's quick about it, that old God of ours!
And in the meantime, be well and have a good trip. Say hello for
me to all our Jews and tell them wherever they are, not to worry:
the old God of Israel still lives! . . .

(1914, 1916)

The Railroad Stories

Stories

TALES OF A COMMERCIAL TRAVELER

TO THE READER

▼

I do a lot of traveling. You'll find me on the road nearly eleven months of the year. Generally I go by train; most often third class; and almost always to towns and villages where there are Jews, since my business doesn't take me to places Jews are barred from.

My goodness, the things one sees traveling! It's a pity I'm not a writer. And yet come to think of it, what makes me say I'm not? What's a writer, after all? Anyone can be one, and especially in a hodgepodge like our Yiddish. What's the big fuss about? You pick up a pen and you write!

Come to think of it again, though, writing is not for everyone. We should all stick to what we work at for a living, that's my opinion, because each of us has to make one. And if you don't work at anything, that's work too.

Still, since we travelers often spend whole days on end sitting and looking out the window until we want to bang our heads against the wall, one day I had an idea: I went and bought myself a pencil and a notebook and began jotting down everything I saw and heard on my trips. I don't mean to boast, but you can see for yourself that I've gathered quite a lot of material. Why, it might take you a whole year just to read it all. What, I wondered, should I do with it? It would be a crime to throw it away. Why not, I thought, publish it in a newspaper or a book? God knows that worse stuff gets into print.

And so I sat down and sorted out my goods, throwing out whatever wasn't up to scratch and keeping only the very best quality, which I divided up into stories—story number one, story number two, and so on, giving each a proper name to make it more professional. I have no idea if I'll turn a profit on this venture or end up losing my shirt. Quite frankly, I'll be happy to break even.

But whatever possessed me, you ask, to invest in such a business in the first place? For the life of me, I can't tell you the answer. Maybe it was a ridiculous thing to do, but there's no going back on it now. I did take one precaution, though, and that's against the critics, because I've kept my real name a secret. They can try guessing it till they burst! Let them criticize, let them laugh at me, let them climb the walls all they want—it will bother me as much as a catcall on Purim bothers Haman. After all, I'm no scribbler, no ten-o'clock-scholar begging for a job—I'm a commercial traveler and I pay my own way!

COMPETITORS

▼

Always, right in the middle of the worst pandemonium, when Jews are pushing to get in and out and fighting for each seat as though it were in the front row of the synagogue, there the two of them are: him and her.

He's squat, dark, unkempt, with a cataract in one eye. She's redheaded, gaunt, and pockmarked. Both are dressed in old rags, both have patches on their shoes, and both are carrying the same thing: a basket. His basket is full of braided rolls, hard-boiled eggs, oranges, and bottled seltzer water. Her basket is full of braided rolls, hard-boiled eggs, oranges, and bottled seltzer water too.

Sometimes he turns up with bags of red or black cherries and green grapes sour as vinegar. Then she also turns up with red or black cherries and green grapes sour as vinegar.

Both always appear together, fight to get through the same door of the same car, and give the same sales spiel, though with different manners of speaking. His is liquid, as though his tongue were melting in his mouth. Hers is lisping, as though her tongue kept getting in her way.

Maybe you think they undersell one another, vie for customers, war over prices? Not a chance! They charge the same amount for everything. The competition between them consists solely of seeing who can make you feel sorrier for whom. Both beg you to have pity on their five orphaned children (his five are motherless, hers have no father) while looking you right in the eye; both shove their goods in your face; and both talk such a blue streak at you that you end up buying something whether you meant to or not.

The trouble is that all their wheedling and whining leaves you confused. Whose customer should you be, his or hers? Because if you think you can get around it by buying from each, they quickly disabuse you of the notion. "Look here, mister," they tell you, "you either buy from one or the other. You can't dance at two weddings at once!"

Worse yet, try to be fair and take turns, once him and once her, and you'll get it from them both. "What's the matter, mister," she'll say, "don't you like my dress today?" Or else he says to you, "Mister! Just last week you bought from me. Do you mean to tell me my goods poisoned you?"

If you harbor humanitarian sentiments, moreover, and start preaching to them that each is a human being who has to eat—in a word, that they should live and let live, as the English like to say— they'll answer you right back, and not in English either, but in a simple Yiddish that may sound a wee bit cryptic though it's really quite understandable: "Brother! You can't ride one ass to two fairs!"

You see how it is, my dear friends. There's no pleasing everyone. It's hopeless even to try, and the more you play the peacemaker, the less peaceful things become. That's something I know from experience. In fact, I could tell you a good one about how once I was foolish enough to butt in on a married couple in order to make up between them—the outcome of which was that I took it on the chin from my own wife! I don't want to digress, though. True, it happens even in business that you sometimes put aside one thing to talk about all kinds of others, in fact, about everything under the sun; but we had better get back to our story.

One rainy day in autumn when the sky was weeping buckets and a black pall hung over everything, the station was crawling

with people. Passengers kept piling in and out, all of them hurry-
ing, all of them jostling, and most of all, of course, our Jews.
Everyone was climbing over everyone with suitcases and packages
and bundles made of bedclothes. And the noise, the sheer commotion—what a racket! Just then, in the midst of all this bedlam,
there they were: him and her, both loaded down with edibles as
usual. As usual, too, both hurled themselves through the same
door of the train at once. Only then . . . goodness me, what had
happened? Suddenly both baskets were on the ground and all the
rolls and eggs and oranges and seltzer bottles were rolling about
in the mud to an uproar of shouts, shrieks, tears, and curses
mingled with the laughter of the conductors and the din of the
passengers. A bell rang, the train whistled, and in another minute
we were off.

There was a babble of voices in the car. Our fellow Israelites
were giving their tongues an airing, everyone gabbling together
like women in a synagogue or geese in the marketplace. So many
different conversations were going on all at once that one could
only make out snatches of each.

"What a massacre of rolls!"

"What a pogrom of eggs!"

"What did he have against those oranges?"

"Why ask? A goy is a goy!"

"How much would you say all that food was worth?"

"It serves them right! It's time they stopped getting on everyone's nerves."

"But what do you want from them? A Jew has to make a living."

"Ha ha, that's a good one!" said a thick bass voice. "What Jews
don't call making a living!"

"What's wrong with how Jews make a living?" piped a squeaky
voice. "Do you have any better ways to make one? Why don't you
tell us about them!"

"I wasn't talking to you, young fellow!" the bass voice thundered.

"You weren't? But I'm talking to you. Do you have any better
ways to make a living? . . . Well, why don't you say something?
Speak up!"

"Will somebody please tell me what this young man wants from
me?"

"What do I want from you? You don't like how Jews make a
living, so I'm asking you to tell us a better way. Let's hear it!"

"Just look how he's leeched on to me!"

"Shhh, all of you! Stop talking about it. Here she comes."

"Who?"

"The basket woman."

"Where? Where is our beauty queen?"

"Right over there!"

Pockmarked and redheaded, her eyes puffy with tears, she struggled through the passengers looking for a place until she finally sat down on her overturned basket, hid her face in her tattered shawl, and resumed crying silently into it.

An odd hush came over the car. Everyone stopped talking. No one let out a peep. Except, that is, for one person, who called out in a heavy bass voice:

"Jews! Why so quiet?"

"What's there to shout about?" someone asked.

"Let's pass the hat around!"

So help me! And do you know who the kind heart was? None other than the same character who had laughed at how Jews make a living, a queer-looking fellow with a queer-looking flat, glossy-brimmed cap and blue-tinted glasses that hid his eyes completely: there simply were none to be seen above his fat, fleshy bulb of a nose. Without further ado he took the cap from his head, threw a few silver coins into it, and went from one passenger to another, booming in his bass voice:

"Give what you can, children! All donations are welcome. *Darovanomu konyu vzuby nye smotryat*—that means, according to Rashi, that we won't look a gift horse in the mouth."

Folks began rummaging through their pockets and purses, and all sorts of coins, both silver and copper, were soon clinking in the cap. There was even a Christian there, a Russian with high boots and a silver chain around his neck, who yawned, crossed himself, and gave something too. In the whole car one passenger alone refused to part with a kopeck—and that, of all people, was the very same individual who had taken up the cudgel for Jewish livings, an intellectual-looking young man with pasty cheeks, a pointy yellow beard, and gold pince-nez on his nose. You could see he was one of those types with rich parents and in-laws who travel third class to economize.

"Young fellow," said the Jew with the blue glasses and big nose, "let's have something for the hat."

"I'm not giving," said our intellectual.

"Why not?"

"Because. It's a matter of principle with me."

"You didn't have to tell me that."

"Why not?"

"Because *vedno pana po kholavakh*—that means, according to Rashi, that you can tell a rotten apple by its peel."

The young man flared up so that he almost lost his pince-nez. "You're an ignoramus!" he squeaked furiously at the man with the blue glasses. "You're a cheeky, insolent, impudent, impertinent illiterate!"

"Thank God I'm all of that and not a two-legged animal that oinks," answered the man with the big nose in a surprisingly good-natured tone of voice before turning to the puffy-eyed woman and saying, "There, there, Auntie, don't you think you've cried enough? You'll ruin your pretty eyes if you don't stop. Here, hold out your hands and I'll fill them with a bit of spare change."

A strange woman if ever there was one! You might have thought that, seeing all the cash, she would have thanked him from the bottom of her heart. In fact she did nothing of the sort. Instead of thanks, a volley of oaths spewed forth from her. She was a veritable fountain of them.

"It's all his fault. I hope he breaks his neck! I pray to God he breaks every bone in his body! He's to blame for everything—I only wish, dear Father in heaven, that everything happens to him! He shouldn't live to cross his own threshold! He should die a hundred times from a fire, from a fever, from an earthquake, from a plague, from an ill wind that carries him away! He should croak! He should burst! He should dry up like a puddle! He should swell like a dead fish!"

Good Lord, where did one person get so many curses from? It was a lucky thing that the man with the blue glasses interrupted her and said:

"That's enough of your kind wishes, my good woman. Why don't you tell us why the conductors had it in for you?"

The woman looked at him with her puffy eyes.

"I only hope he gets a stroke! He was afraid I'd take his customers away, so he tried pushing ahead of me, so I elbowed him out of the way, so he grabbed my basket from behind, so I started to scream, so a policeman came along and winked to the conductors, so they threw both our baskets in the mud. God turn his blood to mud! I swear to you, may I hope to die if I've ever been bothered before or had a hair harmed on my head in all the years I've been working this line. Do you know why that is? It's not from the milk of human kindness, believe me. He should only get a box in the ear for each free roll and hard-boiled egg I've handed out in that station! Everyone, from top to bottom, has to get his share of the pie. I hope to God they get all of it some day: one of them consumption, another a fever, another the cholera! The chief conductor takes what he wants, and the other conductors help themselves too to a roll, or an egg, or an orange. What can I tell you? Would you believe that even the stoker, a pox on his head, thinks he has a bite coming? I wish his ears were bitten off! He keeps threatening to rat on me to the policeman unless I give him something to eat. If only he knew, may the gout get his bones, that the policeman gets a cut too. Every Sunday I slip him a bagful of oranges to buy him off for the week. And don't think he doesn't choose the biggest, the sweetest, the juiciest fruit . . ."

"Auntie," said the man with the blue glasses, interrupting her again, "judging by the volume of business you do, you must be making a mint."

"What are you talking about?" the woman shot back as though her honor were impugned. "I barely manage to meet the overhead. I've been taking such a skinning that I'm at starvation's door."

"Then what do you go on for?"

"What do you want me to do, steal for a living? I have five children at home, may he get five ulcers in his stomach, and I'm a sick woman too, he should only, dear God, lie sick in the poorhouse until the end of next year! Just look how he's killed the business, buried it in the ground—it's a pity he wasn't buried with it. And what a good business it was, too. I couldn't have asked for a better one."

"A good business?"

"As good as gold! Why, I was raking it in."

"But, Auntie, didn't you just tell me you were starving?"

"That's because fifty percent goes to the conductors and the stationmaster and the policeman every Sunday. Do you take me for a gold mine? A buried treasure? A bank robber?"

The man with the blue glasses and the fleshy nose was getting exasperated. "Auntie!" he said. "You're making me dizzy!"

"*I'm* making you? My troubles are making you—they should only make a corpse out of him! I hope to God he's ruined just as he ruined me! Why, he was nothing but a tailor, a needle pusher; he didn't earn enough to buy the water to boil his kasha in. It made him green with envy to see how well I was doing, the eyes should fall out of his head, and that I brought home enough to eat, he should only be eaten by worms, and that I was supporting five orphaned children with my basket, may he swallow a basket of salt that turns to rocks in his belly! That's when he went, I hope he goes and drops dead, and bought a basket too, may I soon buy the shrouds for his funeral! 'What do you call this?' I asked him. 'A basket,' he says. 'And just what do you intend to do with it?' I asked him. 'The same thing that you do,' he says. 'What are you talking about?' I asked him. 'What I'm talking about,' he says, 'is that I have five children who have to eat too, and who aren't going to be fed by you . . .' What do you say to that? And ever since then, as you've seen for yourselves, he follows me around with his basket, may he be followed by the Angel of Death, and takes away my customers, I wish he'd be taken by the Devil, and steals the bread from my mouth—oh, dear sweet God, You should knock the teeth out of his!"

That gave the man with the blue glasses an idea that had in fact occurred to the rest of us. "But why do you both have to work the same train?"

The woman gave him a puffy-eyed stare. "What should we do, then?"

"Split up. The line is big enough for both of you."

"You mean leave him?"

"Leave who?"

"My second husband."

"What second husband?"

The pockmarked red face turned even redder.

"What do you mean, what second husband? The schlimazel we're talking about. A black day it was that I married him!"

We nearly fell out of our seats.

"That man you're competing with is your second husband?"

"Who did you think he was, my first? Eh! If only my first, God bless him, were still alive . . ."

So she said, the basket woman, in a singsong voice, and started to tell us about her first husband. But who was listening? Everyone was talking, everyone was joking, everyone was making wisecracks, and everyone was laughing till his sides split . . .

Maybe you know what was so funny?

(1909)

THE HAPPIEST MAN IN ALL KODNY

▼

The best time to travel by train is . . . shall I tell you? In autumn, right after Sukkos.

It's neither too hot nor too cold then, and you needn't look out all the time at a gray sky sobbing on a gloomy, sulking earth. And if it does rain and the drops strike the window and trickle down the steamy pane like tears, you can sit like a lord in the third-class car with a few other privileged souls like yourself and watch a distant wagon as it labors in the mud. On it, covered with a sack and folded nearly into three, huddles one of God's creatures who takes out all his misery on another of God's creatures, a poor horse, while you thank the good Lord that you're in human company with a solid roof over your head. I don't know about you, but autumn after Sukkos is my favorite time to travel.

The first thing I look for is a seat. If I've managed to find one, and better yet, if it's by a window on the right, I tell you, I'm king. I can take out my tobacco pouch, light up as many cigarettes as I please, and look around to see who my fellow passengers are and which of them I can talk a bit of business with. Usually, I'm sorry to say, they're packed together like herring in a barrel. Everywhere there are beards, noses, hats, stomachs, faces. But a man worth knowing behind the face? Sometimes there isn't even one . . . Yet wait a minute: look at that queer fellow sitting by himself in the corner—there's something special about him. I have a good eye for such types. Show me a hundred ordinary men and I'll pick out the one oddball right away.

At first glance, that is, the person in question was a perfectly unremarkable-looking individual of a type that's a dime a dozen, what we call where I come from a "three-hundred-and-sixty-five-days-a-year Jew." The one strange thing about him was his clothes: his coat was not exactly a coat, the frock beneath it was not exactly a frock, the hat on his head was not exactly a hat, the skullcap under it was not exactly a skullcap, and the umbrella he held in his hand was not exactly an umbrella, although it was not exactly a broomstick either. A most unusual getup.

What struck me most about him, though, was not what he was wearing but rather the animation with which, unable to sit still for a minute, he took in his surroundings on all sides—and above all, the jolly, lively, radiant expression on his blissful face. Either, I thought, his winning number has come up in a lottery, or else he's made a good match for his daughter, or else he's just enrolled a son in the Russian high school that the boy had the luck to get into. A minute didn't pass without his jumping from his seat, peering out the window, saying out loud to himself, "Are we there? No, not yet," and sitting down again a bit nearer to me than before, a jolly, radiant, happy-looking fellow.

At heart, you should know, I'm as averse as the next man to anyone prying into my business and making the who, what, and when of it his affair. I hold with the opinion that if a person has something to get off his chest, he doesn't need to be prompted. And indeed this proved to be the case, because after the second station the lively Jew moved even closer to me, indeed, so close that his mouth was directly opposite my nose, and inquired:

"And where might you be bound for?"

I could easily tell from how he asked, and how he looked around him, and how he scratched himself beneath his hat that hearing my destination concerned him less than telling me his. And I, for my part, was willing to oblige, so that rather than answer his question I asked him one of my own:

"And where might you be bound for?"

That was all it took to set him off.

"Me? For Kodny. Have you ever heard of Kodny? That's where I'm from, it is. It isn't far from here, just three stations away. That

is, I get off at the third station after this one. From there it's still
an hour and a half by cart. That is, we call it an hour and a half,
but it's really a good two, in fact a little more, and that's in the best
of cases, if the road's in good shape and there's a private carriage
to take you. I already telegraphed ahead for one. That is, I sent a
cable that a carriage should be at the station. Do you think I did it
for myself? Don't get ideas about me! I don't mind sharing pot-
luck in a plain wagon with half a dozen other passengers, and if
there's none to be had, taking my umbrella in one hand and my
things in the other and hiking into town on my two feet. Car-
riages, you understand, are a bit beyond my means. In fact, as far
as business is concerned, it isn't so golden that I couldn't just as
well stay home. What do you say to that, eh?"

The fellow paused, let out a sigh, and began to speak again in a
whisper right into my ear, though not before first looking all
around him to see if anyone was listening.

"I'm not traveling alone. I have a professor with me, I do. What
am I doing with a professor? Well, it's like this. Have you ever
heard of Kashevarevke? There's a village called that, Kashevarevke, and there's a rich Jew who lives there, a man who made
himself a pile. Maybe you've heard of him: Borodenko is the
name, Itzikl Borodenko. What do you say to a name like that, eh?
It's a goy's name, not a Jew's. You know what, though? You can
have a goy's name and you can have a Jew's, it's not the name you
have that counts, it's the money. And Borodenko has lots of it, to
put it mildly. The word in Kodny is that he's worth half a
million—and if you were to press me on that, I'd own up to the
other half too. The fact is that he is, you should pardon the
expression, such a so-and-so that he may even be sitting on two
million. You be the judge, because, though I've never seen you
before in my life, I can tell, I can, that you're a man who gets
about more than I do. Tell me the truth, then: have you ever
heard the name Borodenko mentioned in the same breath with
the slightest act of generosity—a contribution to charity, something done for one's fellow Jews, anything? If there ever was such
a thing, the news still hasn't reached Kodny. Well, I'm not God's
bookkeeper and it's easy to be free with someone else's bank account. It's just that I'm not talking philanthropy; I'm talking humanity, that's what I'm talking. If God has been good enough to
let you afford a home visit by a professor of medicine, what harm

would it do you if someone else were to benefit too? No one's asking for your money, only for a good word—why be a wild man about it? Listen to a lovely story.

"It so happened that word reached us in Kodny (there's nothing we Kodny Jews don't know) that the daughter of this Itzikl Borodenko from Kashevarevke, God spare us, was ill. And what do you think was the matter with her? A lot of nothing, a love affair! She had fallen for some Russian and tried poisoning herself when he jilted her. (There's nothing we Kodny Jews don't know!) All this happened just yesterday, mind you. Right away they ran to bring a professor, the biggest there is. What's a professor more or less to a man like Borodenko? Well, that set me to thinking. The professor wasn't going to stay there forever; today or tomorrow he would go home; and when he did he'd have to pass through our station—that is, close to Kodny. Why shouldn't he stop to change trains there and pay us—I mean me—a quick call? You see, I have a sick child at home, it shouldn't happen to you. What exactly is wrong with him? All I can tell you is that it must be something internal. A cough, thank God, he doesn't have. And as far as his heart is concerned, nothing hurts him there either. So what's the problem? There's not a drop of blood in his cheeks and he's as weak as a fly. That's because he doesn't eat a thing. But not a thing. How can someone not eat anything, you ask? But he doesn't, it's a fact. Now and then he drinks a glass of milk, but only when he's forced to. We have to get down on our knees and beg him, we do! He won't even swallow a spoon of soup or a crumb of bread, let alone meat. Why, he can't stand the sight of meat, it makes him turn his head away. He's been like that ever since he spat up blood. That happened over the summer, pray God it doesn't happen again. There was blood just once, but a lot of it. Since then, thank goodness, there's been no more. I only hope it keeps up. You can't imagine how weak he is, though. He can barely stand on his feet. And one other tiny little thing: the boy runs a fever, he's burning up, he is, as though he had the smallpox! That's been going on since late spring: a hundred and two, a hundred and three, nothing makes it go away. I've taken him to the doctors more times than I can count. But what do our doctors know about anything? He needs to eat, he needs a change of air— that's all they ever say. What do they expect me to do? Eating is something he won't even hear about. And as for air, where am I supposed to find it? Air in Kodny? Ha ha, that's a good one! It's a nice little place, Kodny is. A nice Jewish community. We have, knock wood, a few Jews, we have a synagogue, we have a study house, we have a rabbi, we have everything. In fact, there are only two things that God forgot to give us: a chance to make a living and some air. Well, as far as a living goes, we've worked out a system: we all, the Lord be praised, manage to make one from each other. And air? For air we go to the manor grounds; you'll find as much of it as you want there. Once, when Kodny belonged to the Poles, you couldn't set foot in the manor. The Polish squires didn't permit it. Or rather, not the squires themselves, but their dogs. Ever since the manor has been in Jewish hands, though, the dogs are gone and it's a totally different place. Why, it's a pleasure to visit! There are still squires there—big landlords, but at least they're Jewish ones. They speak Yiddish the same as you and I do, and take an interest in Jewish things, and show a friendly face to a Jew. When it comes to Jews, I tell you, they're no different from the rest of us! Not that you should think they're such big saints. You don't see them any more in our synagogue than you do in our bathhouse, and if breaking the Sabbath laws bothers them, they haven't given any sign of it yet. Eating a chicken cooked in butter doesn't frighten them either . . . and I'm not even talking about things like going beardless or hatless, because that's nothing out of the ordinary these days: even in Kodny, thanks be to God, we have our share of young folks whose heads have only the hair on them. To tell you the truth, though, we can't complain about our manor owners. Our Jewish squires don't shirk their duties toward us. On the contrary, they're as generous as can be. Comes every autumn, they send a hundred sacks of potatoes for the poor, and comes every winter, straw to burn in the oven. Every Passover they give money to the Matsoh Fund. Not long ago they even donated the bricks for a new synagogue. Why go on? They're fine, considerate people, one couldn't wish for more from them—if only that chicken weren't cooked in butter, ai, that poor chicken! . . . Don't get me wrong, though. God knows I don't mean to criticize. Why should I have anything against them? Far from it! You won't find them selling me short. Reb Alter (my name is Alter, it is) is tops in their book. Whenever they need anything in the way of things Jewish—a new calendar for the New Year, for example, or matsos for Passover, or a lulav and esrog for

Sukkos—they send for me. And in my wife's store (my wife has a store, she does) there are no better customers for salt and pepper and matches and whatnot. Those are our manor owners . . . while as for their children, the university students—why, there's nothing they wouldn't do for my son! In the summer, when they come home on vacation from St. Petersburg, they teach him whatever he asks them to, they spend whole days with him sitting over some book—and books, I want you to know, are all that boy lives and breathes for! He loves them more than his own father and mother, I'm sorry to say. What I mean is that books will be the death of him, they will. All his troubles began with them, even if my wife still insists that everything started with his call-up from the army. What's she talking about, I ask you? He forgot all about that call-up long ago. Not that it matters: let it be the books, let it be the call-up—the fact remains that I have a sick boy at home, may we all be blessed with good health, who's fading away before my very eyes. God in heaven make him well again . . ."

The man's beaming face clouded over for a second, but no more. A moment later the sun came back out, the clouds vanished, and he was as radiant as before. The smile once more on his lips and the sparkle back in his eyes, he went on with his story:

"Well now, where were we? Yes. And so I made up my mind to run over to Kashevarevke, to Itzikl Borodenko—that's the rich Jew I was telling you about. Naturally, I didn't set out empty-handed just like that. I took a letter with me from our rabbi, I did. (Our rabbi in Kodny is known all over.) A lovely letter it was, too: 'Inasmuch as God in His beneficence has enabled you to bring home a professor in your hour of need, and inasmuch as our Alter's son, may you be spared such sorrow, is all but on his deathbed, may your heart be so moved to pity him that you will trouble yourself to prevail upon the aforementioned professor to pay a call on the sick boy for a quarter of an hour between trains on his way home, which must pass close to Kodny. May the Lord requite you . . .' and so on and so forth. A lovely letter."

Suddenly there was a blast of the whistle, our train came to a halt, and my queerly dressed Jew leaped up and exclaimed:

"Eh, another station! I'd better have a look at the first-class car to see how my professor is doing. I'll tell you the rest when I get back."

He returned beaming more brightly than ever. If I weren't afraid of sounding sacrilegious, I would say he was in a state of divine grace. He leaned forward toward my ear and said to me in a whisper, as if he were afraid of waking someone:

"He's sleeping, my professor. God grant he sleeps soundly, so that his mind will be clear when we reach Kodny . . . Only where was I? Oh, yes, in Kashevarevke.

"I arrived in Kashevarevke, that is, went straight to the man's home, and rang the doorbell once, twice, three times. Out comes a fellow without a hair on his chin and with two blubber lips that he keeps licking like a cat and says to me in Goyish, '*Chto nada?*' 'I should say there is,' I said to him—and in Yiddish, mind you. 'If there weren't, why drag myself here all the way from Kodny?'

"He listened to that, still licking his chops, shook his head, and said, 'We can't let you in now, because the professor's here.' 'But that's just it,' I said. 'It's because the professor is here that I'm here too.' 'What does someone like you want with a professor?' he asks. That was all I needed, to have to tell him the whole sob story! So I gave him our rabbi's letter and I said, 'It's kind of you to take the time to chat with me when you're in there and I'm out here in the rain, but please take this document and deliver it straight to the master of the house.' He took it, he did, and left me standing on the outside side of the door, still waiting to be asked in. I waited half an hour. I waited an hour. I waited two hours. It was pouring cats and dogs and there I was, totally out in the cold. I tell you, it was beginning to annoy me—though not so much for my sake as for our rabbi's. After all, that letter wasn't written by someone who was born yesterday. (Our rabbi in Kodny is known all over!) Well, I gave that bellpull a few good yanks. Out comes Blubber Lips again, this time looking fit to kill. 'The nerve of a Jew,' he says, 'to ring like that!' 'The nerve of a Jew,' I say, 'to let a Jew stand two hours in the rain!' With which I made as if to step inside—wham, bang, I'll be a monkey's uncle if he didn't slam the door in my face! What was I supposed to do now? It wasn't exactly a cheerful situation. To go home with nothing to show for it would not have been very nice. In the first place, it would have looked bad: I happen to be something of a respected citizen in Kodny, far from a no-account, in any case . . . And besides, it broke my heart to think of my poor son . . .

"Well, God is great, as they say. Just then I took a look and what did I see but a droshky pulled by four horses draw up right at the door. I went over to ask the coachman whose it was, and he said it was Borodenko's, come to take the professor to the train. In that case, I thought, things are beginning to look up. Way up, in fact! Before I knew it the door of the house opened and there he was— I mean the professor: an elderly little man, but with a face . . . what can I tell you? An angel, an angel from heaven! After him came the rich Jew, Itzikl Borodenko, as bareheaded as the day he was born, and lastly Blubber Lips himself carrying the professor's satchel. You should have seen that man worth maybe over a million, God help me, with his two google eyes and his hands in the pockets of an ordinary coat just like we wear in Kodny! God in heaven, I thought, is this who You give the millions to? Go argue with God, though! . . . Well, Borodenko saw me standing there, gave me a googly look, and said, 'What do you want?' 'It's like this,' I said. 'I've brought you a letter from our rabbi, I have.' 'What rabbi is that?' he asks. Would you believe it? He didn't even know what rabbi I meant! 'From the Rabbi of Kodny,' I said. 'That's where I'm from, it is. I've come from Kodny,' I said, 'to ask the professor,' I said, 'if he would be kind enough to see my son,' I said, 'for a quarter of an hour between trains. I wouldn't wish it on you,' I said, 'but I have a son who's practically at death's door.' That's exactly what I said to him, I'm not making up a single word of it. What was my line of reasoning? My line of reasoning was, here the man's had a tragedy, his daughter took poison, who knows but it touched a heartstring somewhere that will make him pity a poor father like me. Would you like to know what kind of pity he had? He didn't say a blessed word to me; he just googled Blubber Lips as if to say, 'How about getting rid of this pest of a Jew for me, eh?' Meanwhile my professor had taken a seat in the droshky with his satchel. In another minute I could kiss him good-bye. What was I to do? I saw I had better act fast. It's now or never, I thought; whatever will be will be, but the child must be saved—and so I got up all my nerve and whoops! flung myself at the horses' feet . . . What can I tell you? That I enjoyed those nags breathing down on me? I can't say I did. I can't even tell you how long I went on lying there or if I went on lying there at all. Maybe I didn't. All I know is that in less time than it's taken me to tell you all this, the old professor was standing over me and saying, '*Chto takoye, golubchik?'* He told me to speak up and not be afraid. So I picked myself off the ground and told him everything, with Borodenko standing right there and looking at me cross-eyed. Speaking Russian, you know, is not my strong suit—but God gave me strength and the words came by themselves. I bared my heart to him, I didn't keep a thing back. 'It's like this, Professor,' I said. 'Maybe you were sent by Providence to make me a gift of my child, the one and only son left out of six that were born to me, may he live to a ripe old age. If money is the problem, I can let you have twenty-five rubles—that is, please don't think that they're mine, because wherever would I get so much cash from? They're my wife's, she put them aside to buy stock for her store the next time she went to town. But you can have them,' I said, 'all twenty-five of them. My wife's store can go to the Devil as long as you save the boy's life!' And I began to open my coat to take out the twenty-five rubles. *'Nichevo!'* he says, that little old professor, laying a hand on my arm and helping me into the droshky—may I live to see my son as healthy as every word I say to you is true! I ask you: is an Itzikl Borodenko worth the little finger of a man like that? Why, he would have watched me die in cold blood, he would have! God Almighty came to the rescue in the nick of time, but just suppose that He hadn't . . . What do you say to that, eh?"

There was a bustle of passengers in the car and my Jew all but ran to the conductor.

"Kodny?"

"Kodny."

"Well, be well, and have a good trip, and don't tell a soul who I'm with. I don't want anyone in Kodny to know that I've got a professor. They'll all come running if they do!"

And with those last, confidential words to me, he was gone.

A few minutes later, though, while the train was still at a standstill, I caught a glimpse through the window of a rickety buggy and a pair of careworn, ragged gray horses. In the buggy sat a little old man with a gray beard and youthful red cheeks. Across from him, half in and half out of the vehicle, as though hanging from it by a thread, sat my strange Jew. He was rocking back and forth, his face beaming, his eyes glued so hard to the professor that they were all but popping from their sockets.

It's a pity I'm not a photographer and don't travel with a camera. It would have been a great thing to have taken that Jew's picture. Let the world see what a happy man looks like—the happiest man in all Kodny.

(1909)

BARANOVICH STATION

▼

This time there were no more than a few dozen of us Jews, and we sat in the third-class car in comparative comfort. That is, whoever had found a seat had one; the other passengers stood leaning against the walls of the compartments and joined in the conversation from there. And what lively conversation it was! As usual, everyone was talking at once. It was early in the day. We had all had a good night's sleep, said our morning prayers, grabbed a bite more or less to eat, and even managed to light up a few cigarettes, and we were all in the mood to talk—very much so, in fact. About what? About anything and everything. Everyone tried to think of some fresh, juicy item that would make all the others sit up and listen, but no one was able to hold the stage for long. The subject changed every minute. No sooner did it light on the recent harvest—that is, the wheat and oats crop—than it shifted, don't ask me why, to the war with Japan, while after barely five minutes of fighting the Japanese, we moved on to the Revolution of 1905. From the Revolution we passed to the Constitution, and from the Constitution it was but a short step to the pogroms, the massacres of Jews, the new anti-Semitic legislation, the expulsion from the villages, the mass flight to America, and all the other trials and tribulations that you hear about these fine days: bankruptcies, expropriations, military emergencies, executions, starvation, cholera, Purishkevich, Azef . . .

"A-z-ef!"

The name of that secret police spy who had informed on so many revolutionaries only needed to be mentioned for the whole car to be thrown into a turmoil: Azef, and more Azef, and still more Azef, and Azef once again.

"Mind you, you'll excuse me for saying so, but you're all a lot of cattle, you are! What's so special about Ashev? What bunkum! The whole world's up in arms about him, but who the Devil is he? A young punk, a no-good bum, a nobody, a stool pigeon, a nothing, a big fat zero! If you'd like, I can tell you a story about a stool pigeon, and a hometown boy from Kaminka at that, who makes Ashev look pale by comparison!"

These words were uttered by one of the standees who loomed over us from his place against a wall. I glanced up to have a look at him and saw a generously proportioned individual with a good silk cap on his head, twinkling eyes, a rosy, freckled face, and no front teeth. That is, his two front incisors were missing, which was apparently why he whistled when he spoke, so that "Azef" came out sounding like "Ashev."

I took a liking to the fellow right away. I liked the broad girth of him, the way he talked, even the names he called us. In fact, I like such Jews so much that I'm actually jealous of them.

Having been unexpectedly branded as cattle by the Jew from Kaminka, the whole car was as dumbfounded for a moment as if a bucket of cold water had been poured over everyone's head. It didn't take long, however, for the passengers to recover, exchange a few glances, and say to the Kaminka Jew:

"You want to be asked to tell us a story? All right, we're asking! Tell us what happened in Kaminka, we're curious. Only, what are you standing for? Why don't you have a seat? There aren't any, you say? Jews! Shove over a bit! Make room, please."

Whereupon all of us, though we were already squeezed tightly together, squeezed together even more to make room for the Kaminka Jew. He sat himself broadly down, spreading out his knees like a godfather at a circumcision when the baby is placed in his lap, pushed back the cap on his head, rolled up his sleeves, and commenced in his broad manner of speaking:

"Listen well, my dear friends, because what I'm about to tell you, I want you to know, is not some opera or fairy tale. It's a true story, mind you, that took place right in Kaminka. My own father, God rest him, told it to me himself, and he heard it more than once from his father. I've heard it said that the whole thing was even written down in an old chronicle that was burned long ago. You can laugh all you like, but I tell you it's a crime it was, because it had some fine stories in it—a sight better than what's printed in your magazines and storybooks these days.

"In a nutshell, it happened in the reign of Nikolai the First, back in the days of the gauntlet. But what are you smiling at? Do you know what the gauntlet meant? The gauntlet meant getting flogged while you ran it. You still don't know what it was? In that case, I'd better spell it out for you. Just imagine, then: two rows of soldiers with iron maces stand facing each other, and you go for a little stroll between them some twenty times or more, and in your birthday suit, mind you, while they do what the rabbi did in the schoolroom when you weren't paying attention to your lessons . . . Do you know what running the gauntlet is now? Then we're ready to begin.

"Once upon a time it so happened that the governor—Vassilchikov it was, I believe—ordered a Jew named Kivke to run the gauntlet. Exactly who this Kivke was, or what he had done, are details I can't tell you. Some say he was no great shakes, just a tavern keeper, and an old sourpuss of a bachelor at that. One Sunday, though, when he was chatting with some Russians in his tavern, God put it into his head to argue religion with them: your God, our God . . . until one thing led to another and the village elder and the constable were brought and charges of blasphemy drawn up. All he had to do, that barman, was give them a barrel of vodka and the whole thing would have been forgotten. But on top of everything else, he was stubborn: no, he says, Kivke takes nothing back! What must he have thought? He must have thought he'd be slapped with a three-ruble fine and business would go on as usual. Who could have guessed that he'd be made to run the gauntlet because of a few foolish words? In short, they took the old boy and threw him into the cooler until an honor guard could give him twenty-five good whacks of the mace, as God in His wisdom had decreed.

"Well, I hardly need to tell you what went on in Kaminka once the story got out. And when did the bad news break? At night—and not only at night, but on a Friday night too. The next morning, when everyone came to the synagogue for Sabbath services, the place was in an uproar. 'Kivke's in the clink!' . . . 'He's been given the gauntlet!' . . . 'The gauntlet? How come? What for?' . . . 'For nothing. For a few words' . . . 'He's been framed!' . . . 'What kind of framed? He's a Jew with a mouth that's too big for him!' . . . 'It can be eighteen sizes too big, but the gauntlet? How can they do that to him?' . . . 'Since when do Jews run the gauntlet? And a local Kaminka Jew yet!' . . .

"All day long the Jews of Kaminka stewed as if in a pot. On Saturday night, as soon as the Sabbath was over, they ran crying to my grandfather—Reb Nissl Shapiro was his name. 'Why don't you say something, Reb Nissl? How can you allow a Jew, and a Kaminkan no less, to be flogged?'

"You must be wondering why they all ran to my grandfather. I don't mean to boast, mind you, but I have to tell you that my grandfather, may his soul dwell in Paradise, was the richest, most important, most cultured, most highly thought-of Jew in town, and a very brainy man with high connections. When he heard what the trouble was, he paced up and down the floor a few times (when he was thinking, my father told me, he always liked to pace back and forth), then stood still and announced: 'Children, go home! No one will be hurt. God willing, it will turn out all right; here in Kaminka, the Lord be praised, we've never had a Jew flogged yet, and with His help we never will.'

"Those were my grandfather's very words, God bless him, and it was common knowledge in town that whatever Reb Nissl Shapiro said was as good as done. He just didn't like being badgered about how he intended to do it. When a Jew is rich and has connections, you understand, and he's as brainy as my grandfather, you learn to tread lightly with him. And you know what? It turned out exactly as he said it would. What did? Listen and I'll tell you."

Seeing that the whole car was waiting with baited breath to hear what happened next, the Jew from Kaminka paused, took out a large tobacco pouch from his pocket, and slowly rolled himself a cigarette. So important had he become that several passengers jumped up to offer him a light. Having taken a few puffs, he resumed his story with fresh vigor:

"Now see how a clever Jew operates—I mean my grandfather, God bless his memory. He thought the matter over and cooked up a little plan, which is to say, he persuaded the authorities that the sentenced man, Kivke, should take time out to die while still in prison . . . but why are you all staring at me? Don't you get it? Do you mean to tell me you think he was poisoned? Relax. That's not how it's done in Kaminka. What did happen, then? Something much more elegant: it was simply arranged for the sentenced man to go to bed fit as a fiddle one night and wake up a corpse in the morning . . . do you follow me now? Or do I have to feed it to you from a bottle?

"In a word, early one morning a messenger arrived from the prison with a message for my grandfather: Whereas notification is hereby given that a Jew named Kivke died in prison last night, and whereas Reb Nissl Shapiro is the president of the Burial Society, he, Reb Nissl, is requested to dispose of the deceased, that is, to see to his interment in the Jewish cemetery . . . How's that for a neat piece of work? Not bad, eh? But don't rush out to celebrate yet; it wasn't as easy as it sounds. Keep in mind that the departed wasn't just another dead Jew. There was military brass involved . . . and a governor . . . and a gauntlet waiting to be run . . . do you suppose all that's a laughing matter? The first order of business was preventing an autopsy, which meant going to the doctor and getting him to sign in black and white that he had examined the dead man and determined that the cause of death was conniptions of the heart, that is to say, general apoplexy, it shouldn't happen to you—after which there were various other authorities to be taken in hand too, because they all had to sign the same document. Only then was the dead man really dead. Bye-bye Kivke!

"Needless to say, everyone in this car would be glad to make in a month what it all cost the Jews of Kaminka—and if you have any doubts about the wager, I'll be happy to come in as your partner. And on whose say was the money laid out? On my grandfather's, may he rest in peace. That was a man you could trust. I tell you, the way he had it worked out down to the tiniest little detail was a masterpiece! That evening the sextons of the Burial Society came with a bier to receive the distinguished corpse in grand style and transport it with the highest honors from the prison to the graveyard—that is, with a detail of two soldiers followed by the entire town. You can well imagine that Kivke never dreamed of such a state funeral in his life. And when they reached the gates of the cemetery, the two soldiers were given some vodka to drink and the late departed was brought inside, where Shimon the coachman (I'm passing on his name to you as my father did to me) was waiting for him with a team of four swift horses. Before the cock crowed, mind you, our dead hero was well across the town line on his merry way to Radivil, and from there lickety-split across the Austrian border to Brody.

"It goes without saying that no one in Kaminka slept a wink that night until Shimon the coachman returned from Radivil. The whole town was beside itself with worry, and my grandfather most of all. What if our dear dead Kivke was apprehended at the border and brought back to Kaminka as alive and well as you and me? Why, an entire community might be banished to Siberia . . . With God's help, however, Shimon the coachman and his team of swift horses returned safe and sound from Radivil with a letter from Kivke that said, 'I wish to inform you all that I have arrived in Brody,' and there was great joy in Kaminka. A banquet was given at my grandfather's house, to which the jailkeeper and the constable and the doctor and all the authorities were invited, and a gay time was had by all: a band played music and everyone, mind you, got so drunk that the jailkeeper kissed my grandfather and his whole family as hard and as often as he could and the constable greeted the dawn by taking off his unmentionables and dancing on my grandfather's roof. After all, ransoming a Jew is nothing to sneeze at—and one saved from a flogging yet! Not bad at all, eh? Well, take a deep breath, my good friends, because the real fun has yet to begin. If you want to hear the rest of it, though, you'll kindly wait a few minutes, because I have to ask the station-master here how much time we have left to Baranovich. That's not where I'm going, mind you, but I have to change trains there . . ."

There was nothing to do but wait. The man from Kaminka went to talk to the stationmaster while we passengers in the car discussed him and his story.

"What do you think of him?"

"A swell fellow!"

"No nonsense about him!"

"He sure can talk."

"And no need to be coaxed!"

"What about the story?"

"It's a damn good one."

"Let's hope it's a long one, too."

Incidentally, there were even a few passengers who claimed that the same thing had happened in their towns. That is, not the exact same thing, but something more or less like it. And since every one of them was keen on telling it, the car soon turned into a free-for-all—but only until the Jew from Kaminka reappeared. As soon as he did, we all quieted down, crowded together to form a human wall, and gave him our undivided attention.

"Now where was I? We had just, thank God, said goodbye to a Jew named Kivke, hadn't we? You agree? Well then, you're wrong, my dear friends. A half year or a whole one went by, I can't tell you exactly, and our Mr. Kivke, mind you, sat down and wrote a letter and addressed it to my grandfather. 'In the first place,' he wrote, 'I wish to inform you that I am in good health and hope to hear the same from you. And in the second place, I've been left high and dry here without a cent to my name and no way of earning one, surrounded by Germans in a foreign land. They don't understand my talk and I don't understand theirs. If I can't make a living, I'll have to lie down and die. And so,' wrote Kivke, 'please be so kind as to send . . .' A subtle fellow, no? What he wanted to be sent, of course, was money! Everyone, mind you, had a good laugh, and then that letter was torn up into little pieces and forgotten. Well, before three weeks were up, another letter arrived, again from the late Kivke and again addressed to my grandfather, with an 'I wish to inform you' at the beginning and a 'Please be so kind' at the end, but this time the end had a post-script. Could it be, Kivke wanted to know, that the Kaminkans had something against him? Better to have been flogged and gotten it over with, because his wounds would have healed long ago and he wouldn't have been left penniless among Germans with nothing to do but watch his own belly swell from hunger . . .

"When my grandfather, may he rest in peace, received this letter, he called a meeting in his home. 'What should we do? We can't let a Jew die from hunger.' Well, when you were asked to fork up by Reb Nissl Shapiro, you couldn't be a pig about it. A fine collection was taken up (the biggest contributor to which, needless to say, was my grandfather himself), the sum was sent to Brody, and once more Kaminka forgot that there was such a person as a Jew named Kivke.

"Kivke, however, didn't forget that there was such a place as a town called Kaminka. Another half a year passed, or maybe it was a whole one, I can't tell you exactly, and guess what? Another letter arrived! Once more it was addressed to my grandfather and once more it had an 'I wish to inform you' with a 'Please be so kind' at the end, this time accompanied by some good news. Inso-far and inasmuch, wrote Kivke, as he had recently become be-trothed to a fine young lady from the very best of families, would the town kindly send him the two hundred rubles he had pledged as a dowry, because otherwise the match was off. What a tragedy, just imagine: Kivke would be left without a bride! I hardly need to tell you that the letter made the rounds of Kaminka as though it were a pearl of great price, and people laughed at it until their ribs ached. It became a running gag around town. 'Mazel tov, Kivke is engaged!' . . . 'Have you heard? She's a steal at two hundred rubles!' . . . 'And from the very best of families too, ha ha ha . . .'

"The ha-ha-ing, mind you, didn't last very long, though, because a few weeks later came another letter from Kivke to my grandfather—and this time without the 'I wish to inform you,' just with the 'Please be so kind.' He failed to understand, Kivke wrote, why the two hundred rubles for the dowry had not yet arrived. If he didn't receive them at once, the wedding would have to be called off—in which case his disgrace would be so great that only one choice would be left: either to drown himself on the spot or to come hell-bent back to Kaminka . . .

"Those last words of his, mind you, wiped the laugh off everyone's face. That same evening the town's leading Jews got together at my grandfather's house and decided that the most respected of them, my grandfather too, should go from door to door to raise a dowry for Kivke. What else could they do? And so as not to keep you in suspense, let me tell you that they not only sent him the money, they sent it with a mazel tov and wished the lucky bridegroom, as is the custom, many long years of happiness in which to raise children and grandchildren with his wife-to-be. What were they counting on? They were counting on his being so busy with his new marriage that he'd forget all about Kaminka. But do you think he did? A fat chance of that! Half a year didn't go by, or maybe it was a whole one, I can't tell you exactly, and what do you think came along? Another letter from Kivke! What did he want this time? Insofar and inasmuch as he was now married, he had a God-given wife who would be the envy of any Jew. Nothing was perfect, though—in this case the bride's father, who was such a liar, such a chiseler, such a gangster, such an out-and-out crook beside whom the biggest sinner could be mistaken for a saint, that he had defrauded our Kivke of his two hundred rubles and thrown him into the street with his wife. And so, he wrote, 'Please be so kind as to send'—would his fellow townsmen have the goodness to forward another two hundred rubles to make up for what he had lost. If not, he could either throw himself in the river or come hell-bent back to Kaminka . . .

"This time everyone was good and mad. *Two* dowries? Why, that was already a swindle! And so it was decided to let the letter go unanswered. Well, Kivke waited a week or two, mind you, or maybe even three, and then sent another letter, addressed once again to my grandfather. What, he wanted to know, did they take him for? Why hadn't they sent him the two hundred rubles? He would give them, he wrote, another week and a half—and if he still hadn't received the money by then, they could look forward to having him, God willing, as their guest in Kaminka, Yours Etcetera, amen and amen. He sure was some sheygetz!

"Don't think that didn't kick up a storm! What could anyone do, though? Once more there was a meeting at my grandfather's house, and once more it was decided to send the most respected Jews from door to door. This time, mind you, people made a face, because who wanted to dish out still more money to such a scoundrel—but the fact of the matter was that when Reb Nissl Shapiro said 'Give,' being a pig was out of the question. Nevertheless, everyone swore that this was the last time. And my grandfather himself, mind you, didn't think otherwise, because he wrote Kivke back in no uncertain terms that he wasn't getting another cent and shouldn't dream of it.

"No doubt you think that put the fear of God into the rascal, eh? Well, suppose I told you that one morning, and a Jewish holiday it was too, another letter arrived from the fine gentleman, addressed, naturally, to my grandfather! Insofar and inasmuch, he wrote, as he had struck up a friendship in Brody with a German, a most excellent and honorable fellow, and decided to go partners with him in the china business, which was a very good, very solid line that could support a person nicely, 'Please be so kind as to send' four hundred and fifty rubles—and for heaven's sake, be quick and don't dawdle, because the partner refused to wait, he had ten other candidates lined up, and if he, Kivke, was left without a business, he could either go for a long swim in the river or come hell-bent back to Kaminka . . . In short, the usual. And he signed off with the gentle hint that if he did not have the money in two weeks' time, there would be the Devil to pay—or more precisely, his round-trip ticket from Brody to Kaminka and back. He sure was some shyster!

"I don't have to tell you what kind of upside-down holiday it was—and most of all, mind you, for my grandfather, may he rest in peace, because he bore the brunt of it. At the meeting that was held that night, the whole town was griping and grumbling. 'Enough! How long do we have to go on shelling out? There's a limit to everything; even chicken soup with kreplach can get to be too much. This Kivke of yours will make paupers of us all!' 'Why is he my Kivke?' asked my grandfather. 'Whose Kivke do you think he is?' was the answer. 'Whose idea was it in the first place to have the little bastard go die of a stroke while in prison?'

"Well, my grandfather (he was one smart Jew, he was) saw right away that it was a waste of time to hope for more money from the town, so he went to the local authorities—after all, they were in the same boat as he was—and asked them for a donation to the cause. Do you think they gave him a kopeck? Not a chance! Your goy is not your Jew; such things don't faze him in the least. And so my poor grandfather, mind you, had to swallow his medicine and stake that damned cutthroat to some more cash from his own pocket. You should have seen the letter he sent with it, though! (My grandfather, God rest his soul, could give as good as he got.) Mind you, he gave that sheygetz hell in it. He called him a scoundrel, a degenerate, a know-nothing, a leech, a bloodsucker, a fiend, a traitor, a disgrace to the Jewish people, and whatever-else-have-you. He also told him once and for all not to dare write any more letters or ask for another cent, reminded him that God above sees everything and pays back tit for tat, and ended by begging him (a Jewish heart is still a Jewish heart, after all!) to have pity on an old man like himself and not ruin a town full of Jews, in return for which the Almighty would surely assist him in all his endeavors. That was the letter my grandfather sent, and he signed it with his full name, 'Nissl Shapiro'—which was, mind you, the biggest mistake he ever made in his life, as you'll shortly see for yourselves."

The Jew from Kaminka paused again, reached for his tobacco pouch, slowly rolled himself another cigarette, lit it, and took a few deep puffs without even noticing that the whole car was dying of curiosity. When he had breathed in and coughed out enough smoke, he blew his nose, rolled up his sleeves again, and continued in the same tone as before:

"You must be thinking, my friends, that my grandfather's letter gave that son-of-a-bitch a good scare. Don't kid yourselves! Half a year didn't go by, or maybe it was a whole one, mind you, when along came another letter from that turncoat. 'In the first place,' it said, 'I wish to inform you that my German partner, may his life be one bad dream, has cheated me out of house and home and out of my share of the business. I would have sued him if it hadn't been clear that I didn't stand a Chinaman's chance. Taking a German to court around here means taking your life in your hands. Why, I wouldn't touch one of those bastards with a ten-foot pole! So I went and opened a store near his, right next door to him, in fact, and went into business for myself. With God's help I'll bury that Kraut yet, I'll see to it he ends up eating dirt! The problem is that I need an advance of at least a thousand rubles, so please be so kind as to send . . .'

"That's what Kivke wrote in his letter, which concluded: 'If you don't come up with the money in eight days, I'm taking your last letter signed "Nissl Shapiro" and forwarding it straight to the provincial governor with an unabridged account of all that happened: how I died of a stroke in prison, and how I was resurrected in the cemetery, and how Shimon the coachman brought me to Brody, and how you've kept sending me hush money. I'll write him everything, I'll let him know that we Jews have a great God above who rescued Kivke from the grave . . .'

"How's that for a greeting card? Mind you, as soon as my grandfather, God rest his soul, read those sweet sentiments, he had such a fright that he fainted dead away. It shouldn't happen to anyone, but he lost all control of . . . Jews, where are we? What station is this?"

"Baranovich station!" cried the conductors, running one after another past the windows of our car. "All out for Baranovich!"

Hearing the name Baranovich, the Kaminka Jew jumped from his seat, reached for his belongings, which were in a kind of sack stuffed with God only knew what, and, barely able to carry it, headed for the door. In another minute he was standing on the platform with the sweat pouring off him, struggling through the crowd and asking whomever he stumbled into:

"Baranovich?"

"Baranovich!"

He made me think of a Jew blessing the New Moon in the synagogue courtyard, bumping into his fellow Jews in the darkness and inquiring of each:

"Is that you?"

"Yes, it's me!"

Several passengers from our car, myself included, ran after him and seized him by the coattails. "Hey, there! You can't do this to us! We won't let you go. You have to tell us the end of the story!"

"What end? It's barely begun. Let go of me! Do you want me to miss my train? A strange bunch of Jews you are! Didn't you hear them say Baranovich?"

And before we knew it, the Jew from Kaminka had vanished into thin air.

I wouldn't mind if Baranovich station burned to the ground!

(1909)

EIGHTEEN FROM PERESHCHEPENA

▼

"You don't say! Well, I'll tell you an even better one. There's a man in our town called Finkelstein, a rich Jew, but really loaded, with two sons. If I had his money, I could afford to laugh at the whole business. Do you know what it cost him, though? I wish the two of us were worth half as much . . ."

"I said as much a year ago, damn it all! Just you wait and see, I said, it won't be long before half the Jews in Russia are baptized."

"I couldn't agree with you more! Why, we had a young fellow named Marshak who moved heaven and earth. It didn't do a bit of good; he actually took poison in the end."

"I hate to say it, but you'll soon see the day, damn it all, when there isn't a Jew left in Russia! How can anyone expect us to survive so many troubles, so many quotas, so much discrimination? Every day, every blessed day, there's some new regulation against us. Why, there must be a regulation per Jew already! I'm telling you, before long they'll find a way of turning down everyone. Take Shpole, for example. That's a town with a few Jews in it, wouldn't you say?"

"Why not Nemirov? I had a letter not long ago from Nemirov with the most depressing news."

"Do you mean to tell me it's any better in Lubin?"

"Why, what happened in Lubin?"

"Or in Ananyev, for instance. They used to take at least three Jews from Ananyev each year."

"Who cares about Ananyev? Just look at Tomashpol. In Tomashpol, so I hear, they didn't take a single Jew this year, not for love or money!"

"They didn't? They took eighteen from our town!"

This last remark came from above. My two Jews and I craned our necks to look up at the top berth. A pair of high rubber galoshes hung down from it. The feet in them belonged to a man with a head of unruly black hair and a face that was swollen from sleep.

My two Jews stared at the sleepy-faced man, devouring him with their eyes as though he were a Martian. Both sat up as if given a new lease on life and asked the upper-berther eagerly:

"You say they took eighteen Jews from your town?"

"Eighteen whole Jews, my own son too."

"They took your son too?"

"I'll say!"

"Where? Where?"

"Where I come from, in Lower Pereshchepena."

"In which Pereshchepena? Where exactly is that?"

The two of them were on their feet now, eyeing each other and the Jew in the upper berth, who looked swollen-facedly back down at them.

"You never heard of Lower Pereshchepena? I assure you there is such a place. You really never heard of it? There are even two Pereshchepenas: Upper Pereshchepena and Lower Pereshchepena. I'm from Lower Pereshchepena."

"Pleased to meet you! Why don't you come on down? Why sit up in the sky all by yourself?"

The owner of the high rubber galoshes clambered down with a groan, and the two moved over to make room for him and fell on him like hungry locusts.

"They honestly took your own son?"

"I'll say!"

"But tell us, old man, how did you manage it? It must have cost you a pretty penny!"

"What are you talking about? You mustn't even mention money to them. There was a time, I admit, when they could be bought. And how they could! Oho! Jews came flocking to us from all over in those days. Everyone knew that Pereshchepena was the place for it. For the last several years, though, ever since somebody snitched—it's just my luck it happened when it did!—they haven't taken a cent."

"Then how do you explain it? Someone must have pulled strings!"

"What strings? They simply decided once and for all to take every last Jew automatically."

"You must be joking! Do you realize what you're saying? Are you trying to pull our legs?"

"Pull your legs? Do I look like the type to you?"

All three stared hard as if trying to read each others' faces. Since nothing was written there, however, the two Jews resumed their interrogation.

"Just a minute, now. Where did you say you were from?"

"From Pereshchepena!" The third Jew was beginning to get annoyed. "I've already told you three times. From Lower Pereshchepena!"

"Don't take offense. We've just never heard of your city before."

"Ha ha! Pereshchepena a city? That's rich! Pereshchepena's barely a town. In fact, it's more like a village."

"And from a place like that, you say, they took . . . from Pere-what? What's it called?"

By now the Jew from Lower Pereshchepena was hopping mad.

"I've never seen such queer Jews in my life! Can't you pronounce a Jewish word? Pe-resh-che-pe-na! Pe-resh-che-pe-na!"

"All right, all right. Pereshchepena is Pereshchepena. Why fly off the handle?"

"Who's flying off the handle? I just don't like having to repeat myself ninety-nine times."

"No offense meant. We have the exact same problem. When you said they took eighteen of you, we couldn't believe our ears. That's why we keep asking the same question. The truth of the matter is, we never would have imagined that in Pere . . . Pe-resh . . . that there was even a high school in your town."

The Jew from Pereshchepena gave them an irritable look. "Who said anything about a high school in Pereshchepena?"

They, for their part, stared at him boggle-eyed. "But didn't you just tell us that your own son was accepted as a student there?"

The Jew from Pereshchepena seemed about to have a fit. In the end, though, he merely got to his feet and screamed at them:

"What student? A soldier! He was taken to the army to be a soldier! A soldier, not a student, do you hear me?!"

It was already broad daylight outside. A bluish-gray light trickled through the windows of the train. Passengers were slowly waking up, stretching legs, clearing throats, rearranging bundles for the trip that lay ahead.

My three Jews had parted company. Their brief friendship was over. One had retired to a corner and was having a leisurely smoke. The second had taken a small prayer book and sat down on a front bench, where he was reciting his devotions with one eye open and one shut. The third, the irritable Jew from Lower Pereshchepena, was already having his breakfast.

It was curious to see how the three had become total strangers. Not only had they stopped speaking to each other, they no longer even looked at one another, as if they had done something shameful, something that could never be lived down . . .

(1909)

THE MAN FROM BUENOS AIRES

▼

Riding a train doesn't have to be dull if you manage to fall in with good company. You can meet up with merchants, men who know business, and then the time flies, or with people who have been around and seen a lot, intelligent men of the world who know the ropes. Such types are a pleasure to travel with. There's always something to be learned from them. And sometimes God sends you a plain, ordinary passenger, the lively sort that likes to talk. And talk. And talk. His tongue doesn't stop wagging for a minute. And only about himself, that's his one and only subject.

Once I ended up traveling with such a character for quite a distance.

Our acquaintance began—how else do these things happen on a train?—with a trivial inquiry like "Do you by any chance know what station this is?" or "Excuse me, what time is it?" or "Would you perhaps have a match?" In no time at all, however, we were on as brotherly terms as if we had met in the cradle. At the first station with a few minutes' wait, the man put his arm through mine, steered me to the buffet, and ordered two glasses of cognac without even asking if I drank, and soon after, he urged me with a wink to reach for a fork and help myself. When we were through sampling the hors d'oeuvres that every buffet has to offer, he called for two mugs of beer, so that by the time he had lit a cigar for each of us, we were the best of friends.

"I don't mind telling you frankly and without a bit of flattery," said my new acquaintance when we were reseated in the car, "that I liked you, believe it or not, the minute I set eyes on you. One look at you was enough to make me say, here's someone I can have a word with! If there's one thing I hate, it's having to clam up like a statue when I travel. I like to talk to a fellow human being, which is why I bought a third-class ticket today, because that's where the conversation is. Generally, though, I travel second class. Do you suppose that's because I can't afford to travel first? Believe me, I certainly can—and if you think that's just talk, look at this." And he produced from his rear pocket a wallet stuffed with bills, opened it, thumped it with his hand like a pillow, and put it back again, saying:

"Don't worry, there's more where that comes from!"

No matter how much I looked at him, I couldn't for the life of me guess his age. He might have been about forty and he might have been still in his twenties. His face was round, tanned by the sun, and smooth-shaven, with no trace of whiskers or a beard; his small, beady eyes had a twinkle; and—a short, plump, good-natured, quite vivacious fellow—he cut a sharp figure of the sort I like to see in a spotless white shirt with gold buttons, a stylish necktie with a handsome pin, an elegant blue suit of English worsted, and a pair of smart, lacquered shoes. On one finger he sported a heavy gold ring with a diamond whose thousand facets glittered in the sunlight—which, if it was real, must have set him back a good five or six hundred rubles, if not a bit more than that.

There's no one I admire more than a spiffy dresser. I like to dress well myself, and I like to see others who do. I can even tell by his clothes if a man is a decent sort or not. I know there are people who say it doesn't mean a thing, that you can dress like a count and still be the worst sort of bounder. Tell me this, though: why, then, does everyone still try to look his best? Why does one person wear one kind of outfit and another person another? Why does the first choose a conservative tie of pearl-green silk and the second a loud red one with white polka dots? I could give you still other examples but I think that's enough, because I don't want to waste your time. Let's get back to my new acquaintance and what he has to tell us.

"Yes, indeed, my good friend. You can see for yourself that I could easily travel second class. Do you think I travel third to save money? But money is garbage to me! Believe it or not, I travel third class because I like to. I'm a plain, simple person and I like simple people like myself. You might call me a democrat. I started out a small fish. A very small one, like so." (My newfound friend put his hand near the floor to show me how small he had been.) "And then I grew bigger and bigger." (Up went his hand toward the ceiling to show me how big he was now.) "It didn't happen all at once. It took time. Bit by bit. Step by step. I didn't start out my own boss. Do you think it was so easy even to find a boss to work for? A whole lot of water flowed under the bridge before I got that high up. Believe it or not, when I think of my childhood my hair stands on end! You know, I can't even remember it. And I don't want to, either. Do you suppose that's because I'm ashamed of my origins? Not one bit. I make no bones about who I am. Ask me where I'm from and I'm not embarrassed to tell you that it's a grand metropolis called Soshmakin. Do you have any idea where that is? It's a village in Latvia, not far from Mitava. The whole place was so big that I could easily buy it all up today, lock, stock, and barrel. Maybe it's changed or grown a bit since then—that's something I really can't tell you. In my time, though, the most valuable possession in all of Soshmakin, believe it or not, was a single orange that was lent from house to house to decorate the table for Sabbath guests.

"And do you know what I was raised on in Soshmakin? On whippings, beatings, slaps in the face, boxes on the ear, bloody noses, black-and-blue marks, and an empty stomach. You know, what I recall most is being hungry. I came hungry into this world, and hunger was my best friend ever since I can remember. Hunger and heartache and a cramp in the gut . . . but never mind! Resin, do you know what resin is? It's something from the sap of trees that fiddlers wax their instruments with. Believe it or not, I lived on resin for nearly a whole summer. That was the summer when my stepfather, a tailor with a broken nose, twisted my arm from its socket and chased me out of my mother's house, so that I had to run off to Mitava. Do you see this arm? It's not right to this day."

My new acquaintance rolled up his sleeve to reveal a soft, pudgy, perfectly normal-looking arm and continued:

"After roaming the streets of Mitava, hungry, barefoot, half-naked, and poking through garbage, I found, thank God, a job, my very first. It was being the seeing eye of an old cantor, a famous performer who went blind in his old age and had to beg for a living. I had to lead him around from house to house. It wasn't really such a bad job, you know, but a person had to be made of iron to put up with all his crazy whims. Nothing ever satisfied him. But nothing. He yelled at me, pinched me, tore out whole handfuls of my flesh. He was always complaining that I never took him where he wanted to go, though just where that was is a mystery to me to this day. That was one loony cantor! And to top it all off, you should have heard what he made me out to be. Believe it or not, he went around telling people that both my parents had been baptized and wanted to baptize me too, and that he had risked his own neck to save me from the clutches of the Christians! And I had to listen to all those lies and keep myself from bursting with laughter! As a matter of fact, I was supposed to look glum when he told them.

"I realized pretty soon that there must be better things in life than my cantor, so I said to hell with my job and left Mitava for Libau. I went around hungry for a while there, too, until I ran into a group of poor emigrants who were about to embark for a faraway place called Buenos Aires and asked them to take me with them. *What? Take you with us?* It wasn't possible. It didn't depend on them but on the Emigration Committee that was sending them. So I went to the Committee and put on such an act, but a real tearjerker, that they agreed to pay my way to Buenos Aires.

"Search me if I know why I picked Buenos Aires. Do you think I knew a damn thing about it? Everyone was going there, so I went too. It wasn't until we arrived that I discovered that Buenos Aires was not our real destination; it was simply a transit point from which we were supposed to be shipped still further. And we were: as soon as we landed, we were processed, taken to places where no human being had ever been before, not even in a bad dream, and put to work. You're wondering what sort of work it was? Don't ask! I tell you, our forefathers in Egypt never did half the things that we did, and all the horror stories about them in the Bible don't add up to a fraction of what we went through. It says they had to make bricks out of clay and build the cities of Pithom and Rameses. Bully for them! They should have tried working with their bare hands in the godforsaken pampas that had nothing but thorns growing on them, handling monster oxen that could squash a man to death with one step, breaking wild horses that you first had to chase a hundred miles to lasso, suffering through nights of mosquitos that could eat a human being alive, living on dry bread that tasted like stones, drinking slimy water with worms swimming in it . . . Believe it or not, one day I saw my reflection in the river and was scared half out of my wits. My skin was cracked, my eyes were swollen, my hands were like cake dough, my legs were a bloody pulp, and I was covered all over with hair. Is that really you, Motek from Soshmakin? I asked myself. I couldn't help laughing. That same day I said good riddance to the monster oxen, and the wild horses, and the wormy water, and the godforsaken pampas, and yours truly hoofed it back to Buenos Aires.

"If I'm not mistaken, though, there's a big buffet at this station. Take a look at your train schedule. Don't you think it's time for a bite? It will give us the strength for more talk."

Having feasted royally and washed it down with more beer, we lit up cigars again—good, aromatic, genuine Buenos Aires Havanas, too!—and returned to our seats, where my new friend resumed his story:

"Buenos Aires, you know, is a place the likes of which God never . . . but never mind! Have you ever been to America? Not even to New York? Or to London? No? . . . Maybe Madrid? Constantinople? Paris? None of them, eh? Well, I can't really describe to you then what Buenos Aires is like. All I can tell you is that it's a cesspool. Hell on earth. But a heavenly hell. That is, it's hell for some and heaven for others. If you keep on your toes and wait for your chance, there are fortunes to be made. Believe it or not, there's so much gold in the streets you can trip on it. You only have to bend down and take all you want. Just watch out, though, that your hand isn't stomped on when you do! The main thing is never to look back. Never to have second thoughts. Never to ask yourself, can I stoop this low or not? You have to learn to stoop to anything. Waiting on customers in a restaurant? Do it! Selling in a store? Do it! Washing glasses in a bar? Do it! Dragging a pushcart? Do it! Hawking papers on the corner? Do it! Washing dogs? Do it! Feeding cats? Do it! Catching rats? Do it! Skinning them for their fur? Do that too! In short, do everything. You know, there's nothing I didn't try there, and each time I reached the same conclusion: working for others is for the birds, it's a thousand times better to have others working for you. Is it any fault of my own if God made the world so that someone sweats to brew the beer I drink? Or so that someone gets cramps in his fingers from rolling the cigars I smoke? The conductor gets to drive the train, the stoker gets to shovel coal, the grease monkey gets to oil the wheels, and you and I get to shoot the breeze. What's so bad about that? If you don't like it, go make another world."

I looked at the fellow and wondered, what can he possibly be? A newly made millionaire? An ex-tailor who now owns a big clothing store? Maybe even an industrialist? Or a landlord? Or an investor who lives off his shares? But let's leave the telling to him, because he does it so much better:

"You know, it's a pleasure to live in such a wonderful, well-run world! You just have to make sure that no one spits in your soup. I've tried my hand at a thousand different things, done every possible sort of dirty work. There's not a job that's been too hard or filthy for me. As a matter of fact, there's no such thing as a filthy job. All ways of making a living are legitimate as long as you deal honestly and keep your word. Take it from me. I don't claim to be the Rabbi of Lemberg, but believe me, I'm no thief either. And I'm certainly no swindler or confidence man. I should only live to be as old as I've been square in business! I deal fairly, you know. I never sell anyone a bill of goods. What I promise is what you get, there are no pigs in a poke with me. What exactly is my line, you'd like to know? I'm a kind of middleman, what you might call a jobber. That is, I provide a commodity that everyone knows about but no one ever talks about . . . Why not? Because in this world that's too clever by half for its own good, no one wants to hear a spade called a spade. On the contrary, they would rather hear it called a silver spoon . . . I ask you, what can one do with such people?"

I looked at my companion from Buenos Aires and wondered, good God, what on earth does he do? What is this commodity he provides? What's all this mumbo jumbo about spades? I could have interrupted him and asked, "Look here, my friend, just what do you deal in?"—but that was something I was loath to do. I preferred to let him continue.

"Well now, where was I? Yes: my current business in Buenos Aires. Actually, it's not just in Buenos Aires. I do business, you know, all over the world: in Paris, in London, in Budapest, in Boston—but my headquarters are in Buenos Aires. It's a shame we're not there now, because I'd show you around the office and introduce you to my men. Believe it or not, they live like Rothschilds on the job. They even work an eight-hour day, not a minute more. A man of mine is treated like a man. And do you know why that is? It's because I was someone's man once myself. In fact, I worked for my present partners. There are three of us. There used to be two, before they took me into the business. I was their right-hand man. The whole operation, you might say, depended on me: the buying, the selling, the sorting, the pricing—I had a finger in everything . . . I have a good eye, you know: believe it or not, one look at the merchandise is all I need to tell you what it's worth and where it will sell. But that's only a small part of it. A good eye alone won't get you very far in our business. You need a nose too, you have to sniff some things out a mile away. It takes a sixth sense to tell a good deal from a clinker that can land you up to your neck in such hot water that you'll rue the day you ever fell for it. There are too many sob sisters around, too many eyes looking our way—and ours is a business, you know, that doesn't do well in the limelight. One false step can cook your goose for good. Before you know it, there's such a big stink that it's smeared all over the newspapers. That's all they care about. The papers are in seventh heaven if they can find a bit of muck to rake up. They go to town with it, they turn it into such a federal case that the whole police force is breathing down your neck . . . although just between the two of us, we've got the police in our pockets all over the world. Why, you'd turn pale if I told you what they cost us in a single year! Believe it or not, ten, fifteen, twenty grand in fall money is peanuts to us . . ."

The man from Buenos Aires made a motion with his hand as if throwing thousands into the air, the diamond glittering on his finger. He paused for a moment to see what impression he had made, then went on:

"And if that still won't do it, do you think I can't up the ante? We have complete trust in each other—I'm talking about me and my partners. No matter what one of us spends on such things, no questions are ever asked. It's simply put down to expenses. We never doubt each other's word. We wouldn't dream of welshing on each other—and if one of us tried, he wouldn't get very far . . . You see, we know each other, we know Buenos Aires, and we know all the tricks of the trade. Each one of us has his own plants and canaries. Does that surprise you? But it's always that way in a business based on trust . . . What do you say, though, to our hopping off the train at this station and wetting our whistles a bit?"

My fellow passenger linked his arm in mine and fixed me with a candid look.

Naturally, I had no objection and the two of us hopped off the train to wet our whistles at the buffet. One bottle of lemonade after another popped open to be downed by my companion with a gusto that I envied. All the while, however, I kept wondering the same thing: just what did he deal in, this Jew from Buenos Aires? And how could he have the police in his pocket all over the world? And what did he need plants and canaries for? Was he an international smuggler? . . . A diamond counterfeiter? . . . A fence for stolen goods? . . . Or simply a bull artist, one of that fine breed of gentlemen whose tongues have an odd way of making things swell to many times their true size? We commercial travelers have our own name for these tellers of fish stories: we call them "wholesalers," that is, people who deal only in bulk. In plain Yiddish you'd say, "He's as full of hot air as a steam kettle."

We lit up two more cigars, returned to our seats, and the man from Buenos Aires continued:

"Where were we? I was telling you about my partners. That is, about my current ones. As I say, they used to be my bosses. I hope I haven't made you think they weren't good ones. Why shouldn't they have been good to me, when I was as loyal as a dog to them? I looked after each cent of theirs as though it were my own. And I made some pretty big enemies because of them. Believe it or not, my loyalty almost got me poisoned. That's right, poisoned! You know, forgive me for boasting, but no one could have been any straighter on the job than I was. I don't mean to say I never looked out for my own self, because that's something we all have to do. You can't forget you're only human: today you're alive and kicking—but tomorrow? . . . And the fact is that I never had the slightest intention of working for them forever. After all, didn't I have two hands just like they did? And two feet? And a tongue? I knew they couldn't last a day without me—that they couldn't and mustn't! There were secrets, you know, really big ones, the kind there can be in a business . . . Well, one fine day I made up my mind, knocked on their door, and said to them, 'So long, gentlemen.' 'What's that supposed to mean?' they asked, giving me a hard look. 'It means,' I said, 'that it's been good to know you.' 'What seems to be the problem?' they asked. 'Nothing,' I said, 'except that I'm tired of playing second fiddle around here.' They looked at each other and asked, 'How much can you come in with?' 'However much it is,' I said, 'it will do for starters—and if it won't, God's in His heaven and Buenos Aires is a big town.' You can bet they understood me. They'd have had to have their heads on backwards not to. Right then and there they took me into the business and gave me an equal share of the firm. There are no junior or senior partners with us. 'Let God give and you and me live,' is our motto. Why quarrel when we're making good money and the business, God bless it, is growing? It's a big world and prices keep going up. Each of us draws as much money as he needs from the kitty. All three of us are big spenders. Believe it or not, I can blow three times as much on myself as a married man can on his whole family. Lots of people, you know, would be happy to earn what I give away to charity alone. Everyone puts the touch on me: synagogues, hospitals, immigrant societies, benefits—Buenos Aires is a big town! Don't think it's the only one, though. Believe it or not, I even shell out for Palestine. Not long ago I received a letter from a yeshiva in Jerusalem. A nice letter it was too, signed by lots of rabbis, with a star of David and all kinds of stamps. And it was addressed to me personally, with a terrific beginning: 'To His Illustrious Honor, Reb Mordechai,' etcetera.

Eh, I thought, here are all these fine people sending me a personal appeal—the least I can do is let them have a check for a hundred . . .

"But that's just petty cash. My hometown of Soshmakin is something else. Believe it or not, Soshmakin gets a barrelful of gold from me each year! The day doesn't go by without a letter from there with news of some new cause or emergency—and I'm not even talking about routine things like the Matsoh Fund, which is an automatic hundred every Passover . . . I'm on my way to Soshmakin now, and believe me, this visit alone will set me back at least a thousand. What am I saying, a thousand? I'll be happy to get away with two. Frankly, I'm even ready for three. It doesn't happen every day that a man comes home again after so many years— why, I haven't seen the place since I was a kid! But it's still home to me, Soshmakin is. I can tell you that the whole town will be delirious. Everyone will come running at once. Hallelujah! 'Motek is here, our Motek is here from Buenos Aires!' . . . What a whoop-de-do there'll be! You know, I'm like the Messiah for those poor, hungry devils. Every day I send them a telegram that's signed 'I'm on my way, Motek' to let them know where I am. Believe it or not, I can hardly wait to get there myself. Just to be in Soshmakin again, to kiss the ground, to see my old house! I tell you, you can have your Buenos Aires. You can have your New York. You can have your London. You can even have your Paris. Home for me is Soshmakin . . ."

As he said these words, the face of the man from Buenos Aires underwent a change. It actually became different, younger and handsomer. The beady little eyes glimmered with a glad, selfless love, a love that couldn't have been feigned . . . If only I knew what he did! Before I could pursue the matter, though, he went on:

"You must be wondering why I'm bothering to go to Soshmakin at all. Well, it's partly because I miss the place and partly to visit my parents' graves. I have a father and a mother who are buried there, and brothers and sisters too—a whole family, in fact. I'd like to get married also. How long can I live the single life? And I want to marry a hometown girl from Soshmakin, from my own folks. I've even written friends there to look for the right one . . . and they've written me back that she won't be hard to find once I show up. You can see how crazy I am . . . why, believe it or not, back in Buenos Aires I could have had the greatest beauties in the world. I've been offered women, you know, such as even the Turkish sultan doesn't have—but I turned every one of them down flat. A wife I'll find in Soshmakin. I want someone with character. A good Jewish girl. I don't care if she hasn't a penny to her name: I'll dress her in gold, I'll gold-plate her parents too, I'll make them one big happy family. And then I'll bring her back to Buenos Aires and build her a palace fit for a princess, do you hear? She won't have to lift a finger. Believe it or not, I'll make her the happiest woman in the world. Her whole life will be her house and her husband and her family. I'll send all my sons to the university. One will study medicine, another engineering, another law. The girls will go to a special Jewish finishing school that I know of. Do you know where it is? In Germany . . ."

Just then the conductor came along to check our tickets. He always (it's not the first time I've noticed this) gets it into his head to check tickets just when you least want him to! A commotion broke out in the car. Everyone reached for their bags, myself included. It was time for me to change trains. While the man from Buenos Aires helped me get my things together, we exchanged a few last words, which I present here verbatim, exactly as they were spoken.

The man from Buenos Aires: "My, what a pity you're getting off here. I won't have anyone to talk to."
I: "What can I do? Business is business."
The man from Buenos Aires: "Right you are. Business is business. I'm afraid I'll have to lay out some more money and move to second class. Not, God bless me, that I can't afford to travel first. When I go by train—"
I: "Excuse me for interrupting, but we have only a half minute left. There was something I wanted to ask you."
The man from Buenos Aires: "And what might that be?"
I: "It's . . . but there goes the whistle! I wanted to ask what your business is. What exactly do you deal in?"
The man from Buenos Aires: "What do I deal in? Ha ha! Not in Hanukkah candles, my friend, not in Hanukkah candles!"

Even after I was through the door with my luggage, I still saw him before my eyes, the man from Buenos Aires, with his satisfied, smooth-shaven face and the fat cigar between his teeth, his laughter ringing in my ears:

"Not in Hanukkah candles, my friend, not in Hanukkah candles!"

(1909)

ELUL

▼

"So you're off to the festivities and I'm coming back from them! I've just finished crying my heart out and you're about to begin . . . But why don't I make some room for you? Here, move over this way. You'll be more comfortable."

"Ah, that's better!"

So two passengers sat chatting behind me in the car. That is, one did the talking while the other murmured an occasional word.

"My wife and I go together. That's her, curled up over there. She's asleep, the poor thing; she must have shed enough tears for all the Jews in the world. She didn't want to budge from the cemetery. She simply threw herself on the grave and wouldn't let me tear her away. I tried to reason with her. 'That's enough,' I said. 'Your tears won't bring her back to life again.' Try talking to the wall! And what's the wonder? Such a tragedy! An only daughter, our pride and joy. As pretty as a postcard. And so gifted, bright as they come! Just out of high school, she was. It's been two years now. Don't think it was TB or anything like that. She couldn't have been healthier. No, she did it herself, she went and took her own life!"

"Dear me!"

By now I understood what sort of "festivities" were being talked about. It was, I realized, the beginning of the penitential month of Elul with its midnight prayers, that sad but dear time of year when Jews travel to visit long-dead parents, children, and relatives. Pining mothers, orphaned daughters, mourning sisters, plain grief-stricken women—all go to have a good cry at the graves of their loved ones, where they can let out their sorrow and ease the bitter burden of an afflicted heart.

It's an odd thing: I've been a traveler for years and yet I can't remember ever seeing such a run on the cemeteries as there was last Elul. The trains were doing a landslide business. Every car was jam-packed with somber-faced Jews, with shiny-nosed, puffy-eyed women on their way to or from the "festivities." With the smell of autumn that was already in the air came a powerful, Elulish yearning . . . Without really wanting to, I listened to the conversation behind me:

"Maybe you're thinking she got into trouble like some other young folks—black shirts, red flags, prison, and all that? God forbid! That's one thing I was spared. Or rather, that I spared myself, because I watched her like the apple of my eye. You don't see such a gifted young girl every day, and an only child at that! Pretty as a postcard. Just out of high school. I did everything I could: kept track of where she went, and who her friends were, and what she talked about with them, and even what books she read. 'So you like to read?' I said. 'Be my guest! Just let me know what you're reading . . .' I admit I'm no great expert on these things—but a bit of horse sense, thank God, I have. I don't even care if it's written in French, one look at a book is all I need to tell you what's in it."

"You don't say!"

"I didn't want a child of mine playing with fire—anyone would have done the same. Don't think I browbeat her, though. If anything, I tried making light of it. 'Why pretend we can solve the world's problems?' I said to her. 'Whatever will be, will be, there's nothing you or I can do about it . . .' That's what I said, and do you know how she took it? She didn't say a word. But not a peep out of her, as good as gold she was! So what does the good Lord do? The worst of it was already over, thank God; the Revolution, and the Constitution, and all those troubles were behind us. No more black shirts, no more red flags, no more short hair, no more hell's-a-popping, no more bombs. My teeth could finally stop chattering. Do you think being afraid for her all the time was so easy? An only daughter, our pride and joy, and such a gifted child too. Just out of high school . . ."

"So?"

"In short, the nightmare was ended, God be praised. We could breathe easily again and think of a match for her. A dowry? No problem, if the right young man could be found. And so we began the whole routine: visits to matchmakers, lists of eligibles, and all the rest of it. I could see she wasn't too keen on it. Why not? She wouldn't tell us, not even to say she wasn't interested. What was the matter, then? Wait until you hear the whole story.

"I kept a sharp eye out and one day I made a discovery: she had a book that she was reading in secret. And not alone, either; she was reading it with a friend of hers, the daughter of the cantor of our synagogue, a bright high school girl herself, and with a third person—the boy from Navaredok. Would you like to know who he was? Well, there's nothing worth knowing. An ugly, scruffy, moonfaced, pimple-cheeked, eyebrowless little creep with gold-rimmed glasses—you wouldn't want to eat at the same table with him. And a pest too, a slimy little worm! Do you know what a worm-person is? Then I'd better explain it to you. There are all kinds of people in the world. There are cow-people. There are horse-people. There are dog-people. There are pig-people. And there are worm-people. Do you get it now?"

"Quite."

"How did this worm enter my life? Through the cantor's daughter. He was a cousin of hers, a student of pharmacy, or dentistry, or law, or whatever the Devil it was. All I can tell you is that for me he was the Angel of Death. He and his gold glasses rubbed me the wrong way from the start. I told my wife that too. 'Whatever can you be thinking of!' she said. But I kept my eyes and ears open, and I didn't like their reading together, or their talking together, or their arguing together so excitedly one bit . . . Once I even asked my daughter about it. 'Tell me, missy,' I said to her, 'what's that the three of you are smacking your lips over?' 'It's nothing,' she says, 'just a book.' 'I can see it's a book,' I say. 'I'm asking you what book.' 'And if I told you,' she says, 'would you know?' 'Why shouldn't I know?' I say. Well, she laughed at me and said, 'It's not the sort of book you think . . . it's a novel called *Sanine* by Artsybashev.' 'The artsy pasha?' I said. 'Is he a Turk?' That made her laugh even harder. Ai, missy, I thought, you're laughing your father right into an ulcer! Who knows, I wondered, maybe they're back to planning revolutions again . . . Don't think I wasn't itching to read that book myself!"

"My goodness!"

"I needed a little help, of course. That's when I thought of my shopboy, a real whiz who knows Russian like the back of his hand. I stole the book from my daughter's room one night and brought it to him. 'Here, Berl,' I said. 'I want you to read this tonight and tell me tomorrow what it's all about.' I couldn't wait for it to be morning. 'All right, Berl,' I said, grabbing him as soon as he showed up for work, 'tell me what it says there.' 'Whew, that's some book!' he says, whistling through his teeth. 'I didn't sleep all night, I couldn't put it down for a minute!' 'Is that a fact?' I say. 'In that case, suppose you let me in on it . . .'

"Well, my Berl starts describing the book—what can I tell you? Nothing has anything to do with anything! Listen to a schlock story. 'Once upon a time,' he says, 'there's this goy named Sanine who likes to get drunk and eat pickles . . . And he has a sister, Sanine does, called Lida, who's wild about a doctor, even though she's pregnant by an officer . . . And there's also a student named Yuri, who's crazy in love with a young teacher called Krasavitsa, who goes sailing one night—guess with who?—no, not with the student!—with that boozer, I mean Sanine . . .'

" 'And that's all?' I asked.

" 'Not so fast!' he says. 'I'm not done yet. There's another teacher named Ivan, and he comes along with Sanine to see Krasavitsa take a skinny-dip . . .'

" 'Good for him,' I say. 'But what's the upshot of it all?'

" 'The upshot,' he says, 'is that the boozer, this Sanine, is some stud, and even when he comes home to his own sister, Lida . . .'

" 'Feh,' I say, 'you should be ashamed of yourself! I've had enough of that drunk. Just tell me how it ends. What's the punch line?'

" 'The punch line,' he says, 'is that the officer puts a bullet in his head, and so does the student, and Krasavitsa takes poison, and this Jew, Soloveichik—he's part of it also—goes and hangs himself.'

" 'I wish you'd hanged yourself with him!' I say.

" 'Who, me?' he says. 'What did I do?'

" 'Not you,' I said. 'I meant the artsy pasha.'

"That's what I told my Berl, though I was really thinking of that damned little creep from Navaredok. Don't think I wasn't itching to have it out with him!"

"Well?"

" 'Tell me,' I said to him, 'where did you ever come up with such a schlock story?' 'What schlock story?' he says, turning his gold glasses on me. 'The one about that drunk called Sanine,' I say. 'Sanine is no drunk,' he says. 'Then what is he?' I say. 'He's a hero,' he says. 'What makes him a hero,' I say, 'his eating sour pickles, drinking vodka from a teacup, and carrying on like a studhorse?' That got under his skin, that creep from Navaredok. He took off his glasses, gave me a look with those red, browless eyes of his, and said, 'You may have heard the music, Pa, but you sure can't carry the tune. Sanine lives a free, natural life. Sanine says and does what he wants!'

"And off he goes into a long harangue about the dickens only knows what, freedom and love and love and freedom, waving his hands in the air and sticking out that pigeon breast of his as though he were preaching hellfire. I stood there looking at him and thinking: God in heaven, would you believe a scrawny little twerp like this talking about love?! Suppose I took him by the scruff of his neck and gave him such a shaking that he'd have to pick his teeth up off the floor? Only then I thought, what's the matter with you? So the boy is a bubblehead, so what? Would you rather he had bombs on the brain? . . . Go be a prophet and guess that there are worse things than bombs and that because of that schlock story, I would lose my only daughter, and see my wife go nearly mad with grief, and suffer such shame and heartache that I had to sell my business and move to another town! I can't believe it's been two years already . . .

"But I'm getting ahead of myself. Let me tell you exactly what happened and how it all came about. It started with the peasant riots. We had a good scare in our town when they broke out, because we were afraid pogroms would come next. By some miracle, though, everything turned out for the best. How was that? A regiment of soldiers was sent from the provincial capital, and not only did they restore such order that it was a pleasure, they were a windfall for the whole town. What could be better for business than an entire regiment complete with officers, and adjutants, and quartermasters, and barber-surgeons, and camp followers?"

"That's for sure!"

"Go be a prophet and guess that the cantor's daughter would fall in love with an officer and announce that she was going to baptize herself and marry him! That put the town into a panic.

Not to worry, though: the cantor's daughter wasn't baptized and she didn't marry the officer, because by then the peasant riots were over and he was so involved in decamping with his regiment that he forgot all about saying goodbye to her . . . Except that she couldn't forget about him. Imagine her poor father and mother! It was no joke what they went through. The whole town was in an uproar, wherever you went no one talked about anything else. There were even some bigmouths who spread the word that the cantor's wife had sent for the midwife and went about asking the cantor who he planned to name the child for . . . although to tell you the truth, it's perfectly possible that the whole thing was a figment of their imagination. You know how people in a small town like to gossip . . ."

"Don't they!"

"I felt so sorry for the two of them, the cantor and his wife, that it broke my heart, because when you get right down to it, what fault was it of theirs? I had a daughter of my own, though, and don't think I didn't put my foot down and tell her once and for all, 'Whatever was, was, but from now on you're not friends with that girl any longer!' When I lay down the law, I expect to be obeyed; she may have been an only child, but respect for a father comes first. Go guess that she would go on seeing the girl secretly without anyone knowing about it! When did I find out? When it was already too late . . ."

From behind me came the sound of someone half coughing and half groaning in sleep. The Jew telling the story fell silent for a few moments, then resumed his tale in a lower tone than before.

"It happened at the beginning of Elul. I remember it as though it were yesterday. You should have heard our cantor lead the midnight prayer: why, the way he wept could have moved a stone to tears! No one, but no one, knew what he was feeling as well as I did—believe me, being the father of today's children is no great joy . . . It was already light out when we finished, so I went home, grabbed a bite to eat, took the keys, went to the marketplace, opened the business, and waited for the shopboy to come. I waited half an hour. I waited an hour. Still no shopboy. Finally he appeared. 'Berl,' I said, 'why so late?' 'I was at the cantor's house,' he says. 'What on earth were you doing at the cantor's?' I asked. 'What!' he says, 'Haven't you heard what happened to Chaika?' (That was the cantor's daughter.) 'No,' I said, 'what happened?' 'You won't believe this,' he says, 'but she went and poisoned herself!' "

"Dear me!"

"As soon as I heard that, I ran right home. My first thought was, what will Etke say? (My daughter's name was Etke.) 'Where's Etke?' I asked my wife. 'She's still sleeping,' she says. 'What's wrong?' 'You won't believe this,' I say, 'but Chaika poisoned herself.' The words weren't out of my mouth when my wife grabs her head in her hands and screams: 'Oh, my God! Oh, dear God! Oh, God help her!' 'Who? What?' I said. 'You won't believe this,' she says, 'but Etke spent at least two hours with her just last night.' 'Etke with Chaika?' I say. 'What are you talking about? How can that be?' 'Don't ask me that now!' she says. 'I had to give in to her. She begged me not to tell you that she was seeing her every day. Oh, God! If only this were all a bad dream . . .' And she turns around, my wife, runs into Etke's room, and collapses there on the floor. I ran in after her, straight to the bed. 'Etke! Etke!' I called. What Etke? Who was I calling? She was gone."

"Gone?"

"Dead. In her own bed. There was a bottle on the table with a note beside it, written in her own hand—not in Russian, but in Yiddish. It was a thing of beauty, her Yiddish! 'Dear, darling Papa and Mama,' she wrote. 'Please forgive me for causing you such grief and shame. A hundred times I beg your forgiveness. We promised each other, Chaika and I, that we would die a single death, because we can't live without each other. I know, my dearest ones, that I'm doing a terrible thing to you. I've gone through all kinds of torment. But my fate is my fate, and I must go to meet it . . . I have only one request of you, my dears—that you bury me in a grave next to Chaika's. Be well, and please, please forget you ever had a daughter named Etke . . .' Did you hear that? We should forget we had a daughter named Etke . . ."

There was a sound of stirring behind me, followed by a yawn or a groan and the hoarse, sleep-constricted voice of a woman calling:

"Avreml? . . . Avreml! . . ."

"Gitke, are you up? How did you sleep? Would you like a hot drink? There's a station coming up soon. Where's the thermos? Where did you put the tea and sugar?"

                                                                    (1909)

THE SLOWPOKE EXPRESS

▼

Would you like to know what the best train of all is? The best, the quietest, and the most restful?

It's the Slowpoke Express.

That's what the Jews of Bohopoli call the narrow-gauge local that connects several towns in their district: Bohopoli, Heysen, Teplik, Nemirov, Khashchevate, and a few other such blessed places that are far from the beaten track indeed.

According to the Bohopolians, who have a reputation for being jokesters, the Slowpoke Express is no ordinary train. In the first place, you needn't ever worry about missing it: whenever you arrive at the station, it's still there. Secondly, they say, where else can you find a train on which you never have to fight for a seat—on which, in fact, you can travel for miles all by yourself, stretched out at full length on a bench like a lord and sleeping as much as you please? And they happen to be right on both counts. I've been riding the Slowpoke Express for several weeks now, and I'm still practically in the same place. I tell you, it's magic! Don't think I'm complaining, either. Far from it. I couldn't be more satisfied, because I've seen so many fine sights and heard so many fine tales that I don't know when I'll ever get the chance to jot them all down in my journal.

First, though, let me tell you how this railway came to be built. That's a story in itself.

When word arrived from St. Petersburg that a line was going to be laid (Witte was the minister in charge then), the Jews refused to believe it. What did Teplik, or Golte, or Heysen, need a railroad for? Hadn't they gotten along famously without one until now? And the biggest sceptics were the Bohopolians, who received the news, as was their custom, with a spate of jokes. "Do you see this?" they said, holding up the palms of their hands. "We'll have a railroad the day hair grows here." After a while, however, when an engineer arrived with a team of surveyors, the Jews ate their words and the Bohopolians hid their hands in their pockets. (One good thing about the Bohopoli Jews is that they don't take it to heart when they're wrong. "Even a calendar," they say, "sometimes has the wrong date on it.") Soon the engineer was besieged with documents, references, letters of recommendation, requests for favors—in short, with applications for jobs. A Jew, unfortunately, has to make a living, and it was common knowledge among the good burghers of Teplik, Bershed, Heysen, and Bohopoli that building a railroad was the way to get rich quick. Why, just look at Poliakov in Moscow . . .

There wasn't a Jewish businessman—not just those who dealt in lumber and stone, but wheat and grain merchants too—who didn't try to go to work for the railroad. Overnight the whole district blossomed with contractors, subcontractors, and sub-sub-contractors. "Our Poliakovs," the Bohopolians called them, already busily calculating how they too might get their share of the loot.

In a word, the outbreak of railroad fever spared no one. Even in ordinary times it's hard not to crave an easy ruble, and who can resist becoming a Poliakov quicker than it takes to say one's bedtime prayers?

Indeed, so I was told, the competition among the contractors, the subcontractors, and the sub-subcontractors was so fierce that the contracts had to be raffled off. Whoever was smiled upon by fortune and the chief engineer received one, and whoever didn't had to make do with what could be gleaned from those who did. They were sure to part with something, because the losers had a way of hinting that the road leading to St. Petersburg and the hearts of its officials was open to the general public too . . . To make a long story short, our Jews pawned their wives' pearls and their Sabbath suits to go into the railroad business and ended up by losing every penny and warning their children and grandchildren never to go near a railroad again.

Nevertheless, the one thing had nothing to do with the other. Our Jews, the poor devils, may have been taken to the cleaner's, but a train to travel on they had. And even though, as the reader now knows, the Bohopolians christened it the Slowpoke Express, they can't stop singing its praises and telling its wonders to the world.

For example, they make much of the fact that since the Slowpoke is a slowpoke, there's no danger of the accidents that occur on other lines. The slower the safer, they say—and the Slowpoke is as slow as can be, indeed, a little too slow for comfort. The wits of Bohopoli, who have a tendency to exaggerate, even claim that a local resident once set out on the Slowpoke for his grandson's circumcision in Khashchevate and arrived just in time for the bar mitzvah. And they tell another story about a young man from Nemirov and a young lady from Bershed who arranged to be introduced at a station midway between them; by the time they got there, however, the young lady was toothless and the young man was as gray as a rainy day, and so the match was called off . . .

If you ask me, though, I can do without the Bohopolian joke-sters and their tall tales. When I myself state a fact, it's either something that I've seen with my own eyes or that I've heard from a reliable source like a businessman.

For instance, I have it on good faith from a merchant in Heysen that several years ago, at Hoshana Rabbah time, the Slowpoke was indeed involved in an accident, a veritable catastrophe that sowed panic up and down the line and set the whole district by the ears. The incident was caused by a Jew and—of all people—a Russian priest. I intend to relate it to you in the next story exactly as it was told me by the merchant. I like to pass on items that I've heard from others. You'll see for yourselves when you read it that it's the gospel truth, because a merchant from Heysen could never make up such a thing.

(1909)

THE MIRACLE OF HOSHANA RABBAH

▼

"The Miracle of Hoshana Rabbah—that's what we called the great train accident that took place toward the end of Sukkos. The whole thing happened, don't you know, right in Heysen. That is, not in Heysen itself but a few stops away, in a place called Sobolivke."

With these words a businessman from Heysen, a most compan-ionable fellow, began his jovial account of the catastrophe that befell the narrow-gauge train called the Slowpoke Express, which I described in the last chapter. And since we were on the Slow-poke ourselves—where, being the only passengers in our car, we had all the time and space in the world—he sprawled out as comfortably as if he were in his own living room and gave his narrative talents free rein, turning each polished phrase carefully and grinning with pleasure at his own story while stroking his ample belly with one hand.

"So this is already your second week on our Slowpoke! I suppose you must have noticed, then, that it has a temperament of its own and that once it pulls into a station, it sometimes forgets to pull out. According to the schedule, of course, it mustn't stay a minute longer than it's supposed to. In Zatkevitz, for instance, that's an hour and fifty-eight minutes, and in Sobolivke, which is the place I was telling you about, it's exactly an hour and thirty-two. Bless its sweet little soul, though, if it doesn't stop for over two hours in each, and sometimes for over three! It all depends how long it takes to tank up. Do you know how the Slowpoke's crew tanks up? The locomotive is uncoupled and everyone—the motorman, the conductors, and the stokers—goes off with the stationmaster, the policeman, and the telegraph operator to see how many bottles of beer he can drink.

"And what do the passengers do while the crew is tanking up? That's something you've seen for yourself too: they go stir-crazy, they begin to climb the walls. Some of them just sit there and yawn, some curl up in a corner and grab forty winks, and some walk up and down the platform with their hands behind their backs, humming a little tune.

"Well, it just happened to happen during tank-up time in Sobolivke. One Hoshana Rabbah morning, a Jew was standing by the unhooked locomotive with his hands behind his back—and not even a passenger, don't you know, but a local citizen who had come to have a look-see. How else does a well-off Jew in Sobolivke pass the time on Hoshana Rabbah? He's already waved his palm branch and said his prayers in the synagogue, gone home, and eaten an early dinner. It's only half a holiday, but the next day is a whole one, and there's really nothing much for him to do. What's left but to take his walking stick and go off to meet the train at the station?

" 'Meeting the train,' you have to understand, is a local institution. When the train is due in, a Jew moseys down to the station to have a look at it. Just what does he hope to see that's so exciting—another Jew like himself from Teplik? Or a Jewess from Obodivke? Or a priest from Golovonyevsk? Jewish pleasures! But it was the custom to go, so go this Jew did. And in those days, don't you know, the railroad was new; we weren't used to the Slowpoke yet and we were all still curious about it. Take it this way or that, or any way you like, there by the unhooked locomotive with his walking stick stood a Jew from Sobolivke one Hoshana Rabbah morning, half a holiday it was and half a workday, having himself a look-see.

"Well might you ask: and what of it? Whose business was it if a Jew from Sobolivke stood looking at a locomotive or not? Let him look till the cows come home! It just happened to happen, however, that among the passengers that day was a Russian priest from Golovonyevsk, which is, don't you know, a small town not far from Heysen. And having nothing to do either, he too was walking up and down the same platform with his hands behind his back until he reached the same locomotive. 'Hey, Yudko!' he said to the Jew. 'What are you looking at?'

" 'Since when am I Yudko to you?' the Jew retorted angrily. 'My name isn't Yudko. It's Berko.'

" 'Let it be Berko,' said the priest. 'Tell me, Berko, what are you looking at?'

" 'I'm looking,' said the Jew without taking his eye off the locomotive, 'at one of God's wonders. It's amazing how a ridiculous little thing like turning one throttle this way and another throttle that way can make such a huge engine go.'

" 'What makes you think that turning one throttle this way and another throttle that way will make it go?' asked the priest.

" 'If I didn't know it would, I wouldn't have said so,' said the Jew.

" 'Why, you wouldn't even know how to eat a noodle pudding!' said the priest.

"That got the Jew's dander up so (the Sobolivkan Jews think a lot of themselves) that he said to the priest, 'All right, Father. Suppose you kindly climb aboard with me and let me give you some pointers on how a locomotive runs.'

"Well, by now the priest was pretty damn hot under the collar himself. The idea of that little Jew giving him pointers on anything! And so he said good and loud, 'Go ahead, climb aboard, Hirshko!'

" 'I told you my name isn't Hirshko,' said the Jew. 'It's Berko!'

" 'Fine,' said the priest, 'Berko. Up you go, Berko!'

" 'What do you mean up *I* go?' said the Jew. 'Why me first? Up *you* go, Father!'

" 'It's you who's giving the pointers,' said the furious priest. 'Go ahead!'

"In short, one word led to another, don't you know, and they both climbed aboard the locomotive, where the Jew from Sobolivke began to give the priest driving lessons. He gave one throttle a little twist this way and another throttle a little twist that way, and before they knew it, they were astonished to see that the locomotive was moving and they were off to the races . . .

"I do believe, though, that now is the time to wish them both a pleasant journey and ask ourselves a basic question: exactly who was this Jew from Sobolivke who had the strength of character to board an unhitched locomotive—and with a priest, at that?

"Berl Vinegar—that was the Jew's name. Why Berl Vinegar? Because, don't you know, he makes vinegar, the best money can buy hereabouts. He learned the business from his father, but he himself—I have this directly from Berl—invented a machine that turns out a superior product. If he wanted to, he told me, he could corner the market in three whole provinces. You know what, though? He says he's got time, he's no get-rich-quicknik. That's our vinegar maker. He never studied a day in his life, but there's nothing he doesn't know and no machine he can't take apart. Where did he learn it all? Well, it's no secret that making vinegar has to do with making spirits, and spirits are distilled in a distillery—and a distillery, he told me, has machinery just like a train engine: both work on hot air, so what's the big difference between them? The principle of the thing—Berl used both hands to explain it—is boiling water: you boil the water in a boiler, he says, and when the boiling water's boiled, it turns a shaft, and the shaft, he says, turns the wheels however you want; if you want them to go forwards you turn a gizmo to the right, and if you want them to go backwards you turn a gizmo to the left. Why, it couldn't be simpler, he says! . . . And now that I've introduced you to Berl Vinegar and answered a few questions you may have had about him, suppose we get back to our catastrophe.

"I hardly need to tell you what pandemonium broke out among the passengers in Sobolivke station when they saw the uncoupled locomotive mysteriously take off on its own. That's something you should have no trouble picturing. And the horrified train crew? At first, don't you know, they tried chasing the locomotive. Pretty soon, however, they gave up, because just to show them who was boss, that engine suddenly put on a mad burst of speed. Since the day the Slowpoke made its debut in our parts, no one ever saw it go so fast. The crew came back without it, conferred with the policeman and the stationmaster, drew up a report, and sent out a telegram to all the other stations that said:

" *'Runaway locomotive stop take all necessary precautions stop confirm at once.'*

"It's easy to imagine the panic this telegram sowed all up and down the line. To begin with, nobody understood it. What was *runaway locomotive* supposed to mean? How could a locomotive run away? And secondly, what kind of precautions was anyone supposed to take? What precautions could be taken besides sending out more telegrams? And so the cables began to fly in every possible direction. The wires hummed as if possessed. Every station contacted every other, and the grim tidings spread so far and wide, don't you know, that the whole district was plunged into mourning. In Heysen, for example, our Jews were already quoting casualty counts of how many passengers had been killed. What a horrible way to have to die! And when? On Hoshana Rabbah, just when the Book of Life is being shut for the year! Who can fathom the ways of Providence . . .?

"Well, it was all anyone talked about in Heysen and the villages around. I can't begin to describe to you the mental anguish we all went through. And yet what was that compared to the anguish of the unlucky passengers in Sobolivke station, who were stranded like shepherdless sheep without a locomotive to take them anywhere! What on earth were they supposed to do? It was Hoshana Rabbah, the next day was Simkhes Toyroh, the merriest day of the year—where were they going to be for it? Did anyone seriously expect them to spend it in such a jerkwater? Some fine holiday that would be! . . . The passengers gathered in a corner to discuss their own and the runaway's plight. Who knew what might happen to the schlimazel? It was no joke, an engine like that going for a joyride by itself. And sooner or later it was bound to run into another engine pulling a train from the opposite direction, that is, from Heysen to Sobolivke via Zatkevitz! What would happen to the poor devils aboard? Imaginations ran wild over the horrible collision with all its gory details. It was as vivid as if it had already happened: the overturned cars, the twisted wheels, the mangled bodies, the mutilated limbs, the blood-spattered remains of suitcases . . . at which point another telegram arrived. From Zatkevitz. What did it say? It said:

"Locomotive just passed through Zatkevitz at top speed with two passengers stop one looks a Jew the other a priest stop both waved stop destination unknown stop locomotive headed for Heysen.

"That's when the real shindig started. What could be the meaning of it? A Jew and a priest in a runaway locomotive? Where were they running away to? And why? And who could the Jew be? . . . A few more minutes passed, two and two were put together, and word went around that the Jew was from Sobolivke. *Who? Do you know him? Do I?! Berl Vinegar!* How did everyone know it was Berl? But the fact is that they did. Several Sobolivkans even swore they had seen him standing by the locomotive with a priest, explaining something with his hands. Only what could he have been explaining? What was a vinegar maker doing with a priest by a locomotive? . . . The debate grew so heated that pretty soon it spilled over into the town itself, into Sobolivke, don't you know—and although the town was not far from the station, the story kept growing by such leaps and bounds with each new arrival from there, everyone adding some new touch of his own, that the version reaching Berl's home was so gruesome that Berl's wife must have fainted a good ten times before a doctor could be brought. And simultaneously, don't you know, Jews from Sobolivke began descending on the station like falling stars and raising such a rumpus that the stationmaster had to order the policeman to clear them all out of there—which means that it's time for us to go somewhere else too . . . Suppose, then, that we return to our Jew and our priest in their runaway engine and have a look at what they're up to.

"Having a look at a runaway engine is easier said than done, though. Who's to say what went on in it? All we can do is take Berl Vinegar's word. Granted, his account is full of such wonders that even if only half of it were true, it would be more than enough; still, if I know Berl as I think I do, it's not like him to exaggerate.

"According to Berl, then, his mind went blank when the locomotive pulled out of the station. It wasn't the fright, he says, it was simply not understanding why the engine didn't obey him. Logically speaking, it should have come to a stop with the second turn of the throttle, whereas in actual fact it only picked up more speed. You would have thought that ten thousand devils were pushing it from behind! It was traveling at such a clip that the telegraph poles were dancing like gnats before his eyes, and he felt dizzy and weak all over . . . After a while, though, when he came to his senses, he recalled that a locomotive had a brake. There were indeed—he drew them for me in the air—two brakes: a hand brake and an air brake, which was a kind of wheel that, when given a good turn, did something to the crankshaft, or maybe it was the connecting rod, and brought the engine to a halt. How in the world could it have slipped his mind? And so he took hold of the wheel and was just about to turn it hard to the right when—don't think another hand didn't grab his own. '*Stop!*' Who was it? It was the priest, don't you know, white as a sheet and barely able to talk. 'What are you doing now?' he asked Berl, trembling like a leaf.

" 'Nothing,' said Berl. 'I'm just putting on the brake.'

" 'God help you,' said the priest, 'if you so much as touch another thing! You better listen to me or I'll take you by the collar and throw you out of here so fast that you'll forget your name was ever Moshko!'

" 'It's not Moshko, it's Berko,' said Berl, and tried to explain the principle of the air brake. It didn't do a bit of good, though, because that priest was pretty far gone. 'I don't want to hear about any brake,' he said. 'The only brake that interests me is seeing you break your neck, you little bastard! What did I do to deserve you turning up in my life?'

" 'Father,' said Berl, 'do you think you value your life more than I value my life?'

" '*Your* life?' said the irate priest. 'Who gives a damn for the life of a dog like you?'

"Well, that got Berl's goat so it wasn't even funny, and he gave that priest a piece of his mind. 'In the first place,' he said, 'even a dog has feelings. Our religion forbids us to be cruel to it, because it too is a living creature.' Secondly, said Berl, he wanted to ask the priest something. 'What makes you think that my blood is any less red in God's eyes than yours? Aren't we all descended from Adam? And won't we all be buried in the same earth in the end?' That was number two. And there was something else that Berl told him too. 'Just look at the difference, Father, between you and me. I'm doing my best to stop this locomotive, because I'm trying to save us both, and all you can think of is throwing me out of it— in other words, of murdering your fellow man!'

"He went on laying into him, Berl did, giving that priest such hell that the Father almost had a stroke. He was still going strong, he says, when what did they see go by but Zatkevitz station with its stationmaster and its policeman. They both began waving their hands, but no one seemed to understand them, and there was unfortunately no choice but to head on for Heysen. By now, Berl says, the priest had calmed down a bit, but he still wouldn't let him touch the brake. 'Listen, Liebko,' he said. 'I have a proposal to make to you.'

" 'My name isn't Liebko,' said Berl. 'It's Berko.'

" 'Then Berko,' said the priest. 'Tell me, Berko, what do you say to the two of us making a jump for it?'

" 'What for?' asked Berl. 'So that the two of us can be killed?'

" 'We'll be killed anyway,' said the priest.

" 'What makes you so sure?' Berl challenged him. 'There's no guarantee of that. If God has something else in mind for us—ai, ai, ai, you'd be surprised at the things He can do.'

" 'Such as what?' asked the priest.

" 'I'll tell you such as what, Father,' said Berl. 'We Jews have a day today called Hoshana Rabbah. That's the day on which the fate of every one of us is sealed in the Book of Life for the year— and not only who lives and who dies, but who dies what sort of death. Think of it this way, then: if it's God will that I die, there's nothing I can do about it—what difference does it make to me if it's in a locomotive, or jumping out of it, or getting hit by a thunderbolt? Do you think I can't slip and break my back in the street if that's what God's put me down for? On the other hand, though, if I'm down for another year of life, why kill myself trying to jump?'

"What can I tell you? According to Berl Vinegar of Sobolivke, who swears to the truth of his story with so many oaths that you'd have to believe him even if he weren't a Jew, he can't remember the exact order of things, but as they neared Heysen and saw its big factory chimney in the distance, the locomotive began to go slower and slower until it was going so slow that it decided to stop altogether. What had happened to it? Apparently, says Berl, it had no more coal—and when an engine has no more coal, he says, the water stops boiling, it runs out of steam, and kaput! It's the same, he says, as it is with a man if he doesn't get anything to eat . . . And you can be sure he said to that priest right then and there: 'Well, Father, what did I tell you? If God hadn't written me down for another year of life, who knows how much steam this locomotive might still have and where we might be in it right now?'

"Those were Berl's very words—and the priest, don't you know, just stood there staring at the ground. It was only later, says Berl, when it was time to say goodbye, that the priest stuck out his hand and said to him, 'All the best, Itzko.'

" 'My name,' said Berl, 'isn't Itzko. It's Berko.'

" 'All right,' said the priest, 'Berko. You know something, Berko? I never would have guessed that you were such a—'

"But Berl never heard the rest of it, he says, because the priest hitched up the skirts of his gown and began wending his way home to Golovonyevsk, while he, Berl, walked into town to visit his friends in Heysen. And in Heysen, don't you know, he celebrated the holiday, and thanked God for his deliverance, and told the story of the runaway engine at least a thousand times from A to Z, each time with more miraculous details. All of us insisted on hosting Berl Vinegar in our own homes and hearing about the Miracle of Hoshana Rabbah straight from the horse's mouth, and a merry Simkhes Toyroh was had by all. In fact, we never had a merrier!"

(1909)

THE WEDDING THAT CAME WITHOUT ITS BAND

▼

"I do believe I promised to tell you about another of our Slowpoke's miracles, thanks to which, don't you know, we were saved from a horrible fate. If you'd like to hear about it, why don't you stretch out on this seat and I'll lie down on that one. That way we'll both be more comfortable."

So said my friend, the merchant from Heysen, as we were traveling one day on the narrow-gauge train called the Slowpoke Express. And since this time too we were all by ourselves in the car, which was rather hot, we took off our jackets, unbuttoned our vests, and made ourselves right at home. I let him tell his story in his jovial, unhurried manner, making a few mental notes as he did so that I could write it down later in his own words.

"Once upon a time . . . it happened a while ago, back in the days of the Constitution, when we Jews were getting the glad hand. Actually, though, we in Heysen were never afraid of a pogrom. Shall I tell you why not? For the simple reason that there was no one to do the job. Of course, I don't mean to suggest that if you looked hard enough, you couldn't have found a few public-spirited citizens who would have welcomed the chance to dust off a Jew or two, that is, to break all our bones—the proof of it being, don't you know, that when the glad tidings began to arrive from other places, some of our local patriots dashed off a secret message to whoever they thought it might concern: seeing as how, they wrote, it was time to stand up and be counted in Heysen too, where there was a dearth of volunteers, could they please be sent reinforcements in a hurry . . . And don't you know that twenty-four hours hadn't gone by when word reached us Jews, and again in strictest secrecy, that the reinforcements were already on their way. Where were they coming from? From Zhmerinka, and from Kazatin, and from Razdyelne, and from Popelne, and from a few other places that were equally famous for their roughnecks. How, you ask, did we get wind of such a top secret? The answer, don't you know, is that we had a hidden agent, a fellow called Noyach Tonkonog. Who was this Tonkonog? I'll try to describe him for you, because being a traveler in these parts, you may run into him some day.

"Noyach Tonkonog is a Jew who grew more up than out. And since God gave him a pair of long legs, he learned to put them to good use. He's always on the run and hardly ever at home. He's got a thousand irons in the fire, most of them not his own. His own business, that is, is a printshop. And because it's the only one in Heysen, he rubs elbows with government officials, and with our local gentry, and with all kinds of people in high places.

"It was Noyach who broke the good news to us. That is, he personally spread it around town by whispering in everyone's ear, 'This is strictly for your private consumption, because I'd never

tell anyone else . . .' Before long the word had traveled like wild-
fire that hooligans were being brought in to attack the Jews. We
even knew the exact hour of the attack and the direction it would
come from—it was all planned like a military operation. Well,
there was great gloom in Heysen, don't you know! And it was the
poor who panicked the most. That's not what you'd normally
expect, is it? After all, it makes more sense for a rich Jew to be
scared to death of such a thing, because he's liable to be cleaned
out of house and home. If you own nothing to begin with, on the
other hand, why worry? What's there to lose? Still, you should
have seen them drop everything, grab their children, and run
pell-mell for cover . . . Just where, you ask, does a Jew hide in
Heysen? Either in the cellar of a friendly Russian, or in the attic of
the town notary, or wherever the owner puts you in his factory.
And in fact, everyone managed to find a place. There was only
one Jew who didn't bother, and you're looking at him right now.
I'm not trying to boast, mind you, but you'll see if you think about
it that I had logic on my side. In the first place, what good does it
do to be afraid of a pogrom? You either live through it or you
don't . . . And secondly, even assuming that I'm no braver than
the next man, and that, when push comes to shove, I'd like to be
someplace safe myself, where, I ask you, is safe? Whose word do I
have that, in all the excitement, the same friendly Russian, or
town notary, or factory owner isn't going to . . . do you follow me?
And besides, how can you just go and abandon a whole town? It's
no trick to skedaddle—the whole point is to stay and do something! . . . Of course, you may object, that's easy to say, but what
exactly can a Jew do? Well, I'll tell you what: a Jew can find a
string to pull. I suppose there's someone with the right sort of
influence where you come from, too. In Heysen he's called Nachman Kassoy, a contractor with a round beard, a silk vest, and a big
house all his own. And because he builds roads, he was on good
terms with the prefect of the district, who even used to have him
over for tea. This prefect, don't you know, was quite a decent goy.
In fact, he was a prince of a goy! Why do I say that? Because he
had his price, if you paid it through Nachman Kassoy. That is, he
was perfectly willing to accept gifts from anyone (why be rude,
after all?), but he liked getting them from Nachman best of all.
There's something about a contractor, don't you know . . .

"In short, I fixed things via Nachman, drew up a list of donors, and managed to raise the funds—and a tidy little sum it was too, don't you know, because you couldn't cross a prefect's palm in such a matter without giving it some good scratch . . . in return for which, he did his best to reassure us that we could sleep calmly that night because nothing would happen to us at all. Fair enough, no? The only trouble was that we still had our secret agent, whose reports went from bad to worse; the latest of them, which he of course passed on in such strict confidence that it was all over town in no time flat, was that he, Noyach Tonkonog, had personally seen a telegram that he very much wished he hadn't. What was in it? Just one word, but a most unpleasant one: *yedyem*, it said—here we come! Back to our prefect we ran. 'Your Excellency, it looks bad!' 'How come?' 'There's a telegram.' 'From whom?' 'The same people.' 'What's in it?' '*Yedyem!*' You should have heard him laugh. 'You're bigger fools than I thought,' he said. 'Why, just yesterday I ordered a company of Cossacks from Tulchin for your protection . . .' Well, that put some spunk in us, don't you know: a Jew only needs to see a Cossack to feel so courageous that he's ready to take on the whole world! It was nothing to sneeze at, a bodyguard like that . . .

"In short, there was just one question: who would arrive first, the Cossacks from Tulchin or the roughnecks from Zhmerinka? It stood to reason that the roughnecks would, since they were traveling by train while the Cossacks were on horseback. But we had our hopes pinned on our Slowpoke: God was great, and the only miracle we asked of Him was to make the train a few hours late, which it usually was anyway, in fact, nearly every day . . . Yet for once, don't you know, as though out of spite, the Slowpoke was right on time: it pulled in and out of each station like clockwork. You can imagine how it made our blood run cold to hear from our secret agent that another *yedyem*egram had arrived from Krishtopovka, the last station before Heysen—and this time, for good measure, the *yedyem* had a *yahoo* after it . . . Naturally, we went right to the prefect with the news, threw ourselves at his feet, and begged him not to count on the Cossacks from Tulchin and, if only for appearances' sake, to send a detachment of police to the station so that the hooligans shouldn't think the only law was that of the jungle. His Excellency didn't let us down. In fact, he quite rose to the occasion. What do I mean by that? I mean, he put on his full dress uniform with all its medals and went off to the station with the entire police force to meet the train.

"But our local patriots, don't you know, weren't caught napping either. They had also put on their best clothes and their medals, taken along a pair of priests for good luck, and gone off to meet the train at the station—where, in fact, they asked the prefect what he was doing there, which was the exact same question he asked them. A few words were exchanged, and the prefect made it clear that they were wasting their time. As long as he was in charge, he said, there would be no pogroms in Heysen. He read them the riot act, but they just grinned back at him and even had the cheek to answer, 'We'll soon see who's in charge around here . . .' Just then a whistle was heard. It made our hearts skip a beat. We were all waiting for it to blow again, followed by a loud 'Yahoo!'—and what that 'Yahoo!' meant, don't you know, we already knew from other towns . . . Would you like to hear the end of it, though? There was a second whistle, all right, but there never was any 'Yahoo.' Why not? It could only have happened on our Slowpoke. Listen to this.

"The driver pulled into Heysen station, climbed out of the engine full of prunes, and headed straight for the buffet as usual. 'Just a minute, old man,' he was asked. 'Where's the rest of the train?' 'What rest of the train?' he said. 'Do you mean to say you didn't notice,' he was asked, 'that your engine wasn't pulling any cars?' That driver, he just stared at them and said: 'What do I care about cars? That's the crew's job.' 'But where's the crew?' he was asked. 'How should I know?' he answered. 'The conductor whistles that he's ready, I whistle back that I am too, and off I go. I don't have eyes in the back of my head to see what's following behind me . . .' So he said, the driver—there was nothing wrong with his logic. In a word, it was pointless to argue: the Slowpoke had arrived without its passengers like a wedding without its band . . .

"As we found out later, that train was carrying a merry gang of young bucks, the pick of the crop, each man jack of them, and in full battle gear too, with clubs, and tar, and what-have-you. They were in a gay old mood, don't you know, and the vodka flowed like water, and when they reached their last station, that is to say, Krishtopovka, they had themselves such a blast that the whole train crew got drunk too, the conductor and the stoker and even the policeman—in consequence of which, one little detail was forgotten: to hitch up the locomotive again. And so, right on schedule, the driver took off in it for Heysen while the rest of the Slowpoke, don't you know, remained standing on the tracks in Krishtopovka! Better yet, nobody—neither the roughnecks, nor the other passengers, nor even the train crew—noticed what had happened. They were all so busy emptying glasses and killing bottles that the first they knew about it was when the stationmaster happened to look out the window and see the cars standing by themselves. Did he raise Cain! And when the rest of the station found out, all hell broke loose: the pogromchiks blamed the train crew, and the train crew blamed the pogromchiks, and they went at it hot and heavy until they realized that there was nothing to do but shoulder their legs and tote them all the way to Heysen. What other choice did they have? And that's exactly what they did: they rallied round the flag and hotfooted it to Heysen, where they arrived safe and sound, don't you know, singing and yahooing for God and country. Shall I tell you something, though? They got there a little too late. The streets were already patrolled by mounted Cossacks from Tulchin, who clearly had the whip hand—and I do mean whips! It didn't take those hooligans half an hour to clear out of town down to the last man. They vanished, don't you know, like a pack of hungry mice, or like snow on a hot summer's day . . .

"Well now, suppose you tell me: shouldn't our Slowpoke be plated with gold, or at least written up in the papers?"

(1909)

THE *TALLIS KOTON*

▼

"Speaking of the Drozhne fire—would you like to hear a good one about how a skinflint of a Jew, a rich man who would sooner have parted with his life than with a penny's worth of charity, was made to cough up a hundred rubles for the relief fund?"

The question was put to me one morning by my merchant friend from Heysen, who had finished his breakfast, lit up a cigarette, and extended one to me too. The story he proposed to tell appeared to amuse him greatly, because he burst right out laughing as though he had thought of the funniest thing. In fact, he laughed so hard that I was afraid he would choke. If you don't let a man get it out of his system all at once, though, he'll just laugh his way through everything. And so I waited for him to collect himself, let out a few last wheezes, and begin.

"I've already described a few local characters for you. Now let me tell you about another. His name is Yoyl Tashker and he's certainly nothing to look at. You wouldn't give a plugged nickel for him. A short little, thin little, prim little man with a wisp of a beard, and a walk—why, he scoots down the street as though the Devil himself were after him! And yet he's a wealthy Jew, don't you know. Did I say wealthy? The man is a millionaire! That is, I've never counted his money. He may really have a million and he may not have half that much. Believe me, though, whatever he has is more than he deserves, because the man is the world's biggest tightwad. It's easier to squeeze water from a stone than it is to squeeze a cent out of him. There's not a beggar in town he ever gave a crumb of bread to. In fact, if someone you've given a handout grumbles about the small size of it, the stock answer in Heysen is, 'Why don't you try Yoyl Tashker, I'll bet he's good for more!' That's the kind of rich Jew he is. Please don't get the impression, though, that the man is a cheat, or a lowlife, or a boor. Far from it. He comes from a good family, he's an educated fellow, and he couldn't be any more honest. He goes by the rules in everything and only asks to be left alone: you keep to your side of the fence and I'll keep to mine . . . do you get the picture? He's a moneylender by profession, but he also owns houses and does business with our local gentry. And he's a fiend for work, don't you know, twenty-four hours a day; always traveling, always on the go, never eating or sleeping . . . and quite alone in the world too, without kith or kin, he won't even hire an assistant. That is, he has children somewhere, but—I'll be blamed if I know the reason why—he's cut off every one of them. I've heard it said that they're in America. After the death of his first wife, he simply went and drove them all out. And they say she died of hunger, too! Well, I suppose that's just gossip . . . although who knows if there isn't some truth in it, because the fact is that his second wife didn't last two weeks with him either. Would you like to know why he divorced her? It was on account of a glass of milk. I swear, as I'm a Jew! He caught her with it one day and said, 'One way or another, that does it! If you're drinking milk for your health because you're consumptive, a fat lot I need you around here. And if you're drinking it just for the fun of it, the sooner I get rid of a spendthrift like you, the better.'

"I will say one thing for Yoyl Tashker, though (no one is ever all bad): he's as pious as the day is long. Why, such piety could scare the pants off a preacher! I'm the last person to object to religion in a man: if that's how he wants to live his life, who am I to tell him otherwise? But that's not enough for Tashker. No, he wants the whole world to be as religious as he is, he thinks he's God's legal executor: a Jew going hatless is a personal insult, a married woman's hair makes him see red, parents sending a child to a Russian school can expect to catch hell from him, and so on and so forth . . .

"Well, as fate would have it, this Yoyl Tashker has a tenant living next door to him, a notary public who is not exactly a paragon of devoutness: he goes about shaven and bareheaded, smokes on the Sabbath, and doesn't miss many other tricks, either. Kompanyevitch is the name: a big, tall, slightly stoop-shouldered, baggy-cheeked fellow with the Devil in his eyes—but a quiet one, don't you know, the kind that doesn't flaunt his debauchery. He earns more at the card table than he does at his notary's desk, and his place is a hangout for all our fine youngsters who enjoy a good game of triumph, a snack of pork sausage, and other such similar pleasures . . . Well, it's as I was saying: if you happen to have a neighbor who's no candidate for sainthood, why let him get under your skin? I'm referring to Yoyl Tashker, of course. This Kompanyevitch wasn't proposing to his daughter, so why get all worked up over him? But no, it drove Tashker up the wall. How could Kompanyevitch dare put up his samovar on the Sabbath? Where did he get off serving a seven-course meal on a fast day like Tisha b'Av? Who did he think he was, not koshering his dishes for Passover? And so on and so forth: he poured fire and brimstone on him, he called him every name in the book, he went about telling the whole world, 'Did you ever hear of such nerve in your life? The man pretends to be a Jew and makes tea on the Sabbath like a goy!' . . . When Kompanyevitch heard that, don't you know, he made sure to put up two samovars the next time. Our Yoyl nearly had a heart attack. What a card! He only had to terminate the lease in order to solve the whole problem, but he couldn't bring himself to do it. Of all his tenants, he said, only the notary paid his rent on time. Can you beat that?

"I've already introduced you to two new characters. Now I want you to meet a third, a fellow by the name of Froike-Sheygetz. He's a type too, and has a role to play in our story. In fact, there wouldn't be one without him.

"Froyke-Sheygetz, don't you know, is one of a kind, a hail-fellow-well-met, as they say, who dresses half like a Hasid and half like a Parisian dandy. He wears a long black gaberdine with a derby on his head, is partial to bright-red ties, and goes about with the fringes of his *tallis koton* hanging out of his shirt. There's a rumor around town that he's involved with a woman, and another man's wife at that . . . yet when it's prayer time in the synagogue, he's there faster than a bat out of hell. In a word, he's God's own rascal! What does he do for a living? He's a one-percenter: he brokers checks, loans, IOUs. A lot of rubles pass through his hands—thousands and thousands of them. And he's the one person Yoyl Tashker ever had complete trust in. When it comes to lending money, don't you know, even handing over a hundred gives Tashker the willies, but with the green light from Froyke, you could consider it as good as done. Personally, though, I wouldn't jump from that to the conclusion that our Froyke is a model of financial integrity. He's a shrewd, cunning son-of-a-gun, and one who doesn't take no for an answer. I'd rather wind up in hell itself than in his clutches! Efrayim Katz, by the way, is his real name— and now you know why he's called Froyke-Sheygetz.

"Well, having introduced my three characters, I can get on with the plot. Our story takes place during last summer's fires, when the whole town of Drozhne, God save us, burned to the ground. Letters, telegrams, appeals for help—all began pouring in: we should send as much as we could as fast as we could, because a town full of Jews was sleeping in the streets and going hungry. I don't have to tell you what a yammering there was in Heysen. *Jews, have a heart! How can you just sit there? We have to do something!* Between this, that, and the other thing it was decided to appoint a fund-raising committee. Who was on it? Myself, naturally, along with a few other leading citizens—among them, don't you know, Froyke-Sheygetz, because we needed someone who wouldn't take no for an answer. And so we began to pass around the basket. Who did we pass it to first? To our better-heeled Jews, of course. Which brought us to Yoyl Tashker. 'A good morning to you, Reb Yoyl!' 'And a good morning to you! What can I do for you? Have a seat.' You couldn't have asked for a finer reception. Tashker, don't you know, is the very soul of hospitality: knock on his door and he'll ask you right in, bring you a chair, make you sit down, talk to you about anything at all . . . as long as it isn't money. Try raising *that* subject, and his whole expression changes: one eye slams shut and the entire left side of his face begins to twitch as though he had the palsy. I tell you, it's painful just to look at him! But that's the sort of fellow he is.

"Let's see now, what act was I up to? Yes; our committee called on Tashker. 'Good morning, Reb Yoyl.' 'Good morning to you. Have a seat. What can I do for you?' 'We've come to ask for a contribution.' Down goes one eye, and his cheek gives a jerk that I wouldn't wish on my knee. 'A contribution? Just like that, you want a contribution?' Well, Froyke-Sheygetz didn't take that for an answer. 'It's for a good cause, Reb Yoyl,' he says, 'the best there could be. You must have heard about it. A whole town, it shouldn't happen to us, has burned to the ground. Drozhne . . .' 'What?' cried Reb Yoyl. 'Drozhne's burned down? What are you talking about?! I'm ruined! How can it possibly have gone and burned, with all the uncollected debts I have there? I'm wiped out! . . .' There was nothing Froyke didn't do to convince him that his loans were perfectly safe, because the fire had broken out in the poorest neighborhoods where no one could afford to borrow money—but go try explaining something like that to someone who doesn't want to listen! Tashker just wrung his hands, ran around the room like a madman, and kept moaning out loud, 'It's my luck! I'm wiped out! I can't stand to hear another word! It's the death of me! It's more than a body can bear! . . .'

"How much longer were we going to sit there? We got up, said 'Good day, Reb Yoyl,' and walked out. Once we were in the street again, Froyke-Sheygetz said to us, 'Listen here, all of you: if I don't make that bastard cough up a hundred rubles for the Drozhne relief fund, my name isn't Efrayim Katz!' 'Are you crazy,

Froyke?' we all said to him. 'What's it to you?' said Froyke. 'If I tell you he's giving me the money, it's as good as in my pocket already, because Efrayim Katz is damn well my name!'

"He meant every word of it, too. Listen to what happened. A few days later our rich friend Yoyl Tashker was taking the train to the Tulchin fair. His neighbor Kompanyevitch was aboard too, as were a whole lot of Jews from Tolchin and Uman. There wasn't a seat to be had, and everyone was talking at the top of his voice as usual—everyone, that is, except for Yoyl Tashker, who sat in a corner as usual too, reading a religious book. What did he have to talk about, after all, with any of those Jews? And especially with that degenerate Kompanyevitch, whom he couldn't even stand the sight of. And just as though to get his goat, don't you know, Kompanyevitch had gone and sat right across from him and was giving him the silent stare! Great God Almighty, Reb Yoyl kept thinking, who will rescue me from this pig eater? To move to the second-class car was a sinful waste of good money, but to have to keep looking at the nude chin of an assassin who had the very Devil in his eyes was hardly a more tolerable prospect . . . Only just then, don't you know, the prayed-for miracle occurred: whom did God make board the train at the very next station if not someone Tashker knew—in fact, none other than our good friend Froyke-Sheygetz! The sight of Froyke made Tashker feel like a new man; at last there was someone to have a word with. 'Where to?' he asked Froyke. 'Where to?' Froyke asked him. And so they began to chat. About what? About everything under the sun—until they arrived at a topic that was close to Yoyl Tashker's heart: the sorry state of today's youth. Worthless young men, shameless young women—what could the world be coming to? Froyke-Sheygetz was in perfect agreement; in fact, he even chipped in with a story of his own about a newlywed from Uman who had run away from her husband to take up with a Russian officer. Then he told another about a bridegroom who had married two different women in two different cities, and still another about a youngster who, when struck by his father for refusing to put on his tefillin, had put up his fists and fought back. *'What, hit his own father?!'* That caused an uproar in the car. Everyone was aghast—and no one more than Yoyl Tashker. 'What did I tell you? My very word! It's sheer anarchy. Jewish children won't even pray any more! They won't even put on their tefillin . . .'

" 'Tefillin are one thing,' suddenly said Kompanyevitch, who hadn't let out a peep all this time. 'You can take them or leave them, it's not them I'm concerned about. But a *tallis koton* is something else. It's simply beyond me why young people won't wear it any more! After all, you can't deny that tefillin are a nuisance. You have to put them on, you have to take them off . . . but a simple fringed undershirt such as the Bible tells us to wear—who could possibly object to it?'

"Those words were spoken by our infidel in such a calm, deliberate, assured tone of voice that Tashker, don't you know, couldn't have been more thunderstruck if the train had suddenly turned upside down or been hit by lightning. 'I better have my ears examined!' he thought. 'The Messiah must have come! Would you listen to the pork lover talk about *tallis kotons? Tallis kotons!!!*' And out loud to Froyke he exclaimed, 'What do you say to this sheep in wolf's clothing, eh? Did you hear what he said about *tallis kotons?*'

" 'But what's wrong with it?' asked Froyke, as innocent as a lamb himself. 'Isn't Mr. Kompanyevitch a Jew like you and me?'

"That was already too much for our Tashker. In the first place, since when was it *Mr.* Kompanyevitch? And in the second place, since when was Kompanyevitch a Jew? 'A Jew? Don't make me laugh! A Jew who puts the samovar up on the Sabbath? Who serves a seven-course meal on Tisha b'Av? Who doesn't even kosher his dishes for Passover? That's who's talking *tallis kotons?*'

" 'But why not?' persisted Froyke, still the picture of innocence. 'What does the one thing have to do with the other, Reb Yoyl? If you ask me, a Jew like Kompanyevitch can do everything you say and still wear a *tallis koton* himself.'

" 'What?!!' cried our Tashker at the top of his voice. '*That* beardless wonder? *That* degenerate? *That* living affront to man and God?'

"Everyone fell silent and stared at Kompanyevitch. Kompanyevitch, however, said nothing. Nor, for that matter, did Froyke-Sheygetz. All at once, though, he jumped to his feet like a man throwing caution to the wind and declared, 'You know what, Reb Yoyl? It's my considered opinion that the Jewish soul runs deeper than you think. If a Jew cares about *tallis kotons*, he must be wearing one himself. I'll bet you a hundred rubles that Kompanyevitch is, the loser to donate the money to the Drozhne relief fund. Just

say the word, and I'll ask him to do us the big favor of opening his
shirt and jacket and showing us what's underneath them!'

" 'Bravo!' cried everyone, breaking into such a clamor that the
whole car was hopping with excitement. Kompanyevitch alone
went on sitting there without a word, as if none of this concerned
him in the least. You might have thought that someone else was
being talked about. And our good friend Yoyl Tashker? The poor
devil was as bathed in sweat as if he were turning on a slow spit.
Never in his whole life had he wagered so much as a ruble on
anything—and here he was being asked to risk a hundred! And
suppose—no, it was too horrible even to think of—just suppose
that the scoundrel was wearing a *tallis koton,* after all? . . . On
second thought, though, Reb Yoyl reflected,'Come, now: Kompanyevitch? *That renegade?* I'll be hanged if it's possible'—and, screw-
ing up his courage, he reached into his coat, took out a hundred
rubles, and handed them to the two trustworthy Jews who had
meanwhile been appointed as seconds. They, in turn, requested
of Kompanyevitch that he undress. *Who? Me? Not on your life!*
'What do you take me for?' he asked. 'A schoolboy? A vaudeville
performer? Since when does a grown man strip naked in broad
daylight in front of a crowd of Jews?'

"Kompanyevitch's protests were music to Yoyl Tashker's ears.
'So!' he said to Froyke, his face lighting up. 'Who's right? You
can't fool me! Why, the thought of a Jew like that with a *tallis
koton* . . . what a laugh!'

"Things weren't looking any too good. Everyone turned to
Kompanyevitch. 'How can you do this to us! One way or another,
what do you have to lose? Just think of it: a hundred rubles for the
Drozhne relief fund!'

" 'A hundred rubles for the relief fund!' echoed Yoyl Tashker,
doing his best not to look at his neighbor.

" 'Think of the poor Jews, men, women, and children, without a
roof over their heads!'

" 'Without a roof, just imagine!' echoed Tashker.

" 'Where's the God in your heart?' Kompanyevitch was asked.

" 'Where's the God?' Tashker wanted to know.

"Well, it wasn't easy, but in the end Kompanyevitch was persuaded to remove his jacket, take off his vest, and unbutton his
shirt. Didn't I tell you he was a character? Under his shirt was a
tallis koton, all right—and not just an ordinary *tallis koton* either,

but a big, fancy, superkosher one with a blue border all around it and a double set of fringes that would have done a rabbi proud. It was a *tallis koton* to end all *tallis kotons,* let me tell you! Leave it to a rascal like Froyke-Sheygetz! True, he lost Yoyl Tashker's business then and there. Froyke hasn't dared show his face to Tashker ever since. But he did raise a hundred rubles for the Drozhne relief fund—and from whom? From a rich scrooge of a Jew who never gave a penny's worth of charity in his life, not even a crust of dry bread! Doesn't someone like that deserve a good whipping? I mean someone like Froyke, of course . . ."

(1910)

A GAME OF SIXTY-SIX

▼

The following, which I heard on the train from a dignified gentleman of about sixty whom I took to be a commercial traveler like myself, is related here word for word, as has lately been my habit.

"You know, if you always had to pass the time traveling by making conversation with a fellow passenger, you could go out of your mind.

"In the first place, you never know who you're getting involved with. There are some people who not only like to talk, they like it so much that they give you a headache—and there are others you can't get a word out of. But not a single word! It's anyone's guess why you can't. Maybe they're in a bad mood. Maybe they have an upset stomach, or an attack of gall bladder, or a toothache. Maybe they're even running away from some private hell at home—a house full of brats, a shrew of a wife, problems with the neighbors, a business that can't pay its debts. Whoever knows what goes on inside another person?

"I know what you'll tell me: if I don't feel like talking, why don't I read a newspaper, or take a look at a book? Ah, newspapers: if only they were the same on the road as they are at home! At home I have my regular paper, I'm as used to it, you might say, as I am to my own slippers. It may be that your slippers are newer than mine. In fact, mine are not only old, they're so worn-out that they look, you should excuse the comparison, like a pair of cold blintzes. Still, they have one advantage over yours—namely, that they happen to be mine . . .

"Well, a newspaper, for all the difference between them, is just like a slipper. I have a neighbor back home who lives on the same floor of the same building as I do, in fact, right next door to me. He gets a paper delivered, and so do I. It's just not the same one. One day I said to him, 'What's the point of the two of us getting two different papers? Why not go halves with me in mine, and we'll share one paper between us.' 'Why not indeed?' he says. 'It's a fine idea. Only why not go halves with me in mine?' 'Because your paper,' I say, 'is a rag. Mine is a newspaper.' 'Who says my paper is a rag?' he says. 'It so happens to be the other way around.' 'Since when are you such a big expert on newspapers?' I say. 'Since when are you?' he says. 'Eh!' I say, 'I never realized what an impossible Jew you were. What's the point of even talking to you?' . . .

"In short, he kept getting his newspaper, I kept getting mine, and time went by. Until one day—it was during the cholera epidemic in Odessa (my neighbor and I both do business there)—a funny thing happened. We both went downstairs to meet the delivery boy, both got our newspapers, and were both reading them on our way back up, he his paper and I mine. What's the first thing you read in a newspaper? The news bulletins, of course. So I looked at the first item from Odessa and it said, 'Yesterday there were 230 new cases of cholera and 160 deaths. General Tolmachov summoned all the Jewish synagogue sextons to his residence,' etcetera . . . Well, I could do without Tolmachov and the synagogue sextons. You couldn't even call that news; if he didn't find some new way of hassling Jews every day, his name wouldn't be Tolmachov. What interested me was the cholera. And so I said to my neighbor (he was practically walking down the corridor on my toes—that's how crude he is!), 'What do you say about Odessa, eh? Cholera again!'

" 'It can't be,' he says to me.

"That riled me. What did he mean, it couldn't be? So I took my newspaper and read the bulletin from Odessa out loud to him. 'Yesterday there were 230 new cases of cholera and 160 deaths.

General Tolmachov summoned all the Jewish synagogue sextons to his residence,' etcetera. 'We'll see about that in a minute,' he says and sticks his nose back in his newspaper. That riled me even more. 'What do you think,' I said, 'that your paper has different news from my paper?'

" 'You never know,' he mumbled.

" 'Are you trying to tell me,' I said, getting still madder, 'that your paper writes about a different Odessa, and about a different Tolmachov, and about a different cholera than mine does?'

"He didn't even answer me. He just went right on searching that paper of his for news of the cholera from Odessa. Now go try making conversation with a primitive like that!

"No, sir. There's a better way than that to kill time on a train, and that's with a good game of cards. I mean with a game of sixty-six.

"In general, I'm sure you'll agree with me that cards are the Devil's own invention—but on a long train ride they're a godsend. The time simply flies when you get a game going. Of course, it has to be with the right people. If it isn't, God save you from the mess you're liable to get yourself into! You have to make sure you don't fall in with a bunch of card sharks who can play you for a sucker and take you for all you're worth. It's not all that easy to tell one of them from an honest man. In fact, most of those fellows make believe they're poor innocent saps themselves. They'll pretend to be more dead than alive, or moan and groan over each bad hand—but it's all just an act to get you into the game. And even then they'll let you win a few times . . . until little by little your luck turns bad and you begin to lose. That's when they've got you where they want you. Believe me, before you've seen the last of them you'll have gambled away your gold watch, and the chain that goes with it, and anything else of value you may have. Even after you realize that you've been had by pros, you'll go right on playing like a sheep that can't take its head out of the wolf's mouth. Oh, I know them, I do! And I've paid dearly for the privilege . . . Why, I could tell you no end of stories! When you travel like I do, you get to hear them all.

"For instance, there's the one about the cashier who was traveling with his boss's money—and a nice little bundle it was. He ran into some sharpies, lost the whole caboodle, and nearly jumped out of the train window . . .

"Or else I could tell you about the young man from Warsaw who was coming back from his father-in-law's with his dowry. He was relieved of the entire amount and passed out right on the train . . .

"And then there's the case of the student from Chernigov who was on his way home for the holidays with the few hard-earned rubles he had made tutoring over the summer vacation. The money wasn't for himself either, but for an old mother and a sick sister, the poor things, who were counting on every penny of it . . .

"You can see for yourself that each of these sad stories begins and ends the same way—and no one knows it better than I do. Believe you me, I won't fall for it a second time! Once was more than enough. Why, I can spot one of those birds a mile away now. And I have a strict rule besides: no card games with strangers! I wouldn't sit down to play with you if you offered me the world . . . except, that is, for a little two-hand game of sixty-six. Sixty-six— now that's a different story entirely! What danger is there, I ask you, in a friendly game of sixty-six? And especially if the cards are my own—what's to be afraid of? You see, I never travel without my own pack of cards. Just as a good Jew takes his tallis and tefillin with him everywhere, so I always have my cards.

"To tell you the truth, I like a good game of sixty-six. It's a Jewish game, your sixty-six is. I don't know about you, but I like to play it the old way, with marriages worth twenty and forty. If I've won a trick, I can exchange the nine of trumps for the deck trump, and if I haven't, I can't. Fair enough, no? That's how we Jews play it everywhere, at home and on the road. I may not look the type, but if I get into a game of sixty-six while I'm traveling I can go on playing nonstop, day and night. The one thing I don't like are the kibitzers. God forgive me for speaking frankly, but we Jews are a revolting people. It's practically impossible to play a game of sixty-six with a crowd of Jews around. Before you know it, they're standing all over you and telling you what card to play and whether to trump or not. You can't get rid of them, they stick to you like flies! I've tried saying everything, but nothing makes them go away. 'Look here, my friend, when I want your advice I'll ask for it.' Or, 'Hey, Mr. Buttinski, why don't you keep your opinions to yourself?' Or, 'Would you mind not using me as a leaning post? If there's anything worse than bad manners, it's bad breath.' You might as well talk to the wall!

"Once, you know, a kibitzer got me into such trouble that I was lucky to get out of it again. I can't resist telling you about it.

"It happened one winter. On the train, of course. The car was packed with people and as hot as a Turkish bath. There were as many Jews as stars in the sky, far more than there were seats—why, you couldn't stick a needle between them! And it was then of all times that who should turn up but the perfect partner for a game of sixty-six—a quiet, simple Jew, it so happened, but one every bit as wild for it as I am. We looked for a place to put the cards—there wasn't a square inch available. So what does the good Lord do? Face-down on the bench right across from us is a monk in a sheepskin coat, having himself a snooze. As a matter of fact, he's snoring away so merrily that you can hear him all over the car. I looked at my partner, my partner looked at me—there was no need for words. A big, fat, broad-bottomed monk with a nice, soft sheepskin on him . . . what better table for a game of sixty-six could you ask for? Without wasting any time, we laid the cards on his you-know-what and began to play.

"If I remember correctly, spades were trump. I had the king, queen, and jack, the ace of clubs, the king of diamonds, and . . . but what was my sixth card? I've forgotten whether it was the nine or ten of hearts. I think it was the nine. Or could it have been the ten, after all? Well, it makes no difference. In short, I had a dream hand: forty points before a card was played, with a chance for three game-points. The only question was, what would my partner lead with? If he was a nice enough Jew to lead with a club, he'd make me a happy man. And don't think that isn't what he did! He thought and thought (good Lord, I wondered, how long can you think about a card?) and finally came out with none other than the ten of clubs. I could have kissed him for it! But when I play sixty-six, you know, it's not like me to get excited the way some people do. Easy does it. What's the rush? On the contrary, I like to have a bit of fun. And so I pulled my ear, made a face—why not? Let my partner have the short-lived pleasure of thinking I'm in a fix . . . How was I to know that a Jew was standing behind me and looking at my hand—he should stand on his head until his eyes fall out! Seeing as how I was taking my time, he reached over my shoulder, grabbed the ace of clubs, threw it on top of the ten, gave the deck of cards a whack right on the fat monk's bottom, and shouted:

" 'The ace takes!' . . .

"Well, a nest of angry hornets would have been easier to shoo off than that monk! May all his curses be on him! He kept threatening to get off at the first station and turn us in to the police . . . I ask you: why can't a person be allowed to live?

"But that's neither here nor there. I just wanted you to know what some people will go through for a good game of sixty-six. I've only gotten to the real story now. Listen.

"It happened in winter too, around Hanukkah time, and on the train again. I was on my way to Odessa with some money, a whole big wad of it—I should only earn so much in a month! It's a rule of mine not to sleep when I travel with money. It's not that I'm afraid of thieves, because I keep it—guess where?—right here in my jacket pocket, in a good wallet that's tied twice to be safe. I pity the thief who thinks he can make off with it! It's just that these days, you never know . . . riots, expropriations . . . why take chances? . . . Well, there I was, sitting that winter day all by myself. I don't mean I was alone in the car; there were other passengers too, but none of them were Jews. What good did that do me? There wasn't a soul to play a game of sixty-six with. Just as I was beginning to feel sorry for myself, though, the door of the car opens—we were still quite a few stops away from Odessa—and in walks a pair of our fellow Israelites. You know, I can spot a Jew anywhere, even if he's dressed like a dozen Russians and speaking Russian too, or for that matter, Chinese. One of the pair was an older man and the other was a younger one, and you should have seen what fine fur hats and coats they wore. Fine isn't the word! They put down their luggage, took off their hats and coats, smoked a few cigarettes, gave me one too—and we began to talk, at first, of course, in Goyish, and then in Yiddish. 'Where are you from? Where are you going?' 'Where are you going?' 'To Odessa.' 'To Odessa? That's where I'm going too!' 'Well, then, that makes three of us.' We chatted about this and that until one of them says to the other, 'Say, did you know that today is a holiday?' 'It is?' says the other. 'Have you forgotten that it's Hanukkah?' says the first. 'Hanukkah, eh?' says the second. 'Why, I do believe that it's a Jewish custom on Hanukkah to play a friendly game of cards. How about a little sixty-six?' 'Good idea!' says the younger man, reaching into the older one's pocket and taking out a pack of cards. 'All right, Papa! Let's play a game of sixty-six in honor of Hanukkah . . .'

"So the two of them were father and son: it tickled my funny bone to think of them playing sixty-six together! In fact, I had quite an urge to play with them myself, but I was resolved not to give in to temptation. Just watching them would be entertainment enough . . .

"They upended one of their suitcases, stood it between their legs, and dealt the cards. The father played first hand and the son second, and I sat looking on. After a while the old man turned to me and asked if I knew how to play. I had to laugh at that: it was a good one, all right—why, I had practically invented the game, and here I was being asked if I played it! In fact, it took a will of iron to sit watching quietly, because the way that old codger played his hand could have made you turn over in your grave. Just imagine: the man sits there holding the queen, jack, and nine of trumps, two spades, and the ten of clubs—he only has to take the first trick with the ten and exchange the nine for the deck trump, which happens to be a king, in order to declare a trump marriage. Not him! The old bumblepuppy decides to play the jack of spades instead—and with a perfectly good ten in his hand! So what does his son do? The young rascal takes the jack with a queen, declares two twenty-point marriages, draws the ace of clubs from the deck, tops the old man's ten with it, and goes out as pretty as you please with three game-points, just as God would have wanted!

"That was a hand to remember!

"What followed, though, was even worse; I tell you, it could have made a man scream! Listen to this. The father has six game-points already, he needs just one more to win. His son has only three. Better yet, the old geezer draws a hand with three trumps and a twenty-point marriage to boot. He doesn't declare it, though, even when he takes the first trick; no, he's afraid to play the king or queen, he's worried his son may top them. Well, his son takes the next trick, declares twenty points of his own, closes the stock, breaks up the marriage, and schneiders his father but good! . . . That was already too much for me; such an agonizing Hanukkah I had never yet spent in my life. I couldn't go on watching any longer. 'You'll have to excuse me,' I said to the old coot. 'It's a principle of mine never to kibitz, but I'm dying to know why you played that way. What were you thinking of? If your partner was holding junk, you had it made, no matter what. And if he wasn't—if he happened to have a strong hand—what were you waiting for? What did you have to lose? One game-point at the most, when you were leading six to three anyway. How can a man cut his own throat like that?'

"The old loon didn't say a word. Junior, though, he smiled at me and said, 'Papa doesn't play so well. Papa's not so good at sixty-six.'

" 'Your father,' I said, 'has no business playing sixty-six at all. Tell him to move over and make room for me.'

"But the old hound dog refused to quit. He kept on playing and making such blunders that I thought I'd burst a blood vessel. It was all I could do to convince the old booger to let me play two or three hands. 'After all,' I said, 'it's Hanukkah. Let me celebrate too . . .'

" 'What stakes shall we play for?' Junior asked me.

" 'For whatever you like,' I say.

" 'A ruble a game?' he asks.

" 'Let it be a ruble a game. My one condition is,' I joked, 'that your father promise not to look at your hand and give you any advice . . .'

"Well, he laughed at that and we started to play. We play one game, we play a second, we play a third—I'm going like a house on fire. My partner begins to get flustered. 'Let's double the stakes,' he says. 'If that's your pleasure,' I say, 'then double it is.' Of course, that only made him lose twice as much and get twice as flustered as before. 'You know what,' he says, 'let's double the stakes again.' 'If that's your pleasure,' I say, 'then double again it is.' That meant he was losing quadruple. By now he was foaming at the mouth. 'All right,' he says, 'let's play for twenty-five rubles.' When his father hears that, the old Methuselah, he says he won't allow it, but the young rogue pays him no nevermind. We play for twenty-five rubles—and I win. Well, the old goat is really sore now; he gets up, he sits down, he peeks at my cards, he hums a little tune, he snuffles up his nose—and the boy is mopping his brow as though he's come down with a fever. The more he loses, the more flustered he gets, the more flustered he gets, the more he loses. The old hoot owl was beside himself. He grumbled, he scolded, he hummed, he snuffled, he peeked at my cards, while the young scamp kept losing hand after hand until he was the color of a burning barn. 'I'll be jiggered,' says the father, 'if I'll let you play any more!' 'Papa!' pleads the son, 'just one more game.

I'd sooner die than quit now!' 'Just one more, I promise,' I say to the old buzzard. 'Come on, be a sport . . .'

"In the end the cards were dealt and, thank God, the son won. I was actually glad of it. Right away he wanted another game. What the deuce, I thought: when someone's been losing like he has, you can't be small about it. Well, we played another game, and then another, and another—the shoe, you should know, was now on the other foot. 'So tell me,' I said to the old fox, 'how come you're not blowing the whistle on Junior now?' 'Just wait till we get home,' he says, 'and I'll give him what-for. He'll have something to remember me by, he will!'

"That's what he answers me, the old weasel, peeking at my hand, and humming, and hemming, and snuffling up his nose. Not that I had liked any of that before, either—but as long as the cards were going my way, he could peek-hum-hem-and-snuffle all he pleased; it was only now that they weren't that I began to smell a rat. Meanwhile, though, they kept being dealt and one deal was worse than the next. I was on a real losing streak; I kept having to get up, reach into my jacket, and take out another hundred. What a turnabout! I was beginning to run low on cash. Suddenly the old horse thief grabs my hand and says, 'I'll be jiggered if I'll let you play another game! Why, you're down to your last hundred.' You can be sure that burned me up even more. 'Who says I'm down to my last hundred?' I said—and just to show him how wrong he was, I went and bet my last hundred.

"It was only then, when I was totally cleaned out—when, seeing my partner, flushed with victory, button up his vest, the truth hit home that I was as fleeced as a shorn lamb and as broke as a dropped dish—it was only then that I began to take stock of what had happened. Something told me I had supped with the Devil and gotten stuck with the bill. Too late it dawned on me that the father was no father and that son of his no son—you could tell it from how they looked at each other, and from how the young man went off to one side and waited for the old one to join him. The old pirate whispered something to him, and I could have sworn the young punk slipped something into his hand . . .

"My first thought was to throw myself from the train; my next one: them, not you! You should stick a knife into them, you should put a bullet in them, you should choke the living daylights out of both! . . . Just try it, though, when it's two against one—and meanwhile the train is zipping along, the wheels are going clickety-clack, and my head is spinning too. I felt about to blow a gasket . . . what now? Before I knew it, the train had pulled into a station. What should I do? Who should I turn to? What should I say? . . . I looked up and saw my two fellow passengers reaching for their suitcases. 'Where are we?' I asked. 'In a town called Odessa,' they said. I put a hand in my pocket—there wasn't enough change there to pay a porter. I broke into a cold sweat. My hands shook. There were actually tears in my eyes. I went over to the old vulture and said, 'Look, perhaps you could do me a small favor . . . just twenty-five rubles, that's all I'm asking for . . .'

" 'Why ask me? Ask him,' shrugs the old crocodile, pointing to his companion. But the young con just twirled his mustache and pretended not to hear. The engine whistled. '*All out!*'—we were in Odessa. I don't have to tell you that the first person to jump from that car was me. Or that the shouts that everyone heard were mine too. 'Police!' I screamed at the top of my lungs. 'Po-li-i-ce! . . .'

"In no time one, two, three, four, five, six, seven policemen sprang up out of the ground. By then, though, the young blankety-blank had disappeared from sight. There was only the old hyena, whose arm I had a tight grip on to keep him from getting away. I won't even try to describe the bedlam that broke out in that station. It was like being in the middle of an earthquake. The two of us were brought to a special room, where I told the whole story from start to finish. I poured my bitter heart out, I all but broke down and cried—and it seemed to make an impression, because right away they warned the old shill that he had better come clean. Guess what, though? He didn't know what they were talking about! *Sixty-six? What sixty-six! Cards? What cards! Son? What son!* In fact, he had no son and never had one. 'The man,' says the old bastard, putting a finger to his head, 'is off his rocker . . .'

" 'Oh, I am, am I?' I said. 'Why don't you search him!'

"Well, they took him and turned him inside out right down to his underwear—no money, no cards! His total worth amounted to twenty-two rubles and seventy kopecks, and he really did look like such a poor, harmless beggar that I began to wonder myself if I hadn't imagined it all. Maybe I just dreamed that I met a father and a son and lost a wad playing sixty-six with them? . . . You know what the end of it was? Don't ask! Suppose we forget about the past and play a little game of sixty-six ourselves in honor of Hanukkah . . ."

Whereupon the dignified gentleman, who appeared to be a commercial traveler like myself, produced a pack of cards, cut the deck for first deal, and inquired, "What stakes shall we play for?"

I watched him cut the deck; he did it a little too skillfully, a little too fast. And his hands were a little too white. Too white and too soft. Suddenly I had a most unpleasant thought . . .

"I would be happy," I said, "to play a game of sixty-six with you in honor of Hanukkah, but I wouldn't know how to begin. What actually is this sixty-six you keep talking about?"

My fellow passenger gave me a long, hard look, the barest hint of a smile on his lips, and then quietly, with an inaudible sigh, replaced the cards in his pocket.

He vanished at the next station. On a whim I walked up and down the train twice, looking for him everywhere—he was nowhere to be seen.

(1910)

HIGH SCHOOL

▼

Winter. Across from me, wearing a rather worn skunk-fur coat, sat a middle-aged man whose blond beard was shot with gray. We began to talk.

"You know," he said to me, "a man is his own worst enemy, especially when there's a woman involved—I mean a wife. I happen to be talking about myself. Just from looking at me, what would you take me for? A pretty average Jew, wouldn't you say? You can't tell by the shape of my nose if I'm rich, poor, or down-and-out. For all you know, I may once have had lots of money. And not just money, either—because what's money, after all?—but a solid, respectable business, not one of your flash-in-the-pan operations that make a big hoo-ha while they last. No, sir! It happens to be my personal opinion that slowly but surely is best. Slowly but surely is how I built up my business, slowly but surely is how I watched it go under, slowly but surely is how I paid off my debts, and slowly but surely is how I started all over again. If only God hadn't gone and given me a wife . . . she isn't traveling with me, so I can be frank with you. That is, at first glance she's just a wife like any other, you wouldn't guess there was anything the matter with her. She cuts a pretty imposing figure, in fact, because she's twice as big as I am, and not at all bad-looking either—on the contrary, she's downright pretty. And intelligent too; why, she's sharp as a razor, she thinks exactly like a man . . . which is, you know, the first thing wrong with her, because it's no good for a woman to want to wear the pants in a family. I don't care how smart she is—the fact remains that when God Almighty created the world, He made Adam before He made Eve. Just try telling that to her, though. 'Who God made before who,' she says to me, 'is His affair; that still doesn't make it my fault if I have more brains in my small toe than you have in your whole fat skull.'

" 'Just what do you mean by that?' I ask.

" 'What I mean,' she says, 'is that it's me who does all the thinking around here. Even when it comes to finding a high school for our son, I have to supply the brainpower.'

" 'Where does it say,' I ask, 'that our son has to go to high school? If he wants to be a scholar, who's keeping him from being one at home?'

" 'I've told you a thousand times,' she says, 'that you can't make me fly in the face of the whole world. And in today's world, children go to high school.'

" 'If you ask my opinion,' I say, 'today's world is crazy.'

" 'And you, I suppose,' she says, 'are the only sane one in it! A fine world it would be if everyone went by your opinions.'

" 'Well,' I say, 'they're the only opinions I have.'

" 'All my enemies and friends' enemies,' she says, 'should only have as much in their pockets as you have in your head!'

" 'It's a black day in a man's life,' I say, 'when a woman has to tell him how to run it!'

" 'And it's a black day in a woman's life,' she says, 'when she's married to such a man!'

"Go argue with your own wife! Whatever you talk about, she'll answer you off the wall; say one word to her, and she'll come back at you with ten; try not saying anything, and she'll begin to cry, or better yet, throw such a fit that you'll wish you were never born.

In short, when the dust had settled, she had her way. Between you and me, why pretend? When she wants it, she gets it . . .

"Anyway, what can I tell you? A high school it was! And that meant, first of all, starting him in junior high school. You wouldn't imagine that junior high school was such a big deal, would you? And especially not, I thought, with a whiz kid like mine who ran rings around them all in the rabbi's schoolroom. Why, you could search all of Russia for another child like him! Granted, I'm his father; but the head on that boy's shoulders is something else . . . Why drag it out, though? He applied for the entrance exams, and he took the entrance exams, and he failed the entrance exams. What was the problem? The problem was that he scored only a two in arithmetic. Your child, I was told, has an insufficient mathematical background. I ask you, doesn't that take the cake? You won't find a head like his in all of Russia, and they're talking about mathematical backgrounds! But failed is failed. I don't have to tell you how down in the dumps I was; if he had to take the exams already, I would just as soon he had passed. But being a mere male of the species, I thought to myself: well, we did what we could—he isn't the first Jew who won't go to high school and he won't be the last . . . A lot it helped to tell that to the wife, though. There was no getting it out of her head; the boy was going to high school if it killed her!

" 'Tell me,' I said to her, 'I only want you to be happy, but what do you need all this for? To keep the boy out of the army? But he's an only son, he already has an exemption. To help him make a living? For that he needs high school like a hole in the head. What's so terrible if he has to work in the store with me, or buy and sell like other Jews? And if, God forbid, it's his bad luck to end up a rich businessman or a banker, we'll manage to live with that too.'

"That was the approach I took with her. Did you ever try talking to a wall? 'All right,' she says, 'it's just as well. He can skip the first year of junior high school.' 'What does that mean?' I say. 'It means,' she says, 'that he'll go straight into the second year.' Well, the second year of junior high school is the second year of junior high school—but with a head you can search all of Russia for, who was I to worry if he hadn't gotten into the first year? Listen to what happened, though: when the chips were down, the boy pulled a two again. Not in mathematics; this time the bad news was something else. His spelling left a bit to be desired. That is, he knew how to spell, he just sometimes left out a few letters. As a matter of fact, he didn't even leave them out, he just put them in the wrong places. I was crushed: how would the boy ever go with me to the fair in Poltava or Lodz if his spelling wasn't letter-perfect? But if you think the wife didn't turn the world upside down, you have another guess coming. Off she ran to the director to convince him that the boy really could do it; just give him a chance to take the exams over again! I'm afraid she made about as much of an impression as last winter's snow. The boy had gotten a two and something else called a two-minus—go sue!

"Well, the wife made some scene. How could they refuse to retest him? 'Look,' I said to her, 'that's the way it is. What do you want me to do, kill myself? He's not the first Jew and he won't be the last . . .' That just made her so mad, though, that she gave me a royal tongue-lashing as only a woman can. To tell you the truth, I didn't hold it against her. And my heart went out to the little fellow too, you couldn't help feeling sorry for him. Why, you'd think the sky had fallen in; everyone would be going around in blue blazers with silver buttons except him! 'Stop being a little fool,' I said to him. 'Come to your senses! Was anyone ever born with a written guarantee that he'd get into high school? Someone has to stay home to mind the store, doesn't he? Open admission is only in the army . . .'

"That ticked the wife off but good; she really laid into me this time. 'I suppose that's your idea of being comforting,' she said. 'Why don't you save your words of wisdom for yourself? You'd be a lot kinder if you went and got him another tutor, a real Russian who can teach him Russian grammar.'

"Did you ever hear anything like it? The boy needed two whole private tutors; one tutor and one Hebrew teacher wasn't enough for him! But when the dust had settled, she had her way again. When she wants it, she gets it . . .

"Anyway, what can I tell you? We took a new grammar tutor— and not some measly Jew either, God forbid, but an honest-to-goodness goy. The first-year grammar exam, you should know, is tougher than nails. It's no picnic, your Russian grammar; you have to mind your p's and q's. Just don't ask me what kind of goy God sent us, though, because I'm ashamed to have to say. The damned anti-Semite took a year off my life! He made fun of us to our faces, he practically spat in them. For instance, when he had to pick a word for my son to practice 'to eat' on, all he could think of was 'garlic': 'I eat garlic, you eat garlic, we eat garlic . . .' He should only eat garlic in hell! If it hadn't been for the wife, I would have grabbed him by the seat of his pants and thrown him and his Russian grammar through the window. That's not how she saw it, though. Why take it personally? It was worth it, she said, just to get those p's and q's straight. Imagine, the boy had to go through that torture all winter—in fact, it was nearly summer before he was led to the slaughter again. This time, instead of two twos, he chalked up a four and a five. Glory be! Mazel tov, he'd done it! Or had he? Please to be patient, we wouldn't know until August whether he'd gotten in or not. Why couldn't we be told sooner? Go ask! Well, he wasn't the first or last Jew who had to wait . . .

"Comes August, I see my wife's on pins and needles. She makes the rounds of the director, the inspector, the inspector, the director. 'Why are you running around like a chicken without a head?' I ask. 'What do you mean, why?' she says. 'What world do you live in? Haven't you ever heard of the quota system?' Wouldn't you know she was right, too! The boy was turned down a third time. Would you like to know why? Because he didn't have two fives. With two fives, they said, he might have made it. *Might* have made it—did you ever?! Well, I'll spare you the details of what I had to put up with from the wife. But it was the boy I felt sorry for; he just laid his head on his pillow and cried and cried . . . The long and short of it was that we hired another tutor, a high school student himself, who was to coach him for the second year again—but this time by the intensive method, because your second year is no frolic; there's not only mathematics and grammar, there's geography, and penmanship, and the Devil only knows what. Not that I'd give two cents for the lot of it, to tell you the truth. A page of Talmud, if you ask me, takes more brains than all those subjects put together, and probably makes more sense too. But what could I do about it? He wasn't the first or the last Jew . . .

"Anyway, he began a new regime. Up in the morning—hit the books! Time out for prayers and breakfast—back to the books! All day long—stick to the books! In the middle of the night you could still hear him jabbering, 'Nominative, genitive, dative, accusative'—I tell you, it gave me an earache! Eating and sleeping, it goes without saying, were out of the question. 'To take a human being,' I said, 'and put him through all this for no good reason—why, I wouldn't do it to a dog. It will make the boy sick in the end.' 'Why don't you bite your tongue off!' said my wife. Well, don't think he didn't go off to the wars and bring home a pair of straight fives! And why shouldn't he have? You won't find a head like his in all of Russia! All's well that ends well, eh? Until the big day comes when all the names of the new students are posted on the wall of the school—all of them, that is, except my son's. Was there ever a weeping and wailing! With a pair of straight fives, yet: why, it was cold-blooded murder! The wife ran here, the wife ran there, the wife ran everywhere. In fact, she ran herself ragged until she was told to stop wasting her time—or, to put it more bluntly, to beat it. That's when she began to raise the roof at home. 'You call yourself a father?' she said. 'Why, if you had a father's heart you'd use your influence, you'd look for connections, you'd find some way to the director . . .' There's a woman who thinks on her feet for you, eh? 'Tell me,' I said, 'isn't it enough for me to keep track of a thousand different dates and bills and order forms and memos and other headaches? Do you want me to ruin myself just because of your high school, which is coming out of my ears already?' A man is only human, after all; push him too far and he explodes. Not that she didn't have her way again. You see, when she wants it, she gets it . . .

"Anyway, what can I tell you? I used my influence, I looked for some way to the director—and I took some stiff guff in the process, because everybody wanted to know what I was doing and everybody was right. 'Reb Aharon,' they all said to me, 'you have a nice little business, knock wood, and an only son to take into it—why go looking for trouble?' Go tell them you have a wife at home who has the high school bug so bad that it's high school, high school, high school all day long! Still, if you don't mind my saying so, I'm no shrinking violet; with a bit of luck I found my way to the director. In fact, I walked right into Mr. High-and-Mighty's office and laid it on the line—I can hold my own, praise God, with the best of them, the cat never got my tongue yet. '*Chto vam ugodno?*' he asks me, offering me a seat. '*Gospodin Direktor,*' I say, '*my lyudi nye bogaty, no u nas,*' I say, '*yest malenka sostoyanye i odin khoroshey, zametshatelene maltshik,*' I say, '*katore,*' I say, '*khotshet utshitsa. I ya,*' I say, '*khotshu. Na moya zshena,*' I say, '*otshen khotshet.*' '*Chto vam ugodno?*' he asks again. So I move a little closer and repeat the whole spiel. 'Look here, Professor,' I say, 'rich we're not,' I say, 'but poor we're not exactly either. And we have a boy at home,' I say, 'a fine youngster, who wants to go to school. And I want him to go too. And my wife,' I say, 'would give anything for him to go.' I underlined that 'anything' to make sure he understood, but leave it to the dumb goy not to get it! *'Tak chto-zhe vam ugodno?'* he asks for the third time, beginning to get good and annoyed. So I stick my hand in my pocket real slowly, and pull it out real slowly, and gave my little speech again real slowly too— only this time, while taking all day over the 'anything,' I put my hand into his . . . In a word—success at last! He finally got the point, took out his notebook, and asked me for my name, my son's name, and the year we wanted to enroll him in. Now you're talking, I thought—and out loud I said that the name was Katz, Aharon, and that the boy's name was Moshe, though we all called him Moshke, and that the third year of junior high school would suit us just fine. He read it all back to me—Aharon Katz, Moshke Katz, the third year of junior high school—and told me to bring the boy for enrollment in January. How's that for a change of tune, eh? A little grease helps turn the wheels, doesn't it! The only problem was that January was still a long ways off. What could I do about it, though? If we had to wait, we'd wait. We weren't the first or last Jews . . .

"Well, comes January, the whole merry-go-round begins again. Between this, that, and the other thing, we're told that there's going to be a big meeting of the director, the inspector, and all the teachers, after which there will be an official announcement of who's accepted and who's not. When the day arrived there wasn't a sign of the wife in the house; no hot meal on the table, no samovar, no tea, no nothing. Where was she? In the high school, of course. Or rather, not in it but in front of it, standing out in the cold by herself from early morning. The weather turned freezing, it began to snow, you couldn't see past the tip of your nose—and there she was, still waiting for the meeting to be over. A scene from the opera! 'For God's sake,' I wanted to tell her, 'you know as well as I do that the man not only gave his word, he actually pocketed . . .' Do you follow me? Just try talking to a woman, though! She waited an hour. She waited two. She waited three. She waited four. All the students had already gone home and she was still standing there. At last, when you'd have thought she couldn't wait a minute longer, a door of the building opened and out stepped one of the teachers. She collared him at once and asked him if he knew what the meeting had decided. Indeed he did, he said: eighty-five new students were accepted—eighty-three Christians and two Jews. Who were the Jews? One was named Shepselsohn and one was named Katz. Well, as soon as the wife heard Katz she was off like a shot for home with the grand news. 'Mazel tov! Thank You, thank You, dear God! Oh, thank You! They took him! They took him! . . .' I tell you, she had tears in her eyes. I was pleased as punch myself, of course, but I wasn't about to dance in the streets; that's a woman's way, not a man's. 'You don't look any too thrilled by it,' says the wife to me. 'Just what makes you say that?' I ask. 'Why, you're as cold as a fish!' she says. 'If only you knew how overjoyed your son was, you wouldn't be sitting there like that; you'd already have gone to buy him his uniform, his cap, and his schoolbag, and you'd be planning a party in his honor.' 'What kind of a party?' I ask. 'What is this, his bar mitzvah? His engagement?' I said it calmly enough, because I'm a man, not a woman, but it made her so mad that she stopped talking to me altogether—and a wife who won't talk is a thousand times worse than a nag, since a nag at least has a human voice, while a deaf mute . . . try talking to the wall! To make a long story short, what do you think happened? She had her way again. Oh, when she wants it, she gets it . . .

"Anyway, we had a party to which all our friends came, and the boy was decked out in a fancy uniform with silver buttons and a cap with a dingus on the top. I tell you, he could have passed for the chief of staff! But it really was a lifesaver for the poor little fellow, he looked like a different person. Why, his face was bright as sunshine! We all drank to his health and someone said to me:

" 'He should only finish high school, and nail that sheepskin to the wall, and go right on for the next one!'

" 'Well, now,' I said, 'that's very kind of you, but don't think his future depends on it. Let him stick it out for a couple of years, and then, with God's help, we'll marry him off and the rest will take care of itself . . .'

"The wife just gave me a pitying smile when she heard that. 'Would someone please tell him,' she said to the guests, 'that he doesn't know what he's talking about. He's way behind the times.'

" 'Would someone tell her,' I answered, 'that the times aren't worth catching up with.'

" 'Would someone tell him,' she said, 'that he's nothing but an old f——!'

"That brought the house down. 'Me oh my, Reb Aharon,' they said, 'you've got a Cossack there, not a wife!' Meanwhile the wine kept flowing and we all got so mellow that we started to dance. But I mean dance! The wife, my boy, and I were put in the middle of a circle and everyone cut the rug up around us until, before we knew it, it was dawn . . .

"That same morning we brought him to the school. We arrived so early that the doors were still locked and there wasn't a stray dog in sight. At last, thank God, the doors opened and we came in from the cold and revived. Pretty soon the place was full of youngsters, all with their schoolbags on their backs. There was enough talking and laughing and shouting and hallooing for a country fair. In the middle of it all I'm approached by a man with gold buttons—a teacher, it turns out, with a sheet of paper in his hand. Can he help me? Well, I pointed to my boy and said I had come to enroll him in the rabbi's schoo—I mean in junior high school. 'What year is he in?' he asks me. 'The third,' I say. 'He's just been accepted.' 'And what's his name?' 'It's Katz,' I say. 'Moshe Katz, though we all call him Moshke.' 'Moshke Katz?' says the teacher. 'There's no Moshke Katz in the Third Form. There is a Katz on the list, but his first name is Mordukh, not Moshke . . .'

" 'Well, it's a mistake,' I say. 'It's Moshke, not Mordukh.'

" 'It's Mordukh,' he says to me, waving the list in my face.

" 'It's Moshke!'

" 'It's Mordukh!'

"Well, we Moshked and Mordukhed each other back and forth until the sad truth finally dawned on me; there had been a little error. Do you get the picture? The goy had mixed up the names; he had taken a Katz, all right, it just didn't happen to be mine. There were, it appeared, more ways to skin a Katz than one . . .

"What can I tell you? It would have broken your heart to see my boy's face when he was told to take that dingus off his cap. No stood-up bride ever cried half so hard. He couldn't stop for the life of him. 'I hope you see what you've done now,' I said to the wife. 'Didn't I tell you they'd crucify the boy? I pray to God he gets over it soon, because if not he'll get an ulcer for sure.'

" 'You can save the ulcers for your enemies,' she says. 'That child is going to high school! If he doesn't get in this year, he'll get in next; if he's not accepted here, he will be somewhere else. We'll stop trying over my dead body!'

"How's that for a quick comeback? And who do you think had his way in the end, me or her? Let's not kid ourselves: when she wants it, she gets it . . .

"Anyway, why drag it out? I went to the ends of the earth with that boy—there wasn't a town with a high school that we didn't try. And there wasn't a town with a high school where he didn't take the exams, and where he didn't pass the exams, and where he didn't pass them with flying colors—and where he wasn't rejected. How come? Because of those crazy quotas. Believe me, I started to wonder if I wasn't crazy too. What are you running from town to town for like an idiot? I asked myself. Who the Devil needs it? Supposing he does get in somewhere in the end—so what? Say what you will, though, no one likes to throw in the sponge. And I had become so mule-headed about it that it was an act of sheer mercy on God's part to find me a commercial high school in Poland where they took a Jew for every Christian—that is, where the quota was fifty percent. There was just one little catch: the Jew had to bring his own Christian with him—and only if your Christian passed the exams and you were ready to treat him to tuition did you stand a fighting chance. . . In other words, instead of one millstone around my neck, there were two. Do you follow me? As if it weren't enough to knock my brains out for my own boy, I now had someone else's to worry about, because if Ivan doesn't pass, Yankl can pack his bags too. In fact, that's practically what happened. By the time I found the right Christian, a tailor's boy named Kholyava, I was green in the gills—and when the chips were down, wouldn't you know that he went and flunked flat on his face! And in 'Christian Religion,' of all things! Don't think my own son didn't have to take him in hand and coach him for the makeup. What, you ask, does my son know about Christianity? But with a head you won't find in all of Russia, what's there to wonder at? . . .

"Well, with God's help we made it to the great day: both of them were accepted. Home free at last, eh? Except that when I come to pay the registration fee, my goy doesn't show! What seems to be the problem? The damn Russian would rather croak than see his son with so many Jews. What does he need my commercial high school for, he says, when a Christian boy like his own can get in anywhere he pleases? Go tell him he's mistaken! 'How can I help change your mind for you, Pani Kholyava?' I ask him. 'You can't,' he says. So I sat him down and had a little talk with him about all men being brothers, etcetera—I even took him to a tavern for a drink or two, which turned out to be nine or ten—I tell you, I managed to get a few gray hairs before I finally heard from the school that young Kholyava was enrolled there. Thank God, I thought, at last it's over and done with!

"Well, I came home that day to get a new shock. What was it this time? The wife had thought it over and decided that she couldn't leave our precious one-and-only all by his lonesome in Poland. How could she ever look herself in the mirror if she did? 'But what else can you do?' I asked her. 'What else can I do?' she says. 'Do I have to spell it out for you? I'm going with him.' 'But who'll look after the house?' I ask. 'The house,' she says, 'is only a house . . .' Just what was I supposed to say to that? And don't think she didn't pick up and go with him, leaving me all by myself! Imagine, a whole house with no one in it but me—it shouldn't happen to my worst enemies. My life went to pieces; the business went to the dogs; everything went to hell around me while we sat and wrote each other letters: 'my dear wife,' 'my dear husband'— oh, it was a first-rate correspondence! 'For God's sake,' I wrote her, 'how long can I go on like this? I'm only human. A house without a woman is no house . . .' It did as much good as last winter's snow, of course. In the end it was she who had her way again. When she wants it, she damn well gets it . . .

"There's not much left for me to tell. One day I caved in, I couldn't take it any longer. I sold the business, which was already in ruins, for a song, took my last few rubles, and went to join her in Poland. Once I settled down there, I began to look around a bit to get the lay of the land—it wasn't easy, but I managed to put myself back on my feet and even to strike up a partnership with a respectable Jew, a fine fellow from Warsaw who was president of the synagogue. How was I supposed to know that he would turn out to be a purse snatcher, a swindler, a racketeer, who would leave me holding the bag? I don't have to tell you that I was at the end of my rope . . . Well, strangely enough, who do I see as I'm walking home one day but my son, all red in the face and without the dingus on his cap. 'Hey, Moyshele,' I say, 'where's the dingus?'

" 'What dingus?' he says to me.

" 'Your school button,' I say.

" 'What school button?' he says.

" 'The button on your cap,' I say. 'Just a while ago you bought a new cap with a new button.'

" 'I threw it away,' he says, turning even redder.

" 'What do you mean, you threw it away?' I ask.

" 'I'm free!' he says.

" 'What do you mean, you're free?' I ask.

" 'We're all free!' he says.

" 'All right,' I say, 'so you're all free. What does that mean?'

" 'It means no more school,' he says.

" 'And what does no more school mean?' I ask.

" 'It means,' he says, 'that we all voted to walk out.'

" 'What do you mean, you all voted to walk out?' I say. 'Who asked you to vote? Walk out where? Do you mean to tell me I've ruined myself just for you to start a revolution? God help us all! I only hope they don't pin it on us Jews, because we're always the first to take the rap.'

"Well, I gave it to him but good, as only a father can. I just should have known that the wife, God bless her and keep her from me, would come running with a mouthful of her own. I had better, she said, brush the cobwebs off of me—I had better wise up, she said—I had better realize, she said, that the old days were gone forever. In the new world that was coming, she said, we would all be free and equal. No more cats, no more mice, no more whips, no more horses, no more dogs, no more lice, no more slaves, no more bosses . . .

" 'My, my, my,' I said to her, 'fancy you reciting poetry. Modern times, modern rhymes, eh? I suppose you'd like to open their cages and set the chickens free too. No more pens, no more hens, just imagine!'

"Well, you'd have thought from the way she blew her stack at me that I had poured boiling water on her. There was nothing to do but hear her out to the bitter end. The only trouble was that there was no end. 'You know something?' I said. 'That's enough. If you'll just stop, I'll agree to anything you say. It's my fault, I'm to blame for everything, it's all because of me—*but won't you please be q-u-i-e-t!*'

"It just went in one ear and out the other, though. Nothing doing! She had to know why, and how could I, and who said, and

by what right, and since when, and did it ever, and on and on and
on and on and on . . .

"I ask you, whose idea were wives in the first place?"

(1902)

THE AUTOMATIC EXEMPTION

▼

"**W**here am I coming from?" said the tall, thin, heavily bearded
Jew with the felt hat on his head. He had just finished his morning
prayers and was putting away his tefillin and his prayer shawl.
"Where am I coming from? It's just my luck to be coming from
the army, that's where I'm coming from! The young man
stretched out on that seat over there is my son. We stopped in
Yehupetz on our way home to see a lawyer and a doctor—to get
an opinion, that's what we stopped for. A fine lot I needed the
army in my life! This is the fourth time he's been before the draft
board and he isn't done with it yet. And the boy is an only son, he
has an automatic, a guaranteed, a one-hundred-percent lifetime
exemption . . . but why are you looking at me like that? Did I say
something wrong? Wait, just wait till you hear the whole story.

"A lot of ancient history, that's what you're going to hear. You
see, I come from Mezritch, though I grew up in Mazapevke, but
Vorotolivke is where I'm still registered. That is, I grew up in
Mazapevke, but I lived in Vorotolivke, though Mezritch is where
I'm from now. Not that my name and address make a difference;
my son's name, though—now that's something else again, that has
everything to do with it. I'll say it does! It's Itsik, his name—that's
short for Avrom-Yitzchok, though he really goes by Alter, which is
what his mother, God bless her, took to calling him for good luck,
being an only child and all that. That is, he wasn't always an only
child, because there was another boy a year or so younger, Eisik is
what his name was. We had a tragedy with him when he was little,
though—I mean with Eisik, not with Itsik. One day when we left
him alone in the house (it happened in Vorotolivke, because we
hadn't moved to Mezritch, and it couldn't have been in Maza-

pevke), he knocked over a boiling samovar and burned, he actually burned himself to death! That's when we began to call him Alter— Itsik, I mean, not Eisik—that is, bless his soul, Avrom-Yitzchok . . .

"You must be wondering what it wants, the army, what it wants with an only son. But that's just it! Maybe you think he's such a fine specimen, God forbid, that they decided to take him anyway? Don't you believe it: why, you wouldn't sell him a penny of life insurance, he's so sick that he looks like a ghost! That is, sick may not be the right word for him; he's not really sick, he just isn't very healthy either. It's a crime to wake him now, because he's sleeping, but you'll see when he gets up what a bag of bones he is. He's all arms and legs, as thin as a stick, a dried fig has more color than he does . . . and the height of the boy: good grief, he's a regular beanpole! That's because he takes after his mother, God bless her. What I mean is, his mother is tall and thin too, she's what you might call the refined type . . . But I ask you: with a spindleshanks of a son who has an automatic exemption, *I* should have to worry about the army?

"A lot it helped, though, that exemption, when the boy got his call-up. What exemption? It didn't even exist! Why not? Because there happened to be a small problem—namely, that when my son Eisik was burned to death by the samovar, his name was never struck from the register. Well, I ran to that dunce of a government rabbi that we have and let him know just what I thought of him. 'You grave robber! You body snatcher! How could you have done this to me? Why didn't you make out a death certificate for my Eisik?'

" 'Who's Eisik?' the dumb clunk asks.

" 'What?' I say. 'You don't even know who Eisik is? My son Eisik, who knocked over the samovar.'

" 'What samovar?' he asks.

" 'Wake up and die right!' I say. 'Welcome to Mezritch! Do you call that block of wood of yours a head? You could put it to better use as a nutcracker! Who around here doesn't know that my Eisik was burned to death by a samovar? I'll be blamed if I know what we need you for in this town. When a live Jew has a problem, he finds a real rabbi to go to—I'd think the least you could do is keep track of the dead. Why are we paying the taxes for your salary?'

"Do you know what finally dawned on me, though? It dawned on me that I was wasting my breath on our right reverend, because what happened with the samovar wasn't in Mezritch at all, it was back in Vorotolivke. The things that slip a person's mind!

"But that's all a lot of ancient history. By the time I was through running to Vorotolivke and getting all the necessary papers, they had taken away my Avrom-Yitzchok's—I mean my Itsik's—that is, my Alter's—exemption. They wouldn't even give him a deferment. Not even a deferment? Now we were in for it! I nearly tore my hair out: an only, a one-hundred-percent draft-proof son, eligible for induction! Well, go cry over spilled milk . . .

"Leave it to God to come through in the pinch, though. When it's time for the draw, my Alter—I mean my Itsik—picks the highest number there is: six hundred and ninety-nine. You should have seen that draft board go wild. The chairman even slapped him on the back and said, 'Bravo, Itsko, *molodyets!*' I was the envy of the whole town. Six hundred ninety-nine—it was the winning ticket, that's what it was. Everybody wanted to shake my hand. Congratulations, mazel tov! You'd have thought I'd won a million in the sweepstakes . . .

"I don't have to tell you about our Jews, though. When it's time for the physical, the disqualifications come faster than you can count. Suddenly every boy in town's a hopeless invalid. There wasn't one who didn't claim to be a cripple . . .

"Well, that's all a lot of ancient history. They ran through all the numbers until they reached six ninety-nine and my poor Itsik—I mean my poor Alter—had to pick himself up and go off to the induction center like any butcher or baker's son. My wife was a nervous wreck, my daughter-in-law almost fainted. How, why, who ever heard of an only son with an automatic, a guaranteed exemption being taken for a physical—and without even hope of a deferment? The boy himself wouldn't let on that he was worried—'If other Jews can be soldiers,' he said, 'so can this one'—but I was sure that he was shaking in his boots. Wouldn't you have been?

"Leave it to God to come through again, though. My Alter— that is, my Itsik—was stripped to his bare bottom, begging your pardon, and brought in to the doctor, who measured him, weighed him, pinched him, poked him, and told him to go home. 'You'll never make a soldier out of a mutt like this,' he says. 'He doesn't have what it takes. Why, he has barely thirty inches in the chest.' (Thank God it takes what he has, I thought, not to have

what it takes!) Back comes my Itsik—I mean my Alter—with a
white card in his hand . . . hallelujah, it's mazel tov again. The
whole family got together, broke out a bottle, and drank a toast to
the boy's health. The Lord be praised, we could finally forget
about the army . . .

"You know our Jews, though. Don't think one of them didn't find
a Russian to complain that I had bribed the doctor! Would you believe that before two months had gone by there was a letter in the
mailbox telling my Alter—that is, my Itsik—to report for another
physical? How's that for good news? Happy days are here again!
My wife was a nervous wreck, my daughter-in-law almost fainted.
How, why, who ever heard of an only son with a guaranteed, a one-
hundred-percent exemption having to go for two physicals?

"That's all a lot of ancient history, though. The fact of the
matter was that a personal invitation from the governor was not
something you turned down just like that. As soon as we came to
the capital, I began to run around like mad. I went looking for
people I knew, for someone to put in a good word; I climbed on
my soapbox each time I mentioned my delicate, my one-and-only
son . . . and do you know what it was good for in the end? It was
good for a few good laughs, that's what! And the boy himself?
Frankly, I'd seen better-looking corpses—although, to listen to
him, the trouble wasn't the army at all. For the army, he said, he
didn't care a fiddlestick; if he had to go, he would go. So what was
getting him down? The situation at home—that is, the female
hysterics . . . I tell you, there we were at the governor's and I
didn't know if I was coming or going. You know what, I thought:
life is one big lottery, that's what!

"But leave it to God to come through a third time! My Itsik—I
mean my Alter—is brought in to the governor as naked, begging
your pardon, as the day he was born, and this time a whole committee is there to perform the laying on of hands. They measure
him, they weigh him, they pinch him, they poke him, and do you
know what conclusion they come to? That he doesn't have what it
takes. (Thank God it took what he had not to have it!) At first one
of them thought otherwise. 'He passes!' he said. 'He fails!' said the
doctor. Passes, fails, passes, fails—it went on like that for a while
until the governor himself got up from his chair, went over to
have a good look, and said, 'Passes? The hell he does! . . .' '*Mazel
tov.*' I cabled home at once, '*goods declared definitely damaged . . .*'

"Listen to this, though. I happen to have a cousin with the same name as mine who lives in Mezritch too. He's a rich Jew who deals in cattle, that's who he is, and, if I may say so, a bit of a bastard on the side. Not that that's such an unusual combination—but wouldn't it be my luck that the telegram I sent was delivered to him by mistake, and just when he was all on edge waiting to hear about a big shipment of oxen he had sent! You can imagine what it did to his blood pressure to be handed a cable that said, '*Mazel tov, goods declared damaged*'—why, when I got back to Mezritch I thought he would eat me alive! Do you know what it's like to be in Dutch with a rich bastard of a cattle dealer? As if it wasn't enough for him to walk off with my telegram, he had to blame me for sending it yet . . .

"But let me get back to the time in Vorotolivke when my Itsik— I mean my Alter—was still a small boy. One fine day it was decided to have a census in town. The census takers went from house to house and wrote down who lived there, and how many children they had, and whether they were boys or girls, and what were their names—and when my wife, God bless her, was asked about our Itsik, she went and said that he was Alter. Well, there are no two ways about it: if you're a census taker and you're told 'Alter,' what do you write down? You write down 'Alter.'

"And so a year after my Itsik was excused from the army, we got another letter in the mail: would my son Alter kindly report to the draft board in Vorotolivke. In my worst dreams I should never have such a nightmare! Would you believe it? A new Jew is born: welcome to the world, Reb Alter!

"Well, that's all a lot of ancient history. My boy Itsik—I mean Alter—had to go see the draft board again. My wife was a nervous wreck, my daughter-in-law almost fainted. How, why, who ever heard of an only son with an automatic, a guaranteed, a one-hundred-percent exemption having to appear three times before a draft board? A lot of good it did to explain that to anyone, though—I might as well have been talking Turkish. I had to run to our local community council and beat my breast before they would agree to have ten Jews sign an affidavit swearing that my Itsik was my Avrom-Yitzchok, and that my Avrom-Yitzchok was my Alter, and that my Alter, my Itsik, and my Avrom-Yitzchok were all one and the same boy.

"Affidavit in hand, I went to Vorotolivke. I arrive there—*Well,*

well, well, look who's here! What's new, Reb Yosl? To what do we owe the pleasure? That's all I needed, for them to know what I was there for! The less Jews know about your business, the better. 'Nothing special,' I said. 'I just wanted a word with your squire.' 'What about?' they ask. 'About some grain, that's what,' I say. 'I bought a consignment from him and paid him for it in advance. The grain never came, my money is gone—the dish ran away with the spoon . . .' What I actually did, though, was go to the town hall, where I gave the affidavit to a clerk. He took one look at it, the clerk, and hit the ceiling. *'Stupaytye!'* he says—in other words, I can go to hell, me and all my dirty Jew tricks. 'If you scheming sheenies think you can dodge the draft,' he says, 'by turning Avrom into Yitzchok, and Yitzchok into Itsik, and Itsik into Alter, it's time you realized that sort of hanky-panky doesn't cut any ice around here!' . . . Aha, I thought, hearing him say 'hanky-panky,' he's out to line his own pocket—and I took out a coin, slipped it into his hand, and said to him in a whisper, 'For your trouble, Your Worship.' 'What's this,' he roars at me, *'bribery?'*—and don't think every clerk in that building didn't come on the double to show me the way out in a hurry! It was just my luck to run into someone with principles . . . although to tell you the truth, that's only in a manner of speaking. One is never at a loss among Jews; it didn't take me long to find one whose money that clerk was less finicky about. The only trouble was that it did as much good as chicken soup does a dead man—when all was said and done, there I still was, stuck with a son named Alter. And since Alter is what his name was, would he kindly report to the draft board in Vorotolivke . . . What a mess!

"Believe me, I must be made of iron to have lived through all that. And yet looking back, what was a fool like me so afraid of? The boy could have been called up a hundred times, he still didn't have what it took. (Thank God, I thought, that it took what he had not to have it!) In fact, he had already been turned down twice . . . though on the other hand, I couldn't help thinking: here I am in a strange town, and one with principles yet—who knows what's liable to happen . . .

"Leave it to God to come through another time, though! My Alter—I mean my Itsik—drew a new number, went for a new physical, and managed to fail this one too. Now, with God's help, we had three white cards . . .

"Well, the boy returned to Mezritch—what a welcome! We threw a big party, the whole town was invited, and we danced and whooped it up all night long. What could anyone do to me now? I wouldn't have changed places with a king!

"But I had better get back to my Eisik, God rest him, who knocked over the samovar when he was little. Listen, just listen to this: who could have guessed that because the right reverend of Vorotolivke had forgotten to file a death certificate for my Eisik, I would find a letter in the mailbox one day telling him to please report for the draft? Talk about bolts from the blue! What did they want from my poor life? How could I bring my Eisik to the draft board when he was with the angels in heaven? That's just what I told that government rabbi too; what, I asked him, what was I supposed to do now? 'You have a problem,' he says to me. 'You don't say!' I say. 'And just what do you think it might be?' 'Your problem,' he says, 'is that Itsik and Eisik happen to be the same name.' 'Oh, they do, do they?' I say. 'And how does a genius like you figure that?' 'Why, it's very simple,' he says. 'Itsik is Yitzchok, and Yitzchok is Isaac, and Isaac is Eisik, so Eisik is Itsik.' Elementary, no?

"To make a long story short, why bother with a lot of ancient history? My Eisik was wanted by the draft board—it would make my life miserable until I produced him, that's what it would do! At home the hysterics started all over again. Hysterics? The end of the world! In the first place, the mere mention of Eisik reopened my poor wife's old wounds. 'If only he could go to the army,' she wept, 'and not have to rot in the grave . . .' And besides, she was scared to death that the draft board, God forbid, would reason the same as the rabbi—namely, that Itsik was Yitzchok, Yitzchok was Isaac, Isaac was Eisik, so Eisik was Itsik. Wouldn't that be just dandy! The thought of it made her a nervous wreck, my daughter-in-law almost fainted. It was really no joke: an only son, with an automatic, a guaranteed, a one-hundred-percent lifetime exemption, three times before the draft board, three white cards to show for it—and he still wasn't out of the woods . . .

"Well, I took myself in hand, that's what I did, and went to Yehupetz to see a good lawyer. And I brought my son with me to see a professor of medicine who could tell us if he had what it took or not, though I knew very well that he didn't. (That is, it took what he had to have what it took not to have it!) With a legal and a medical opinion, I thought, I could finally sleep soundly at night . . . but do you know what I found out? I found out that those lawyers and doctors didn't know which end was up. Whatever one said, another said the opposite; they couldn't agree on a thing. It was enough to drive me out of my mind. Just listen to this.

"The first lawyer we saw was a real pinhead, though you would never have guessed it from the size of his noodle, which had a bald spot big enough to fry an egg on. He was so brainy, that man, that he couldn't even understand who was Itsik, who was Alter, who was Avrom-Yitzchok, and who was Eisik. I had to keep telling him that the first three were one boy, and that it was Eisik who knocked over the samovar in Vorotolivke, where I lived before moving to Mezritch, after I left Mazapevke. At last, when I thought he had finally gotten it, he asked, 'Just tell me one thing, though: which of them is the eldest—Itsik, Alter, or Avrom-Yitzchok?'

" 'Try to concentrate,' I said. 'I've already told you fifteen times that Itsik, Avrom-Yitzchok, and Alter are all the same person, that's who they are—that is, Itsik is really Avrom-Yitzchok, but his mother called him Alter for good luck. It was Eisik who knocked over the samovar in Vorotolivke, I mean before I moved to—'

" 'Just tell me when,' he says, 'that is, in what year, Avrom-Alter—I mean Yitzchok-Eisik—was first asked to report for the draft.'

" 'But you're all bollixed up!' I say. 'You're mixing kasha with borscht. I've never in my life met a Jew like you, with such a goy's head on his shoulders. I'm telling you that Yitzchok, and Avrom-Yitzchok, and Itsik, and Alter are all the same person. The same, do you hear me? The same!'

" 'All right, all right,' he says. 'You don't have to shout. What are you shouting for?'

"Would you believe it? *He* wants to know why *I'm* shouting . . .

"Well, I said to the Devil with him, that's what I did, and I went to see another lawyer. This one turned out to be a real logic chopper—in fact, he chopped it a little too fine. He listened to my story, stroked his forehead, waggled his thumb, and began to explain to me that there was a statute on the books that said that the authorities in Mezritch had no right to call the boy up in the first place, although on the other hand, there was another statute that said that since he was called up, the authorities in Vorotolivke could be requested to issue a waiver, which did not mean, however, that the authorities in Mezritch could not be required to waive the request, provided that in the meantime, of course, the authorities in Vorotolivke had not waived the right to have the waiver waived . . .

"In short, he kept waiving me such waivers that I waved good-bye to him and went to see a third lawyer, that's where I went. Some meatball he was too, a young fellow fresh out of law school, still wet behind the ears, so to speak! Not that he wasn't quite charming, with a voice as clear as a bell—the problem was that it didn't stop ringing. He must have been taking voice lessons, because he kept listening to himself talk as if it were on doctor's orders. In fact, he was having such a fine time making speeches that I had to interrupt him and say, 'That's all very well, and I wouldn't doubt it for a moment, but what good does your yatata do me? I want some advice from you, that's what I want, about keeping my son out of the army . . .'

"Well, that's all a lot of ancient history. In the end I found an honest-to-god lawyer, a gentleman of the old school who knew exactly what the score was. He sat there listening with his eyes closed while I told him the whole story and when I was finished he said, 'It that all? No more? Then go home and forget it, it's all nonsense. The worst you can get is a three-hundred-ruble fine.'

" 'Eh?' I say. 'That's the worst? If only I had known that's all they can stick me with! And here I was worried sick for my son, it's my son I was worried for.'

" 'What son?' he asks.

" 'What do you mean, what son?' I say. 'My Alter—I mean my Itsik!'

" 'What had you so worried?' he asks.

" 'What do you mean, what?' I say. 'What happens if he's called up again, then what?'

" 'But he has a white card,' he says.

" 'He has three of them!' I say.

" 'Then what more do you want?'

" 'What more do I want? I don't want anything,' I say. 'I'm just afraid that since they're looking for Eisik, and there is no Eisik, and Alter—I mean Itsik—is registered as Avrom-Yitzchok, and Yitzchok, according to that dodo of a rabbi, is Isaac, and Isaac is Eisik,

they may try to claim that my Itsik—I mean my Avrom-Yitzchok—
that is, my Alter—is really my Eisik!'

" 'Well, what if they do?' he says. 'So much the better. If Itsik is
Eisik, you won't even have to pay the fine. Didn't you say he had a
white card?'

" 'Three of them,' I say. 'But the white cards are Itsik's, not
Eisik's.'

" 'But didn't you just tell me,' he says, 'that Itsik *is* Eisik?'

" 'Who says that Itsik is Eisik?'

" 'You just told me he was!'

" '*I* told you?' I say. 'How can I have told you such a thing when
Itsik is Alter, and Eisik is who knocked over the samovar in Vo-
rotolivke, that is, before I moved to Mezritch, I mean, after I left
Mazapevke . . .'

"Well, that's when he lost his temper and said, '*Stupaytye, vi
nodoyedlive yevrei!*' Did you get that? He called me a nuisance,
that's what he did. Would you believe it? Me, a nuisance? *Me?!!!*"

(1902)

IT DOESN'T PAY TO BE GOOD

▼

"It doesn't pay to be good," said the quite proper Jew with the
mole on his nose as he accepted the cigarette I offered him. "Do
you hear me? It doesn't pay. It was being too good, too much of a
soft touch, that made me nourish a viper at home—in fact, two of
them. Just listen to what I got myself into.

"God wanted to see how good I could be, so He sent me a pair
of orphans, a boy and a girl. Because He punished me with no
children, I took two of them into my house. I cared for them, I
gave them nothing but the best, I made human beings of them
both—and how did they thank me for it? With a knife in the back!

"First let me tell you about the girl. Where did I find a girl
orphan? It happened like this. My wife had a younger sister
named Perl who was, let me tell you, something special. It ran in
the family—my wife is an attractive woman to this day. There

were men dying to have Perl and keep her in clover just for her looks alone. And that's not the half of it, either!

"When my sister-in-law got married, we all thought she had hit the jackpot, that it was a stroke of good luck such as comes a woman's way once in a blue moon. Her husband was born with a silver spoon in his mouth, the only heir of a rich father, and of a rich grandfather, and even of a rich, childless uncle—there was money wherever you looked. What a windfall! And that wasn't the half of it, either. There was only one little hitch, which was that he had the Devil in him. I don't mean to say that he wasn't a fine fellow: there was nothing stupid or crass about him, and he was as friendly, as likable, as good company as they come. So what was the matter? The boy was a bum! (May he forgive me for being truthful—he's in the other world now.) What do I mean by a bum? I mean he had a passion for cards. Why, passion isn't the word for it: cards were his be-all and end-all, he would have walked a hundred miles for a hand of them! At first it was just a round of sixty-six, or, once a month on a long winter night, a harmless game of challenge or klabberjass among friends . . . except that he began to play more and more—and with all kinds of riffraff, the worst loafers, drifters, and grifters. Take it from me, once a man starts with cards there's no telling where he'll end up. Who even thinks then of praying three times a day, or wearing a hat on his head, or observing the Sabbath laws, or anything else that smacks of being a Jew? And as if that wasn't bad enough, my sister-in-law Perl was a strictly religious woman who couldn't put up with her husband's shenanigans. She took to bed for days on end, she cried such buckets over her fate that it actually made her ill. At first it was nothing serious, then it got worse and worse— until one day, I'm sorry to say, poor Perl passed away. And that's not the half of it, either!

"Perl died and left behind a child, a little girl of six or seven. Her husband was off somewhere in Odessa, the Devil only knew where; he had sunk so low that he had gambled away every cent of the family fortune—a hopeless derelict, that's all that remained of him. For a while he was even rumored to be in jail. After that he mooched around here and there until he died of God only knows what and was buried in a potter's field. That's the family history in a nutshell. And so the poor little orphan, Rayzl was her name, ended up with us. I took the child in, you see, because I had none myself; God wouldn't give me one of my own, so why not her? I only wanted to be good—the trouble is that being good gets you nowhere. In any other uncle's house, an orphan girl like her would have grown up in the kitchen; she would have been put to work, made to serve tea, sent on all kinds of errands. I, though, treated her like my own child: I dressed her in clothes as good as my wife's, I bought her the same shoes, I gave her the same food to eat. She even sat with us at the table like our own flesh and blood—why, flesh and blood isn't the word for it. And that's not the half of it, either!

"When Rayzl grew older, I sent her off to a scrivener to learn to read and write. There's no denying that she was a good, a hardworking, a well-behaved girl . . . and beautiful too, a real stunner! I really did love her like a daughter. But children, you know, grow like toadstools; before I knew it, the time came to think of a match for her. And on top of all that, my little niece had blossomed: she was as tall, as lovely, as striking as a rose. My wife had begun to lay away a few things for her—clothes, linens, blankets, pillows—and I myself had every intention of putting up a few hundred rubles for a dowry. We even began to discuss possible husbands. Who could an orphan girl whose father, may he forgive me, was not exactly a savory character and whose stepfather was no Rothschild hope to marry? We had to look for someone suitable who would be able to support her. Only, where would we ever find him? A young man of independent means was setting our sights too high, while I myself didn't want an ordinary working boy—after all, the girl was almost our own, she was my wife's sister's daughter. It was a godsend that we came across a salesman, a young fellow in his twenties, who brought home a few rubles, and had put away a few rubles, and was worth a few rubles in the bargain. Well, I had a little talk with him—yes, he was interested, and how! My niece was just his cup of tea. Next I went to have a talk with her—if you can call what I had with her a talk . . . why, talking to a tree stump would be easier! What seemed to be the problem? Nothing; she just didn't want him—she didn't need him—she would thank me to leave her alone. 'All right,' I said, 'if not him, then who else? The Baron de Hirsch's grandson?' If you've heard a tree stump talk, you'll know what she answered me. She just gave me a silent stare. And that's not the half of it, either! . . .

"Here, though, I have to interrupt my story to tell you another one, which has to do with the first. That is, the first story and the second story make one story between them.

"All in all I had only one brother, Moyshe-Hirshl, who was younger than I was. One day something happened (why does it always have to happen to me?) that shouldn't happen to a soul. On a Friday morning in the bathhouse, when he meant to give himself a cold shower, he grabbed a bucket of boiling water by mistake and poured it over his head. He was scalded so badly that he died eight days later in terrible pain, leaving behind a wife and a six-year-old child, a small boy named Paysi. Before half a year had gone by, there was talk of the woman remarrying. That irked me so much that I went to her and said, 'If you can't wait to find another husband, I want you to let me have the child.' At first she balked at the idea, she wouldn't even think of it. Little by little, though, I got her to come around. She brought me the boy and went off to Poland to get married. In fact, I've heard she's not doing badly there. Only that's not the half of it, either!

"Well, now I had, with God's blessing, a son as well. I say I had a son because I actually adopted him and took out all the official papers. And a gifted boy he was, too—why, gifted isn't the word for him! Of course, he was my nephew, it goes without saying that I'm prejudiced; take it from me, though, you won't find another youngster like Paysi, I won't say in the world, but certainly in our town, and in any other town in the district, and up and down the whole province, and maybe in a few more. You just name it. Reading? The tops! Writing? The tops! Arithmetic? The tops! How about French, you say? The boy spoke it like a Frenchman! How about music? You should have heard him play the violin! And good-looking . . . and with a way of putting things . . . and a personality . . . and . . . and . . . I tell you, gifted isn't the word! And when you add the fact that I was ready to give him a wedding gift of a few thousand rubles, since he was my brother's child and mine by adoption, that is, practically my own natural-born son, in other words, far from a nobody . . . you'd think he could have had his pick of brides, wouldn't you? You can bet that he was offered the best, the finest matches available—and you can bet I didn't jump at any of them. Why should I? You don't give away a young man like that every day. And that's not the half of it, either!

"In short, I began getting offers from all over the world: from

Kamenets, and from Yelisavet, and from Gomel, and from Lubin, and all the way from Mogilev, and from Berdichev, and Kaminka, and even Brody. They were throwing cash at my feet: ten thousand, twelve thousand, fifteen thousand, eighteen thousand—I didn't know where to look first! But then I thought it over and decided: why go to the ends of the earth for someone you don't even know? Better, as they say, the cobbler next door than a rabbi far away. And in fact there was a rich Jew in our town with an only daughter he was prepared to settle quite a few thousands on, a lovely girl too, she was . . . and the man was all for it . . . why shouldn't we call it a deal, could anyone tell me that? And especially since both matchmakers in town were working on it day and night, running back and forth between the two of us until their tongues were hanging out, because they were in a hurry, you understand, they had daughters of their own to marry off, and not such spring chickens at that. And that's not the half of it, either!

"Well, it was agreed that the two families should get together. Things aren't what they used to be, though. Once, matches were made behind a child's back; you came home from shaking hands with your in-laws, you wished the bride or groom a mazel tov, and that was that. But today it's the fashion to talk to the children first; they even expect to be introduced and decide if they like each other. You're not allowed to tell them anything—they're supposed to make up their own minds. Well, and why not? So I took the lad aside and said to him, 'Tell me, Paysikins, what do you think of So-and-So's daughter?' He turned as red as a beet and didn't say a word. Aha, I thought, silence is golden; no news is good news, as they say. Why else would he have blushed like that? It could only be because he was too embarrassed to talk. And so it was decided that one evening the same week we would first pay a call on the bride's family and then have them over to our place. What else remained to be done? Only to bake a honey cake and make dinner as usual. Except that wasn't the half of it, either!

"The day came, and no sooner had I risen that morning than I was handed a letter. By who? By a coachman who brought it. I took it, I opened it, I started to read it—and I saw black before my eyes! What did it say? Listen and I'll tell you. It was from my Paysi, who asked me not to be angry that he and Rayzele—did you ever?!—had eloped without letting us know. I shouldn't try to look for them, he wrote, because they were already far away. I tell you, I never! Once they were married, he wrote, they would, God willing, come home again . . . What do you say to a friendly note like that, eh? And I'm not even talking about my wife, who passed out three times, because the scandal was really hers: Rayzl, after all, was her niece, not mine. 'Well,' I said to her, 'how do you like the bitch your sister whelped now?' I took it all out on her, I gave it to her for all she was worth. And that's not the half of it, either!

"You can imagine for yourself what a white-hot rage I was in. Just the thought of having taken in a strange girl as a poor, hungry orphan, of having done all I could to make her happy, only to have her go make an ass of my own brother's son! I ranted, I raved, I had a fit, I damn near went berserk. On second thought, though, I said to myself, 'What good does it do to lose your temper? Is stamping your feet going to help any? Why don't you think of something constructive, some way to catch them in time?' . . . My first move was to go to the police; I slipped them a modest retainer and informed them that a niece of mine who was living in my house had stolen some valuables and run off God knows where with my adopted son. Then I laid out some more money and sent telegrams left and right, to every town and village in the area. Sure enough, with God's help they were caught. Where? In a little town not far from us. Bravo!

"When the good news reached me that they had been nabbed, I went with the police to the town they were found in. I won't bother to tell you how I felt on the way—worried isn't the word for it! My greatest fear was, who knows, perhaps they already were married—in which case, as they say, the horse had been stolen before the barn door was locked . . . But God was with me: the wedding hadn't taken place yet. It's just that now there was a new problem: since I had told the police that I was robbed, the two of them were being held in jail. Jail—a bad business! I raised the rafters, I went about telling them that the real thief was my niece and that he, my adopted son, was innocent—but when I finally talked them into releasing my Paysi, what do you think he said? 'If one of us is a thief, so is the other!' Did you ever?! It was she, the little bitch, who put him up to it. What a tart! . . . I ask you, does it pay to be good? Who in his right mind would have pity on an orphan? Where's the percentage in it? I tell you, it cost me a year of my life before I could free them both and take them back with me, because he wouldn't budge unless she was let out too. And that's not the half of it, either!

"Naturally, I forbade her to set foot in our house again. I paid a cousin of ours, a country bumpkin named Moyshe-Meir, to put her up in his village, and my Paysi came back home to live with us. I gave him a talking to, I did. 'For God's sake,' I said to him, 'here I've taken you and adopted you as my own son, I've put aside a couple of thousand for your wedding gift—how could you spring such a scandal on me?' 'What scandal?' he said. 'She's your niece, I'm your nephew—we're cut from the exact same cloth.' 'But how,' I asked, 'can you even compare yourself to her? Your father was my brother, and a man of character too, while hers, may he forgive me, was nothing but a bum, a lousy card fiend!' . . . Just then I glanced at my wife—she's about to pass out again. Did she let out a squawk: I mustn't dare say a bad word about her sister's husband—the two of them were in the other world now, we should let them rest there in peace! Did you ever?! 'That still, may he forgive me, doesn't make him any less of a degenerate,' I said. That did it: she went out like a light! What has the world come to when a man is such a stranger in his own home that he can't open his mouth any more? And that's not the half of it, either!

"Well, I took my Paysi in hand and watched him like a hawk to make sure he didn't pull any more stunts. And, with God's help, he shaped up and even agreed to be engaged—not to any great world-beater, it's true, but still, to a girl from a decent family, with a good reputation, with money for a dowry, with . . . with . . . with what a man like me had coming to him at last! I was in seventh heaven. All's well that ends well, eh? Be patient, there's still more.

"One day I came home from the store to have a bite of lunch. I washed up, I sat down to eat, I said the Lord's blessing, I looked up from the table—no Paysi! The first thought to cross my mind was that he'd bolted again. 'Where's Paysi?' I asked my wife. 'I have no idea,' she says. As soon as I finished eating I ran back into town; I looked here, I looked there, I looked everywhere—he was gone without a trace. Right away I sent a message to our cousin Moyshe-Meir to ask what was doing with Rayzl. Back came a letter with the news that she'd left his house the day before, saying she was going to visit her mother's grave in town. Was I fit to be tied! I took it all out on my wife again, because she was to blame for

everything: the girl, after all, was her niece. And that's not the
half of it, either!

"I ran to the police, I spent a fortune on telegrams, on search
parties—not a clue, there wasn't a sign of them. I ranted, I raved,
I had a fit—it didn't do a bit of good. Take my word for it, in the
three weeks that followed I damn near went berserk! Suddenly a
letter arrived: mazel tov, all was well; with God's help they were
married, there wasn't a thing I could do. Did you ever?! Would I
kindly call off my dogs, they wrote, all they asked was to be left
alone; they had loved each other since childhood, and now, thank
God, they had all their hearts desired. I tell you, I never! . . . How
did they intend to make a living? We shouldn't worry about them:
he was preparing for his entrance exams in medicine, and she was
studying to be a midwife. Did you ever?! Meanwhile, both were
doing private tutoring and earning, with God's help, up to fifteen
rubles a month; the rent cost them six and a half, food was eight
more, and as for the rest—God was great . . . I tell you, I never!
Well, well, I thought, when you're starving to death and come
crawling to me on all fours, we'll see who's boss then! 'I hope you
see now,' I said to my wife, 'what a bad seed she is. From a bum
like her father, from a card fiend like that, what else could you
expect?' . . . That wasn't all I said, either—I was just waiting for a
word of her back talk. 'Since you like to faint whenever I mention
your dear brother-in-law,' I said, 'how come you're not doing it
now?' . . . Did you ever hear a stone talk? That's how she answered me. 'Do you think I don't know,' I said, 'that you're in
cahoots with them, that you're the brains behind this whole
thing?' . . . Not a peep out of her—as quiet as a mouse, she was.
Well, what could she have said when she knew damn well I was
right? She could see what a state I was in. What, besides being
good, had I done to deserve all this? And that's not the half of it,
either!

"I suppose you think that's the end of the story. Wait, now
comes the best part.

"In short, a year went by. They wrote us now and then, but
never a word about money. Suddenly they sent us good news—a
son had been born and we were invited to the circumcision. 'Congratulations,' I said to my wife. 'It's an occasion to be proud of! No
doubt they'll name the boy after your dear brother-in-law.' She

didn't answer me; she just turned white as a sheet, put on her coat, and stalked out of the house. She'll be back soon enough, I thought; so I waited an hour, and then another, and another—it was already evening, it was the middle of the night, and still no wife in sight. A fine state of affairs it was turning out to be! . . . Wouldn't you know it, she had gone off to them, and ever since then—it's been nearly two years—she hasn't been back and hasn't given any sign of coming back. Have you ever heard anything like it? At first I waited for a letter from her, but when I saw none was coming, I sat down and wrote her myself. 'Do you know what you've done?' I asked. 'Do you have any idea what the whole world is saying about us?' Back came the answer that her place was with her children—did you ever?!—and that her little grandchild (whose name, by the way, was Hirshele, after my brother) meant more to her than ten whole worlds. In fact, you could search ten whole worlds, she wrote, and never find another child like him. And at the bottom she wished me health and happiness—without her. I tell you, I never!

"Well, I wrote her again, and still another time, and let her know in plain language that she wasn't going to get a penny out of me. Back came the answer that she didn't need my money . . . did you ever?! In that case, I wrote, I was disinheriting her and cutting her off without a cent till hell froze over. Back came the answer that she couldn't care less . . . I tell you, I never! Her life with the children, she wrote, lacked nothing, it should only always be as good, because Paysi was already in medical school and Rayzl was working as a midwife; in fact, they were earning seventy rubles a month—did you ever?! If I wanted to cut her off, she wrote, I could do it whenever I wished, I could even will my money to the Church. I tell you, I never! And at the bottom she wrote that I was out of my mind. The whole world, she said, was making a laughingstock of me. 'You would think it a tragedy,' she wrote, 'that your brother's son has married my sister's daughter. If you don't like it, you old fool, you can lump it!' Did you ever?! 'Why, if you could only see little Hirshele,' she wrote, 'pointing to his grandfather's picture on the wall and saying "gra'papa," you'd give yourself a swift kick in the pants!' I tell you, I never! That's how she writes to me. And that isn't the half of it, either!

"What do you say, does a man need nerves of steel or doesn't he? Do you think it doesn't stick in my craw to come home to an empty house with only the four walls to talk to? It makes a man wonder; I ask you, who am I living for? Why has this happened to me? For what do I deserve an old age like this? For being good? For being such a big soft touch? . . . You'll have to excuse me, but when I begin to talk about it I get such a lump in my throat that I can't go on anymore . . .

"Oy, it doesn't pay to be good. Do you hear me? It doesn't pay!"

(1903)

BURNED OUT

▼

"May God not punish me for saying this," I heard a Jew behind me tell some passengers, "but our Jews, our Jews, do you hear me, are an *amo pezizo*. Do you know what that means in plain Yiddish? It means they're safe to eat a noodle pudding with, to sit next to in the synagogue, and to be buried beside in the graveyard—but as for the rest, to hell with them all and forget it! . . .

"You'd like to know what I have against Jews and why I'm running them down? But if you'd been through with them what I have and had done to you what I've had, you'd be running amuck in the streets! . . . Well, forget it; I'm not one to go around bearing grudges. With me it's a principle to let the other man have his way, *oylom keminhogoy,* as it says. What does that mean in plain Yiddish? It means that I'll leave it to God to settle accounts with them—and as for the rest, to hell with them all and forget it! . . .

"Listen to this. I wouldn't wish it on you, but I happen to come from a nice little town by the name of Boheslav, one of those places of which it's said, sow a bushel and you'll reap a peck. In fact, if there's anyone you really want to punish, don't send him to Siberia, that's nothing; send him to us in Boheslav, and make him a storekeeper, and give him enough credit to run up a nice debt, and see to it he has a fire that burns him out of house and home, and have all the Jews in town go around saying that he personally gave the match a scratch, because he wanted . . . but you can guess for yourselves what a Boheslav Jew is capable of thinking, and of saying, and even of writing to the right places—and as for the rest, to hell with them all and forget it! . . .

"You can guess for yourselves who you're looking at, too—at a man whose rotten luck it is to have been a three-time loser. Three strikes is what I have against me: in the first place, I'm a Jew; in the second place, I'm a Jew from Boheslav; and in the third place, I'm a burned-out Jew from Boheslav—and burned out to a fine crisp too, a whole-offering to the Lord, just as it says in the Bible! It happened this year. The whole place went up in smoke like a straw roof. I came out of it *bekharbi uvekashti*—that means in plain Yiddish, with nothing but the shirt on my back. And the fact of the matter is that I wasn't even there when it happened. Where was I? Not far away, in Tarashche, at my niece's engagement party. It was a first-rate party too, with a banquet, with fine guests—none of your Boheslav trash. You can guess for yourselves that we drank a good barrel and a half of vodka, not to mention the beer and the wine. In short, the time went by *kidibo'ey*—that's swimmingly to you, in plain Yiddish. All of a sudden I was handed a telegram. It was in Russian and it said, '*Wife sick, children sick, mother-in-law sick, you come quick.*' I don't have to tell you that I picked up my feet and cleared out of there in a hurry. I come home—surprise, surprise! The store is gone, the stock is gone, the house is gone, and everything in it is gone, down to the last pair of socks. *Begapoy yovoy uvegapoy yeytsey*— do you know what that means in plain Yiddish? It means that some go from rags to riches and I go from rags to rags . . . The poor wife stood there crying; the children just stared at her, they didn't have a place to lay their heads. It was a lucky thing it was all insured, and well-insured too—only that, you can guess for yourselves, is what smelled fishy. It wouldn't have looked so bad in itself; but the worst part was that it wasn't the first time, I'd already had a fire before— and also at night, and also when I wasn't at home. Then, though, everything went smoothly. The inspector came, made a list of the burned rubble, gave an appraisal, haggled with me fair and square, a ruble more, a ruble less, until we reached an agreement—and as for the rest, to hell with them all and forget it! . . .

"That was the first time. God save all Jews from the inspector they sent me this time, though: a mean bastard if ever there was one! And to make matters worse, an honest one too, there was no way I could slip him a bribe. Doesn't that beat all? The man's incorruptible, go do something about it! He poked and picked and puttered around, he kept asking me to explain to him how the whole thing had happened, and what exactly was burned, and where everything was, and why there wasn't a trace left of any- thing, but not an iota . . .

" 'But that's just my point!' I said to him. 'I've been totaled. If you want to know why, don't ask me, ask God.'

" 'I don't like the looks of it,' he said. 'Don't think that getting us to pay up will be easy.'

"That's one smart sleuth for you, eh? He thought he'd play the big bad wolf with me. And ditto the police detective who came to see me next. He kept trying to trip me up, he was sure he'd got his hands on a first-grader. 'So tell me, Moshke,' he says, 'how come things have such a way of burning down with you?'

" 'How come?' I say. 'Because they catch fire.'

" 'Then suppose you explain to me,' he says, 'how come you took out insurance just two weeks before it happened?'

" 'When should I have taken it out, Officer,' I say, 'two weeks after it happened?'

" 'Well,' he says, 'how come you weren't at home?'

" 'And if I had been,' I say, 'you'd be happier?'

" 'But how come,' he asks, 'you received a telegram telling you that your family was sick?'

" 'Because,' I say, 'they wanted me to come quick.'

" 'Then how come they didn't tell you the truth?' he asks.

" 'Because they didn't want to scare me,' I say.

" 'All right,' he says. 'I've had enough of this! I want you to know that I'm running you in.'

" 'But what for?' I say. 'What did I ever do to you? You're taking a perfectly innocent man and ruining his good name! Does it make you feel good to cut a man's throat in cold blood? Well, if that's what you want, I can't stop you. Just remember, though, that there's a God above Who sees everything.'

"Did he blow his top at that! 'Just who do you think you're talking to about God, you little so-and-so?' he said. That didn't scare me, though—not when they had nothing on me, because I was clean as the driven snow. How does the saying go? *Al tehi boz lekhoyl bosor:* in plain Yiddish that means that you don't smell of garlic when you haven't eaten it—and as for the rest, to hell with them all and forget it! . . .

"In fact, everything would have been just fine if it weren't for Boheslav. Do you think a Boheslav Jew can stand to see another Jew come by money? That's when the poison pen letters began to circulate. Some sent them by mail and some brought them down to the insurance company in person, but everyone said it was me who gave the match a scratch . . . how's that for sheer finkery? They said I had purposely left home that night so that . . . doesn't that beat all for low-downness? They even claimed I never had the stock I put in for and that my account books were faked—they tried to pin such a bum rap on me that it would have made a Haman blush—they . . . they . . . but as for the rest, to hell with them all and forget it! . . .

"That didn't scare me, though, not when they had nothing on me, because I was as clean as the driven snow. After all, to say it was me who gave the match a scratch was ridiculous. Any child understands that if you do such a thing you don't dirty your hands yourself, not when three rubles will get you a good angel to do the job for you . . . isn't that how it's done where you come from? And as for the rumor that I purposely left home that night because of it, nothing could be further from the truth, because I was at my sister's party. I have an only sister in Tarashche, she was marrying off her middle daughter—are you telling me I shouldn't have gone? What kind of a brother would that make me? I ask you: suppose you had an only sister whose daughter was getting engaged—would you have stood her up and stayed home? Of course not! It's not as if I had any way of knowing it was the night my house would burn down. It's a lucky thing I happened to be insured. And the reason I was is that lately, fires have been breaking out all over. Every summer each little town has too many of them for comfort. It's one fire after another; if it's not Mir, it's Bobroisk, if it's not Bobroisk, it's Rechitsa, if it's not Rechitsa, it's Bialystok—the whole world is going up in flames! . . . So I thought to myself, *koyl yisro'el khaveyrim*—do you know what that means in plain Yiddish? It means that if Jews are burning out everywhere, who's to say it can't happen to me! Why be a booby and trust in miracles to save a store that can be insured? And if I was already taking out insurance, why not the maximum? You know what they say: if you have to eat pork, you may as well eat it till you burst. The company wouldn't lose its shirt or even grow a

cent poorer because of my monthly payments—and as for the
rest, to hell with them all and forget it! . . .

"And so I toddled off to my agent and I said to him, 'Listen
here, Zaynvel, it's like this: the whole world is burning out, why
take chances? I want you to insure my store.'

" 'You don't say,' he says, giving me a weird grin.

" 'How come you're smiling at me like a freshly laid-out corpse?'
I ask him.

" 'Because I'm feeling so good and so bad,' he says.

" 'If you're feeling so good, how come you're feeling so bad?' I
ask him.

" 'I'm feeling so bad,' he says, 'because I insured you before.
And I'm feeling so good because I'm not doing it again.'

" 'How come?' I ask.

" 'Because,' he says, 'you already bamboozled me once.'

" 'When did I bamboozle you?' I ask.

" 'When you burned out the last time,' he says with the same
grin.

" 'You might at least say you're sorry it happened, you young
jerk!' I say.

" 'Am I sorry it happened!' he says—and he laughs right in my
face.

"Doesn't that beat all for sheer crust? You can guess for yourselves that I went somewhere else. Who did he think he was scaring? *Hamibli eyn kvorim bemitsrayim*—in plain Yiddish that means
that there's more than one insurance company in Russia. Good
lord, there are as many agents around as fleas on a dog! And so I
found a young fellow who had just landed his first job and was
looking for business. You can guess for yourselves that he was
happy to insure me, and for a good ten thousand at that—and
why not? Don't I look like a man who might have ten thousand
smackers' worth of goods in his store? *Tovar voborotye*, as the
goyim say—that's easy come, easy go in plain Yiddish . . . Now
they're all saying, those Boheslav Jews, that I never carried that
much stock in the first place. Who do they think they're scaring?
Let them talk, let them squawk, let them just try to prove it—and
as for the rest, to hell with them all and forget it! . . .

"It was a lucky thing that at the time, when I took out the
policy, no one in Boheslav knew a thing about it, so that it went

through without a hitch. It was only after the accident, when I was burned out a second time, that our brother Jews began running to the agents. What company was I insured with? And when was the policy taken out? And how much was it for? . . . And when they discovered that it was for ten thousand rubles, the fur began to fly. Great God Almighty! *Ten* thousand rubles? Our Moyshe-Mordechai is going to get away with *ten* whole thousand rubles? . . . A black plague take them all! What was it to them if I got my ten thousand? Was it any skin off their noses if some cash came my way? Suppose the opposite had happened and the fire had left me flat broke—would they have given me a refund? . . . But no, you don't fool around with Boheslav! In Boheslav they run a clean town! It's a town of such great saints, Boheslav is, that you better not try any funny stuff! . . . As if they couldn't see with their own eyes what a tragedy I had had—why, we barely escaped with our lives, not to mention the damage! . . . And supposing it wasn't as great as all that, so what? You'd think they would sooner break every bone than see me get paid for any of it . . . Although even supposing I get it all, the full ten thousand, I ask you: what of it, what? Why should anyone lose any sleep over it? The man burned? Let him burn! If you don't like it, you can go and burn too! Put yourselves in his shoes and you would see what this means to him. Did it ever occur to you that he might have children at home? That he might have a daughter to marry off, an absolute pearl of a child who's everything a father can ask for? That he might have to watch her become an old maid, because he can't afford to pay a matchmaker? That he might also have a son, a boy with a brain that's one in a million, who's wasting away because there's no money to send him to school? That he might literally be killing himself, bleeding himself white—and for who? For his own family! . . . But no one even thinks of that! Everyone looks at me crosswise and says, *ulai yerakheym*—shall I tell you what that means in plain Yiddish? It means that maybe, God forbid, I may end up with something in the bank. That's what they're afraid of—and as for the rest, to hell with them all and forget it! . . .

"You know what, though? I'll be honest with you. If some poor storekeeper like me begrudges me the money, that doesn't bother me so much; it's only natural for him to be jealous when he'd like to have it himself. But what excuse does a rich Jew have? And the person who burns me up the most is the son of the richest Jew in town. He's a real know-it-all, but a good Jew, a warm Jew, a smart young fellow with a heart of gold who won't take a penny's interest on a loan and gives to charity like there's no tomorrow; in short, a decent, a fine human being; it's just that whenever he sees me, he stops me and says, 'What's new with your claim? I hear you lost a bundle in that fire'—and he puts his hands in his pockets, lets his tummy hang out, gives me a look like a satisfied cow, and makes a face I'd love to stick a fist in . . . and I have to grin and bear it! What else can I do? *Pshoyt neveyloh*, it says, *ve'al titstoreykh*—do you know what that means in plain Yiddish? It means that a pinch in the cheek brings out the color . . . If only the police investigation would be over already. Have I ever been given the third degree! The detective keeps calling me back, each time he's got some new question . . . Of course, it's all water off a duck's back, since what's there to worry about? They can't scare me, because they have nothing on me, not when I'm as clean as the driven snow . . . They even made me sign a paper that I wouldn't leave Boheslav, but you can see that I travel when and where I please, just to show those Boheslav Jews what I think of them. *Koyl dikhfin yeysey veyitzrokh*—in plain Yiddish that means that if they can't stand to be without me, they'll just have to travel with me—and as for the rest, to hell with them all and forget it! . . .

"Maybe you think that with a claim like mine, the company won't come to terms? Well, Mr. Know-it-all should only get a smack in his fat puss for every thousand rubles I could have gotten already! Then why haven't I taken them, you ask? That just shows how little you know me! I happen to be, you should know, a tough customer myself, I'm not such an easy nut to crack. My philosophy is, *hekhiloysoh linpoyl*—that means once you've gone the first step in plain Yiddish—then *nofoyl tipoyl*—you may as well go the whole hog . . . What about the investigation? But an investigation never hurt anyone. Why let it scare me when they have nothing on me, because I'm as clean as the driven snow? . . . It's just a crying shame that they're holding up my money, because I happen to be good and hard-pressed, my creditors have me by the throat. That's what hurts! I swear, it drives me up the wall; after all, in the end I'll get the money anyway, there's not a thing they can do about it, so why drag it out for no good reason? All I want is what I have coming. Why take it out on my kids, you child-murderers? Am I asking for so much? Give me my ten thousand rubles, my children's money! Do you think I want it for myself? It's for them, I tell you! Give me their money and leave me in peace! You go your way and I'll go mine—and as for the rest, to hell with it all and forget it! . . .

"But what good does it do to argue? What good does it do to shout? It doesn't make things any better, not when they couldn't be worse. The business is gone, my daughter has no dowry, my son can't go to school, and just staying alive, just staying alive, praise God, costs an arm and a leg. My life is sheer hell! Who can sleep at night? Who can even think of it? . . . Don't imagine I'm worried, though. Why let them scare you when they have nothing on you, because you're as clean as the driven snow? . . . Still, you're only human, you can't help wondering; there's the investigation, and there's the state prosecutor, and there are the Jews in Boheslav who will swear on the witness stand that they saw you with a candle in your attic late that night . . . No, you don't fool around with Boheslav! Believe me, we have a Jew in town called Dovid-Hirsh—all of us together should only earn in a week what I've had to pay him to keep his mouth shut! And he's a good fellow too, and from a good home; it's all done with a smile, with a 'please God' and a 'God willing'—and as for the rest, to hell with them all and forget it! . . .

"Now do you see what Boheslav is like? Am I right or not to be down on our Jews there? Just you wait until I get my money, I'll show them a thing or two then! First of all, I'll let the town have a contribution—I can't tell you the exact sum, but it won't be a cent less than our richest Jews give. I won't take a back seat to any of them; when I'm called up to the Torah on the Sabbath and the sexton sings out loud and clear what I've given the synagogue, there'll be some shocked faces, believe me! The Hospital and the Talmud Torah Funds go without saying: the first will get half-a-dozen new linen smocks, and the second a brand-new set of *tallis kotons* for the children . . . And then I'll marry off my daughter. But what a wedding it will be! I suppose you think I'm planning an affair like everyone has these days? Eh, I can see you still don't know me. Why, I'll throw the wedding of the century—Boheslav won't ever have seen the likes of it! I'll put up a tent over the whole synagogue courtyard. The band will come all the way from Smila. There'll be a table big enough for three hundred beggars with the very best food, and the fanciest rolls, and the most expensive liquor, and a five-spot for each . . . And as for the guests themselves—the whole town will be there, every last mother's son of them, and at the table of honor I'll sit the very bastards who would have liked to see me croak, and I'll drink to their health, just see if I don't, and we'll dance, and we'll dance, and we'll dance! . . . Jews, dance harder! Musicians, give it all you've got! . . . That's the sort of Jew I am! You don't know me yet, but you will. Do you hear me? You don't know me yet! When I celebrate, money is no object—it's another quart of vodka and another quart of vodka and *tomus nafshi im plishtim.* Do you know what that means in plain Yiddish? It means drink till you burst, children, and then off you go—and to hell with you all and forget it! . . ."

(1903)

HARD LUCK

▼

"You're talking about thieves!" exclaimed a nattily dressed gentleman who was clutching an attaché case for dear life. (It was nighttime and there were three of us in the second-class waiting room at the station. While keeping an eye out for the mail train, which was an hour and a quarter late, we had struck up a conversation about crime.) "So it's thieves you want to hear about? Then you've found yourselves the right man! Where else in the world do you have as many thefts as you do in my line of business? Diamonds aren't small potatoes. They can do such things to a person that sometimes your own customer will try stealing one from under your nose. And especially if it's a female. We never take our eyes off a woman we don't know. It's not so easy to steal from a diamond dealer. If I may say so myself, in all the years I've been one I've never lost a stone yet. Although once, as luck would have it, I had a close call. If you'd like, I'll tell you about it.

"To tell you the truth, I'm not exactly a diamond dealer. That is, I deal in diamonds, but I have nothing to do with the cutting; I just buy and sell, generally wholesale, and generally at trade fairs that I go to. Sometimes, though, when there are serious private clients, I take my display case, this one right here, and pay a special call on them.

"One time I happened to hear about a rich Jew in Yehupetz who was marrying off a daughter. That meant diamonds for sure. Not that, in case you're wondering, there weren't plenty of diamond dealers in Yehupetz already—in fact, too many of them—but what did that have to do with it? Lock me up in a room with a thousand dealers and one customer, and you'll soon see who rings up the sale. Selling diamonds is an art. You have to know just what to show, and how to show it, and who to show it to. I don't mean to boast, because publicity is the last thing I'm after, but ask anyone who knows the least thing about it and he'll tell you that I'm in a class by myself. If someone else can sell you X amount of diamonds, I can sell you 3X. It's an art and I'm an artist.

"Well, then, I took the train to Yehupetz. The merchandise I had with me fitted right into this little case, but believe me, the three of us together should only be worth as much as it was. I found myself a place and sat myself down with my case pressed tight against me; I needn't tell you that I didn't leave it for a second. Sleeping, of course, was out of the question. You don't sleep when you're traveling with merchandise. My heart gave a thump every time a new passenger entered the car. Could he be a thief? No one has it written on the tip of his nose.

"With God's help, after a day and a night without food or sleep I arrived at the rich Yehupetz Jew's house, took out my goods, and launched right into my sales pitch. I talked and talked until I was blue in the face—and, as luck would have it, got nothing but a headache for my pains.

"Far be it from me to complain about our rich Jews, but for my part they can all catch the cholera! A slow boil is all they ever give you. They look at each item, they turn it every which way, they ooh and they ah over it—but when it's time to do business, one big goose egg is all you end up with. Well, what could I do about it? You make a sale, you lose a sale—the main thing is to keep hustling. Who knows what you might be missing out on elsewhere? Most probably nothing, but that's no reason not to get there as fast as you can. So I hailed a cab and asked to be rushed to the station. Just then I heard someone shout, 'Hey, mister! Hey, stop!' I turned around to look—a young man was running after me with an attaché case in his hand that looked exactly like mine. 'Here, you dropped this,' he says.

"I could have died! It was my case. How could I have dropped it? When? Where? As luck would have it, the case turned out to have slipped from my hand just as the young man happened by; he picked it up and . . . but I've already told you that part, what more is there to say? I climbed out of the cab, shook his hand, and said, 'I don't know how to thank you. May God give you health and happiness. Thank you, thank you ever so much!'

" 'Don't mention it,' he says to me.

" 'How can I not mention it?' I say. 'You've saved my life. You've done such a good deed that no reward in the whole world would be big enough. Just tell me what I owe you. Speak up, don't be shy.'

" 'But if it's really the good deed you say it is,' he says, seeing me reach into my pocket, 'why should I sell the rights to it for money?'

"Well, when I heard that, I took that young man and actually gave him a kiss. 'God Himself will reward you for what you've done,' I said. 'Please come with me now, though, and at least let me treat you to a glass of wine and some food.'

" 'A glass of wine,' he said, 'I'll have with pleasure. Why not?'

"And so we both climbed into the cab and I told the driver to forget about the station and take us to a good restaurant instead. When we got there I asked for a private booth for two, ordered a fine meal from the waiter, and began to chat with my companion. Not only had he saved my life, he was, I now saw, an extremely likable young man with an attractive face and deep, dark, earnest eyes—in short, a peach of a fellow. And bashful to beat the band! I kept having to tell him not to be embarrassed to ask for whatever he craved without worrying about the cost. And whatever he ordered, of course, I asked the waiter to bring twice as much of. We ate and drank like kings. Not, God forbid, that we were drunk. That isn't like a Jew. But when I was feeling just a little balmy I said to him, 'Do you have any idea what you've done for me? I'm not even talking about the cash value of what you found, although we should both only be worth what I owe for it. My life belongs first to God and then to my creditors. And you've saved not only it but my honor as well, because if I had come home without this case, my creditors would have thought it was just a diamond dealer's trick. (Pocketing the goods and crying "thief" is something we dealers have a name for!) The one thing left for me to do would have been to buy a rope and hang myself from the nearest tree. To your health!' I said. 'God grant your every wish! Be well, and let me give you one more kiss, because I really have to be off.' And, saying goodbye to the young fellow, I paid the bill and reached for my case—*what case? What young fellow?* There wasn't a sign of either.

"At that point I fainted dead away.

"As soon as I was revived, I promptly lost consciousness again. It was only when I came to a second time that I began to scream so loud that the whole Yehupetz police force came running. I promised them a fat reward and they took me with them to every thieves' den in town, to every underworld rathole—but my young man was nowhere to be found. By now I was thoroughly exhausted and at the end of my tether. I went back to my lodgings, lay down on the bed there, and wondered how to take my life. By hanging? With a knife? Or by throwing myself in the Dnieper? As I was trying to decide, there was a knock on the door. *Who is it?* It was someone come to take me to the police station. My fine feathered friend had been caught—and with the goods still on him!

"Is there any need to tell you how I felt when I saw my case with all the diamonds in it? Before I knew it, I had blacked out once more. (That's something I have a way of doing.) When I came around this time, I went over to the young man and said to him, 'I simply don't understand it. Please, explain it to me before I go crazy: where's the logic in first running after me with my case and refusing to take even a cent for it, and then, the minute my back is turned, walking off with it again? Why, my whole life was in it, it was everything I had in the world! You almost ruined me. I was a hair's breadth away from putting an end to it all!'

"He looked at me, that young man did, with those earnest brown eyes of his and said as calmly as you please, 'What does one thing have to do with the other? A good deed is a good deed, but stealing is my profession.'

" 'Young man,' I said to him, 'just exactly who are you?'

" 'Who am I?' he said. 'I'm a Jewish thief with a house full of children and the worst luck you ever saw. Not that I've chosen a hard line of work—I'm just a total bungler. Don't think I'm complaining. Stealing, thank God, is no problem. The problem is getting caught. That's where I never have luck.'

"Only when I was already on the train did it occur to me what an ass I had been. For a pittance I could have bought that thief his freedom. Why should I have been his Waterloo? Let someone else have it on his hands . . .

"Could I interest you in some reasonably priced diamond earrings? Here, let me show them to you. Stones like these you've never even seen in a dream—they're something extra-special, let me tell you . . ."

(1910)

FATED FOR MISFORTUNE

▼

Taking his time as if weighing each word, a cultivated, rather worried-looking Jew with a broad, pale, wrinkled forehead, a good black Sabbath frock coat, and a hat with a wide silk ribbon around it told the following story about himself:

"If you're fated for misfortune, there's no place you can run to. You can try eighteen different ways to escape it—none of them will do any good. Take me, for example: I'm a quiet, peaceable Jew who minds his own business, never makes a fuss, and hates being in the public eye. I'll do anything to avoid being made president of the synagogue, or the godfather at a circumcision, or the guest of honor at a wedding, etcetera, etcetera, etcetera . . .

"Well, just listen to what happened anyway. One day a Jew died in our town. We called him 'Menashe-Goy,' because he was, God forgive me, a simple soul. He couldn't read or write, he didn't know a Hebrew letter from the sign of the Cross, he was barely able to recite a few prayers, etcetera, etcetera, etcetera . . .

"In short, he was a real Simple Simon, but a decent fellow and honest to the core; his word of honor was sacred to him, and the next man's money—sacrosanct. Was he ever stingy with his own, though! He would rather have given up his eyeteeth than a penny.

He spent his whole life accumulating more and more, and he was still going strong when suddenly he upped and died. Well, dead is dead—and since that's what Menashe now was, I was approached with the suggestion that, as he had left behind no small amount of money, plus some outstanding loans, plus some other assets, plus some property, etcetera, etcetera, etcetera, and as there was no one to manage it all—she, his widow, being only a woman and his children being too small (there were five of them, four boys and a girl)—I should agree to be their fiduciary, that is, their guardian. Of course, I wouldn't hear of it. Their fi-*who*-ciary? What did I need it for? . . . But that only made them pester me more. 'How,' I was asked, 'can you possibly refuse when you're the only one in town who can be trusted,' etcetera, etcetera, etcetera. 'Don't you realize what a crime it is to let such wealth go unmanaged? What will the poor children, the four little boys and the girl, have left when they grow up? What are you so afraid of? Be the fi-who-ciary, and let the widow, their mother, be the fi-who-ciary-ess!' I did my best to beg off: what did they want from my life? What kind of fi-who-ciary would I make when I didn't even know how to spell it? That just added fuel to the fire, though. How could I, and what kind of person was I, and where was my sense of duty, etcetera, etcetera, etcetera . . .

"Well, in the end I had to give in: I became a fi-who-ciary, that is, the children's legal guardian, together with her, the widow. And since a fi-who-ciary is what God had made me, the first thing I did was try to determine just what the poor orphans were worth. I went about locating every asset, store, house, horse, cow, etcetera, etcetera, etcetera, and converting it all into cash . . . which was easier said than done, mind you, because Menashe, may he rest in peace, was one well-fixed miser of a Jew! However much people had guessed he was worth, they hadn't guessed enough by half—and to make matters worse, he hadn't put down a single thing in writing, because he was, God forgive me, an illiterate. New loans he had made kept turning up all the time. Wherever you looked, you found someone else who owed him money. And of course, you understand, I had to walk around with it all in my head and get every penny that I could for it—what other choice did I have? And I had to do it all by myself too, because she, my fi-who-ciary-ess, was a cow of a housewife who didn't know left from right—a perfectly nice cow, it so happened, but a cow all the same. She couldn't have told a good IOU from a bad one if her life depended on it, etcetera, etcetera, etcetera . . .

"Well, I put together ruble after ruble until there was quite a pile. And having gone to no small trouble to put it together, I next had to think of investing it, because if the family used it to live off, what would become of it? Children, it so happens, need clothing and shoes, etcetera, etcetera, etcetera, to say nothing of having to eat— and once you start eating up your capital, you eat your way through it in no time. And then what? A responsible person, you understand, had to put the money to work. And so I began to look around for somewhere to put it. Should I open a store for the family? But who was going to run it when my fi-who-ciary-ess, it so happened, was a cow, and the children were only children? . . . Should I lend it out at interest? But supposing the borrower went bankrupt—who would be held accountable? The fi-who-ciary! . . . Until finally I decided, what more solid business could there be to sink it in than my own? What safer borrower was there than me, eh? . . . Credit, God be praised, I had everywhere, at every fair in the country, while as for my reputation—it should only be as good all my life! Wasn't it the best solution by far to put the money into my own store? What better way to guard its value than to keep turning over the stock with it, eh? . . . And if you buy with cash, you should know, you're in a different league entirely, because it commands a good premium. Hard cash, you understand, is a rare commodity these days; everyone pays with paper, with notes, a signature here, a signature there, etcetera, etcetera, etcetera . . .

"Well, I put the money into my business and it wasn't such a poor idea, because things didn't go badly, they didn't go badly at all. My gross, you understand, grew very nicely, since a well-stocked store draws a different type of customer. It's the bait that makes them bite, as any fisherman will tell you. There was just one little problem: my expenses! They were now double what they used to be, because I was supporting two whole households . . . My own family, knock wood, was nothing new; but she, the widow, kept needing things too, as did all five of her children, four boys and a girl who weren't even mine. That was no joking matter! There were clothes to buy, and shoes to buy, and a school for the boys, and a private tutor for the girl, to say nothing of a family outing here and a snack for the kids there, etcetera, etcetera, etcetera—there simply was no way of avoiding it. What would everyone have said? A fine fi-who-ciary he is, taking all the money for himself and not sparing the poor orphans even a kopeck for candy! . . . There I was, you understand, slaving away, beating my brains out, on the road all the time buying merchandise, with a ledger full of debts and bad news—and no one could have cared less. She, the widow, never once lent a hand; all she wanted was her half of the income . . . But after all, you say, it was her money I was using? In the first place, though, her money was tied up in stock; in the second place, I wasn't just using it, I was planning to pay her good interest; and however you look at it, it wasn't worth the bother of having it on my mind day and night, etcetera, etcetera, etcetera—if you don't believe me, go be a fi-who-ciary yourself! Try making it your business how somebody else's children are doing in school, and whether they are where they should be, and if they aren't where they shouldn't be, etcetera, etcetera, etcetera—who did they all think I was, their governess? It's all you can do these days to look after your own kids, especially if you've been blessed with a bad egg. Menashe, may God forgive me, was a simpleton of a Jew, but the very soul of honor; his children, though—Lord have mercy! One was worse than the other . . . The two older ones, at least, were halfway manageable; the first, who was deaf and a real sad sack, I managed to apprentice to a trade, and the second, though a total idiot, was at least quiet and kept out of people's hair . . . The third, on the other hand, was gifted enough as a child, but fell in with a bad crowd when he grew older and turned into such a scoundrel himself that it was best to give him a wide berth. He bothered and badgered and blustered and bedeviled and etcetera-ed me so that I finally gave him a few rubles and packed him off to America, which had been his great dream since he was little; good riddance was all I could say! . . . As for the girl, I married her off with nearly a thousand rubles' dowry, bought her a trousseau, stood her to a fine wedding with a band, etcetera, etcetera, etcetera—I gave her everything a bride could desire, almost as if I were her own father . . . and what, what other choice did I have, would someone please tell me that? They had no father of their own, she, their mother, was a cow—who was there, if not me, to break his neck for them? . . . 'You're a damn fool!' my wife kept saying to me. 'As if you had nothing better to do than sacrifice yourself for someone else's children! Just wait and see, they'll thank you like a ton

of bricks for being such a fi-who-ciary.' That's what she said, and
she couldn't have been more right: a ton of bricks is what I feel
I've been hit with—why, every brick weighs a ton! Just wait till you
hear what I've been through. Believe me, I must be made of iron
if I can still sit here and tell you about it . . .

"Well, of all the children Menashe left behind, there was one,
the youngest, a boy called Danielchik, who really took the cake; he
was the wrath of God in person. From the time he was a tot, he
was a terror. At the age of five he thought nothing of beaning his
mother with a boot—and on a Sabbath morning before prayers,
of all times!—while ripping off her shawl in the presence of
strangers was second nature to him. I tell you, she must have had
the skin of an elephant to put up with him! Day in and day out we
had our hands full with Danielchik. Whenever I dropped by, I
found her, the widow, sitting and sobbing her heart out: what
ever had she done to deserve such a child? Why couldn't he have
rotted away in the womb instead of having to be born? The things
that Danielchik did to her defied all description. He stole whatever he could get his hands on: her jewelry, her rings, her earrings, her pearl necklace, her silk kerchief, her lamps, her kitchen
knives, an old pair of eyeglasses, etcetera, etcetera, etcetera—
everything was fair game; he swiped it all and sold it to buy candy,
or nuts, or watermelons, or expensive tobacco for himself and his
friends. You can imagine the sort of friends they were! Thieves,
drunks, hoodlums—the Devil only knows where he found them.
He gave away everything he owned to them: his new boots, his
best cap, the shirt off his back . . . 'Danielchik,' you'd ask him,
'what's wrong with you? How can you just go and give away a
brand-new pair of boots?' 'Screw them!' he would say. 'Have a
heart, the poor guy was going barefoot . . .' A big-hearted little
fellow, no? And I'm not even talking about money; every cent he
got hold of, he simply passed on to that gang of his. 'Danielchik,
for God's sake, what are you doing?' 'Screw it! The guy's human
too, he's got to eat just like you do . . .' Quite the little philanthropist, eh? There was nothing halfway about him, he was a
one-hundred-percent pure freak of nature! Don't think he was
stupid, though, or some kind of ugly duckling. Far from it; he was
a clever, handsome, healthy, high-spirited boy, a talented singer
and dancer—he just happened to be a thoroughbred hell-pup . . .
What didn't we try with him? We tried the carrot—and the stick:

we locked him in his room for three days and three nights, we thrashed him with a cat-o'-nine-tails, we even broke a good bamboo cane over him that I had paid three whole rubles for . . . it was all spitting into the wind! I tried apprenticing him to every kind of tradesman, making a watchmaker, a goldsmith, a carpenter, a musician, an ironsmith, etcetera, etcetera, etcetera, out of him— not a chance! You could cut him in two with a carving knife before he'd do a stitch of work. 'But what will you be when you grow up, Danielchik?' you'd ask. 'A free bird,' he would say with a laugh. 'A free bird? A jailbird is more like it!' 'Screw it!' he would say—and before you could open your mouth again, he was gone.

"Well, we washed our hands of him and let him grow up as he pleased—which meant, you can imagine, as a perfect black sheep. Not that he continued stealing; in any case, there was hardly anything left to steal. It was rather the way he carried on in general, the fine company he kept and all his monkeyshines, plus the getup he went around in: a red blouse hanging down over his pants, high boots up to his knees, hair as long as a priest's, chin as smooth as a goy's—quite the young gentleman he was! . . . He never had the cheek to come see me himself, though. Whenever he wanted something from me, he put her, his mother, up to it— and she, the widow, was such a cow that she actually went right on loving him, her precious darling couldn't do wrong! Until one day when I came to my store, my fair-haired boy was waiting there for me.

" 'Well, well, a guest!' I said. 'Welcome, Danielchik. What's the good word?'

" 'The good word,' he said, 'is that I'm getting married.'

" 'Congratulations,' I said. 'Who's the lucky girl?'

" 'Osna,' he said.

" 'What Osna?'

" 'Our Osna, who worked in our house.'

" 'Holy God!' I said. 'You're marrying a housemaid?'

" 'Screw that!' he said. 'Don't you think a housemaid's human too?'

" 'God help your poor mother,' I said. 'Have you come to invite me to the wedding?'

" 'No,' he said. 'I've come to talk to you about clothes. We sat down together, Osna and me, and drew up a list of what we need: for me, one flannel winter suit, one sailcloth summer suit, a dozen undershirts, and half-a-dozen shirts; and for Osna, some calico for a summer dress, a woolen winter dress, a few yards of ging-ham for house frocks, a fur muff, two shawls, half-a-dozen hand-kerchiefs,' etcetera, etcetera, etcetera . . .

" 'And is that all?' I asked when he was done, doing my best not to smile.

" 'That's all,' he said.

"Well, I couldn't hold it in any longer; all of a sudden I burst out laughing so hard that I nearly fell off my seat. My employees took one look at me and began to laugh too. We laughed until the walls shook. And when I had laughed so much that I couldn't laugh any more, I said to my fine young Romeo:

" 'Danielchik, sweetheart, just tell me one thing: is it because you and me are such partners in the store that you think you can hand me a list like this?'

" 'As a matter of fact,' he said, 'I can't tell you exactly what my share of your store is. But if you take my father's money and divide it five ways, there should be enough to cover the clothes with plenty to spare for after the wedding . . .'

"Well, what can I tell you? Hearing him say that was like being shot in the heart, or having a fire lit under me, or God only knows what. I saw stars in front of my eyes! Do you get me? As if it wasn't enough that I had spent all those years of my life supporting a widow and five children, and attending to all their needs, and marrying them all off, etcetera, etcetera, etcetera—now along comes this little upstart and thinks he can lecture me about shares he has in my store . . .

" 'What did I tell you?' said my wife. 'Didn't I say they would thank you like a ton of bricks?'

"Well, you may as well know that I gave him everything he asked for. Why argue with a snotnose like that? It was beneath my dignity. Let him take his money and go hang—all I wanted was to get rid of the little pest . . . Do you think I did, though? Then you better think some more. A month after the wedding he came to see me again, did my clean-cut young friend, to demand the sum of two hundred twenty-three rubles.

" 'Just how did you arrive at two hundred twenty-three rubles?' I asked him.

" 'That's what they're asking,' he says to me without batting an eyelash, 'for the beer hall and the billiard parlor.'

" 'What beer hall? What billiard parlor?'

" 'I'm going into business,' he says. 'I've bought a beer hall with a billiard parlor. Osna will run the bar and I'll keep an eye on the billiard tables. We can make a good living from it.'

" 'And a very respectable one too,' I told my young provider. 'A beer hall with a billiard parlor—I must say it's just your style.'

" 'Screw that!' he says, 'I don't want to be a sponge, that's all. I don't mind eating dry bread once a day, just as long as it's mine . . .'

"Introducing Danielchik the philosopher! Isn't that a scream? 'Congratulations!' I said. 'You can sell beer and play billiards all you want. What does it have to do with me, though?'

" 'It has to do with you,' he says, 'because of the two hundred twenty-three rubles you're giving me.'

" 'What do you mean, I'm giving you?' I say. 'Just where am I supposed to take them from?'

" 'From my father's money,' he says without a blush.

"Would you believe it? At first I had a powerful urge to grab him by the neck and throw him right to the Devil! . . . On second thought, though, I said to myself: for heaven's sake, who are you rolling in the mud with? Let him have the money and the deuce take him! 'Tell me, Danielchik,' I said to him, 'do you happen to have any idea how much your father left you?'

" 'No,' he says. 'What do I need to know for? In a year from now, when I turn twenty-one, you and I will go over the books. In the meantime, let me have my money and I'll go.'

"That made me see more stars. Would you like to know why? It wasn't because I was afraid of anyone, since what was there to be afraid of? Hadn't I spent more than enough on them already? I tell you, it was no trifle to have supported a widow and her five children all those years, to have attended to their every need, to have married off each one of them, etcetera, etcetera, etcetera—and now here was this little crumb wanting to go over my books!

"Well, I took out two hundred and twenty-three rubles and gave them to him with the prayer that from now on he would leave me alone . . . and in fact, quite a while went by without his showing his face again. Until one day when I came home—there he was! My heart sank when I saw him. I'd be blamed, though, if I was going to show it, so I said to him perfectly naturally:

" 'Eh, a guest! Where have you been hiding, Danielchik? How's your health? How's business?'

" 'Screw my health!' he said. 'And since you ask, business isn't so hot.'

"You don't say! I thought to myself. Well, better luck next time! A little bird tells me, though, that I'm about to be hit for more cash. And out loud I said to him, 'Why, what seems to be the matter? Aren't you making any money?'

" 'What money? Who cares about money? Screw it!' he said. 'I'm through with the beer hall, I'm through with the billiard parlor, and I'm through with my wife. She ditched me, Osna. Screw her too! I'm going to America. My brother's been wanting me to come.'

"Was it a weight off my mind to hear that! Suddenly I even found myself liking the boy. If I hadn't been embarrassed, I would have hugged him on the spot . . . 'America?' I said. 'A fine idea! America is the land of opportunity. People find happiness there, they find money. And if you have family there already, it's even better . . . Did you come to say goodbye to me? That's very decent of you. Don't forget to drop us a line. After all, we're practically next of kin . . . Daniel, do you need any money for the trip? I'll be glad to help out a bit . . .'

" 'As a matter of fact,' he said, 'that's what I've come about. You can let me have three hundred rubles. That's what the ticket costs.'

" 'Three hundred rubles?' I said. 'Isn't that a bit steep? How about one hundred and fifty?'

" 'Why waste your time haggling?' he said. 'Don't you think I know that if I asked you for four hundred you'd give me that too, and five and six also, for that matter? But screw it, I don't need all that much. I just need three hundred for the passage.'

"I tell you, butter wouldn't have melted in his mouth! Three hundred lashes, I thought to myself, is what you deserve! If only I could be sure that this was really his grand exit and that I was seeing the last of him and of all his etcetera, etcetera, etcetera . . .

"Well, I counted him out those three hundred rubles and even bought a present for his brother—a whole pound of Russian tea, a carton of good cigarettes, and a few bottles of Jewish wine from Palestine. We gave him a food hamper too, with a duck my wife roasted, some rolls, some oranges, etcetera, etcetera, etcetera, and off we went to the train station to kiss him and our troubles goodbye. We hugged him like a son and, so help me, even cried— why, the boy had grown up on my knees, and a fine young lad he had turned out to be, why deny it? A little on the brash side perhaps, but with a heart of gold, I declare! True, I was a wee bit relieved that he had gone and left me with one headache less . . . but I was also a wee bit sorry: a young boy like that and little more than a vagabond—who knew where he might wind up and what might become of him? If only he would remember to write now and then . . . although perhaps it was just as well that he didn't. Let him have a long life and a happy one! There was nothing I would have wished for my own child that I didn't wish for him, believe me . . .

"Well, lo and behold—two years hadn't passed since he left for America when one day the door opens and who should walk in but some stranger in a top hat, a handsome, ruddy, brawny, merry young fellow who grabs me in his arms and begins to cover me with kisses! 'What's the matter with you?' he says to me. 'Are you just pretending, or do you really not know who I am?'

" 'Well, I'll be! It's Danielchik!' I said, trying to look glad, though I was boiling inside. Why the Devil, I thought, couldn't you have been killed in America, or better yet, on the train we saw you off on, or best of all, drowned in the ocean? But out loud I just said, 'When did you get here, Danielchik, and what brings you back?'

" 'I blew in this morning,' he says. 'What brings me? I've come to settle the accounts with you.'

"When I heard him say 'the accounts,' I thought I would rupture an artery. What accounts did that gangster think he was talking about? But I managed to pull myself together and say to him, 'Why trouble yourself to come all the way from America for that? My goodness, if you wanted to pay me what you owe me, you could have mailed it to me from there . . .'

" 'What I owe you?' he says with a grin. 'Don't you mean what you owe me?'

" 'What *I* owe *you?*' I say. 'What makes you think I owe you?'

" 'Me, and my brothers, and my sister, and all of us,' he says. 'I've come from America on behalf of the whole family. I want a full accounting of my father's money. You can deduct whatever you laid out for us and give us the balance. We won't go to court over a ruble more or less; screw that, we'll work it out between us . . . How the heck are you? How are your children? I've brought each one of them a present . . .'

"I thought I would keel over, or else take a chair and bash his head in with it . . . but I got a grip on myself and invited him to come, God willing, on Saturday night to go over the books with me. Then I went to see some lawyers. How, I asked them, could I get him off my back? The Devil take them if I could get a straight answer! One said that since ten years had gone by, I could claim the statute of limitations; another said no, being a fi-who-ciary meant I had to give an accounting even after a hundred years . . .

" 'But how can I give an accounting,' I said, 'when I kept no books and have no receipts?'

" 'In that case,' says the lawyer, 'you're in trouble.'

" 'I didn't need you to tell me that,' I say. 'What I want to know is, how do I get out of it?'

"A blank, that's all I drew from him. I must be made of iron, do you hear me, to have gone through all this! I ask you, what did I need such a miserable mess for, this whole etcetera, etcetera, etcetera? What in the world ever made me agree to be someone else's fi-who-ciary? Don't you think I would have been a thousand times better off coming down with pneumonia, or breaking a leg, or having some terrible accident? Anything, anything, but this fool fi-who-ciation of five children, of a widow, of a Danielchik, of no account books, of etcetera, etcetera, etcetera, etcetera, etcetera! . . ."

(1902)

GO CLIMB A TREE IF YOU DON'T LIKE IT

▼

Across from me, by the window, sat a man with a smile on his face and the kind of eyes that try to crawl under your skin. I could see he was waiting for me to break the ice, but I preferred to keep to myself. After a while, though, it was simply too much for him to sit in silence with a fellow Jew. He laughed to himself abruptly, then turned to me and said:

"You're wondering what made me laugh? I just happened to think of a joke that I played on Yehupetz, ha ha! You'd never guess it from looking at me, Moyshe-Nachman from Kennele, a Jew with a cough and with asthma, would you? Well, did I put one over on Yehupetz—but one that will give them something to remember me by! If you'll just excuse me for a moment while I cough . . . ai, Purishkevitch should only have a cough like this . . . there! Now let me tell you what a Jew can do.

"One fine day I had to go to Yehupetz. Why does a Jew with a cough and with asthma have to go to Yehupetz? To see the doctor, of course. With my cough and my asthma, I don't have to tell you, Yehupetz gets to see a lot of me, even if it's not supposed to, since what business do I, Moyshe-Nachman from Kennele, have in Yehupetz without a *pravozshitelestvo,* that is, a residence permit? . . . But when you have a cough and asthma and you need to see the doctor—well, that's life: where else but Yehupetz can you go? You get there in the morning, you slip away at night, and you're in a panic all day long, because if you're caught and served a *prokhodnoyo,* that is, an expulsion order, you're right back where you started from. Still, that's nothing compared to an *etap;* an *etap,* you should know, is a criminal arrest—why, I'd die of shame three times before I could live through one of those! After all, I am, as you can see, a pretty solid citizen, praise God. I own my own house, I can afford my own cow, and I have two daughters, one married and one engaged. What can I tell you? That's life. . .

"And so I came to Yehupetz to see the doctor—or rather, the doctors, because this time I meant to have a consultation with at least three of them. I wanted, you see, to have it out with them once and for all and to know what I was, fish or fowl. There wasn't any question I had asthma, but how you get rid of it when you have it—that, you see, was a different story entirely. Each doctor had run all the tests on me. Each had tried everything. And each was at his wits' end. For example, the first, a prince of a fellow named Stritzel, wrote me out a prescription for *codeini sacchari pulverati;* it wasn't expensive and it even tasted sweet. The second doctor prescribed *tinctura opia*—why, you could have passed out from a drop of it! Then I went to see a third doctor; the medicine he gave me tasted almost the same, but it wasn't *tinctura opia,* it was *tinctura tebiacca.* If you were me, you'd have called it quits by now, no? Well, I went to still another doctor; what he prescribed was as bitter as wormwood and went by the name of *morphium aqua amig-dalarium*. Does it surprise you that I know all that Latin? In fact, I've studied Latin the way you've studied Greek, but that's life: when you have a cough with asthma, and a touch of tuberculosis on the side, picking up Latin is a breeze . . .

"And so I came to Yehupetz for a consultation. Where does a Jew like me stay in Yehupetz? Not in a hotel, of course, and not in a boardinghouse either. First of all, they fleece you but good there. And second of all, how can I stay in a hotel when I don't have a *pravozshitelestvo*? The place I always go is my brother-in-law's. I happen to have, you see, a schlemiel of a brother-in-law, a miserable beggar of a heder teacher; Purishkevitch should only be as poor. And children—God save us from such a litter! You know what, though? The lucky devil has a *pravozshitelestvo,* and a perfectly good one at that. How did he come by it? Because of Brodsky; he's got a little job with Brodsky on the side. Don't think that means he runs a factory. In fact, he's just a backbencher in Brodsky's synagogue, but he happens to be the Torah reader there. That makes him an *obradchik,* which is someone with clerical status, and gives him the right to live on Malovasilkovsky Street, not far from the ex–chief of police, though it's all he can do to keep body and soul together. The one bright spot in his life is me. I am, so to speak, the moneyman in the family—and whenever I come to Yehupetz I stay with him, eat lunch and supper at his house, and find him some errand to run that will earn him a ruble or two; Purishkevitch should only earn as much. But that's life . . .

"This time, though, as soon as I saw him and my sister, I could tell that something was wrong; they both looked like they'd just seen a ghost. 'What's the matter?' I asked.

" 'We're in for it,' they said.

" 'How come?' I asked.

" 'Because there's an *oblave*,' they said.

" 'Pshaw!' I said. 'Who's afraid of an *oblave?* The police have been rounding up Jews since Adam was knee-high to a grasshopper.'

" 'You're wrong there,' they said. 'It's not just any *oblave*. This *oblave* is for real. There have been dragnets every night. If a Jew gets caught, they don't care who he is—it's an *etap* and no questions asked!'

" 'We'll pay them off, then,' I said.

" 'Impossible!'

" 'They won't take a ruble?'

" 'Not a chance!'

" 'How about three?'

" 'Not even a million!'

" 'In that case,' I said, 'we're over a barrel.'

" 'You're right,' they said. 'And not just any barrel, either. This barrel is for real. First, there's the jail sentence. Then there's the criminal record. And then there's having to face Brodsky . . .'

" 'Look,' I said, 'as far as Brodsky is concerned, I can either take him or leave him. I don't intend to gamble with my health for Brodsky's sake. I came here for a medical consultation, and I'm not going home without it.'

"Well, between one thing and another, the clock wasn't standing still; I had to consult with my doctors. Did someone say doctors? Not when the first could only make it Monday morning, the second Wednesday afternoon, and the third the following Thursday—and go climb a tree if you don't like it! I could see I was in for a long siege; why do a favor for Moyshe-Nachman of Kennele just because he has a cough with asthma and can't sleep at night? (Purish-kevitch should have insomnia like mine!) . . . Meanwhile it was getting late. We ate supper and went to bed. I had just dozed off when bing! bang! there's a knocking on the door. I opened my eyes and asked, 'Who is it?'

" 'We're done for!' my poor sap of a brother-in-law says to me. He looks like a corpse and he's shaking like a branch in the wind.

" 'What do we do now?' I ask.

" 'What do you suggest?' he says.

" 'I don't know,' I say. 'It looks like we're in a jam.'

" 'You're right,' he says. 'And not just any jam, either. It's a real sour-apple jam.'

"Bangety-bang! goes the knocking on the door. By now all the poor little children are awake and screaming for their mama, who's running around trying to hush them—what can I tell you, it's a regular carnival! Oy, Moyshe-Nachman from Kennele, I say to myself, are you ever between a rock and a hard place! Why couldn't it have happened to Purishkevitch? . . . Just then, though, I had a brilliant idea. 'Listen, Dovid,' I said to my brother-in-law, 'I have it! You'll be me and I'll be you!'

"He looks at me like the dumb bunny he is and says, 'How's that?'

" 'I mean,' I say, 'that we'll pull the old switcheroo. You'll give me your pass and I'll give you mine. You'll be Moyshe-Nachman and I'll be Dovid.'

"A pumpkin head if there ever was one! He doesn't know what I'm talking about, he stands there with a helpless stare. 'Dummy!' I say to him. 'What don't you get? It's as simple as can be. Any child would understand. You'll show them my pass and I'll show them yours. That's life. Has it gotten through your thick skull now, or do I have to knock it in with a hammer?'

"Well, it must have gotten through, because he agreed to the switcheroo. I gave him my pass and he gave me his. By then the door was nearly coming off its hinges. Bangety-bang! Bingety-bangety! 'Hey, what's the hurry?' I called out. 'Where's the fire?' Then I said one last time to my brother-in-law, 'Now just remember, Dovid, you're not Dovid any more, you're Moyshe-Nachman'—and I went to open the door. 'Come in, gentlemen, come in, what a surprise!' In charges a whole company, Captain Flatfoot and all his little flatfeet. There'll be a gay time in the old town tonight, I thought . . .

"Naturally, they all made a beeline for my poor sap of a brother-in-law. Why him and not me? Because I stood there with my chin up—it's when the fat is in the fire that you can tell the men from the boys—while Purishkevitch should only look as bad as he did. '*Pravozshitelestvo, Gospodin Yevrei!*' they demanded, pouncing on him. He couldn't get out a word. 'Damn you,' I said, trying to help him out of a tight spot, 'why don't you say something? Speak up! Tell them you're Moyshe-Nachman from Kennele.' And turning to the police, I begged them to go easy on him. 'Please try to understand,' I said, 'he's just a poor cousin of mine from Kennele, we haven't seen each other in ages.' I was trying so hard not to laugh that I thought I would burst. Just picture it: there I was, Moyshe-Nachman from Kennele, begging for mercy for Moyshe-Nachman from Kennele, who was standing right next to me, ha ha! The only catch was that it did as much good as last winter's snow, because they grabbed the poor sap like a sack of potatoes and quick-marched him off to the cooler. At first they wanted to take me too. That is, they took me, but I was released right away. What, I ask you, could they do to me? I had a perfectly good *pravozshitelestvo*, I was an *obradchik* in Brodsky's synagogue, and I left behind a few rubles at the station just to be on the safe side, do you get it? That's life!

'*Khorosho, Gospodin Obradchik,*' they said to me. 'Now run on home and finish your noodles. Let this be a lesson to you not to harbor illegals on Malovasilkovsky Street!' . . . A lesson that hurt like a slice of fresh bread in the kisser, ha ha! . . .

"Do you want to hear the rest of it? The consultation, of course, had to be called off. Who could think of consultations when a brother-in-law had to be bailed out? I suppose you think I'm referring to the *etap*. I wish I were! There was no standing bail for that; the poor sap had to sit in jail—and believe me, he didn't sit very pretty! It should only happen to Purishkevitch. We didn't grow any younger in Kennele waiting for him to be let out—and when we finally brought him back there, our real troubles first began. Don't ask me what I had to go through to arrange new papers with a new name for him. I only wish I earned in three months what it cost me, not to mention the fact that I'm now saddled with his entire upkeep, that is, with supporting his wife and children, because he claims I'm to blame for the whole pickle. It's all my fault, he says, that he lost his *pravozshitelestvo* and his job with Brodsky. And he may even have something there. He's just missing the point, ha ha. The point's the quick thinking, the old switcheroo, do you get it? Just imagine: a Jew with a cough and asthma that Purishkevitch should only have, a touch of tuberculosis on the side, and no *pravozshitelestvo*—that's life!—comes to Yehupetz anyway, stays on Malovasilkovsky Street right under the ex–police chief's nose, and go climb a tree if you don't like it!"

(1911)

THE TENTH MAN

▼

There were nine of us in the car. Nine Jews. And we needed a tenth for a prayer group.

In actual fact, there was a tenth person there. We just couldn't make up our minds if he was a Jew or a Christian. An uncommunicative individual with gold pince-nez, a freckled face, and no beard. A Jewish nose but an oddly twirled, un-Jewish mustache.

Ears that stuck out like a Jew's but a neck that was red like a goy's. From the start he had kept his distance from us. Most of the time he just looked out the window and whistled. Naturally, he was hatless, and a Russian newspaper lay across his knees. And not a word out of him! A genuine Russian, the real McGoy, no?...On second thought, though, how could he be a goy? Who did he think he was fooling? The idea! It takes a Jew to know one; a Jew can smell another Jew a mile off on a moonless night. For goodness' sake, God's written it all over us! . . . No, the man was a Jew for sure, I'd stake my life on it! Or was he? These days you never can tell . . . By the time the nine of us were through conferring in whispers, it was decided that we had seen his type before. What to do, though? If a Jew wanted to pass for a Christian it was nobody's business but his own—yet just then we needed a tenth man and needed him badly, because one of us had a deathday to observe and wanted to say the mourner's prayer. And it wasn't any ordinary deathday either, the kind we all have for a father or a mother. No, this was the anniversary of the passing of a child; an only son's, that's whose it was . . . It had been a struggle, the boy's father told us, just to get the body returned by the prison so that it could be brought to a Jewish grave—and the youngster, he swore, was perfectly innocent, he had been railroaded at his trial. Not that he hadn't been in thick with the other revolutionaries, but that was still no reason to hang him. Hang him they did, though; and his mother died soon after. Not as soon as all that, however. Oh, no! First she ate her heart out bit by bit—and while she did, made her husband gray before his time.

"How old would you say I am?" the man asked us.

We all looked at him, trying to guess his age. It was impossible. While his eyes were young, his hair was gray. His heavily lined face seemed on the verge of either laughter or tears. There was in fact something strange about his whole appearance. He was wearing a smoking jacket that was much too long for him, the hat he had on was pushed way back on his head, and the beard on his chin was an oddly rounded goatee. And those eyes of his . . . ah, those eyes! They were the kind of eyes that once you've seen, you'll never ever forget: half-laughing and half-crying they were, or half-crying and half-laughing . . . if only he would unburden himself and let the tears out! But no, he insisted on being the very soul of gaiety. A most peculiar fellow.

"Well now, where are we going to find a tenth man?" asked one of us out loud, with a glance at the pince-nezed passenger, who gave no sign of having heard. He simply looked out the window and went on whistling some Russian tune.

"What do you mean, where?" asked someone else. "Don't we have ten already?" And he began to go around the car with his finger: "One, two, three . . ."

"Count me out!" said the whistler—in Yiddish.

We stared at him openmouthed.

"You mean you're not a Jew?"

"I am a Jew. I just don't happen to believe in such things."

For a long moment we sat there dumbfounded, looking at each other without a word. The bereaved father alone did not seem put out in the least. With his half-laugh, half-cry of a smile, he said to the whistling young man:

"The more power to you! You deserve a gold medal."

"I do? What for?"

"To tell you the truth, that's a rather long story. But if you'll agree to be a tenth for prayers, so that I can say the kaddish for my son, I promise to tell it to you afterwards."

With which our good-humored mourner took out a large handkerchief from his pocket, twisted it into a belt, girded his waist in the manner of a pious Jew, turned his face to the wall of the car, and began the afternoon prayer:

"*Ashrey yoyshvey veysekho, oyd yehalelukho seloh . . .*"

I don't know about you, but there's nothing I like better than a simple afternoon prayer. I prefer it any time to all the do-re-mi operatics that the synagogues are full of on Sabbaths and holidays. And our mourner led us in it with such feeling, with such soulfulness, that we were all touched to the quick—even, I daresay, our conscripted tenth man. Listening to a father pray on the occasion of his son's deathday is not something that can leave a person cold, especially when the words are chanted in such a sweet, heartfelt voice that they're like balm to one's weary bones. And above all—the kaddish. The kaddish! A stone couldn't help but be moved by a kaddish like that . . .

In a word, that was an afternoon prayer to remember!

Having finished praying and removed his makeshift belt, the mourner sat himself down opposite our tenth man and, with the same gaily tragic expression as before, commenced his promised story. He stroked his round little beard as he told it, speaking slowly like a man who has time.

"The story I'm going to tell you, young man, is actually not one story but three. Three little stories in one.

"The first story happened to an innkeeper in a village. Once, that is, an innkeeper lived with his wife in quite a large village. There were many Russians in it but no other Jews; they were the only ones. Not that it troubled them; far from it, it meant they could earn a good living without fear of competition. Better rich among Christians, as they say, than poor among Jews . . . In fact, they lacked only one thing: children. For years they had prayed for them in vain, and this made their life sorrowful. Finally, when they were nearly past childbearing age, God had mercy; the innkeeper's wife conceived and gave birth to a healthy child. And a male child, too—what happiness! Of course, it was necessary to circumcise the boy. And so, on the eighth day, the innkeeper gladly harnessed his horse to his wagon, drove off to town, and came back with the rabbi, the circumciser, the beadle, and five other Jews. Naturally, his wife had a magnificent banquet ready for them when they arrived. Everything was just fine until the time came for the circumcision—at which point, it was discovered that they were missing a Jew. There were only nine of them. What had happened? Leave it to a country innkeeper: in counting to ten he had made the mistake of including his own wife! You can imagine what a good laugh the guests had. Meanwhile, though, the time was passing; what were they supposed to do now? It was a big village full of goyim, but there was nary another Jew. What a predicament! . . . Just then, however, someone looked out the window—and what did he see but a coach heading straight for the inn. In it was sitting a coachman. Well, let it be even a coachman as long as it was a Jew . . . 'Welcome, stranger!' 'Sholem aleykhem!' 'A Jew! You're just in time, we need a tenth for a minyan . . .' No words can describe the joy there was! Tell me now, don't we have a great God in heaven? A whole village of goyim couldn't save the day—along comes a single Jew and sets everything right!

"The second story, my dear fellow, took place not in a village but in a town, and in a solidly Jewish one, too. It happened on the Sabbath, that is, on a Friday night, after the candles had been lit. A father came home from the synagogue, blessed the wine, washed his hands—and just as he was sitting down to eat with his family, a candle had the bright notion of breaking in two. They tried propping it up with the hallah to keep it from toppling over—to no avail; the burning candle fell on the tablecloth and threatened to set it afire. In a minute the whole house would be in flames. What were they supposed to do now? Put it out? But it was the holy Sabbath! By now the neighbors had come running, the whole street was gathered there; a great hue and cry broke out. 'Jews, we'll be ruined!' . . . Just then, however, someone glanced up the street—and who should be coming down it but Chvedka the goy! '*Chvedka, serdtse,*' they cried, being careful not to overstep the Law, 'did you ever see such a queerly burning candle?' And Chvedka, dumb goy though he was, got the hint at once, spat on his hands, grabbed the burning candlewick between two callused Christian fingers, gave it a pinch—and the fire was out. I ask you: don't we still live in an age of miracles? A town full of Jews couldn't save the day—along comes one goy and rescues them all!

"And now I have to tell you my third story. This one concerns none other than a famous rabbi. This rabbi had an only son, an exceptionally capable youngster who was all a rabbi's son should be. He was married off when still young, given a handsome dowry, and encouraged to study Torah all day long at his father-in-law's expense. Indeed, that's just what he did, and everything would have been perfect if there hadn't been such a thing as the draft. On the face of it, of course, the boy had nothing to worry about: to begin with, he was an only son—and secondly, if it was a problem of money, money was no problem in this case. But the times, the times were bitter! Even only sons were being taken to the army, and ten thousand rubles couldn't buy a boy's way out of it. The authorities were ruthless, the doctor had a heart of stone; I tell you, it was a bad lookout. Just imagine, my dear young fellow, the rabbi's son was stripped to the bone and brought before the draft board—why, never before in his whole life had he been without a hat on his head! And that's what saved him, because he happened to have a canker there, a real running sore; there was nothing make-believe about it. He must have had it since childhood without knowing it—he had been so stubborn as a boy that he had refused to have his hair washed even once . . . Well, I needn't tell you that the draft board sent him packing in a hurry!

"And now tell me, my dear young friend, do you understand your true worth? You were born a Jew, you'll soon be a goy, and you're quite a running sore already. Don't you think you deserve a gold medal?"

At the very next station our tenth man slipped away.

(1910)

THIRD CLASS

▼

This is not so much a story as a little chat, a few words of admonition and farewell from a good friend.

As we are about to part, dear reader, I would like to show my gratitude for your having borne with me for so long by giving you some useful advice, the fond counsel of a practical man. Listen carefully.

If you must go somewhere by train, especially if the trip is a long one, and you wish to have the feeling of traveling, that is, of having enjoyed the experience, avoid going first or second class.

First class, of course, is out of the question anyway. God protect you from it! Naturally, I'm not referring to the ride itself. The ride in first class is far from unpleasant—indeed, it's sumptuous, comfortable, roomy, and with every possible convenience. It's not that I'm talking about; it's the people, the passengers. What can be the point, I ask you, of a Jew traveling in total solitude without a living soul to speak to? By the time you've reached your destination, you can have forgotten how to use your voice! And even if once in a blue moon you happen to run into another passenger, it's either some vulgar country squire with crimson jowls like a trombonist's, or some stuck-up lady who's as sniffy as a mother-in-law, or some foreign tourist in checked pants whose eyes are glued so tightly to the window that not even a fire in the car could tear him away from it. When you travel with such types, you begin to have the most depressing thoughts—why, you may even find yourself ruminating about death. Who needs it?

Do you think second class is any better, though? There you are, surrounded by all sorts of people who are obviously no different from yourself, with the identical human passions. They would like nothing better than to talk to you; in fact, they're dying of curiosity to know where you're going, where you're from, and who you are; but they sit there like so many tailor's dummies and so do you, and all that happens is one big exchange of stares. The whole car has taken a vow of silence—shhh, watch out you don't break it!

For example: across from you is a young dandy with manicured nails and a smart mustache whom you could swear you know from someplace, you just can't remember where. Indeed, he shows every sign of stemming from Mosaic lineage, that is, of being a fellow tribesman of yours. What good does that do you, though, when you can't get a word out of him? He's finished twirling the ends of his mustache, and now all he wants is to look out the window and whistle.

If you'd like to take a few good years off such a person's life—in fact, bury him so thoroughly that not even the Resurrection can put him back on his feet—all you need to do, provided there's a Christian sitting next to him, or better yet, a young lady, is turn to him in any language at all, though Russian is preferable, and inquire, *"Yesli ya nye oshibayus, ya imyel udovolstvye vstryetitsa s'vami v'Berdichevye?"* (In Yiddish we would say, "If I'm not mistaken, didn't I once have the pleasure of meeting you in Berdichev?") Believe me, that's a thousand times worse than any name you might call his father!

On the other hand, if you run into such a type in Podolia or Volhynia, Polish might be the better gambit. *"Pszepraszam, Pana! "Jesli się nie mylę znalem ojca Pana z Jarmelyncu, który byl w laskach u jasnie wielmożnego Potokego?"* (Roughly speaking that's, "Excuse me, sir, but if my memory doesn't betray me, I'm an old friend of your father's from Yarmelinetz; wasn't he in the service of Count Potocki there?") That may not seem like any great insult, but Yarmelinetz and the service of Count Potocki just happen to spell J-e-w . . . Enough of this, though! Let me tell you a story I happened to witness myself.

It happened on the mail train. Since there's no third class there, I had no choice but to travel second. Across from me was sitting a gentleman who could have been either a Christian or a Jew. To tell the truth, though, Jew seemed the more likely . . . or did it? Who could say? He was a handsome young fellow, smooth-shaven and sportily dressed with a black sash around his white pants—

and a bit of a Don Juan in the bargain. Why do I call him that? Because he was showering his attentions on a pretty young thing, a mademoiselle with a high chignon and pince-nez on her small, turned-up nose. Although newly acquainted, they were already fast friends. She kept offering him chocolates while he amused her with funny jokes, first Armenian and then Jewish ones, until both of them were holding their sides. And they laughed hardest of all at the Jewish jokes, which the young man in the white pants told with a decidedly Christian-like relish without showing the slightest appreciation of the fact that I might be a Jew myself who could be offended by them . . . In short, the romance was getting on famously. Soon he was sitting beside her and looking deep into her eyes (at first they had been opposite each other) while she played with the chain of his watch, which was tucked into his sash. All of a sudden, at some remote station whose name I can't even recall, the train was boarded by a lame, sallow-faced, perspiring Jew carrying a white parasol who stuck out his hand to the young sport and said in a plain, earthy Yiddish:

"Well, hello there! I recognized you through the window. I have regards for you from your Uncle Zalman in Manestrishtch . . ."

Needless to say, the young man made his exit at the same station and the pretty young thing was left sitting all by herself. But that's not the end of the story. The mademoiselle—she must have been a Christian, because otherwise why would our Don Juan have made such a hasty getaway?—began to collect her things a few stations later and prepared to leave the train too, still without having said a word to me, or even so much as glanced in my direction. It was as if I didn't exist. Yet waiting for her on the platform at the stop where she got off were—a patriarchal Jew with a beard as long as Father Abraham's and a Jewess with a wig and two huge diamonds in her ears. "Riva darling!" the old couple called out, and fell upon their daughter with tears in their eyes . . .

No commentary is necessary. I simply wanted to introduce you to some of the types who travel second class and to persuade you not to go that way yourself, because even among your own, you're always a stranger there.

When you travel third class, on the other hand, you feel right at home. In fact, if you happen to be in a car whose passengers are exclusively Jews, you may feel a bit too much at home. Granted, third class is not the height of luxury; if you don't use your elbows, you'll never find a seat; the noise level, the sheer hubbub, is earsplitting; you can never be sure where you end and where your neighbors begin . . . and yet there's no denying that that's an excellent way to meet them. Everyone knows who you are, where you're bound for, and what you do, and you know the same about everyone. At night you can save yourself the bother of having to fall asleep, because there's always someone to talk to—and if you're not in the mood to talk, someone else will be glad to do it for you. Who expects to sleep on a train ride anyway? Talking is far better, because you never know what may come of it. I should only live another year of my life for each time I've seen perfect strangers on the train end up by making a business deal, arranging a match for their children, or learning something worth knowing from each other.

For instance, all the talk you hear about doctors, indigestion, sanatoriums, toothaches, nervous conditions, Karlsbad, and so forth—you'd think it was all just a lot of malarkey, wouldn't you? Well, let me tell you a story about that. Once I was traveling with a group of Jews. We were talking about doctors and prescriptions. At the time, it shouldn't happen to you, I was having problems with my stomach, and a fellow passenger, a Jew from Kamenetz, recommended a medicine that came in the form of a powder. It so happened, said the Jew, that he had been given this powder by a dentist rather than a doctor, but the powder, which was yellow, was absolutely first-rate. That is, it wasn't yellow, it was white, like all powders; but it came in a yellow wrapper. He even swore to me by everything that was holy, the Jew did, that he owed his life to the yellow powder, because without it—no, he didn't even want to think of it! And I didn't need to use a whole lot, either. Two or three grains, he said, would make me feel like a new man; no more stomachaches, and no more money-grubbing, bloodsucking physicians; I could say to hell with every one of the damn quacks! "If you'd like," he said, "I can give you two or three grains of my yellow powder right now. You'll never stop thanking me . . ."

And that's what he did. I came home, I took one, two, three grains of the stuff, and after a while—it didn't happen at once, but later on, in the middle of the night—I had such pains that I thought I was kicking the bucket. I swear, I was sure I was on my last gasp! A doctor was called, and then another—it was all they could do to bring me back from death's door . . . Well, now I know that if a Jew from Kamenetz tries giving you a yellow powder, you should tell him to take a powder himself. Every lesson has its price.

When you go third class and wake up in the morning to discover that you've left your tefillin and your prayer shawl at home, there isn't any cause for alarm—you only need to ask and you'll be given someone else's, along with whatever else you require. All that's expected of you in return, once you're done praying, is to open your suitcase and display your own wares. Vodka, cake, a hard-boiled egg, a drumstick, a piece of fish—it's all grist for the mill. Perhaps you have an apple, an orange, a piece of strudel? Out with it, no need to be ashamed! Everyone will be glad to share it with you, no one stands on ceremony here. A train ride and good company, you understand, are two things that create an appetite . . . And of course, if you happen to have a wee bit of wine with you, there's no lack of volunteer tasters, each with his own verdict and name for it. "It's a Bessarabian muscat," says one. "No, it's an imported Akerman," says another. "What kind of muscat?" says a third, getting angrily to his feet. "What kind of Akerman? Can't you tell it's a Koveshaner Bordeaux?" At which point a fourth fellow rises from his corner with the smile of a true connoisseur, accepts the glass of wine with an expression that says, "Stand back, you duffers, this calls for an expert," takes a few sips, and pronounces, his cheeks flushed a merrymaker's red:

"Jews, do you know what this is? No, I can see that you don't. It's neither more nor less than a pure, simple, honest, no-nonsense, homemade Berdichev kiddush wine!"

And everyone realizes that the man is right, a Berdichev kiddush wine it is. And since quite a few tongues have been loosened by the time the wine has made its rounds, suddenly everyone is telling everybody everything, and everything is being told to everyone. The whole car is talking together at once in a splendid show of Jewish solidarity. Before long each of us not only knows all about the others' troubles, he knows about every trial and tribulation that ever befell a Jew anywhere. It's enough to warm the cockles of your heart!

When you travel third class and arrive in some town and don't know where to stay, you have a car full of Jews to help you out. In fact, the number of different places recommended will tally exactly with the number of Jews in the car. "The Hotel Frankfurt," says one of them, singing the praises of his choice. "It's bright and it's cheery, it's clean and it's breezy, it's the biggest bargain in town." "The Hotel Frankfurt?" exclaims someone else. "God forbid! It's dark and it's dreary, it's sordid and sleazy, it's the biggest gyp joint around. If you really want to enjoy yourself, I suggest you try the Hotel New York." "The only reason I can think of for staying in the New York," puts in another traveler, "is that you're homesick for bedbugs. Here, hand me your bag and come with me to my favorite, the Hotel Russia. It's the only place for a Jew!"

Of course, having given him your bag you had better keep an eye on him to make sure he doesn't make off with it . . . but I ask you, where in this wonderful world of ours aren't there thieves nowadays? Either you're fated to meet up with one or you're not. If it's in your crystal ball to be robbed, you can be cleaned out in broad daylight, and no amount of prayers or policemen will make the slightest difference. If anything, you'll thank your lucky stars that you got away with your life . . .

In a word, go third class. Those are the parting words to you of a good friend and a practical man, a commercial traveler.

Adieu!

(1902)

▲

Glossary and Notes

▼

Entries in this glossary appear in the same order as in the text, according to page number. Included are translations, source attributions, and when necessary, explications of Tevye's Hebrew quotations and of those made by the narrator of "Burned Out"; explanations of Jewish customs that may not be familiar to the general reader; and identifications of historical personages and events mentioned in *Tevye* and *The Railroad Stories*. Glossarized words, phrases, and names appearing more than once in the volume are generally cross-referenced—unless they occur in the same chapter or story, in which case they are listed only once. English translations of Biblical quotations use the King James text, with occasional emendations to suit the context. Translations of other Hebrew sources are my own. In the case of fragmentary quotations from the Bible, the prayer book, etc., the English translation often includes the entire verse or passage from which these are taken; in such instances, the English words that correspond to the Hebrew fragment in the text appear in italics. Quotations not translated in the glossary have already been translated in the text itself.

As mentioned in the Introduction, Tevye's Hebrew is transliterated here according to the East European pronunciation. Readers wishing to pronounce it as he did should follow these rules:

"Kh" is a guttural pronounced like the "ch" in "Bach" or the Scottish "loch." (In proper names like Chava or Menachem Mendl, the "ch" is pronounced in the same way.)

"Oy" is as in "boy."

"Ey" is as in "grey."

"Ai" and "ay" are like "ie" in "pie."

"O" and "oh" are like "aw" in "law."

"I" is like "ee" in "seen."

"U" is like "oo" in "boot."

"A" is as in "father."

"E" and "eh" are as in "get."

In multisyllabic words, the next-to-last syllable is generally stressed.

T e v y e   t h e   D a i r y m a n

PAGE

3 / Revakh vehatsoloh ya'amoyd layehudim—"For if thou holdest thy peace at this time, *then shall enlargement and deliverance arise to the Jews* from another place"; Esther, 4:14.

3 / Shavuos—Shavuoth or Pentecost, a two-day holiday in late spring commemorating the giving of the Torah.

4 / Rashi—The acronymic name of Rabbi Shlomo Yitzchaki of Troyes (1040–1105), whose popular commentary on the Bible is commonly read by observant Jews on the Sabbath in the course of reviewing the weekly portion from the Pentateuch.

4 / Targum—The first-century Aramaic translation of the Bible by Onkelos the Proselyte that, like the commentary of Rashi, is traditionally studied with the weekly Torah reading.

4 / Perek—The Mishnaic tractate of *Pirkey Avot, The Ethics of the Fathers.* (See Introduction, p. xxviii.)

4 / Zon umefarneys lakoyl—"For He is a God *who nourishes and supports all life*"; from the grace regularly recited after meals.

5 / Mi yorum umi yishofeyl—"Who shall be raised up and who shall be brought low"; from the *unesaneh toykef* prayer on the High Holy Days, in which God is described as deciding the fates of everyone for the coming year. In the prayer book the phrase occurs as *mi yishofeyl umi yorum,* "who shall be brought low and who shall be raised up."

5 / Atoh bekhartonu—"For *Thou hast chosen us* among all the nations"; from the holiday prayer book.

5 / Vayehi hayoym—"And it came to pass"; a common Biblical phrase introducing a new story or episode in a narrative.

6 / Shimenesre—The "eighteen benedictions," a lengthy devotion recited as part of the morning, afternoon, and evening prayers and structured around nineteen (originally eighteen) blessings, the first of which begins, "Blessed art Thou, O Lord, our God and God of our fathers, God of Abraham, God of Isaac, and God of Jacob." When praying by himself, a Jew says the *shimenesre* silently and without moving from his place—which only heightens the comedy of Tevye's shouting the prayer out loud while running after his horse.

6 / Mekhalkeyl khayim bekhesed—From the second benediction of the *shimenesre*, as is *umekayeym emunosoy lisheyney ofor*.

6 / Re'ey-no be'onyeynu—From the seventh benediction.

6 / Refo'eynu veneyrofey—From the eighth benediction.

6 / Boreykh oleynu—From the ninth benediction.

6 / Velamalshinim al tehi tikvoh—From the twelfth benediction.

6 / Ov harakhamon—From the sixteenth benediction.

6 / Shma koyleynu—"Hearken to our voice"; from the sixteenth benediction.

6 / Khus verakheym oleynu—"Have mercy and pity us"; also from the sixteenth benediction.

7 / Retsey—"*Accept* Thy people Israel, O Lord, our God, and hearken to its prayers, and restore its worship to Thy holy temple"; from the seventeenth benediction.

14 / Hamavdil beyn koydesh lekhoyl—"Blessed art Thou, O Lord, our God, King of the Universe, *who separateth the holy* [Sabbath] *from the profane* [week]"; from the *havdalah*, the prayer formally ending the Sabbath that is said on Saturday night. Tevye's comic rhyme implies that God not only keeps the Sabbath and the rest of the week well apart from each other, but also does the same with the rich and the poor.

14 / Bemokoym she'eyn ish—"*In a place where there are no men* [of moral or religious stature], *try to be a man*"; from *The Ethics of the Fathers*. Tevye's rhyme stands this adage on its head: whereas the original quotation means that in a place where ideals of conduct are disregarded one must nevertheless try to live up to them, he himself is saying that when the reality falls short of the ideal, one makes do with what there is.

16 / Vehayeled eynenu—"And he returned unto his brethren and said, '*The child is not*' "; Genesis, 37:30.

17 / Yom Kippur songs—Being a penitential fast day, Yom Kippur, the Day of Atonement, does not have festive songs, though some of its prayers are sung in the synagogue. Tevye's choice of these inappropriate melodies reflects how drunk he is.

17 / "King Solomon wasn't joking"—Tevye is referring to the verse in Ecclesiastes, 7:28, "One man among a thousand I have found; but a woman among all those have I not found."

20 / Koyl oyreyv lemineyhu—"Every raven after his kind"; Leviticus, 11:15.

20 / Raboys makhshovoys belev ish—Proverbs, 19:21.

21 / Kulom ahuvim, kulom brurim—"*All are beloved, all are elect,* all are intrepid, all are holy, all perform the will of their Maker in awe." From a description of the angelic hosts in the morning prayer.

22 / Yehalelkho zor—"*Let another man praise thee,* and not thine own mouth." Proverbs, 27:2.

22 / Odom yesoydoy mi'ofor—"Man is but dust." From the High Holy Day prayer.

23 / Hakoyl hevel—"All is vanity." Ecclesiastes, 1:2.

24 / Koyl dikhfin yeysey veyitzrokh—Tevye is jokingly misquoting the opening line of the Passover seder ritual. According to the Haggadah, the seder liturgy, Jews sitting down to the ceremonial meal begin by inviting the homeless and hungry to join them, saying, *Koyl dikhfin yeysey veyeykhul; koyl ditzrikh yeysey veyifsakh*—"Let all who are hungry come and eat; let all who are needy come and observe the Passover." Tevye's version, however, means, "Let all who are hungry come and be needy."

24 / "If you don't mind my quoting King David"—Tevye is clowning, for he knows perfectly well that this verse from Ecclesiastes is attributed to King Solomon, not to King David, who is traditionally considered to be the author of Psalms.

25 / Akudim nekudim uvrudim—"And behold, the rams which leaped upon the cattle were *streaked, speckled, and grizzled.*" Tevye likes these words from Genesis 31:10 because of their rhythm and internal rhyme, and uses them to refer a series of something without being overly pedantic about their literal meaning.

26 / *Begapoy yovoy uvegapoy yeytsey*—"*If he comes* [to his master] *with nothing, he shall depart with nothing.*" Exodus, 21:3, from a passage dealing with the Israelite laws of slavery and manumission.

26 / Rashi—See note to p. 4. The "commentary" on the verse from Exodus attributed to him by Tevye is, of course, Tevye's own invention.

27 / "I'm talking Purim costumes and you're talking Hanukkah candles"—On Purim, the holiday celebrating the foiling of Haman's plot to kill the Jews, it was a custom in parts of Eastern Europe to dress in costume and go mumming; on Hanukkah, which celebrates the victory of the Maccabees, candles are lit on each of the eight nights of the holiday.

28 / *Hazoyrim bedimoh berinoh yiktsoyru*—"They that sow in tears shall reap in joy." Psalms, 126:5. Tevye's misattribution of the verse to Abraham is again deliberate buffoonery.

28 / *Lav akhboro ganvo*—"*It's not the mouse that's the thief,* but the hole [that beckons to it]." A Talmudic proverb.

30 / *Revakh vehatsoloh ya'amoyd layehudim*—See note to p. 3.

30 / *Vayisu misukoys*—"*And they journeyed from Succoth* and encamped in Etham, on the edge of the wilderness." Exodus, 13:20.

31 / *Oylim veyordim*—"And he dreamed, and behold a ladder set up on the earth . . . and behold the angels of God *ascending and descending* on it." Genesis, 28:12. Tevye seems to be associating the words either with the rotary motion of wheels or with the coming and going of supplicants to a rich man's house.

31 / *Eyn oymer ve'eyn dvorim*—"Day unto day uttereth speech, and night unto night showeth knowledge. *There is no speech nor utterance* where their voice is not heard." Psalms, 19:3.

32 / *Vehayeled eynenu*—See note to p. 16.

32 / *Vayivrakh Ya'akoyv*—"*And Jacob fled* with all that he had." Genesis, 31:21.

33 / *Ka'asher ovadeti ovadeti*—"If I perish, I perish." Esther, 4:16.

33 / *Loy dubim veloy ya'ar*—Literally, "neither bears nor woods"; a rabbinic expression (based on the story of the prophet Elisha and the bears in Kings II, 24) that means, "There's neither hide nor hair of it," "It's a figment of the imagination," etc.

34 / Lekhayim veloy lamoves—"For life and not for death, for a blessing and not for a curse." From the prayers for dew and rain.

34 / Al tis'haleyl beyoym mokhor—"Boast not of tomorrow, for thou knowest not what today may bring forth." Proverbs, 27:1.

34 / Vetso'akoh hane'aroh—"For he found her in the field [and abused her] *and the maiden cried,* and there was no one to save her." Deuteronomy, 22:27.

34 / "The Lord giveth and the Lord taketh away"—Job, 1:21.

34 / Li hakesef veli hazohov—"*The silver is mine and the gold is mine,* saith the Lord of Hosts." Haggai, 2:18.

34 / Be'al korkhekho atoh khai—"Regardless of thy will thou art conceived, and regardless of thy will thou art born, and *regardless of thy will thou livest,* and regardless of thy will thou diest." From *The Ethics of the Fathers;* a favorite quote of Tevye's.

35 / Koyl ha'odom koyzev—"I said in my haste, *all men are liars.*" Psalms, 116:11. Apparently Tevye is referring to the bill of goods that Menachem Mendl has sold him—unless he is confusing the verb *koyzev,* "lie," with *koy'ev,* "hurt."

35 / Bonim gidalti veroymamti—"*I have nourished and brought up children,* and they have rebelled against me." Isaiah, 1:2.

37 / Loy mi'uktsokh veloy miduvshokh —"Neither from your sting nor from your honey"; a rabbinic expression meaning, "Just do me no harm and I'll gladly do without your favors."

37 / Askakurdo dimaskanto dikarnaso difarsmakhto—This is a sheer nonsense phrase, although one whose Aramaic prefixes and suffixes give it a Talmudic sound.

39 / Odom koroyv le'atsmoy—"A man is closest to his own self"; a rabbinic saying.

39 / Im eyn kemakh eyn Toyroh—"If there is no flour, there is no Torah"; from *The Ethics of the Fathers,* meaning that before one can study, one has to eat.

40 / Rashi—See note to p. 4. Here again Tevye is putting his own words in the commentator's mouth.

40 / Rokheyl mevakoh al boneho—"A voice is heard in Ramah, lamentation and bitter weeping; *Rachel weeping for her children,* refusing to be comforted for her children, for they are gone." Jeremiah, 31:15.

40 / Gemara—The larger and more difficult part of the Talmud, consisting of lengthy and involved Aramaic commentary on the shorter and simpler Hebrew Mishnah.

40 / Haggadah—See note to p. 24.

43 / Haneshomoh lokh—"The soul is thine and the body is thine." From the penitential prayers said before the High Holy Days. For the sake of the witticism, Tevye overlooks the second half of the verse.

43 / Tsoholoh vesomeykhoh—"And the city of Shushan *rejoiced and was glad.*" Esther, 8:15.

43 / The *hallel* prayer—A prayer of praise and thanksgiving to God, composed of Psalms 113–118, that is recited in the morning service on major holidays. All Tevye's quotations on this and the following page are from it.

43 / Hashomayim shomayim ladoynai—"The heavens are the Lord's." Psalms, 115:16.

43 / Veha'orets nosan livney odom—"But the earth He hath given to the children of men." Psalms, 115:16.

43 / Loy hameysim yehallelu yoh—"The dead praise not the Lord." Psalms, 115:17.

43 / Ve'anakhnu nevoreykh yoh—"But we will bless the Lord." Psalms, 115:18.

43 / Ohavti ki yishma—"I love [the Lord], *because He hath heard* my voice and my supplications." Psalms, 116:1.

44 / Ofafuni khevley moves—"*The sorrows of death compassed me,* and the pains of hell got hold upon me: I found trouble and sorrow." Psalms, 116:3.

*44 / Ani omarti bekhofzi—*See note to p. 35.

44 / Koyl ha'odom koyzev—". . . all men are liars." Psalms, 116:11.

44 / Oydkho ki anisoni—"I will praise Thee, for Thou hast answered me* and art become my salvation." Psalms, 118:21.

*45 / Hakoyl hevel—*See note to p. 23.

46 / The Four Questions—At the beginning of the Passover seder the youngest child present customarily asks four questions about the nature of the occasion that are designed to elicit from those present the recital of the story of the exodus. The Four Questions begin with the words *ma nishtanoh—*"how is this [night] different?"

50 / Solakhti kidvorekho—"And the Lord said, *I have pardoned according to thy word.*" Numbers, 14:20.

50 / Vehashtiyoh kedos—"And the king made a feast . . . *and the drinking was according to custom.*" Esther, 1:5,8.

52 / Borukh shelo osoni ishoh—"Blessed be [God] that hath not made me a woman"; a blessing in the morning prayer, recited by males.

52 / Bonim gidalti veroymamti—See note to p. 35.

52 / Veheym poshu vi—"And they have rebelled against me." See note to p. 35 on *bonim gidalti veroymamti.* Here Tevye supplies the second half of the verse that he omitted at the beginning of the story.

53 / Odom yesoydoy mi'ofor vesoyfoy le'ofor—See note to p. 22 on *Odom yesoydoy mi'ofor.* Tevye completes the quote here by adding the words *vesoyfoy le'ofor*—"and dust is all that remains of him."

53 / Kabdeyhu vekhoshdeyhu—A rabbinic adage meaning literally, "Respect him and suspect him," i.e., some people must never be trusted even though you honor them.

53 / Haneshomoh lokh vehaguf shelokh—See note to p. 43.

53 / Ki toyvas mar'eh hi—"For she was fair to look on." Esther, 1:11.

54 / Kulonu khakhomim, kulonu nevoynim—"And even though *we all are wise, we all are learned,* we all are versed in the Torah, we are commanded to recite the story of the exodus from Egypt." From the Passover Haggadah.

54 / Al tishlakh yodkho—"And he said, *lay not thine hand* upon the lad." Genesis, 22:12 (see Introduction, pp. xxix).

54 / Vesomakhto bekhagekho—"Thou shalt observe the Feast of Tabernacles seven days . . . *and thou shalt rejoice in thy feast.*" Deuteronomy, 16:13–14.

54 / Vayehi hayoym—See note to p. 5.

55 / "Help the jackass of your neighbor"—"If thou see the ass of him that hateth thee lying under his burden . . . thou shalt surely help him." Exodus, 23:5.

55 / Vaya'as eloyhim—"And God made . . . every thing that creepeth on the earth." Genesis, 1:25.

56 / Kulom ahuvim, kulom brurim—See note to p. 21.

57 / *Bekhoyl levovkho uvekhoyl nafshekho*—"And thou shalt love the Lord thy God *with all thine heart, and with all thy soul,* and with all thy might." Deuteronomy, 6:5.

57 / *Vehayeled eynenu*—See note to p. 16.

58 / *Vayehi erev vayehi voyker*—"And there was morning and there was evening." Genesis, 1:5 and passim.

58 / *Revakh vehatsoloh ya'amoyd layehudim mimokoym akher*—See note to p. 3. Here Tevye completes the verse by adding *mimokoym akher*, "from another place."

59 / *Akudim nekudim uvrudim*—See note to p. 25.

59 / *Yo'oh aniyuso leyisro'eyl*—"Poverty is becoming to Israel." The Talmudic adage implies that God gave the Jews poverty as a gift because it is spiritually good for them, but Tevye reverses its meaning.

60 / *Im eyn kemakh eyn Toyroh*—See note to p. 39.

60 / *Loy bashomayim veloy ba'orets*—"Not in heaven or on earth." While the phrase *bashomayim uva'orets,* "in heaven and on earth," occurs in the Bible and other Jewish sources, its formulation in the negative is Tevye's own.

61 / *Bo'u mayim ad nefesh*—"Save me, my God, for *the waters are come in unto my soul."* Psalms, 69:1.

61 / *Ohavti es adoyni es ishti*—"I love my master, my wife." Exodus, 21:5.

63 / *Eyn Esther magedes*—"*And Esther spoke not* of her nativity or her people." Esther, 2:20.

64 / *Eyn koyl ve'eyn kosef*—Tevye is thinking of the verse in Kings I, 18:29, "And it came to pass, when midday was past, they [the priests of the Baal] prophesied until the time of the evening sacrifice; yet *there was neither voice . . . nor any heed [e'eyn koyl . . . ve'eyn koshev]"*— but, whether intentionally or not, he has confused the word *koshev,* "heed," with *kosef,* "money," so that he ends up by saying, "There was neither voice nor money."

65 / *Kerakheym ov al bonim*—"*Like as a father pitieth his children,* so the Lord pitieth them that fear Him." Psalms, 103:13.

65 / High Holy Days—The solemn holidays of Rosh Hashanah, the New Year, and Yom Kippur, the Day of Atonement, which occur ten days apart in early autumn.

65 / Sukkos—The seven-day holiday of Sukkoth or the Feast of Tabernacles, occurring five days after Yom Kippur, during which observant

Jews eat and sometimes sleep in a sukkah, a thatch-covered hut or
booth erected especially for the festivity.

65 / *Atoh . . . veshorkho . . . vekhamorkho*—"But the seventh day is the Sabbath of the Lord thy God: on it thou shalt not do any work, *neither
thou,* nor thy son, nor thy daughter, nor thy manservant, nor thy
maidservant, *nor thine ox, nor thine ass,* nor any of thy cattle, nor the
stranger that is within thy gates." Deuteronomy, 5:14. Taking advantage of the fact that the verse fails to mention one's wife, Tevye
parses *veshorkho,* "thy ox," to mean "thy wife"—and since the verse
makes no mention of horses either, he interprets *vekhamorkho,* "and
thy ass," to refer to his nag.

66 / *Al keyn ya'azoyv ish es oviv ve'es imoy*—"*Therefore a man shall leave his
father and his mother* and shall cleave unto his wife." Genesis, 2:24.

67 / *Lomoh rogshu*—"Why do the heathen *rage?*" Psalms, 2:1.

67 / The Book of Life—The divine register in which, according to both
rabbinic tradition and popular Jewish belief, God annually inscribes
the fate of every individual. The predestined year is said to run from
one Yom Kippur to the next, the ten-day period between Rosh
Hashanah and Yom Kippur being set aside for entering the next
year's fates, which can still be changed for the better by penitence
and good works. At the end of Yom Kippur God's decision is
stamped and sealed—yet the Book of Life is left open for last-minute
changes until Hoshana Rabbah, the last day of Sukkoth, thus creat-
ing a grace period of several additional days in which one can still
ward off a cruel destiny. It is only on Hoshana Rabbah that the Book
is shut irrevocably for the year; hence the custom referred to by
Tevye of staying up all night in prayer and study on Hoshana Rabbah eve.

69 / *Hoydu lashem ki toyv*—"Give thanks to the Lord, for He is good."
Psalms, 136:1.

69 / *Tsa'ar gidul bonim*—"The sorrows of child raising." A rabbinic expression.

69 / *Ad kan hakofoh alef*—"That's the end of the first *hakofoh.*" A *hakofoh* is
a circling of the synagogue with the Torah scrolls on the holiday of
Simkhat Torah, the Rejoicing of the Law. Seven such rounds, accompanied by singing and dancing, take place. At the end of each the
sexton announces, "That's the end of the ——*hakofoh,*" and the
Torah scrolls change hands for the next round.

70 / Eyl rakhum vekhanun—"And the Lord passed by before him and proclaimed, The Lord, The Lord *God, merciful and gracious,* long-suffering and abundant in goodness and truth." Exodus, 34:6.

70 / Hamekhaseh ani mey'Avrohom—"And the Lord said, *Shall I hide from Abraham* that thing which I do?" Genesis, 18:17.

70 / Rotsoh hakodoysh borukh hu lezakoys—"Rabbi Hananiah ben Akashya said, *The Holy One Blessed Be He wished to bestow merit* upon Israel and so He gave them many laws and commandments." From *The Ethics of the Fathers.*

71 / Midrash—See Introduction, p. xxix.

71 / Gorky—Maxim Gorky (1868–1936), Russian writer and revolutionary supporter. Gorky, who burst spectacularly on the Russian literary scene in the 1890s with his stories about the Russian lower classes, was especially popular with young Jewish readers because of his outspoken opposition to anti-Semitism and his sympathy for the Jewish victims of Czarist persecution.

72 / Yegia kapekho ki toykhal—"For thou shalt eat the labor of thine hands." Psalms, 128:2.

72 / Meyayin boso ule'on atoh hoyleykh—"Akavia ben Mehalelel said, Keep in mind three things and you will not fall into sin: know *whence you come, and whither you go,* and to Whom you will owe an accounting." From *The Ethics of the Fathers.*

72 / Ish kematnas yodoy—"Every man as he is able." Deuteronomy, 16:17.

73 / Hanoyseyn lasekhvi binoh—"Blessed art Thou, O Lord God, King of the Universe, *Who giveth the rooster knowledge* to tell the dawn from the night." From the opening blessings of the daily morning prayer.

73 / Shivoh dvorim bagoylem—"*The fool has seven traits* and so does the wise man: the wise man does not speak to his superior in knowledge without being spoken to, and does not interrupt his companion, and does not answer rashly, and replies to the point, and puts first things first and last things last, and says 'I do not know' when he does not know, and always admits to the truth; and the fool does just the opposite." From *The Ethics of the Fathers.*

75 / Holakh Moyshe-Mordekhai—"Off went Moyshe-Mordekhai"; a parodistic pseudo-verse.

75 / Ma pishi uma khatosi—"And Jacob answered and said to Laban, *what is my trespass? What is my sin?*" Genesis, 31:36.

75 / *Mah onu umeh khayeynu*—"What are we and what is our life?" From the morning prayer.

76 / *Kerakheym ov al bonim*—See note to p. 65.

77 / *Al tiftakh peh lasoton*—"Do not open your mouth to the Devil." A rabbinic proverb meaning, Do not speak of what you do not wish to happen, lest the evil eye bring it to pass.

77 / "And against the Children of Israel not a dog stuck out its tongue." Exodus, 11:17.

78 / The Lord giveth and the Lord taketh away—See note to p. 34.

78 / *Loy omus ki ekhyeh*—"*I shall not die, but live,* and declare the works of the Lord." Psalms, 118:17.

79 / *Be'al korkhekho atoh khai*—See note to p. 34.

79 / *Odom kiveheymoh nidmeh*—"Man . . . that understandeth not *is like the beasts that perish.*" Psalms, 49:20.

79 / *Oylom keminhogoy noyheyg*—"The world goes on its accustomed course." A rabbinic saying.

80 / *Al tistakeyl bakankan*—"Rabbi [Yehuda Hanasi] said, *Look not at the storage jar* but at what it stores." From *The Ethics of the Fathers.*

81 / *Kerakheym ov al bonim*—See note to p. 65.

81 / The *ashrey*—The opening section of the afternoon prayer, which begins with the verse, *Ashrey yoyshvey veysekho, oyd yehalelukho seloh* , "Blessed are they that dwell in Thy house; they will still be praising Thee, Selah." Psalms, 84:5.

81 / The *shimenesre*—See note to p. 6.

82 / *Ish lefo'aloy ve'odom le'avoydosoy*—"Man goeth forth unto his work and to his labor." Psalms, 104:23.

82 / *Ad kan oymrim beshabbes hagodol*—"Thus far one says on the Great Sabbath." On the Sabbath before Passover, "the Great Sabbath," as it is called, it is customary to recite the opening section of the Haggadah. At the end of this section, therefore, many Haggadahs bear the notation "Thus far one says on the Great Sabbath," in order to indicate where to stop.

82 / *Vayishkokheyhu*—"And the chief butler did not remember Joseph. *And he forgot him.*" Genesis, 40:23.

82 / Pogroms in Kishinev—See Introduction, p. xiv.

82 / The new Constantution—Tevye is referring to the Constitution of 1905 (see Introduction, p. xiv), but mispronounces the Russian word. And Sholem Aleichem has made a mistake of his own here, too: since "Hodl" was published in 1904, "Chava" in 1905, and "Shprintze" in 1907, it is inaccurate for Tevye to say in "Shprintze" that the two of them have not met since the time before the 1903 Kishinev pogroms.

82 / Harey ani keven shivim shonoh—"Rabbi Elazar ben Azaryah said, '*Lo, I am nearly seventy years old,* and never did I know that one is obliged to mention the exodus at night until I heard it from ben Zoma." From the Passover Haggadah.

83 / Be'al korkhekho atoh khai—See note to p. 34.

83 / Rotsoh hakodoysh borukh hu lezakoys—See note to p. 70.

83 / Borukh merakheym al ha'orets—"Blessed is He Who hath mercy upon the earth." From the prayer book.

83 / Vayisu vayakhanu, vayakhanu vayisu—"And they journeyed and they camped, and they camped and they journeyed." This is not an actual verse but rather Tevye's version of the Biblical account of the wanderings of the Children of Israel in the desert, with its oft-repeated formula of "And the Children of Israel journeyed from — and camped in ——."

83 / Vayehi hayoym—See note to p. 5.

85 / Shavuos—See note to p. 3. It was traditional among East European Jews to eat dairy foods on Shavuos, unlike other holidays, when meat (if affordable) was the preferred main course.

85 / Lo blintzu avoyseynu bemitsrayim—Tevye has creatively taken the Biblical verse (Numbers, 10:5), "We remember the fish, the cucumbers, the melons, the leeks, the onions, and the garlic which we did eat in Egypt," made a Hebrew verb out of the Yiddish word *blintz,* and said quite Biblically to Ahronchik, "My wife will serve you such blintzes fit for princes as *our forefathers never blintzed in Egypt.*"

86 / Kesef vezohov ma'asey yedey odom—"The idols of the heathen are *silver and gold, the work of men's hands.*"—Psalms, 115:4.

86–87 / Hashomayim shomayim ladoynai—See note to p. 43.

87 / A Jew doesn't ride on Shavuos—Among the activities that are prohibited to observant Jews on Sabbaths and most major holidays is traveling in any form except by foot.

88 / *Hashleykh al hashem*—"*Cast upon the Lord* thy burden." Psalms, 55:22.

88 / *Vayehi erev vayehi voyker*—See note to p. 58.

89 / "The wise man has eyes in his head." Ecclesiastes, 2:14.

90 / *Holakh Moyshe-Mordekhai*—See note to p. 75.

91 / *Raboys makhshovoys belev ish*—"Many are the thoughts in a man's heart but the counsel of the Lord shall prevail." Proverbs, 19:21.

92 / *Keshoyshanoh beyn hakhoykhim*—"*As a lily among thorns,* so is my love among the daughters." Song of Songs, 2:2.

93 / *Sheli shelkho* and *shelkho sheli*—"What's mine is yours and what's yours is mine." Tevye is alluding to the saying in *The Ethics of the Fathers* that goes, "There are four kinds of men. [He who says,] 'What's mine is mine and what's yours is yours' is the average man . . . [He who says,] 'What's yours is mine and what's mine is yours' is the artless man. [He who says,] 'What's mine is yours and what's yours is yours' is the righteous man. [He who says,] What's yours is mine and what's mine is mine' is the wicked man."

93 / There's a time for everything, as King Solomon once said—"To every thing there is a season and a time to every purpose." Ecclesiastes, 3:1.

95 / My tongue clove to my mouth, as the Bible says—"If I forget thee, O Jerusalem, let my tongue cleave to my mouth." Psalms, 137:5.

97 / *Koyl zman shehaneshomoh bekirbi*—"*As long as the soul is in me,* I shall thank Thee, O God and God of my fathers." From the daily morning prayer.

97 / Two mountains never meet . . .—A rabbinic proverb.

97 / *Al tistakeyl bakankan*—See note to p. 80.

98 / *Im kevonim im ka'avodim*—"Judge us *whether as* [Thy] *sons or as* [Thy] *servants:* if as sons, pity us as a father pities his sons; and if as servants, our eyes are cast to Thy mercy." From the Rosh Hashanah service. Tevye first wrenches the phrase out of its religious context and then, in his next sentence, restores it there.

99 / *Ki zeh koyl ha'odom*—"Let us hear the conclusion of the whole matter: fear God and keep His commandments, *for that is the whole of man.*" Ecclesiastes, 12:13.

99 / *Mah onu umeh khayeynu*—See note to p. 75.

99 / I hired a Jew to say the mourner's prayer—During the year following a death in his immediate family, a male Jew is required to recite the kaddish, the mourner's prayer, several times daily in the synagogue. (The kaddish is one of the few prayers that cannot be said in solitude.) Since there is no synagogue in Tevye's village and a daily trip to Boiberik or Yehupetz is impractical, he has no choice but to pay someone else to say the prayer for him—a common practice in such circumstances.

99–100 / Charm is a liar and Beauty a cheat—"Charm is deceitful and beauty is vain; but a woman that feareth the Lord, she shall be praised." Proverbs, 31:30.

100 / Makdim rakhamim leroygez—"For all men believe that He is slow to anger: the Merciful One *Whose pity comes before His wrath.*" From the High Holy Day service.

100 / Vayehi hayoym—See note to p. 5.

101 / The name rings a bell from the Bible—Tevye is thinking of Gamliel the son of Pedahtsur, the head of the tribe of Menasheh. (Numbers, 2:20.)

102 / Lanokhri toshikh—"*Unto a stranger* [Gentile] *thou mayest lend upon usury;* but unto thy brother [Israelite] thou shalt not." Deuteronomy, 23:20. The Bible permits the Israelite to lend money at interest only to the non-Israelite, since to his brother he is commanded to lend it free; Tevye, however, humorously construes "usury" to mean bribery.

102 / Loy orkhu hayomim—"Before many days went by." A pseudo-verse: the phrase *orkhu hayomim*, "the days went by," occurs in the Bible, but not in the negative.

103 / Holakh Moyshe-Mordekhai—See note to p. 75.

104 / Vayeyleykh khoronoh—"And he [Jacob] went to Haran." Genesis, 28:10.

104 / Mah zeh ve'al mah zeh—"Then Esther called for Hatach, one of the king's chamberlains . . . and gave him a commandment to Mordecai to know *what it was and why it was.*" Esther, 4:5. Here Tevye makes a question of it, i.e., what's the point of it all?

104 / Lehoyshivi im nedivim—"He raiseth the poor man up out of the dust . . . *that He may set him with princes,* even with the princes of his people." Psalms, 113:7–8.

104 / Royv godloy veroyv oshroy—"The multitude of his riches and wealth." Tevye is misquoting, apparently unintentionally: the verse he has in mind (Esther, 5:11) reads, "And Haman told them of the glory of his riches, and the multitude of his children, and all the things wherein the king had promoted him [*gidloy;* Tevye reads it *godloy*—"his wealth"]."

106 / Lomoh zeh anoykhi—"And she [Rebecca] said, If it be so, *why am I thus?*" Genesis, 25:22.

106 / Mah yoym miyomim—"What is [different about] this day among days?" A rabbinic expression.

106 / Mekimi mi'ofor dal—"He raiseth up the poor out of the dust . . ." Psalms, 113:7. From the *hallel* prayer. (See note to p. 43.)

106 / Meyashpoys yorim evyoyn—". . . And lifteth the needy out of the dung-hill." Psalms, 113:7.

107 / Shloyshoh she'okhlu—"Rabbi Simeon says, *Three men who eat* together at the same table and speak no words of Torah may as well have eaten the flesh of a pagan sacrifice." *The Ethics of the Fathers.*

107 / "A righteous man knows the soul of his beast." Proverbs, 12:10.

108 / Marbeh nekhosim marbeh da'ogoh—"He [Hillel the Elder] used to say, Much meat, many worms, *much possessions, many worries.*" *The Ethics of the Fathers.*

109 / Loy dubim veloy ya'ar—See note to p. 33.

109 / Holakh le'oylomoy—"He has gone to his world." A rabbinic euphemism for saying someone has died.

110 / What Onkelos has to say in his Targum—See note to p. 4.

110 / Miznavto dekhazirto loy makhtmen shtreimilto—A comic concoction of Aramaic and Yiddish meaning, as Tevye tells Podhotzur, that one cannot make a shtreimel, a Hasidic round fur hat, out of the tail of a pig.

110 / Wailing Wall—The western wall of the Temple Mount in Jerusalem, the one remaining feature of the destroyed Temple and the holiest of Jewish shrines.

110 / Rachel's Tomb—A small mausoleum near Bethlehem supposedly containing the grave of the matriarch Rachel, who died in childbirth, according to the Bible, on her way to that city. It is traditionally a place where Jews, particularly women, come to ask for their prayers to be granted.

110 / Cave of the Patriarchs—A structure in Hebron which is a shrine for Jews and Moslems. According to popular belief it houses the graves of Abraham, Sarah, Isaac, Rebecca, Jacob, and Leah.

112 / Kheyt shekhotosi lefonekho—"The sin that I have sinned before Thee." A recurrent phrase in the confessional section of the Yom Kippur prayer.

112 / Vayisu vayakhanu—See note to p. 83.

113 / Im eyn ani li mi li—"He [Hillel the Elder] said, *If I am not for myself, who will be? And if I am for myself what am I? And if not now, when?*" *The Ethics of the Fathers.*

115 / Veyoda shor koyneyhu—"*The ox knoweth his owner* and the ass his master's crib." Isaiah, 1:3. Tevye is punning here, as *koyneyhu*, "his owner," can also mean "his buyer."

115 / Zeh khelki mikoyl amoli—"And this was my portion of all my labor." Ecclesiastes, 2:10.

116 / Each of the hundred-and-seven-and-twenty lands of King Ahasuerus—Esther, 1:1.

117 / Harey ani keven shivim shonoh—See note to p. 82.

117 / Shmo'eyni—"And Abraham . . . spoke unto Ephron, saying . . . I pray thee, *hear me.*" Genesis, 23:12–13.

117 / What Bible reading—The Pentateuch is traditionally divided into fifty-four weekly readings (there are occasional doublings), each chanted in the synagogue on one Sabbath of the year. Each reading is named for one or two of the words occurring in its first verse; thus the third reading in Genesis, which starts with Genesis, 12:1, is called Lekh-Lekho, "Get thee out."

117 / Lekh-lekho . . . meyartsekho . . . umimoyladitkho . . . el ha'orets asher arekko—"And the Lord said unto Abram, *Get thee out of thy country, and from thy kindred, and from thy father's house, unto a land that I will show thee.*" Genesis, 12:1.

117 / Al tashlikheynu le'eys ziknoh—"Cast us not away [O Lord] in our old age." From the penitential and High Holy Day prayers.

118 / Al hatoyroh ve'al ha'avoydoh—"Simeon the Just . . . said that the world rests on three things: *on Torah and on work* and on charity." *The Ethics of the Fathers.* Tevye is being ironical, of course: the only "Torah" Motl knew was work itself.

118 / Vayomos Moysheh—"And Moses died." Deuteronomy, 34:5.

119 / The *hallel* prayer—See note to p. 43.

119 / Mekimi . . . mi'ofor dal—See note to p. 106.

119 / Oylim veyordim—See note to p. 31.

120 / Be'al korkhekho atoh khai—See note to p. 34.

120 / Nakhzor le'inyoneynu harishon—"Let us return to our original matter." A rabbinic expression used to terminate a digression in a scholarly discussion.

120 / The story of the Amalekites—Exodus, 17.

121 / "Then came Amalek and fought with Israel." Exodus, 17:8.

121 / Bo'u mayim ad nefesh—See note to p. 61.

122 / Ka'asher ohavti—"And Isaac . . . called Esau, his eldest son, and said unto him . . . make me savory meat, *such as I love.*" Genesis, 27:1,4. Tevye, however, means "such as you love."

122 / Vayehi bimey Mendel Beilis—"And it came to pass in the days of Mendel Beilis." On the Beilis case, see Introduction, p. xiv.

123 / Zdrastvoytye—"Good day" in Russian.

124 / Tsoras rabbim khatsi nekhomoh—"The troubles of others are half a comfort [for one's own]." A rabbinic proverb.

125 / Mah onu umeh khayeynu—See note to p. 75.

125 / Li hashomayim veli ha'orets—"The heavens are mine and the earth is mine." Psalms, 89:12; there, though, it says, "The heavens are Thine and the earth is Thine too."

125 / Lekh-lekho meyartsekho—See note to p. 117.

125 / El ha'orets asher arekko—See note to p. 117.

128 / Ad kan oymrim beshabbes hagodol—See note to p. 82.

129 / Kerakheym ov al bonim—See note to p. 65.

129 / Eyl erekh apoyim—A long-suffering God. See note to *eyl rakhum vekhanun* on p. 70.

129 / Solakhti kidvorekho—See note to p. 50.

130 / Bonim uvney vonim—"Sons and sons of sons." A rabbinic expression for "sons and grandsons."

130 / Mi ke'amkho yisro'eyl goy ekhod—"*And who* in the whole earth *is like the one nation, thy people Israel?*" Samuel II, 7:23. A vintage Tevyism. Whereas in the Bible the word *goy* simply means "nation" and refers here to the Israelites themselves, Tevye construes it in the postbiblical sense of "Gentile" and ungrammatically but ingeniously reinterprets the verse to mean: how can even one goy (*goy ekhod*) be like a Jew (*ke'amkho yisro'eyl*)?

130/Ashrekho yisro'eyl—"*Happy art thou, O Israel*; who is like unto thee, O people saved by the Lord?" Deuteronomy, 33:29.

T   h   e   R   a   i   l   r   o   a   d   S   t   o   r   i   e   s

135/ Places Jews are barred from—See Introduction, p. xi–xii.

136/ "As much as a catcall on Purim bothers Haman"—On the holiday of Purim, when the Book of Esther is read in the synagogue, it is customary for the congregation to boo, stamp its feet, and jeer whenever the name of Haman is mentioned.

139/Darovanomu konyu vzuby nye smotryat—Russian: "One doesn't look a gift horse in the mouth."

139/ Rashi—See note to p. 4.

140/Vedno pana po kholavakh—Russian: "You can tell a squire by his boots."

143/ Sukkos—See note to p. 65.

147/ Eating a chicken cooked in butter—Jewish dietary laws forbid the eating of meat and dairy products together.

147/ Going beardless or hatless—Not shaving one's beard and keeping one's head covered at all times are two of the hallmarks of the Orthodox Jew and (a litmus test mentioned more than once in *The Railroad Stories*) the chief signs by which he is immediately recognized as such by other Jews.

147/ Matsoh Fund—In the days before Passover it was customary in Jewish communities to collect money for the poor to enable them to buy matsos—the flat, unleavened bread eaten on the holiday—and other necessities.

147/ A lulav and esrog—The lulav, or palm shoot, and esrog, or citron, are both part of the Sukkos ritual. Since neither was grown in Russia, they had to be brought by special dealers from abroad.

149/Chto nada—Russian: "Is there something [that you want]?"

150–151/Chto takoye, golubchik—Russian: "What is the matter, my pigeon?"

151/Nichevo—Russian: "There's no need."

152/ Purishkevich—V. N. Purishkevich (1870–1920), leader of the anti-Semitic faction in the Duma, the Russian parliament, and founder of "the Black Hundreds" (see Introduction, p. xiv).

152/ Azef—Yevno Fishelevich Azef (1869–1918), a secret agent of the Russian police planted in the illegal Social-Revolutionary Party, where he rose to a top position while informing on its members and activities.

154/ Nikolai the First—Czar of Russia from 1825 to 1855.

162/ Blessing the New Moon—In accordance with the lunar nature of the Jewish calendar, it is customary among Orthodox Jews to hold a prayer for the new moon at the beginning of every month. The ceremony is held outdoors—where, the moon being young, there is little light in the absence of artificial illumination.

169/ Emigration Committee—An arm of the Jewish Colonization Association, an organization established by the Jewish philanthropist Baron Maurice de Hirsch (1831–1896) for the purpose of encouraging Jewish rural settlement in Argentina.

174/ Yeshiva—An advanced school for Talmudic studies and the training of Orthodox rabbis.

177/ Hanukkah candles—See note to p. 27.

177/ Elul—The last month of the Hebrew year, occurring in late summer; it is followed by the month of Tishri with its High Holy Days. During Elul it is customary for observant Jews to rise each day before dawn for special penitential prayers in the synagogue and to visit the graves of loved ones.

179/ Artsybashev—See Introduction, pp. xxxv.

184/ Bohopoli, Heysen, etc.—Towns in the southern Ukraine, several hundred miles southwest of the Kiev ("Yehupetz") region.

184/ Witte—Count Sergei Yulievich Witte, Russian statesman and a railroad engineer himself. He served as minister of communications in 1892.

185/ Poliakov—Lazarus Poliakov, a rich Russian Jewish banker who lived in Moscow.

186/ Hoshana Rabbah—See note to p. 67 on the Book of Life.

186/ Sukkos—See note to p. 65.

187/ Waved his palm branch—See note to p. 147 on "lulav and esrog."

187/ It's only half a holiday—The major Jewish holidays, such as Sukkoth, are divided into *yomim toyvim* (singular, *yom tov*), days on which most of the restrictions in force on the Sabbath, including that on work and travel, apply, and *khol hamo'ed*, days on which they do not. Hoshana Rabbah is a *khol hamo'ed* day, but the following day, Shemini Atzeret, the Day of Solemn Assembly, is a *yom tov*. It is followed by Simchat Torah.

190/ The Book of Life—See note to p. 67.

190/ Simkhes Toyroh—The holiday of Simchat Torah (see note to p. 187 on "it's only half a holiday"), which celebrates the completion of the yearly cycle of Torah readings (see note to p. 117 on "What Bible reading"). It is a day on which there is much dancing, singing, and sometimes drinking, and is considered the merriest festivity of the Jewish year.

201/ A married woman's hair—Among Orthodox Jews a married woman's hair must be covered at all times. (Among the extreme Orthodox, it is commonly shaved before marriage, the bare scalp being covered by a kerchief or wig.)

201/ Put up his samovar on the Sabbath—Among the many Sabbath restrictions is one on lighting fires and cooking food.

201/ Tisha b'Av—A fast day, commemorating the destruction of the Temple, occurring in midsummer.

201/ Koshering his dishes for Passover—In accordance with the prohibition on keeping any leaven or leavened foods in the house during the eight days of Passover, observant Jews either change all their dishes for the holiday or else "kosher," that is, ritually purify, the dishes they have been using.

202/ *Tallis koton*—A small, rectangular undergarment that slips over the head and has fringed tassles hanging from each of its four corners. It is worn at all times by observant male Jews, in obedience to the commandment, "And the Lord spoke unto Moses saying, Speak unto the Children of Israel and bid them that they make them fringes on the borders of their garments, throughout their generations, and that they put upon the fringe of the borders a riband of blue." Numbers, 15:37.

204/ Tefillin—The phylacteries, or leather thongs, to which are attached small, hollow cubes containing verses written on parchment, that a Jew binds to his arm and forehead every morning when praying. This is in accordance with the biblical commandment, "And thou shalt bind them for a sign upon thine hand, and they shall be as frontlets between thine eyes." Deuteronomy, 6:8.

208/General Tolmachov—The governor of Odessa and a well-known anti-Semite.

209/Sixty-six—A two-handed card game belonging to the pinochle family. It is played with a 24-card deck, containing the ace, king, queen, jack, ten, and nine of each suit, and the cards rank in that order except for the ten, which is next-highest to the ace. Points are scored for king-queen melds or marriages (40 for a trump marriage, otherwise 20) and for tricks taken, and the first player to score 66 points wins the hand. If his opponent has over 33 points, the winner is awarded one "game-point"; under 33, two game-points; and none at all, three game-points. Seven game-points generally win a match.

210/Tallis—The fringed prayer shawl worn by observant Jews during the morning prayer.

210/Tefillin—See note to p. 204.

212/Hanukkah—See note to p. 27.

219/A two in arithmetic—In the Russian system, students were graded on a scale of one to five.

222/*Chto vam ugodno*—Russian: "What is it that you want?"

222/*Gospodin Direktor,* etc.—These words, spoken in broken Russian, are translated by the father himself in the lines that follow.

223/*Tak chto-zhe vam ugodno*—Russian: "But *what* is it that you want?"

229/A guaranteed . . . exemption—Only sons, according to Russian law, were automatically excused from the army.

229/Itsik—An affectionate form of Yitzchok, the Hebrew for "Isaac."

229/Alter—When a child was seriously ill or otherwise feared for, it was the custom among East European Jews to change his name for good luck. Alter, which means "old one" in Yiddish, was one of the substitute names most frequently used, the belief being that it would throw the Angel of Death off the child's tracks.

229/Eisik—The Germanized form of "Isaac," which also had currency among Yiddish-speaking Jews as a name.

230/Government rabbi—As a way of tightening its control over the Jewish communities under its rule, which preferred to conduct their internal affairs with minimal recourse to civil authority, the Russian government enacted a law in 1857 requiring each community to employ a publicly licensed or "crown" rabbi, who was a graduate of a state-run rabbinical school. Such rabbis, who acted as go-betweens for the community and the government bureaucracy, were held in low esteem by the Jewish population, which made as little use of them as possible.

231 / Molodyets—Russian: "wonderful!"

234 / Stupaytye—Russian: "Get out of here!"

238 / Stupaytye, vi nodoyedlive yevrei—"Get out of here, you Jewish pest!"

240 / Baron de Hirsch—See note to p. 169.

247 / Amo pezizo—"The impulsive people." A rabbinic epithet for the Jews, based on a traditional commentary on the Israelites' answer to Moses when making ready to receive the Law at Mount Sinai (Exodus, 24:7), "We will obey it and hear it"—for, as the rabbis pointed out, "We will [first] hear it and [then, if it suits us] obey it," would have been the more prudent response. On the narrator's use of Hebrew quotations, see Introduction, p. xxvii–xxviii.

247 / Oylom keminhogoy—See note to p. 79.

248 / Bekharbi uvekashti—"Moreover, I have given to thee one portion above thy brethren, which I took out of the hand of the Amorite *with my sword and with my bow*." Genesis, 48:22.

248 / Kidibo'ey—"As is proper." A common Talmudic term.

248 / Begapoy yovoy uvegapoy yeytsey—See note to p. 26.

249 / Al tehi boz lekhoyl bosor—"Show disdain for no man"; a misquotation from *The Ethics of the Fathers,* which has *odom* instead of *bosor*. Although *bosor* also means "man," its primary meaning is "flesh" or "meat," which may be why the narrator associates it with garlic. In any case, though, he clearly does not know what he is saying.

250 / Koyl yisro'el khaveyrim—"All Jews are brethren." A rabbinic saying.

251 / Hamibli eyn kvorim bemitsrayim—"And they said unto Moses, *Are there not enough graves in Egypt* that thou hast taken us to die in the wilderness?" Exodus, 14:11.

251 / Tovar voborotye—Russian: "The merchandise is moving."

252 / Ulai yerakheym—"Perhaps He will have mercy." There seems to be no traditional source for this quote.

253 / Pshoyt neveyloh . . . ve'al titstoreykh—"[Better to] *skin carcasses* in the marketplace [for a living] *rather than depend on* others." A Talmudic proverb.

253 / Koyl dikhfin yeysey veyitzrokh—See note to p. 24.

253 / Hekhiloysoh linpoyl . . . nofoyl tipoyl—"Then said his wise men and Zeresh his wife unto him [Haman], If Mordecai be of the seed of the Jews, before whom *thou hast begun to fall,* thou shalt not prevail against him, but *thou shalt surely fall* before him." Esther, 6:13.

254 / Tallis kotons—See note to p. 202.

255 / Tomus nafshi im plishtim—"Let me die with the Philistines." Judges, 16:30.

270 / Purishkevitch—See note to p. 152.

271 / A heder teacher—The heder was a schoolroom in which small children were taught beginning subjects, mostly religious ones.

271 / The Torah reader—Reading the weekly portion of the Torah in the synagogue (see note to p. 117) is a highly specialized task, as the reader must know by heart the chant notes, vocalization, and punctuation of the text, none of which appear in the Torah scroll itself.

273 / Pravozshitelestvo, Gospodin Yevrei—Russian: "Your permit, Mr. Jew!"

274 / Khorosho, Gospodin Obradchik—"All right, Mr. Cleric."

274 / Prayer group—Though any Jew can pray privately, ten male Jews (a minyan) are needed for public prayer to be held.

275 / Deathday—On the Hebrew anniversary, the *yortsayt,* as it is called in Yiddish, of a family member's death, a memorial candle is lit and the male survivors are expected to say the kaddish—which (see note to p. 99) can only be recited in a minyan.

276 / Girded his waist—Extremely pious Jews belt their jackets at the waist when they pray, in order to symbolically divide the upper or "spiritual" part of themselves from the lower or "animal" part.

276 / Ashrey yoyshvey veysekho . . . —See note to p. 81.

277 / On the eighth day—The day of life on which, barring illness, all Jewish male children are circumcised. The circumcision too must be performed in the presence of a minyan.

277 / Sholem aleykhem—See Introduction, p. ix–x.

277 / After the candles had been lit—The lighting and blessing of the Sabbath candles on Friday evening marks the onset of the day of rest.

278 / Hallah—The braided bread that is blessed after the wine and the ritual washing of hands at the beginning of the Sabbath meal.

278 / But it was the holy Sabbath—Among the many acts prohibited on the Sabbath are lighting and extinguishing a fire. Jewish law, of course, permits the Sabbath to be violated when human life is endangered, but to a sufficiently pious Jew the mere burning down of his house does not fall into that category. Furthermore, though a non-Jew is allowed to put out the fire, the Jew must not openly request him to do so, for that too would be a violation of the Sabbath laws.

278 / *Chvedka, serdtse*—Russian: "dearest Chvedka."

278 / Never before . . . had he been without a hat—See note to p. 147.

283 / Tefillin—See note to p. 204.

283 / Kiddush wine—The wine, generally sweet, that is blessed at the beginning of Sabbath and holiday meals.